Reflexions

by Richard Olney

For my brothers and sisters–
Margaret
Norris
John
James
Elizabeth
Frances (in memoriam)
Byron.

Brick Tower Press
New York

Brick Tower Press
1230 Park Avenue
New York, NY 10128

Library of Congress Cataloging-in-Publication Data
Olney, Richard
Reflexions
Includes biographical reference and index.
ISBN 978-1-59687-486-2 Hardcover. ISBN 1-883283-43-4 Trade Paper
1. Olney, Richard, 1927-1999—
Art/Autobiography/Cooking/Wine
Hardcover, Adult/General
Nonfiction

Catalog Card Number: 99-94556

First Edition, Trade Paper, June 2005

Acknowledgements

In addition to family and other friends, who figure in the text of this book, to whom my gratitude is implicit, I would like to thank: J.D. McClatchy, editor of *The Yale Review*, who published an excerpt from *Reflexions* in the January 1999 issue; Liz Clark, whose determination to see *Reflexions* in print exceeded my own, her publisher, John Colby, and his wife, Betsy, who, in March 1998, scoured the hillside with me to collect the first wild asparagus of the season for our luncheon omelette before returning to New York with the manuscript and a carton of photos and menus from which to choose illustrations; and Chip Kidd, for his inspired jacket design of a troubled-looking person hovering over distant reflexions of Time Past.

Contents

Appreciation

This lavishly rich and detailed chronicle of Richard Olney by Richard Olney, begins in New York in 1951 where, as a struggling artist, he waited tables in Greenwich Village. It then moves to Paris and weaves a magical description of food that becomes so real—as if you were there with him: "My first meal in Paris was in a glum little dining room for boarders...the plat du jour was 'gibelotte, pommes mousseline'—rabbit and white wine fricassee with mashed potatoes. The gibelotte was all right, the mashed potatoes the best I had ever eaten, pushed through a sieve, buttered and moistened with enough of their hot cooking water to bring them to a supple, not quite pourable consistency—no milk, no cream, no beating. I had never dreamt of mashing potatoes without milk and, in Iowa, everyone believed that, the more you beat them, the better they were." This book is not just a memoir, it is a guide created by the best food and wine writer of our time.

"Among his friends were many other American expatriates, including the writer James Baldwin, the filmmaker Kenneth Anger and the actor Gordon Heath. At the same time he was exploring food and wine he astonished the editorial team of Cuisine et Vins de France by the extent of his knowledge while on a tour of the Bordelais vineyards. Richard corrected them on their ideas about the traditions of French cooking, quoting Escoffier to prove his points. He began writing for the journal under the heading of Un Américain (gourmand) à Paris in 1962, each time presenting a menu with accompanying wines.

"A year earlier, he had bought a rugged hillside above the village of Solliès-Toucas, complete with a ruined shack without electricity or sanitation: this was to become Richard's home. Over several years he worked, slowly, as funds permitted, to make it habitable, labouring with the local masons, carpenters and plumbers. He restored the ancient terraces on the slope above and made a large garden. Later Richard and his brothers Byron and James hewed out a wine cellar beneath the rock.

"A piece in the Sunday Times magazine introduced Richard to British readers in the mid sixties. At about the same time he started giving courses on cooking and on wine at Lubéron College in Avignon. He taught the essentials, the techniques of classic cooking, knowing that once understood they gave the cook great personal freedom. The French Menu Cookbook (1970), with menus for different seasons and occasions, and wines to accompany them are detailed and precise; he encouraged readers to regard them as blueprints which could be varied with different garnishes or flavourings. His masterpiece Simple French Food (1974) followed, one of the half dozen books that should be on every kitchen shelf. Its title is deceptive: simple to Richard never meant fast or easy: simplicity is the sign of perfection. The book reinforces the message that once the basic rules have been mastered, they can be adapted, even broken. His painter's eye illuminated his perception of food and his writing. You, the cook must also be the artist, bringing understanding to mechanical formulas, transforming each into an uncomplicated statement that will surprise or soothe a gifted palate...for such is creativity, be it in the kitchen or in the studio.

"From 1977-1982 he edited the 27 volume series, The Good Cook, for Time-Life—by far the most intelligent cookery course ever published—which made his name familiar to a huge readership, especially in the United States. Then followed scholarly, elegant books on two of France's greatest wines: Yquem (1985) and Romanée-Conti (1991). In between came Ten Vineyard Lunches (1988), later Provence the Beautiful Cookbook (1993) and Lulu's Provençial Table (1994). Reflexions is his last book.

Richard Olney

"Richard lived a solitary, orderly life. He disliked leaving his hillside, but friends were always welcome; he was generous, thoughtful, forever hospitable. He did not drive, had no radio or TV, and wrote on an ancient typewriter. He couldn't be bothered with a computer, but he had long installed a fax on which he wrote regularly to his four brothers and two sisters in the States and to friends all over the world: fellow writers Elizabeth David and Sybille Bedford, chefs Alice Waters, Jeremiah Tower, Simon Hopkinson, and most of France's greatest winemakers and restaurateurs. He was enormously admired and respected by the French gastronomic community. In England and the United States, his growing intolerance of things sham or pretentious gave him the label of 'difficult.'

"The kitchen, the central part of his house, is dominated by a large fireplace built by Richard, again with Byron's help; copper pans hang on the walls, an armoire faces the door, shelves are filled with earthenware and books, a rough-tiled counter with a stone sink fronts the long window. Here he lived and entertained in bad weather; the rest of the year meals were taken out of doors: 'relaxed summer lunches shared with friends' and indeed on a vine-covered terrace, lit at night by a row of coloured lights.

"For Richard a meal, however simple, was always a celebration, the atmosphere relaxed, the talk ranging widely for many hours. His excellent palate, good taste and fastidiousness always ensured his guests a harmonious meal."

—Jill Norman, The Guardian,
London, August 1999.

Introduction

by Alice Waters

Almost thirty years ago, when I was becoming a *restauratrice*, one of my partners gave me a copy of Richard Olney's first book, *The French Menu Cookbook.* We had recently dared to open a restaurant with a simple format: At Chez Panisse we offered our guests no choice, serving instead one meal only, at a fixed price, composed of four or five courses, using only the best ingredients we could find. The menu changed daily, following the seasons and the market; our culinary inspiration was the regional cooking of France. We were amateurs and wildly inexperienced, but we were impassioned by food and wine.

Reading *The French Menu Cookbook* was like receiving unexpected validation. With intense conviction, it articulated precisely what we were struggling to demonstrate: that "one can only eat marvelously by respecting the seasons," that menus must be composed "in terms of what may be called a 'gastronomic aesthetic,'" and that "good and honest cooking and good and honest French cooking are the same thing." The gastronomic aesthetic revealed throughout the book was exuberant, sensual, and, at the same time, deeply knowledgable and rigorously uncompromising. We immediately began cooking recipes from the book, but it yielded more than additions to out repertoire: it reminded us that we had much to learn, and it gave us courage by confirming our implausibly high standards.

Naturally, I wanted to meet the author, and a few years later, when *Simple French Food* was published and Richard traveled to San Francisco to promote his new book, I managed to invite him to Chez Panisse and arranged a surprise reunion with his old friend Kenneth Anger, whom he had not seen for twenty years. This endeared me to Richard and helped get me invited the following summer to his Provençal *mas*, hidden away in the rocky hillsides above Toulon.

Richard Olney is known primarily as a writer of cookbooks. However, he has also written indispensable books about wine, and, what is more, he is a painter, a mentor, a guide, and a gardener. In a word, he is an artist, and one whose artistry is evident in everything he has created, from his wine cellar, hewn with his own hands from the rock and stocked with irresistible vintages, to his elegant prose, with its occasional Gallic turns of phrase. His artistry as a host is unforgettable.

My first visit to Solliès-Toucas began in that state of extreme self-consciousness and absorbent, heightened awareness that sometimes accompanies a first visit to the house of someone who is very important to you. I remember every detail: the climb up the steep hill to his little house set amid terraces of ancient olive trees; the clicking of the cicadas, the rustle of the leaves in the wind, the aroma of the wild herbs all around us, mixed with the smell of Richard's Gauloise.

Richard received us wearing nothing but an open shirt, his skimpy bathing suit, a kitchen towel at his waist, and a pair of worn espadrilles. He invited us into his house, which consists basically of one room in which he works, eats, and entertains when weather prohibits dining on his idyllic terrace. I can close my eyes and see the boulders with which Richard and his brothers had built the fireplace at the head of the house, the copper pots hanging above, the marble mortars on the mantlepiece, the column by the table papered with wine labels, the lovely platters and tureens displayed on hard-to-reach shelves, the windows out to the garden where the table under the grape arbor had been laid with beautiful linens. He served us a spectacular salad, full of Provençal greens that were new to me–rocket, anise, hyssop–with perfectly tender green beans and bright nasturtium flowers tossed in, and dressed with the vinegar he makes himself from the ends of bottles of great wine. (That salad was a revelation, and inspired countless *salades composées* in the years to come.) My first visit ended, many hours later, in the same way all my subsequent visits have ended: in a kind of ecstatic paralysis brought on by extraordinary food, astonishing wines, and dancing until dawn to seventy-eights of Edith Piaf and *bal musette* music.

In conversation, Richard can be blunt in his judgments–and he is always right. In print, on the other hand, although he is still always right, his judgments are expressed with discretion and finesse. He has never pursued celebrity; he has neither the patience nor the appetite for it. He has lived to please himself, and in doing so, he has created an irreplaceable body of work. His generosity to like-minded gastronomes is legendary. Through Richard I have made the acquaintance of some of the soulful and spirited people in this book, including the remarkable Peyraud family of the Domaine Tempier at Bandol, who have become my surrogate family in France. Twenty-five years ago, scarcely anyone in America knew what an Hermitage or a Bandol or a Côte-Rôtie was, but because he took an interest in the education of my friend Kermit Lynch, an audacious young wine importer, and introduced him to many of France's most steadfastly traditional winemakers, today there is a thriving market in this country for their wines. During the same quarter-century, the demand for fresh, local produce that has led to the rebirth of farmers' markets has surely been stimulated by Richard's fervor for the seasonal and the authentic.

My proudest moment as a seasoned restauratrice took place one afternoon at Chez Panisse several years ago, when Richard rose to speak to a group of French winemakers he was accompanying on a tour of California wineries. We had just cleared away the remnants of the last course of a special lunch over which we had taken great pains. Richard's appreciation of the wines, as always, was eloquent and succinct, but when he spoke of the food, he praised Chez Panisse with particular warmth. Readers of this book will have some sense of what it must be like to receive a tribute from someone whose discrimination is so artful and whose enthusiasms are so passionate; and, above all, they will learn something of what it means to lead a life so honest, so pure in taste, and so fine in judgment.

Alice Waters
Chez Panisse
Berkeley, California
April 20, 1999

One

1951-1956
Paris. Clamart. Summers on Ischia.
Travels in Italy and Greece. Magagnosc.

It was the summer of 1951. I painted days and waited tables nights at 17 Barrow, a Greenwich Village restaurant whose cuisine wanted to be international, its atmosphere bohemian; on the walls were nostalgic travel posters from the '20s and '30s, the tables were lit by candles stuck into Chianti fiascos and, in the background, Edith Piaf and Billie Holiday sang of love and heartbreak. It fitted my mood and I liked the work, but Europe was on my mind. Father wanted his children to be happy but he could not understand why I had deliberately chosen a pattern of life that promised no stability. He believed, as a matter of principle, that we should be supported as long as we pursued the noble goal of higher education, but it had for long been clear that higher education and I were hopelessly incompatible; he decided that European travel might be important to a painter's education. I chose to sail on the *De Grasse*, the oldest and slowest of the French Line's ships, for its last voyage, 10 November. I was enchanted by the formal menus, the briny clean air that flowed through the open port hole at the head of my bed, the wondrous awareness of the ocean's vastness, the out-of-space, out-of-time renditions of swing, jazz, and French music hall tunes by the ship's orchestra and the rough sea, which nearly emptied the dining room and stretched our crossing from seven to nine days.

My first meal in Paris was in a glum little dining room for boarders, in the Hôtel de l'Academie, at the corner of the rue de l'Université and the rue des Saints-Pères. The plat du jour was "gibelotte, pommes mousseline"—rabbit and white wine fricassee with mashed potatoes. The gibelotte was all right, the mashed potatoes the best I had ever eaten, pushed through a sieve, buttered and moistened with enough of their hot cooking water to bring them to a supple, not quite pourable consistency—no milk, no cream, no beating. I had never dreamt of mashing potatoes without milk and, in Iowa, everyone believed that, the more you beat them, the better they were.

The first few weeks, my days were spent mostly in museums and, for lunch, I ate as cheaply as possible. Good food was everywhere. A dollar bought 500 francs and could pay for a meal, including wine. Small family restaurants, with husband or wife in the kitchen, the other taking orders and tending bar, while the teen-age offspring waited table, were commonplace. The floors were scattered with sawdust and, for the regular clientèle, numbered pigeon-hole napkin racks hung at the entrance; the napkins were laundered once a week. Petit salé (brine-cured pork) cooked with lentils was a favorite main dish; others were gibelotte, pot-au-feu (called "boeuf gros sel" when served without its broth), poule-au-pot, potée (with sausage, cabbage, and aromatic vegetables), blanquette de veau, boeuf bourguignon, tripes au vin blanc or tête de veau, slow-cooking dishes based on inexpensive ingredients, which required only a talent for controlling the heat source to be perfect. I liked Chez Augustin, in the rue de Seine, a long, narrow room, lined on either side with banquettes and marble-topped, wrought iron tables, strung end to end. Before the entrance door was unlocked, the tables were set up with covers, bread, one of a variety of hors d'oeuvre and a carafe of red wine at each place. As the customers settled in, they began shuffling plates of hors d'oeuvre from one place to another, choosing what they wanted. Main course orders were taken, cheese and dessert followed and, on the way out, each client paid 700 francs. The wine was not good, but a bottle of good wine would have been no incentive to passing the afternoon in the Louvre.

In the evening, I preferred seeking out, with new-found friends, bistrots with good cellars. One of the best in the quartier was the Chope Danton, at the Carrefour de l'Odéon, where habitués stood at the "zinc" downstairs to drink house wines by the glass and a spiral stairway led steeply up to the dining room. The tables were dressed with paper and the food was Burgundian or Lyonnaise in spirit. Except for a few Bordeaux and some of the grander Burgundies, the patron, Monsieur Moissonnier, chose his wines at the vineyards where they were raised in casks until the month of April following the vintage, before being shipped to Paris, bottled in the restaurant's cellars and drunk within the year. I have never drunk prettier Beaujolais than his Chiroubles, Saint-Amour, Fleurie or Côte de Brouilly.

The hotel was a few minutes' walk from the crossroads of Saint-Germain-des-Prés, around which were clustered the Café de Flore, Les Deux Magots, the Café Royal, Brasserie Lipp and La Reine Blanche. I had no time to suffer from linguistic failings or solitude. At the Flore and the Deux Magots, English and American habitués table-hopped and a new-comer was instantly drawn into their insular society. A young English film-maker, Peter Price, asked if he might join me for coffee, then invited me to dinner at the home of cinéaste friends, the Lovetts (their names were spelled differently), from whom he rented a room. Charles Lovett was English, lean, languid and elegant; Thad was American, stocky, affected to be tough and thumped around in cowboy boots. They had a housekeeper-cook, described by Thad as a famous cordon-bleu. At table, cheap red wine was poured from exquisite antique decanters into crystal tulips. Their other locataire was Kenneth Anger, whose first film, *Fireworks*, was then enjoying a great success at the avant-garde French Cinémathèque. Kenneth offered me a room in the rue Jacob, which he rented but had abandoned at winter's approach for, amongst other inconveniences, it was unheated and had no running water. I moved in but not for long. Most nights, John Craxton, a young English painter, arrived to share my bed; we kept each other warm. He moved in a bucolic dreamworld, peopled with beautiful Greek goat herds. Soon he left for Greece.

La Reine Blanche was a deep tunnel, lit brightly and crudely. Physically, it had no charm. The only feminine presence was Madame Alice, the patronne, an impassive mountain of stone, surmounted by a tightly pulled and smoothly sculpted mound of cold stone-grey hair. Her flesh was grey and she dressed in grey. But for a twitch at the corners of her mouth, Madame Alice's welcoming smile disturbed no muscle in her face. She rarely moved from the high seat before the cash register at the far end of the bar; when she did, she moved slowly, but she could effortlessly manhandle the roughest of her clients. She needed no bouncer. The bar, thickly populated by trade, was cruising territory. Beyond it were tables and booths where friends gathered; there, I met Sacha Neuville, Bill Aalto and Elliott Stein.

Sacha, né Albrecht Niederstein, was then in his late forties. He had come to Paris from Berlin in the early 1930s and, during the war, had lived in the south of France with falsified papers in the name of Sacha Neuville, an identity that he chose to retain. He lived in the avenue de Ségur. A vast studio was hung with paintings by André Lhote and Moïse Kisling and a small kitchen was hung with heavy copper; Sacha was a fastidious cook. His days were circumscribed by habit and ritual, from the precise fragment broken from a rough cube of unrefined sugar for his morning coffee to the hour spent playing patience before dressing for the day, the cigarettes, meticulously rolled from tabac bleu in stickumless, tan papier maïs and lit by a temperamental antique lighter, visits to the flea market and to a shop in the rue Washington for freshly roasted moka, where the patron sternly advised his clients to use only Evian water for preparing his coffees, drinks at the end of the day with his friend, Robert, a second-hand book dealer in the rue Mazarine, who was more often with collegues at Juju's bar next door than in his shop, to the after-dinner coffee and glass of red wine at La Reine Blanche. At our first meeting, Sacha asked, "Have you met Jimmy Baldwin?" The name meant nothing to me. He said, "Well, he is out of town now, but you are bound to meet him as soon as he returns." Because the question recurred so often during the following months, I became conscious long before the event that "meeting Jimmy" was a major part of one's induction into life on the Left Bank.

Bill Aalto, a disheveled, sentimental giant, who had lost a forearm in the Spanish Civil War and always looked as if he had just surfaced from a brawl, was a gentle poet who suffered cruelly from the infidelity of his muse. Volcanic eruptions after a drink too many had earned him the nickname, "Big Etna," which wicked friends promptly transformed into "Big Edna," and often simplified to plain "Edna" to fuel his rage. Bill was a loyal drinking companion. It was he who introduced me to Chez Inez, a club in the Latin Quarter where Inez Cavanaugh, accompanied at the piano by Aaron Bridges, sang beautiful blues.

Elliott Stein, poet and editor of a recently defunct little magazine, *Janus*, had lived since 1947 in the Hôtel de Verneuil and suggested that I take a room there. Seen from the outside, the ancient building, at the corner of the rue de Verneuil and the rue de Beaune, was beautiful, architecturally sober and pure. Inside, the Corsican owners, Monsieur and Madame Dumont, three children and a kindly grandmother, who later retired to Corsica, lived on the ground floor, above which were five floors and twenty-seven rooms. Room no. 1 was rented out by the hour, many of the others were let to writers of various nationalities. Mine was banal and badly lit, but the daily rate was 300 francs and most of my time in the hotel was spent in Elliott's room, no. 27, a book-lined cocoon, whose windows, set deeply into the slanting walls, opened onto both streets. The only toilet was on the second floor, a "squat-john," or hole in the floor, furnished with torn-up newspapers and a violent flushing system, which encouraged one to stand outside the entrance before pulling the chain. Each room contained a sink but the hotel had no bath; the sheets were changed once a month and the minuterie was adjusted to illuminated phases so brief that one often arrived at a landing in the dark before pushing a button to light the succeeding flight of stairs. When I moved in, the first question asked by Madame Dumont was, "Do you know Jimmy? He lived here, you know, and, when he was sick, it was I, personally, who nursed him back to health by cooking porridge for him every day!" (Many years later, on a brief visit to Paris, I stuck my head in to say hello and found Madame Dumont simmering. "Did you know," she said, "that Jimmy was in Paris and he didn't even come by to say bonjour to me—I, who saved his life.")

Elliott and I were rapidly recognized as a couple. However, no declarations of everlasting fidelity had been sworn and Elliott was determined to impose the concept, if not the fact, of his independence. His favorite method was to recount in lurid detail the antics at organized orgies that he attended, either with Harriet Sohmers, a tall, handsome American girl, who was always looking for trouble, or with an English film-maker, whose name I forget; I could never sift out the fact from the fantasy.

Elliott, at a tender age, had devoured more literature than I could imagine absorbing in a lifetime. He was, then, methodically re-reading all of Henry James, but his greatest passion was the cinema. He disliked grade "A" films, admired grades "B" and "C" and, I think, considered *King Kong* to be the greatest film ever made. He, naturally, had much to discuss with Kenneth Anger and they became, for a while, great friends. Amongst Elliott's friends in the hotel was a self-styled "avant-garde playwright," Daniel Maroc, whose proudest possession was a notebook in which he ticked off the number of men he had seduced. They were nameless and without sentimental value. He cruised the streets nightly, bringing one, then another, to his room and, as each departed, another mark was added to the book. The number was into the thousands. Annette Michelson, John Ashbery, Otto Friedrich and Ned Rorem, with whom Elliott was working on a short opera, often came by.

Peter Watson, the angel behind *Horizon*, the literary magazine edited by Cyril Connally, and the principal benefactor of the ICA (Institute of Contemporary Art) in London, came often to Paris to sit for a portrait, commissioned from Giacometti. Peter was immensely likeable and, in an elegant bird-of-prey fashion, quite beautiful, lean and angular with sharply drawn features. Giacometti, in frustration, wiped out the features after each sitting. Giacometti was intense. I've never met anyone so possessed, tortured and innocent. He seemed to be crying out for help and to believe that every banal phrase uttered over a passing drink might contain an important message.

Elliott decided that my allowance was inadequate and that I should take a job cooking dinners for his friend, Tommy Michaelis, a middle-aged lawyer who loved being surrounded by young men. Tommy's first words, when I arrived, were, "Do you know Jimmy Baldwin?—No?—You must meet him as soon as he returns to Paris—he is a genius!" Once, Bill Aalto came to dinner but, mostly, the company was trade, pleasant enough but with limited conversation and indifferent to the food and the wine, which were gobbled and guzzled. I left after a couple of weeks.

In February 1952, Peter Watson asked Elliott and me to spend a week with him in London. The visit coincided with the death of the King; London may never have been so packed, but the crowds had little effect on attendance at the National Gallery, where we were able to admire the Piero della Francescas in peace. We kept off the streets and made no attempt to eat in restaurants. I was surprised, after the lush French markets, to discover England still on wartime food rationing. Blue duck eggs were unrationed but chicken eggs and butter were rare. I cooked, we ate well, drank good wine and the conversation was relaxed; it could not have been a nicer introduction to London.

With the approach of spring, I intended to head for Italy. Elliott planned to join me later. Bill Aalto, who had spent a lot of time in southern Italy and, in particular, in Forio, on the island of Ischia, where his friend, Wystan Auden, held court, insisted that we pass the summer in Forio. Another friend, Bernie Winebaum, who was passing through Paris, enthusiastically agreed and both sent off letters to Auden announcing our arrival some months hence. I wanted, above all, to visit Florence but, because Kenneth Anger was leaving for Rome and had promised to hold me a room in his pensione, I began there. I put Kenneth on the train, with the drama that has always attended him: we lingered too long over dinner and, upon arriving at the quai in the Gare de Lyon, his train was pulling out; he managed to fling himself through an open door onto the platform while I hurled his suitcases in after him. A few days later, it was Bill Aalto who put me onto the same train. The restaurant in the Gare de Lyon, in which we had dinner, has since been named Le Train Bleu, a souvenir of the defunct Paris-Nice, all-sleeper, luxury train, once famous for its food. The high vaulted ceilings, with murals of plump goddesses and ponderous bearded gods flitting around in the clouds, looking very much like well-to-do citizens of the Second Empire, are wonderfully silly, the cuisine is comfortably bourgeoise and the wine list good.

I was too impatient to arrive in Florence to do justice to Rome on that first trip. My clearest memory is of the Etruscan terracotta sarcophagus of the almond-eyed couple in the Villa Giulia. We ate at Ranieri, where the aging proprietor recounted the visits of Ronald Firbank, who contented himself with peeling a couple of grapes for his meal but tipped like a grand seigneur.

Most of what I knew about Florence and the early Italian Renaissance I had learned from Mary Holmes, art history lecturer at the University of Iowa during the 1940s. She was everyone's favorite teacher and instilled in hundreds of students an enduring passion for the Italian masters of the 15th century. From the lecture podium, through clouds of cigaret smoke, she held the auditorium in a trance and, when lecturing on Masaccio or Piero della Francesca, she could never leave them.

Upon arriving in the railway station in Florence, I checked my bags and began wandering, aimlessly, until my steps led me to the church of Santa Maria del Carmine. At the left-hand entrance to the Brancacci chapel, in the right arm of the transept, the first thing one sees is the most moving expulsion from the Garden of Eden in the history of art. Masaccio painted it in 1427. This boy, who died before the age of thirty, had a vision whose power has never been surpassed.

My friend, Lucia Vernarelli, with whom I had studied under Tamayo at the Brooklyn Museum Art School, was in Florence and had held a room for me, overlooking the Arno, at the Pensione Bartolini, a small family affair on the top floor of an old palace on the lungarno Guicciardini, at the foot of ponte Santa Trinità; pitchers of hot water were delivered to the rooms for morning toilets, but a bath had to be ordered in advance so that the wood stove in the bathroom could be stoked to heat the water. In the years to follow, I never attempted to stay elsewhere and, most often, Lucia was a fellow guest at the Bartolini.

Lucia's friends were artists and writers. Except for Giovanna Crema, an adorable, high-spirited girl, whose lip often curled in contempt of middle class mores, and her companion, Mario who later committed suicide, my memory of them is vague—my Italian was inadequate and their English non-existent; we stumbled along in a sort of French. Usually we ate in a small restaurant, frequented by artists where Giovanna, who was seduced by the American habit of drinking orange juice for breakfast, insisted on having freshly squeezed blood oranges for dessert. To celebrate—anything was an excuse—we ate at Cammillo, a trattoria in borgo San Jacopo, a few stops from the Bartolini. This was before the official "D.O.C." laws (Denominazione di Origine Controllate) dictated that Chianti must be red and before red Chianti assumed pretensions to grandeur. The proprietor, Bruno, owned vines in the Chianti region and served his red and white Chiantis, fizzy and cool, in carafes. Cammillo was known for its bistécca alla fiorentina, a thick T-bone steak grilled over wood coals. I remember also their trippa alla fiorentina, thin strips of tripe, braised with white wine, tomatoes and oregano, sprinkled with grated Parmesan and passed beneath the grill. Late autumn, they always had fresh white truffles to shave over risotto or taglierini.

Forio d'Ischia was a couple of hours' boat ride from Naples. The white, sandy beaches were vast and unpeopled. There was a small outdoor market. The butcher, who had no refrigeration, sacrificed one animal a week, which he called "carne"; it was neither beef nor veal or, in his view, it was both. I reserved the brain each week in advance; the meat was too fresh, but the tougher cuts made good stews. Each morning, a peasant led a nanny goat from door to door, squirting into a bowl the necessary amount of milk for breakfast coffee. The social center was the terrace of Maria's caffè. Inside, the walls were covered with magazine photos of her most famous client, signor Auden. Of course, Bill Aalto had given me a letter of introduction to Maria, a dumpy, bubbling, good-natured lady, who painted her face with abandon and dyed her hair jet black. Her business partner was her older sister, Gisella, an affectionate, motherly woman, who never gave a thought to her gray hairs, from whom I rented our house for the season. I met Auden on Maria's terrace and we spent a pleasant evening, while he reminisced about old friends, announced the imminent arrival of his friend, Chester Kallman, of Pavel Tchelitchew, whom he considered to be the greatest living painter, and, perhaps, of Brian Howard, "a brilliant and dear friend, but a lapsed poet," and described his pattern of living: writing poetry from 7 'til 10, correspondence from 10 'til noon, after which he was free. He asked me to come around to his house the next day at noon. At the apéritif hour, I mistakenly assumed that I had been asked to drink a glass of the local white wine. Instead, he pulled several small hotel-breakfast jars of honey and jams from his pockets, explaining that he always carried them with him, should the opportunity present itself, and that he liked to smear the stuff on boys' cocks and lick it off. He wondered if I would like to try it. I declined. The air became abruptly hostile, I said good-bye and we never spoke again. A couple of days later, Chester Kallman, whom I had known in New York, arrived; he cut me dead. When Elliott arrived, I explained that we were social outcasts—he giggled. The only entertainment in Forio was Maria's terrace of an evening, for the most part observing the flirtatious, animal activity of the local boys; Elliott and I took a table on one side of the terrace, while Auden and Chester, surrounded by English professors, occupied the other side. One day, a note was delivered from Pavel (Pavlik to everyone) Tchelitchew, who, with his friend, Charles Henri Ford, had rented a house across the road, asking us to come for drinks. There were no preliminaries—Pavlik explained immediately that Wystan had warned him that we were out-of-bounds and that he must avoid us at all cost, which, as he said, with much chuckling and chortling, only whetted his curiosity. Pavlik was very funny—I never stopped laughing whenever we were together. He would say, with child-like glee, "Oooh! I have a big one, you know!" He attributed his great success with ballet dancers to "the big one." He bemoaned the cruel pitfalls of love—Edith Sitwell, he said, was hopelessly in love with him, which was a great bore, whereas he suffered agonies of unrequited love for Peter Watson. His letters, mostly about mystical concepts that he hoped to convey in his paintings, were written in a small hand, which diminished in size as it approached the bottom of the page, when he would begin turning the paper around, writing sidewise and upside down, smaller and smaller, a couple of times around, before turning it over, repeating the process and beginning another page. I saw him whenever he was in Paris, until his death, five years later.

Tommy Michaelis planned to arrive on an early evening boat and spend a couple of days with us. The preceding day, I bought a mature, young cock from a neighbor, killed, plumed and cleaned it and put it into the ice-box to relax. The next morning, by miracle, a peasant came down from the mountain, peddling a crate of freshly-picked wild mushrooms. I recognized none of them, but they were beautiful and I bought the lot—more than half were Caesar's mushrooms (*Amanita caesarea*), some still enclosed in a fragile grayish white membrane (volva), the size and shape of a chicken's egg, others freshly opened, the half-sphere caps bright orange with lemon-yellow gills. The unopened egg-shapes, when split, present the compact, embryo mushrooms in a striking design of orange lines, white bands of flesh and yellow stripes, encircling the white stem. At this stage, or freshly burst from the membrane, raw, thinly sliced and seasoned to taste at table with olive oil, a drop of lemon juice, a pinch of fine gray sea salt and freshly ground pepper—or, larger, with the caps spread wide, anointed with olive oil, grilled over wood coals and seasoned at table—they are exquisite. Then, I didn't know what to do with them, so I threw them into a large pot with the chicken and a dab of olive oil, covered, and moved things around occasionally over very low heat. Tommy arrived at 11:30; he had missed the old steamer and hired a private boat. During its lifetime, the chicken had not been pampered, but it had run free, developed some muscle and tasted like chicken. Thanks to Tommy's lateness, it was meltingly tender, it tasted like mushrooms, the mushrooms tasted like chicken and the juices were heaven. Tommy and Elliott tasted nothing—they began to quarrel, for no apparent reason, the moment we were at table; before the meal was finished, Tommy left in a rage. Elliott appeared to be quite pleased with the evening's outcome; I was convinced that he had planned the rupture in advance.

We left Ischia for a couple of months of dedicated tourism in Greece, Sicily and Tuscany. Then, one could wander freely in the Parthenon and the Acropolis was open 'til midnight on the night of the full moon, the night before and the night after. The bleached white monuments, washed in white moonlight, were other-worldly. I took off my sandals and was wandering barefoot around the

Parthenon in this eerie atmosphere, when a guard, in garbled French, roughly ordered me to put my sandals on; he said I was showing lack of respect—whether for him or for Athena was unclear.

A writer friend, who rather grandly claimed to have been poisoned in several Paris three-star restaurants, insisted that we eat in a restaurant in Piraeus, the Athens seaport, which, he said, served the best food in Europe. It was an odd place. Except for the staff, there were no Greeks present. The food was banal, but they had created the formula, a quarter of a century before the nouvelle-cuisine loonies launched le menu dégustation, of the non-meal—fifteen or twenty little dabs of unrelated foods, served in interminable succession, one after the other, the whole lot accompanied by turpentiny retsina wine, for a fixed price. One day we had lunch in a primitive workers' restaurant in one of the little streets near the foot of the Acropolis. The tables were oil-cloth-covered boards, supported by sawhorses, with benches to either side. The food, mostly stews and baked dishes, was on view and one had only to point to order. I forget what we began with, but we both pointed to a huge vat of snails, the same small, white shelled snails that are, misleadingly, called "limaces" in Provence and prepared "à la suçarelle." These were prepared in much the same way, first cooked in a court-bouillon, then simmered for a couple of hours in a ragoût of sausage meat, garlic, onions, herbs, tomatoes and white wine. They were so good that even the retsina was a pleasure–the price of the meal, translated from drachma, was less than fifty cents. I have never eaten better in Greece.

Except for the stark, melancholy remains of Greek temples in Agrigento, a section of moulded plaster ceiling, which collapsed over our bed in a Taormina hotel room and left me limping for two weeks, and some spooky catacombs near Palermo, packed with remarkably well-preserved corpses, my memories of that first trip to Sicily are vague.

Lucia and I had traveled to Arezzo to study Piero della Francesca's "Story of the True Cross," in the church of San Francesco, and to Piero's home town, Borgo San Sepolcro, to gaze in awe at his Resurrection. Back in Florence, Elliott and I did the

Richard Olney. Portrait of Sacha Neuville, 1953. Oil on canvas.

"Piero tour" again, this time adding to the itinerary Piero's mother's home town, Monterchi, to see the Madonna del Parto. In his book on Piero, published in 1951, Kenneth Clark writes, "It is one of the few great works of art which are still relatively inaccessible, and to visit it offers some of the pleasures of a pilgrimage. Only after much wandering and misdirection do we reach a rustic cemetery on a hill a few miles outside the village of Monterchi, where the custodian seems to understand the nature of our quest; and it is with skepticism and apprehension that we see her open the doors of a tiny graveyard chapel. In this heightened state of perception we are suddenly confronted with the splendid presence of the Madonna, rising up, 'full without boast,' only a few feet away from us. That this effect, as of a sudden revelation, was in Piero's mind, is evident from the device of the two angels pulling back the curtain." We experienced the same "wandering and misdirection," finally entering a little bar-caffè at a country cross-roads to ask directions once again. Three or four men at the bar first had a good laugh at the crazy Americans looking for a cemetery, then pointed to a road; "about a kilometer," one said. The custodian of the cemetery led us, through a labyrinth of ancient gravestones, to the tiny chapel, proportioned to contain no more than three people, which was believed to mark the grave of Piero's mother; the back wall was hidden by faded blue double curtains. When we were correctly positioned, she dramatically pulled a cord, which drew back the curtains in perfect imitation of those in the fresco, parted by the angels to present the pregnant earth goddess, head-on and close-up, delicately opening, beneath a partially unlaced bodice, the front of her gown to announce the coming of the god-child. We gasped. The custodian was delighted with the success of her presentation; it was a marvelous bit of theatre. She asked us to sign the guest book; the signature preceding ours was Kenneth Clark's, dated more than a year earlier. (Four years later, my sister, Elizabeth, and I visited Monterchi. The magical little chapel had been demolished, a hideous tall brick chapel had been erected near the entrance to the cemetery and Piero's fresco was fixed, high above the altar, against the naked, raw-red brick wall, never again to be seen as it was conceived.)

Reflexions

Back in Paris, I met Jimmy Baldwin, probably at the beginning of 1953. I remember that he was very excited because Knopf had accepted *Go Tell It on the Mountain*, which was to be published that spring. I was again living in the Hôtel de Verneuil and the urgency of finding a place of my own, where I could paint, cook and receive friends, was pressing. I visited a fly-by-night agency, culled from the want-ads, where I was told that a "distinguished" retired actress had a flat to rent in Clamart, a Parisian suburb, for 10,000 fr. ($20) a month. I met her there, late afternoon, the following day—the three bare attic rooms, with a tiny kitchen, no bath, no toilet and no heating, were depressing at first sight, but I took it. The house, in ill repair, surrounded by an unkempt garden and courtyard, protected from neighbors and the street by high stone walls, dated from 1820 and was beautiful. I didn't meet the landlady, Mlle (Suzanne) Marty, until the next day. She seemed pleased to find me there, offered me several pieces of furniture and a coal stove and showed me the cellar, one room of which, she said, was for my use. The toilet, on the ground floor, emptied into a septic tank and was flushed with a pitcher of water. I bought a portable, galvanized bathtub at the flea market, a replica of the narrow, elongated tub in which Bonnard stretched an immersed nude in one of his most famous paintings. It barely fitted into the kitchen on the diagonal and had to be filled from heated pots and pans of water, emptied, scrubbed and hauled back to its corner in the storeroom, all of which was very tiresome but seemed to make the soak, itself, more luxurious and precious. I also acquired an antique bathing device, familiar to everyone from Degas paintings of the bath, a sort of galvanized tray resembling a giant tastevin. Without a servant to pour over pitchers of hot water and scrub one's back, it was useless. I think I was suffering from "Impressionist fever."

I painted one wall of the main room with an amateurish viticultural map of France (clusters of grapes here and there), presenting major vineyard regions, and began to settle in. The actress always arrived to collect the rent in the late afternoon, when Mlle Marty was out. I had been there for several months when Mlle Marty rather timidly asked me why I never paid any rent; She said the actress had paid none for two years but that, when I moved in, she thought things might be different. The actress was supposed to be paying 5,000 fr. a month, so I suggested that we split the difference; I would pay 7,500 fr., reimburse Mlle Marty for the previous months and we could say good-bye to the actress. She like the solution but was terrified of a confrontation; I promised to deal with the lady alone. When the time came, accusations of dishonesty, abuse of good faith, etc. were hurled at me, but it was the last we saw of her. Mlle Marty was euphoric.

Mlle Marty was the daughter of a retired army general, who had died a few years earlier, leaving her the house but not much else. Her mother had died young. She had dreamt of being a classical actress but her father rejected the possibility of a general's daughter dabbling in the theater. She lived with two cats, minou and minette; they were not always the same, for minou prowled and often returned badly torn up from nocturnal battles—or failed to return. She hennaed her hair about once a month and, for days after, her hands and forearms were orange. She adorned herself with costume jewelry, unusual hats from past eras and gowns discovered in the flea market, entertained a high disdain for the bourgeoisie, and the neighbours thought that she was mad. She claimed to respect all life and disapproved of swatting flies, but could often be heard, from behind half-closed shutters, to cheer a cat, stalking a bird, with the words, "Vas-y minette, attrape-le!" Mlle Marty had no friends, but she revered artists. I asked her sometimes to dinner and, in the years to come, painted a number of portraits of her.

The cellar was cool the year round and humid, ideal for storing wine. Great wines were not expensive then—I remember buying several cases of Château Ducru-Beaucaillou 1947 for 700 fr. ($1.40) a bottle. Each year, in April, I bought a keg each of Pouilly-Fumé, Beaujolais-Villages, and one of the Beaujolais first growths, Côte de Brouilly, Morgon or Chiroubles, which, after a few weeks' rest in the cellar, I put into bottles.

Bill Aalto had returned to New York, Peter Price to England, Elliott continued to live at the Verneuil but was often in Clamart, sometimes with Serena Rothstein, an American painter. Sacha was a regular dinner guest, Kenneth Anger came occasionally and Peter Watson came when he was in Paris (his Paris visits became less frequent—in the spring of 1956, he was discovered drowned in his bathtub). I often exchanged meals with an American couple, Tom and Ulla Hubble, who lived on the ground floor of Mlle Marty's house. Annette Michelson, of whom I was painting a portrait, stayed for lunch on the days of the sittings; Elliott and I often visited her and her companion, Bernie Frechtman who was Jean Genet's translator, at their flat in Paris. Bernie was a gentle scholar. I liked him and conscientiously read his translation of *Notre Dame des Fleurs*; privately I thought it had more the odour of the polite classroom than of the rough underworld which was Genet's milieu. (After Elliott and I parted ways, Annette, Bernie and I drifted apart. In 1965, Genet quarreled with Bernie, he and Annette separated, she returned to America and, in 1967, Bernie hanged himself.)

Harriet Sohmers moved in circles unfamiliar to me. She had told me that she and other friends were into writing pornographic novels ("such fun!") and that she knew the group who had launched a little magazine, *Merlin*, a year earlier. (All of this information went in one ear and out the other—it was only recently, upon reading *Exiled In Paris*, published in 1995 by James Campbell, that the pieces of the puzzle fell into place and I realized that *Merlin* had been associated with Maurice Girodias of Olympia Press and that several of the editors of *Merlin* had amused themselves by writing "dbs"—dirty books—for Olympia under various pseudonyms.) The *Merlin* people gathered in the Café de Tournon, where I had taken coffee a couple of times with an American writer, Eugene Walter, who lived across the street from the café. Eugene's conversation was determinedly whimsical—he talked a lot about monkeys—and the atmosphere of the café was uncongenial to me; I returned to the Flore.

Harriet decided that it would be a wonderful idea to invite several of her friends to dinner in Clamart. I was not taken with the idea of entertaining a lot of strangers, "but," she said, "they're all so brilliant and interesting— you'll adore them." I guess Elliott knew them. As it turned out, one of my guests, a lovely girl named Jane Lougee, I knew by name and rumor, because an old college friend had been in love with her. I didn't like the men, whose names and faces I promptly forgot. They swilled the food and the wines and, before the cheese platter and its accompanying wine arrived, began to roll marijuana cigarettes. Elliott, I'm sure, had never smoked the stuff before; he was unleashed, totally out of control, dancing wildly around and pounding out drum beats on a large canvas I had just begun. I was disgusted and depressed.

At more civilized gatherings, when Mlle Marty was present, Elliott would beg her to play Phèdre, while he gave the réplique. He often was so fascinated by her performance that he forgot the réplique–and she would scream, "La réplique! Vite, donnez-moi la réplique!" while he frantically fumbled pages to find it. Her props—handkerchiefs and scarves—were in shreds by the end of the performance.

Auden's nonsense didn't discourage us from renting Gisella's house again in summer 1953. Serena Rothstein also took a house there. Brian Howard and his friend, Sammy, arrived and, intrigued by the Auden ban, promptly paid us a visit. (Brian, an American raised in England and educated at Eton and Oxford, was a legend, famous for his sultry good looks, his precocious brilliance and his tantrums—everyone who knew him or had known him described bad scenes, which became worse with the passage of time—gratuitous insults, overturned restaurant tables, tearful apologies....) That day, and few other times we saw Brian, the air was tense, for he was obsessed by the idea that Sammy and I should sleep together. Sammy was a sea of calm; he shrugged and smiled. (A few years later, on the Côte d'Azur, Sammy died by gas, Brian from an overdose of drugs.)

The night before leaving Ischia, we gave a party; it lasted late and was a passably drunken affair. Except for Serena and Sammy, I have no memory of the guests—Brian wasn't there. Sammy and I were curled up in a corner when Serena saw us and hastened to report the horrible news to Elliott. A couple of hours later, on the boat to Naples, the floodgates opened to a barrage of invectives, anguished accusations and furious denouncements: I was a traitor; didn't I know that love was sacred; life was no longer worth living.... All the way to Naples, Elliott threatened to jump

overboard. I couldn't understand what all the drama was about—mainly, I was perplexed that, after having regaled himself for a year and a half with tales of daisy-chains and sworn vows of non-fidelity, such fury could be ignited in Elliott's breast by a non-event. That scene marked the beginning of the end of our togetherness, but he cooled down and we continued to Florence.

At La Pietra, an ancient villa outside of Florence, whose most recent façade was 17th century, we visited Harold Acton, whom I had known in New York in the spring of 1951. He was a fascinating companion, a born conversationalist and raconteur, who seemed to know or to have known everyone whose name had appeared in print in this century, whether in literary publications or the society pages. His speech and his movements lilted in unison, at times giving the impression that he might take flight; he believed, above all, in the supremacy of **art**. Many claim that he was the model for Ambrose Silk in *Put Out More Flags* and for Anthony Blanche in *Brideshead Revisited*; Evelyn Waugh wrote, "The characters in my novels often wrongly identified with Harold Acton were to a great extent drawn from (Brian Howard)." His father had died recently and Harold was heir to La Pietra, its formal gardens and outdoor theatre, caretaker of his father's famous collection of early Italian paintings and guide to daily visitors, a suffocating responsibility for a carefree spirit. He and his mother, once American, then in her early eighties, a wisp of elegance, whose extravagantly high-heeled shoes caused her to totter slightly, received us, with three or four other guests. No sooner had tea been served than the butler arrived and began to prepare dry martinis; he appeared to be about to empty the bottle of vermouth into the cocktail pitcher when Harold's mother hastened to snatch it away, exclaiming, "Oh, these Italians are impossible—they will never understand how to make a martini!" She proceeded to add a drop of vermouth to the pitcher and to serve the martinis herself, while the butler, properly chastened, stood to the side. (Subsequent visits confirmed my suspicion that they had carefully rehearsed this little act for the guests' entertainment.) Harold's conversation was urbane, witty and amusing, but the spark of joyous abandon that I had known in New York was missing.

Late one night, with Jimmy Baldwin at La Reine Blanche, I met Bernard Hassell, a black American dancer at les Folies-Bergère. When we touched, there was something like an electrical explosion, so we hopped a taxi to Clamart to touch again. It was a lunatic adventure, for Bernard needed a sugar daddy, not a penniless painter, we nonetheless battled our way through a number of years to come. When he chose to exercise it, Bernard had great charm and he was often very funny. For a couple of months, we went often to Le Boeuf sur le Toit to listen to Garland Wilson, a friend of Bernard's, whom I had known in New York when he, Norene Tate and Mae Barnes entertained in Jimmy Daniels's club on 8th Street. Garland died at the piano late 1953.

The Hubbles were planning to return to California. Jimmy asked if I could arrange with Mlle Marty for his painter friend and "adopted father" from Greenwich Village days, Beauford Delaney, who had recently arrived in Paris, to move in. Mlle Marty lived on the ground floor in the back of the house. The first floor was occupied by a French woman and her German husband, with whom we did not socialize. The door to Beauford's quarters, just inside the entrance to the house, led to a former anteroom, transformed into a kitchen-dining area, beyond which was a large room stretching the length of the house, with tall, double French windows opening onto the courtyard in front and the garden behind. He spread the floor with white bed sheets "to improve the light." Mlle Marty, Beauford and Bernard were all lunar personalities; for years to come, every month on the night of the full moon, the house was quaking with irrational activity—loud rumblings, bumps and shrill scraping noises suggested that Mlle Marty was displacing heavy furniture at 3 or 4 a.m., Beauford was slamming doors and Bernard was leaping out of bed every few minutes on mysterious missions.

Beauford wrapped himself in the cloak of a gentle, beatific philosopher; he spoke in honeyed, mystical tones of the wondrous jewel beneath all things, which only the artist could uncover, while his hands seemed to be unveiling this very jewel in the air before one's eyes. In the cafés of Saint Germain or Montparnasse, many sat rapt, listening and watching; others may have considered it good entertainment, worth the price of a drink. Most of these people Beauford categorized as "darling friends." Some came to Clamart bearing gifts of cast-off clothes or other useless gimcracks; when he had closed the door on them with sweet blessings, he would turn his back to the door, stoop over, fling symbolic skirts in the air and then paw the ground with his feet. The exorcism was completed with a raucous witch's cackle and, then, we could relax with a drink. Beauford rubbed black shoe-polish into his hair and never discussed his age. Jimmy confided to me that he had sneaked a look at Beauford's passport and that the birth year, 1900, had been incompetently altered to 1910.

At about the same time, I met Jimmy's friend, Mary Painter, a Marshall Plan economist with the American Embassy, who was in the process of moving from her flat in the rue Bonaparte to more spacious quarters in the rue des Carmes, near the Place Maubert and the Latin Quarter. Mary had a passion for the table and she adored ortolans, the little birds which were captured in nets in the southwest of France (now illegal) as they migrated north in the spring and, again, in autumn as they flew south, fattened in cages for a couple of weeks before being force-fed a few drops of armagnac for the sacrifice, plumed and packed in cases to be shipped to Paris. In the ortolan season, spring or fall, we went to Chez l'Ami Louis, a simple, even rather slummy, bistrot in appearance, which may have been the most expensive restaurant in Paris. The floors were spread with sawdust, the tables with newssheet, the dining room was heated by a coal stove and stove-pipes, the walls were dusky from their emanations and there was no wine list beyond the half-dozen wines scribbled to the side of the menu. A large proportion of the clientèle was American. Monsieur Antoine, the Swiss chef-proprietor, who was alone in the kitchen, except for a dishwasher, was a madman; he hated all sauces—in fact, he hated most French food and was contemptuous of all his colleagues. At Easter-time, he served legs of milk-lamb, roast to order, and, in late autumn, rare-roast wood-cock. We began with his duck foie gras, firm and pink, accompanied by a slice of raw country ham, cured on the bone; the ortolans were merely sautéed in butter for a few minutes.

Richard Olney. Portrait of Annette Michelson, 1953. Oil on canvas.

Mary's stock of PX scotch was unlimited but, in those days, she was disciplined in the sense that she drank strong spirits only on the week-end. Friday evening, Jimmy, Beauford and I would arrive, sometimes Jimmy's friend, Lucien, who lived in Switzerland but was often in Paris—the Folies kept Bernard away until midnight—and the whisky would flow to the accompaniment of blues and jazz, punctuated by meals, which I prepared, often until Sunday night. These gatherings were baptized "Saturday Night Function," after one of the records that was often played. Beauford worshipped these sessions, waiting impatiently each week for Friday evening to arrive. Mary had a Siamese cat named Caesar. Beauford didn't like Caesar, but he hoped it would please Mary if he were to show some interest in the beast. He never attempted to touch it, but he would approach it, repeating, in soothing, incantational tones, "Nice Caesar…nice Caesar…." One evening, Caesar casually lifted a paw and split Beauford's nose open. It was a dramatic moment, there was a lot of blood, first-aid was administered and, henceforth, Beauford was very nervous about being in the same room with Caesar.

Mary and I had dreamt for some time of making a pilgrimage to Alexandre Dumaine's restaurant at l'Hôtel de la Côte d'Or, in Saulieu (Burgundy) a two or three hour drive on the old Paris-Nice route. Jimmy, Beauford and I squeezed ourselves, along with Caesar, disgruntled in his wicker basket, into Mary's mini-car. Mary wanted to let the cat prowl freely in the car, but Beauford was so terrified at this prospect that we kept it imprisoned and yowling until we arrived in Saulieu, late morning, in time to settle into our rooms—one for Mary and Caesar, another with two single beds and a roll-away cot for the rest of the party—and to discuss the dinner menu with Dumaine before going to lunch.

A chatty, anecdotal, sometimes cranky, book of recipes, *La Table au Pays de Brillat-Savarin*, published in 1892 by a lawyer and amateur cook, Lucien Tendret, was often reflected in Dumaine's menus. His sumptuous pâtés and terrines, intricate mosaics, in cross-section, of pistachio-speckled dark and light forcemeats, alternating with striped layers of dark game and white meats, punctuated with fingers of red tongue, white back fat and black truffle, were adapted from Tendret. "La Poularde à la Vapeur de Lucien Tendret," a truffled Bresse chicken, placed on a plate and a tripod and steamed in the vapors of a double consommé within a hermetically sealed earthenware marmite, was always on the menu, but had to be ordered in advance. That was our main course for dinner, preceded by "Filets de Sole Eminence," an assemblage of folded, poached sole fillets, slices of lobster tail and pike quenelles, with a creamed lobster "à l'Américaine" sauce. The quenelles, composed of the pounded and sieved pike flesh, egg-white and cream, were firm, but light as a soufflé. The first wine, a Montrachet 1934, was a golden, voluptuous dream. The chicken arrived in its marmite, the cover sealed by a dampened ribbon of cloth wound round and round the rim, which, when unwound, released a flood of truffle fragrance. The chicken was served with its juices, which had collected in the plate, and accompanied by creamed morels. The wine, a Beaune Dames Hospitalières 1947, was good, but not memorable. With the cheeses, we wanted to be astounded, so we asked Madame Dumaine to consult with the master (who never left the kitchens during the service); he sent to table a cool bottle of La Tâche (Domaine de la Romanée-Conti) 1951, a despised vintage with no more than a year of bottle age; it was transcendent—I had never tasted anything like it. (1951 was such a disastrous vintage that the proprietors of the Domaine decided not to pick La Tâche at harvest time—in late October, the sun came out, the grapes ripened and La Tâche, alone, was bottled with the Domaine's label.)

No one smoked in Dumaine's dining room. In the bar, with the apéritif, one smoked and, again with coffee and digestif. After the service, Dumaine would leave his kitchens and settle into the bar to smoke a Gauloise and converse; his conversation never strayed from the technical aspects of cuisine and how he had adapted classical techniques to his own sensibilities—his mirepoix, for instance, was never cooked in fat, for he had discovered the flavor to be purer if the chopped vegetables were sweated, covered, in the oven, until they rendered their juices and began to colour at the edges, before being deglazed with white wine. We drank 1904 cognac with him and liked it so much that we carried some to our rooms. Beauford dozed off, Jimmy's glass was empty and he reached stealthily for Beauford's when, suddenly, Beauford opened his eyes. The scene was re-enacted several times before, finally, Beauford's eyes failed to open and Jimmy emptied his glass. Like so many things remembered, the incident is meaningless, yet when I think of Dumaine, of the steamed chicken or La Tâche 1951, I see Jimmy's hand moving toward Beauford's glass and I hear Beauford saying, "...just resting my eyes."

The aura of Clamart, then, was that of a provincial village. The entrance to a forest, le Bois de Clamart, an extension of le Bois de Meudon, was a block from La Place Marquis, near Mlle Marty's house. Parisians came there on weekends to wander in nature or to picnic. Facing the forest's edge was "la Guinguette," a café-bar with an arboured terrace and the ambiance of an impressionist painting, which belonged to Pierre and Pierrette Vimont, former proprietors of a bar in Pigalle, about which Pierrette reminisced sentimentally. For Clamart, she was pretty exotic: she wore high-heeled "wedgies" and heavily mascaraed false eyelashes, painted a beauty spot on her face, kept within reach a glass of Champagne, which she de-gassed with a swizzle-stick, spoke in a gravelly voice and had a distinctly bawdy sense of humour. Pierrette's father had been a professional chef and she offered me his battery of copper pots. She had learned to cook from her father; I remember a sumptuous coq-au-vin, prepared with a giant, year-old cock, cut up and marinated in red wine and aromatics before being put to cook for a couple of hours, cooled over-night, degreased and simmered with its garnish of lardons, little onions and mushrooms.

Tommie Greaves, with whom I had waited tables at 17 Barrow, spent a few weeks in Paris. She came often to dinner in Clamart, I shared a number of restaurant meals with her in Paris and she joined the Saturday Night Function crowd; she had known both Jimmy and Beauford during their Village days. I was reading Henry James, whom Tommie suspected of being a tiresome old snob and windbag. I insisted that she read *Portrait of a Lady* and was comforted to find her in tears as she finished it.

Then Julius Goldstein, with whom I had shared a lower East Side coldwater flat during our Brooklyn Museum Art School days, arrived. Like Tommie, he was critical of my reading material and, again, I imposed *Portrait of a Lady*; as he finished, the tears were flowing so abundantly that he fled to the Bois de Clamart to have a good cry. We often visited la Guinguette. Pierrette, who had just finished one of the Simenon "Maigret" novels, in which Maigret visits Texas, where, in every bar, he is greeted with "Have a drink, Julius!," never failed, as we entered to claim this phrase, which she pronounced," avoondrinkjuliousse," following it with peals of laughter.

Henry Miller, who had written of Beauford in dithyrambic terms, was passing through Paris. Beauford was proud to count the famous writer among his friends and wanted me to meet him—I invited them to lunch, after which we went to the Guinguette for coffee and digestif. Miller uncritically worshipped France and everything French; Pierrette and her Guinguette were a huge success.

Mary commissioned a portrait of Jimmy. He was a conscientious sitter. Jimmy's speech was punctuated with endearing, kiddish exclamations—he said, "Wow, baby! That is FAN-TAS-TIC!" (In spring 1990, I received a phone call from London; Christopher Hitchens introduced himself and asked if I had ever painted a portrait of James Baldwin—I described a black jersey pullover with sleeves pushed up to the elbows, one arm slung over the back of a small, straight-backed chair–"That's it!" he said and explained that he had received a book to review, *James Baldwin, The Legacy* (Quincy Troupe, S&S, 1989), in which the portrait was reproduced and attributed to Beauford Delaney. My brother, James, sent me a copy of the book—and there it was, a bad reproduction with the top of the head and half a hand, at the bottom of the painting, chopped off, bearing the caption "Beauford Delaney's portrait of Baldwin, early 1950s." S & S declined to publish an apology. It was reproduced, with the correct attribution, in the *London Times Literary Supplement*, June 8-14 1990.)

To celebrate the portrait's completion, I organized a lunch with Mary, Jimmy, Beauford and Bernard at Lapérouse, one of the hallowed gastronomic temples of the day, in a private "salon." I went around in advance to discuss the menu with the maître d'hôtel and the wines with the sommelier. The maître d'hôtel recommended petits pois with the duck— "But," I said, "it's not the season." He assured me that tinned peas were superior to fresh peas, so I figured we had nothing to discuss. The sommelier was of the old-fashioned breed—he pocketed a commission from négociants on the wines he sold and he pushed them hard. We drank a négociant's Corton-Charlemagne and I don't remember the reds. The food was restaurant cuisine, marked by the taste of basic sauces, but we had a good time, partly because of the 19th century aura of the private room, the opposite walls of which were mirrors on which had been scratched with diamonds the names of hundreds of cocottes and their gentlemen. We had no diamonds with which to leave our mark, but the maître d'hôtel always knocked before unlocking and entering, lest any indiscretions be revealed.

Noah Greenberg, a friend from New York arrived in Paris, on tour with his group of musician performers, the Pro Musica Antiqua, where they presented the *Daniel Play* in the church of Saint-Germain-des-Prés. Critics and public were ravished by the performance and by Russell Oberlin's angelic counter tenor. Noah was a big man, with a big laugh, a big appetite and a huge love of life. He wanted to invite me to dinner and I chose la Boule d'Or in the Place d'Aligre, where the food was bigger than life—trolleys laden with charcuterie and a tub of unpasteurized butter were rolled around for clients to serve themselves and the main courses, rustic in spirit, were served abundantly. Noah was in heaven. I invited the group to a buffet-dinner party in Clamart to celebrate their success. Mlle Marty and Beauford were present, Bernard arrived at midnight and the weather was beautiful. Pouilly-Fumé and Beaujolais flowed, the table was spread with ratatouille, roast legs of lamb, warm salad of white beans, cheeses, and I forget...the party was up and down stairs and mostly in the garden. Russell and I still retain sentimental memories of that evening. Noah died, too young, from a heart attack a few years later.

Sacha brought Eda Lord to lunch one day. Eda was American. (She published two enchanting autobiographical novels, *Childsplay* and *A Matter of Choosing*, one about a turbulent childhood, the other about growing up strong willed.) She married young, moved to China, left her husband and, in 1932, arrived in

Berlin, where she met Sacha, a Swiss friend, Lili Turel, and others; they all moved to France a year later. Eda's World War II was spent with Resistance friends in the south of France. Her last novel, *Extenuating Circumstances*, describes those years. Eda was gentle and comfortable to be with, her conversation was quietly ironic, sometimes punctuated with innocent wonderment, her voice and laugh corrugated by a dedication to cigarettes. Doctors had forbidden her to drink; she carried a thermos of hot water and a jar of instant coffee, from which she concocted endless infusions while her friends drank harder stuff. She loved the table and was fascinated by wine, sniffed it, but dared not taste it.

Lili Turel shared a house in Magagnosc, a village near Grasse, with Philippe Wehrlé, a brilliant theoretical physicist in the view of those better versed than I to judge. Their bond was opium, which Philippe believed was God's greatest gift to man; Lili claimed to hate it, but couldn't live without it and was incapable alone, of preparing a pipe. Sacha and Lili had been lovers, in all but the physical expression, since their days in Berlin. Each autumn, he visited Magagnosc, and again in the spring. Lili asked me to come along with Sacha in the fall of 1954. It was my first glimpse of the south of France. I was stunned by the light, the colours, the scents of wild herbs, the beauty and activity of the open-air markets, the terraces of olive trees.... I knew that I must, eventually, live there. In the following years, I, too, spent a couple of weeks, each autumn and spring, with Lili and Philippe, sometimes overlapping with Sacha's visits, sometimes alone, painting days and cooking in the evenings.

Philippe had been director of the Vichy government's weather bureau. Many of his friends, formerly in the Resistance, who came by to smoke, praised his usefulness in the enemy camp; he shrugged that off with the observation that a diplomatic pouch was invaluable for searching out opium and traveling freely with it. Although their conversation was polite, Sacha didn't like Philippe. He blamed him for the death, in the 1930s, of René, a young man he had loved, because Philippe taught him to smoke opium (René died in a Montparnasse dive by swallowing heroin, bought from Kiki, the artists' model whose nude back Man Ray transformed

Richard Olney. Portrait of James Baldwin, 1954. Oil on canvas.

Richard Olney. Portrait of Mlle Marty, 1955-56. Oil on canvas.

into a bass fiddle for posterity.) and he blamed him for Lili's addiction.

Philippe came down to breakfast just before noon, after spending mornings in his rooms, smoking and working on a scientific treatise. (Two heavy volumes were published in Switzerland shortly before his death.) For relaxation, he read Saint-Simon and the intrigues at the court of Louis XIV occupied much of his conversation at table. Alba, the housekeeper, who was there from 9 to 5, prepared lunch. Philippe and Lili smoked together at the end of the day in an extra bedroom. Lili went upstairs at six, insisting that she would smoke only one pipe and, day after day, begged me to do nothing in the kitchen until she came down and we could prepare dinner together. I soon realized that there was no such thing as "only one pipe." I prepared the meals, except for last minute details, and carried my drink upstairs around 10 o'clock to announce that dinner would be ready when they were. More pipes were smoked. The ambiance was eerie and fascinating, the conversation lucid, analytical and, I thought, brilliant, the awareness of time passing non-existent; as often as not, it was 2 a.m. before we sat down to table—my menus were conceived with that in mind. Philippe was not interested in rare and beautiful pipes—they were nothing but long rubber tubes with a simple bowl stuck to one end, the sticky opium concentrate dabbed into a tiny hole. The lamp burned peanut oil, whose flame, Philippe claimed, was less hot than that of other oils. All of his cardigans had heavy patches sewn to the right elbow, on which he leaned while preparing pipes. Lili lay flat on her back while Philippe fed her the tube and held the bowl to the flame; I didn't like to see Lili smoke. She told Philippe that, if he ever encouraged me to smoke, she would kill him—that was all right with me because opium scared me to death.

Lili and I often took a morning bus into Grasse to shop. She loved searching out the freshest and tenderest vegetables. (It was in Magagnosc that I discovered the beauty of small violet artichokes, picked before the choke begins to form, eaten raw, dipped in fruity olive oil and homemade vinegar—and of freshly picked fava beans, the size of a little finger nail, their skins still tender and bright, shiny green, the flesh juicy with no trace of starchiness, eaten raw dipped in salt, with rough country bread and unsalted, unpasteurized butter.) With our shopping baskets loaded, Lili was no longer game for a bus ride and she needed a fortifier; before taking a taxi, we would stop in a café, where she threw down several cognacs in rapid succession. Philippe told me that I must never permit Lili to drink cognac but, for certain things, she was strong-willed and I was powerless to stop her. For the most part, she was never seen to drink anything except wine at table but, on mornings that we didn't go shopping, she was often confined to her bed with a mysterious illness that, I thought, bore all the earmarks of a hangover from clandestine drinking in her room at night; on these days, she didn't come down to lunch, but was sufficiently revived by evening to assist at the smoking session. She bemoaned the loss of her youth and beauty, associated her recurrent illness with that phenomenon, and traveled several times to Switzerland to be treated by a doctor, who specialized in rejuvenescence by means of ewes' placenta injections. When she was sober and feeling well, Lili was an angel; she could spend hours collecting wild flowers, with which she composed exquisite, ephemeral bouquets to scatter throughout the house.

I visited family in June 1955. (Margaret and I had studied painting together at the University of Iowa and, later, lived in New York at the same time. I came to know my other brothers and sisters, one by one, as they began to grow up. Byron, the youngest, was not yet five years old when I left home for college.) John was in the army in Korea, Norris was in the navy. Margaret and her husband, Tom McBride, were living in New York on West 23rd Street. James, Elizabeth, Frances, Byron and I gathered there and I got to know Byron for the first time—he was still in high school. Jimmy Baldwin was in town and came to dinner. He and Tom glanced around the table, looked at each other and began howling with laughter; the joke, apparently, was that, except for them, everybody at table looked alike.

Bill Aalto and his young friend, Donny, were living on 39th or 40th Street near 9th Avenue, a slummy neighborhood with a wonderful market and a butcher who sold real mutton. Bill asked

Byron and me to dinner. Byron remembers that, with great guffaws, he made much mock to-do about our celebrating Flag Day. The other guest was Joan Colquhoun, who arrived with several bottles of Pommard. (Joan had moved to New York because Bill was there; while he was in Paris, she had lived in London but often crossed the channel bearing him gifts of teddy bears stuffed with ten pound notes—then, the English were permitted to carry only small amounts of money out of the country.) The leg of mutton was roast medium-rare. It was delicious until Bill and Donny began quarreling, a mild difference of opinion swelling to violent altercation, at which point Donny picked up the carving knife and began to swing it around. I pulled Joan aside and told her to get Byron out of there and down to Margaret's and that I would join them as soon as possible. I waited until I was certain that Joan and Byron would have turned onto 9th Avenue, then started down the stairs, with Bill following, Donny riding him piggy-back, knife in hand. (In Byron's memory, Donny emptied the platter of carved meat over Bill's head, it was Bill who picked up the knife and it was I who rode him down the stairs.) I headed for the piers, until I lost them, and caught a taxi to Margaret's where I found Joan, drinking a whisky and quite elated by the evening's excitement. After a drink or so, she thought we should have another across the street in a bar called The Idle Hour, a louche hangout for drunken longshoremen, where the clientèle was mesmerized, not for the first time, by Joan's brittle British accent and raucous laugh. Of course Bill came by the next day with soul-racked apologies.

Jimmy returned to Paris that autumn with a new lover, Arnold, a jazz musician who had left his vibraphone in New York, a gentle, sweet boy who drifted easily with the tide. They moved into a flat on Avenue de Versailles and asked Mary, Beauford, Bernard, and me to Saturday lunch. Mary arrived from her first riding lesson in the Bois de Boulogne looking like a fashion ad for the ultimate horsewoman, in riding breeches, boots, headgear and tailored jacket, swinging a crop. It may have been her only riding lesson, as the Saturday morning sessions fitted badly with the Saturday Night Functions, which began on Friday evenings; I never again saw her in the horsey getup. Arnold's innocence was captivating: once, when he, Jimmy, and Beauford came to dinner, I accompanied a boned, stuffed and braised lamb shoulder with a purée of celeriac, potatoes, garlic, onions and turnips; Arnold exclaimed, "Gee, Richard–those are the most fantastic mashed potatoes I've ever tasted!"

In spring 1956, my sister, Elizabeth, planned to spend a couple of months in Europe. I decided to pick up her ship in Barcelona, on its way to Naples. On the train from Paris, I shared a compartment with a young man from Barcelona. Upon arriving, I expected him to be met by family or friends, but he seemed to be at loose ends and suggested that he show me "Barcelona by night." I deposited my bags at a hotel near the port and we visited a half-dozen bars, all laden with tapas. I don't know what we drank, but I remember an ongoing cephalopod feast—little cuttlefish sautéed in their ink, squid fritters and bite-size fragments of octopus, braised in a variety of sauces. Then he said that, since Barcelona was famous for its whorehouses, we should visit one. The girls, none in their first youth paraded in half-dress, their fronts covered with gowns which fell to their ankles their behinds uncovered to display flabby bouncing buttocks. I felt like an intruder and wanted to get out; my friend was perfectly willing. He had not been flirtatious with me nor was he interested in the whores. As far as I could tell, he was, above all, pleased to have been able to present "his" Barcelona to a stranger; the cephalopods rated higher than the whorehouse but it was a nice experience.

The ship docked the following morning; Elizabeth and I continued to Naples, from which in the days to follow we made the usual excursions to Pompeii, Herculaneum, and to Paestum, whose 6th and 5th century B.C. Greek temples rising from the plain and from the mists of time, unenclosed and uninfested by tourists were magic. (On later visits they were penned in by high fences and visitors queued to pay entrance fees.) From the railroad station, the site of the temples was a long walk on a deserted country road bordered by fields of artichokes, whose buds were at the perfect stage of development to be eaten raw. We filched a few and, that evening in Naples, had dinner in one of the terraced restaurants surrounding the port of Santa Lucia, where boats float indolently as, hour after hour, their musician occupants play and sing "Santa Lucia." I was uncertain how the maître d'hôtel would take to clients' producing their own food. To pave the way, we ordered a bottle of white wine and some prosciutto crudo (cured on the bone and delicious) before I uncovered the artichokes and asked him to bring us some olive oil and vinegar. He was astonished and delighted that foreigners should want to do anything so quintessentially Italian as to eat raw artichokes and proceeded to give us very special service throughout the meal. The ham and artichokes were followed by a tomatoey stew of cuttlefish, crustaceans and shellfish.

Elizabeth's European tour was an abbreviated version of my traveling experience from preceding years: we did our duty by ancient Rome and baroque architecture, found Lucia in Florence, settled into the Bartolini, traveled the Piero della Francesca circuit, visited Siena, Assisi and La Pietra, where Mrs. Acton and the butler reenacted the martini scene, and headed for France, where we left the train in Dijon to take a bus to Saulieu. The distance is barely forty-five miles, but the bus took three hours, meandering through every village within reach; none of the other passengers traveled further than from one farm to another or to the closest village. The driver knew everyone but us. When the bus stopped, across the street from l'Hôtel de la Côte d'Or, Mme Dumaine hastened over to greet us; I was convinced that it was the first time in the restaurant's history that clients had arrived by the local bus.

I had telephoned in advance to order the truffled steamed chicken for our dinner. The "éminence" assemblage of quenelles, lobster and sole fillets in creamed Américaine sauce had been too complicated for my palate; I asked Dumaine to prepare quenelles au beurre blanc, with which we drank a young Chateau Fuissé; my beloved La Tâche 1951 was poured with the chicken and the cheeses. The next day, we lunched on a slice of terrine, an omelet and a bottle of Beaujolais—very silly to travel to Saulieu to eat an omelet when one could have been feasting on truffled, stuffed pigs' trotters, but a voice told me that I owed it to myself to see how the master made an omelet; I learned nothing except that Dumaine's omelet and mine were the same, eggs broken up with a fork, yolks and whites imperfectly mixed, golden outside and semi-liquid inside.

The Dumaines waved us off on the rickety old bus to Dijon, whence we continued by train to Paris, its museums, the Saturday Night Functions, meals in Clamart, drinks at Pierrette's, my first and last visit to the top of the Eiffel Tower, and the Saint-Germain-des-Prés café life. We attended an Edith Piaf concert at the Olympia. Cocteau had told Piaf that she must never forsake her waif-like, street-urchin appearance. She was tiny, her head too large for its frail body and her hair was sparse. Whenever I saw her, she wore a shapeless black rag and her feet were tucked into worn, ugly flat sandals; but for arms sometimes raised, as if to carry her in flight, she stood motionless before the microphone. Half her public was Parisian working class; the rest was everyone else—underworld, aristocracy, artists, writers, theatre people.... When she began to sing, the audience went wild.

Elizabeth returned and, in June 1956, our brother, John, having just graduated from college, arrived and adjusted himself to a pattern of Saturday Night Functions, posing for portraits, drinks at Pierrette's and the Café de Flore, and gastronomic adventures in Clamart, Paris and Saulieu. At Summer's end, John got a job with the U.S. Army in Orléans as "budget and fiscal officer." He bought a car, spent weekends in Clamart and at Saturday Night Functions; and I sometimes returned with him to Orléans, once with Beauford, another time with a friend from college days, Marjorie Beck, who had become a fashion model in New York before moving to Paris and becoming Chanel's favorite. I remember that she always addressed John as "Old Cock." (When I last heard, years ago, Marjorie was preparing to launch an avant-garde literary review from her home town, Elsworth, Iowa.) In Orléans we often ate, in a comfortingly provincial atmosphere, at l'Auberge Saint Jacques, whose specialties were quenelles de brochet, game in season and Touraine wines—Vouvray, Chinon, and Bourgeuil.

After nearly ten years in Paris, the U.S. government decided to transfer Mary to Washington, D.C.—-she thought the world had come to an end. The last Saturday Night Function was celebrated on the weekend preceding Thanksgiving 1956. She was sailing the day after Thanksgiving and asked me to prepare Thanksgiving (mid-afternoon) dinner for her going-away party. Jimmy and Arnold were in Corsica. Bernard, Beauford, John, a couple of Mary's Embassy friends, Mary and I were the party. The day before, I laced the surface of a leg of venison with little strips of pork back fat, weaving them in and out of the flesh, dribbled over some white wine and olive oil and left the leg to marinate overnight. We began with frog's legs, briefly poached in white wine court-bouillon and served in poulette sauce; the leg was roast pink, accompanied by a buttery chestnut purée, finished with diced crisp celery heart. Roederer Crystal was served before the meal, Chevalier-Montrachet with the frogs, Nuits-Saint-Georges with the venison, Chambertin with the cheeses and I prepared almond souffléed crêpes to accompany a Château Guiraud 1942.

During the 1940s, Lucia and her husband, Ernest Hacker, often had parties in their New York loft on lower 5th Avenue, where cherished records played endlessly. One, sung by Damia, of selections from Kurt Weil's *L'Opéra de Quat' Sous*, I loved. I had never heard of Damia and they knew nothing of her. When I arrived in France, I discovered that she had been a great name among café-concert and music-hall artists during the First World War, the 1920's and '30's and I added all of her available records to my collection, along with Frehel (whom Piaf claimed as her greatest inspiration), Lys Gauty, Mistinguett, Germaine Montéro, Catherine Sauvage and others in the same tradition. Late in 1956, Damia, then in her seventies, returned to the Olympia stage–for a comeback or a good-bye.... Sacha and I went to see her. I thought she was wonderful as she swept dramatically across the stage, arms spread in supplication, a sob in her voice, singing *La Rue, J'ai Perdu Ma Jeunesse*, or other songs of anguish and ardour about poor street girls helplessly in love with their sailors or other fleeting amours. When we left the theater, Sacha said, "I didn't know that you really liked her—in the '30s we used to go to her concerts to laugh at her."

Two

1957-1960
New York. Return to Clamart.

Father was a banker and a lawyer; although he did not trust doctors, medicine was the only other métier that he considered to be altogether respectable. Painting seemed rather far out to him and, in any case, the purpose of the métier was to earn an honest living. (These sentiments were not his, alone; my former brother-in-law, Tom McBride, also a lawyer, once unburdened his feelings to the effect that painting was all right for women—i.e., Margaret, who was raising a family and had little time to paint—but that it was not a "man's work.") In Spring 1957, Father decided that I had wasted enough time in Europe and that there would be no more allowance. I had, in fact, been working hard and had exhibited in salons and in group shows in Paris and London, but he was right in the sense that none of that promised to earn me a living. I booked space to New York on *Le Flandre* for the second week of July and arranged with Mlle Marty to keep the flat in Clamart, determined to return as soon as possible.

Not long before sailing, Byron, who had just graduated from high school, wrote that he was coming to Europe for two months before enrolling in college that fall. We crossed paths on the ocean. Byron remembers arriving in Paris on Bastille day. I have never understood how he, Father, and I could have been so uncoordinated nor have I forgiven my own blind stupidity; why I did not beg Father for a two-month reprieve so that I could travel with Byron and return with him—or why Father did not insist that I do this—I don't know. Byron settled in Clamart, Beauford loved his company and Bernard introduced his "brother-in-law" to all his friends in Saint Germain-des-Prés. John's vacation was in August;

he and Byron visited Italy and returned to Orléans by way of Geneva to pick up John's girl friend and co-worker, Elfriede, who had been vacationing with her family in Austria.

In summer 1957, Jimmy was in and out of New York. I had found a converted coldwater flat on the corner of Houston and West Broadway and was looking for night work that would leave my days free for painting. Mary, who was living in Georgetown, longing to eat crayfish à la nage and to see friends, asked Jimmy and me to join her for a weekend. She had received, I think from Wisconsin, a metal container filled with water and a couple of hundred crawdads, more often sold to fishermen to be used as bait. They were small but lively, I threw them into a boiling white wine court-bouillon for five minutes and we had a feast.

I took a job selling books, from 5 p.m. 'til midnight, at the Doubleday book and record shop, then at 5th Avenue and 52nd Street. Most of my co-workers were young theatre people, holding ends together while looking for work. The shop was always busy and the work was pleasant, except for the inspectors from the main office, who came around occasionally, pompous idiots who acted like army sergeants–"Straighten that tie!"; "Stand up straight!" etc.) We had half an hour for dinner, the others went out, but I prepared something at home and brought it along with a half bottle of wine, to eat downstairs in the stock room. Once, during my dinner break, one of the idiots came prowling around and began to bellow nonsense about "drinking on the job" and getting me fired immediately. I told him that he was interrupting my meal, that I was not on the job and that I could not eat dry—someone must have protected me, for I heard nothing about the incident and my dinner was never again interrupted. My favorite customers were Marlene Dietrich and Lena Horne, both of whom seemed especially human and had the courtesy to treat an anonymous book salesman as a friend. Dietrich often stopped by to pick up a book between five and six o'clock, dressed simply and carelessly, with little or no makeup; when she appeared late, after the theatre, always accompanied by Noel Coward, she was very much her public self, the goddess of artifice in swirls of feathers; then, they headed for the record department and, after having chosen, there was inevitably an argument about whose account the records should be charged to—they were always charged to Dietrich.

I was sent to the Doubleday shop in Grand Central Station as "night manager" which meant that I was alone in the shop and after locking the doors at midnight, had to count the money and "balance the books." It was called a "promotion"; I hated it. Sale rules ware rigid: the sale had to be rung up on the cash register to open it, the bills put in before change was made and the cash register closed before the purchase was wrapped and handed to the customer. A certain type of creature obviously on the Doubleday payroll, never the same but hardly distinguishable from his colleagues, trying to imitate a harried businessman but succeeding better in the role of a cheap movie G-man, sometimes entered the shop, snatched up a book, threw down the exact change (always odd because of added taxes), mumbling something about being in a hurry, and hastened out before pausing to turn and spy lest the sale not be rung up. The charade was revolting, but transparent.

I was shuffled, in the same role, to the Penn Station shop, even more sinister, in a long, darkly lit corridor, with shops the length of one side, facing a wall splattered with advertising and graffiti. Clients were rare and the other shops were closed at night, a neat setup for robbery. One night, Arthur Bell came in. I had known Arthur, a black American dancer, in Paris, at the height of his glory, when he was premier danseur with a French ballet company and, for a season, had received rave reviews; on stage, he was beautiful—his body could do anything effortlessly. Arthur didn't take himself seriously, but he loved to play games of grandeur—he became so grand that the ballet company had to separate itself from him. He was out of work and had no place to live. He asked if he could stay in Clamart for a while and I foolishly said, "sure." He spent long periods each afternoon douching himself "to be clean for the orgy," which he faithfully attended every night in Paris. When he began to hand out the Clamart address, I told him he had to go. Later, Bernard told me that Arthur was in jail and going to be deported: he had boarded a train without a ticket, settled into the dining car and, after the meal, when the maître d'hôtel made out his bill, he had torn it up and contemptuously flung the bits of paper in the man's face; he was handed over to the police at the next stop.

When Arthur sidled into the Penn Station shop, glancing neither to his left nor to his right, the caricature of a shifty thief, he didn't see me. A spook, poured in the same mould as the fake G-Man at Grand Central, was stationed across the corridor. When I walked over to Arthur and said, "hello," he jumped as if he had been stabbed, then recognized me and said, "Oh, hi Richard." He looked awful, dressed in dirty, ragged gym sweat clothes, his face swollen, bruised and scarred as if he had been badly beaten. He said he had been released from prison that day; I didn't ask why he had been in—I knew that it was for some meaningless, self destructive gesture. (And I thought that he had come into the bookshop, knowing that he was being watched, hoping to be arrested for theft and sent back to prison.) I told him there was a plainclothes man across the way and begged him not to try lift-

Bernard, Lucia and me.
In the Tuileries, 1959.

ing anything, he promised, we chatted a while and I walked him to the door, where we shook hands. The spook barged in, demanding loudly, "Who was that and why were you talking to him?" I hadn't the presence of mind to ask who he was or by what right he was being insolent, but mumbled something about an old friend from Paris. He was enraged because I had clearly cheated him of an arrest...but there was nothing he could do about it. I told the Doubleday management that they could move me back to 5th Avenue or I would quit; they moved me back.

Margaret and Tom were still in New York, James had just enrolled at Columbia for graduate studies, I saw Bill Aalto often, Lucia and Ernst were in the 5th Avenue loft and Harriet Sohmers was back in New York. Harriet asked Lucia and me to dinner one Sunday night, my only free evening. She was then married to a seaman (whom I never met) and had a son, not yet at the walking stage, crawling around, undiapered; one had to pee in the sink because the toilet bowl was packed full of dirty diapers. When we arrived, Harriet gaily informed us that there was nothing to eat in the house, but that she had a bottle of gin and "wouldn't it be fun to just sit around and get drunk?" She had no ice. Lucia and I went out and scrounged around the Lower East Side until we found a shop open where we could buy some spaghetti, tins of tomatoes, bread, a fiasco of Chianti and a few ice cubes; it was not a three-star meal but, at least, we ate and drank honestly. I have a confused memory, also, of a party uptown to which Harriet invited Bill Aalto and me. We were, I think, the only males present. Harriet's girlfriend, Irene, appeared to be more interested in Susan Sontag than in Harriet. There was a certain amount of quarreling and some rather wild dancing, during which Harriet was flung across the room and broke her nose. I forget who raced her off to the nearest hospital, where they refused to treat her "because of her filthy language." A more subdued Harriet finally got patched up in another hospital.

Bill Aalto went into the hospital with cancer. Joan was nearly always there when I went by; I never saw Donny. One day, Chester Kallman's father visited—he told me what a wonderful friend Bill had been to Chester. On my last visit, Bill was unconscious, the hideous death rattle announcing his delivery that night.

Robert Isaacson, a friend from earlier New York days, commissioned me to paint his portrait. Lucia and Ernst gave a party to celebrate the portrait's completion and Robert planned a mock ceremony, at party's end, to hand over a check. At 4 a.m. everyone gathered around, while Robert drew out pen and checkbook and proceeded, with flourishes and ill-suppressed giggling, to scribble out the check and pass it to me (applause); it was written out to the order of "Poor Richard" and the signature was illegible, but it passed the scrutiny of his bank.

In early September 1957, returning from France, Byron stopped for a few days in New York, en route to begin college at the University of Iowa, in Iowa City. In December, John returned to begin medical studies in Iowa City; at the same time, Bernard persuaded John to pay his passage to New York, where he moved into West Broadway to share a single bed and deflate my precarious economies. Elfriede arrived a few months later, she and John were married and shared a large house in Iowa City with Byron and Frances, who had suffered her first bout of Multiple Sclerosis while still in high school, but was momentarily, well enough to begin college.

I put Bernard to work, posing for figure paintings. Inez Cavanaugh was in New York. She had opened a night club near Wall Street, too far from central Manhattan to attract anyone but the old Parisian clients. It failed. She came by West Broadway afternoons to gossip. Bernard and I usually met Jimmy for drinks after my working hours; drinks embraced a circuit of Village bars and lasted until 4 a.m. Early in 1958, Jimmy moved into Horatio Street. Although he habitually scattered money with abandon, memories of penury must have prompted him to begin furnishing the new flat with a discarded sofa found in the street. Bernard, outraged that his famous writer friend would stoop to collecting trash found in the streets, refused to help carry it up. I, and I forget who else, helped. It never shook the lingering scent of stale urine.

Jimmy kept the flat in Horatio Street for several years but continued to move back and forth between France and America. I lent him the flat in Clamart. When he returned to France in June 1958, Bernard, for whom the glamour of New York was wearing thin, twisted Jimmy's arm for an extra fare and moved into a vacant flat in Montmartre that belonged to a former lover.

I painted portraits, some commissioned, some not—James, Lucia, a couple of Bernie Winebaum, one of which, spread out on a canapé in a pose unconsciously imitating that of Mme Manet on her blue canapé, I especially liked; another of an interior decorator friend of Bernie's, who also commissioned several decorating jobs—most interesting was the vast, high-ceilinged lobby of a Central Park West apartment building, surrounded by plaster-cast doric columns to be transformed into false marble. The painting contractor asked me what preparation base the painters should give to the columns; "Mat, off-white," said I, as if I knew what I was about. I felt quite silly arriving to work the first morning with a bag full of rags, some bottles of turpentine and damar varnish and a paint box, but the workers treated me like a vedette. I used my rags to smear all the columns messily with a thin wash of earth colour and, with small, pointed watercolour brushes dragged irregular dark lines through the wash, some jaggedly criss-crossing, smearing here and there with the palm of my hand to muddy the definition, and adding occasional lines of white accent. One day, I was atop a tall ladder, smearing, when Lena Horne walked into the lobby, looked up and waved with a great smile of recognition; I climbed down to say hello, touched and pleased that she could place me out of the Doubleday context. When I stepped back to look at the result of my muddling, I was delighted, as was the contractor; he told me that painting false marble was a "lost art" and that, in New York, I could make a fortune. I remembered that Braque had been a professional false marble painter before becoming an *artiste-peintre*; I didn't intend to pattern my career on Braque's in reverse, but I appreciated the compliment.

John, Elfriede, Elizabeth, and Byron visited New York at Easter-time 1959 and Byron was back that summer, living with James and attending summer school at N.Y.U. Carol Terrell, whom I had met through Tommie Greaves, was dreaming of Paris. In late summer, Carol and I booked passage on *Le Flandre*. Margaret,

Richard Olney. Portrait of Robert Isaacson, 1959. Oil on canvas.

James, Byron, Lucia and Tommie were among those who drank Champagne with us until the great horn blasted and the loudspeaker announced, "All Guests Ashore."

A few days before I arrived in Clamart, Jimmy moved to friends' rooms in Paris. Mlle Marty met me at the gate and began to babble a complicated tale, at first incomprehensible because of her diversions: "Oh, Monsieur Olney," she said, "You have no idea...it was so amusing...they must have had a quarrel...the day before he left, Monsieur Baldwin had some friends in your flat...at two o'clock in the morning, they all ran down the stairs, completely naked, and began chasing each other around the Place Marquis." A few weeks later, Jimmy rented rooms above Pierrette's Guinguette and moved back to Clamart where he organized a Thanksgiving-day party around a stuffed turkey and all the traditional American garnishes. There was a crowd but I knew no one except for Bernard and Beauford.

Doug Davis, a young American painter who had been around Paris for several years, was in New York when Piaf collapsed on stage and was hospitalized. He brought her flowers and she promptly fell in love. Photos in the French newspapers of Piaf leaving the hospital on Doug's arm, radiant with joy, carried headlines in the spirit of "Snatched from the Grave by the Miracle of Love." They returned to France together and she hired a gallery near Saint-Germain-des-Prés to give him a show, whose opening she attended to meet all his friends. Jimmy also adored Piaf and wanted to interview her; Doug smoothed the path. Jimmy envisioned the meeting of two lions but discovered that, in Piaf's view, she was the only lion; his enthusiasm waned. Doug's and Piaf's idyll was short-lived—he complained that she wanted to own him, to dress him (he particularly disliked her taste in ties, which he was obliged to wear) and that her sexual demands exhausted him. (A couple of years later, he died in a plane crash and the papers were again full of photos and the tragedy of Piaf's life—an earlier lover, the prize fighter, Marcel Cerdan, had also died in a plane crash.)

My fall and spring visits to Magagnosc settled into the old pattern, painting landscapes, flower paintings, a portrait of Philippe, and preparing late dinners after smoking sessions.

Bernard took Carol under his wing. His methods of protection and instruction were often brusque; a vignette remains with me of Carol, Bernard and me, wandering in the streets of Montmartre, when Carol lit a cigarette. Bernard: "Put that cigarette out, girl! Ladies don't smoke in the street!" Carol: "But Lucia smokes in the street." Bernard: "That's different—Lucia's an artist." (I thought of my grandmother who, when I was a child, told me that my great-grandmother had smoked a pipe. "It was all right at that time and at her age," she said, "but ladies never smoke cigarettes." After a pause, she added, except, of course, for theater people.")

Eda Lord was living in rural England with Sybille Bedford. She visited Paris briefly in December at the same time that Marlene Dietrich's *One Woman Show* was opening at the Théâtre de l'Etoile. Eda, Sacha, and I attended. It is difficult to understand—impossible to explain—how anything so silly as a music hall chorus line of girls, with Dietrich at the center, in top-hats and tails, holding batons and doing synchronized high kicks, Dietrich's discreetly higher than the girls', can be transcendental. Eda and Sacha were as entranced as I–the evening was magical.

Robert lsaacson visited me in Clamart to choose paintings for a one-man show, planned for early 1961. (It is always a pleasure to receive—or to be received by—Robert, not only because he keeps me laughing, but because he knows what he is eating and drinking—he willingly makes fun of his fancy friends who think of themselves as exquisite gourmets but he is one of the best cooks I know and his wines are always carefully chosen.) For most of the year to come, I rummaged through flea markets and second-hand shops, searching out and touching up old frames.

Lili came to Paris, where she always stayed with Sacha. Because she couldn't conveniently smoke away from Magagnosc, she carried a phial of brown liquid, which she took to avoid the effects of opium withdrawal, but the satisfaction was not the same and she compensated with clandestine doses of cognac. Lili, Sacha, Bernard, and I planned to have dinner at a favorite bistro, Chez Maître Paul (the owner's name was Paul Maître) in the rue Monsieur le Prince, and had held a table in the small room upstairs, above the main dining room, which accommodated only a couple of tables. Lili told Sacha that she had some errands to run and would meet us at the restaurant. When Sacha, Bernard and I arrived, a group of five occupied the other table, we ordered a bottle of white wine while waiting for Lili, who arrived quite late—she had stopped at the bar next door to fortify herself with a few cognacs. She spurned the wine and ordered a cognac. Her conversation, quite incoherent, evolved into a tirade against the hateful bourgeoisie and, with no warning, she hurled her glass of cognac at the other table, where, fortunately, it shattered against the wall, only splattering the occupants. I asked Sacha to order something for me while I took Lili back to his studio. I managed to lead her out through the kitchen exit to avoid extra scandal, got her into a taxi, where she tried to drag me to the floor in a confused reenactment of distant escapades (the next day, I'm sure, she had no memory of this sad nonsense)—I asked the driver to wait for me, got her into the studio and returned to the restaurant. The scene had dampened our spirits. The group at the other table eyed us warily. When we stopped at the cash register, la patronne, Mme Maître, permitted us to pay the bill before inviting us to never again set foot in her establishment. (Paul Maître bought vines in the Touraine, sold the restaurant, which still bears his name, and retired to make wine.)

Three

1961-1966
European tour with Byron and James.
Solliès-Toucas. *Cuisine et Vins de France.*

In January 1961, Piaf opened at the Olympia, a ghostly wisp of flesh in a black rag, clinging to the microphone for support, but the magical voice soared and the audience was in a frenzy; among the new songs was *Je ne regrette rien*.

The show at the Isaacson gallery opened in February. Robert was cross with me for not coming to New York. I needn't think, he said, that paintings would sell themselves, the artist had to be present and deploy some charm. Of course he was right; the only explanation for my behavior—the discomfort of being an object of public attention—was unacceptable as an excuse. Robert proposed me for an Ingram-Merrill fellowship, which I received.

Byron sailed the end of February to spend six months in Europe before beginning medical school. James would finish his studies at Columbia in June and planned to join us. I met Byron's boat train at the Gare St.-Lazare. We checked his bags and walked to Au Petit Riche in the rue Peletier, a bistrot specialized in food and wine from the Touraine, whose decor has remained unchanged for well over a century. Byron ate grilled andouillette (chitterling sausage) for the first time, loved it, and we drank pitchers of young Vouvray and Chinon.

The next few weeks were devoted to museum-going, wandering the Paris streets, drinks at the Flore, meals in favorite bistrots, shopping and cooking in Clamart and visits to the Guinguette. The rue Paul Vaillant-Couturier, in which I lived, was blocked off Tuesday and Saturday mornings for the street market which began setting up at 6 a.m. to the clanking cacophony of metal rods, erected to form the framework, over which awnings were spread, of the merchants' stalls. We shopped to the tune of the hawkers' chants. My cheese merchant furnished us with lovely Crottins de Chavignol and voluptuous Pont l'Evèque cheeses. (Today, Crottins de Chavignol are industrialized and banal; I haven't tasted a decent Pont l'Evèque in 25 years—it is not I who have changed, it is Pont l'Evèque.) Bernard was not working—he and Beauford shared our dinners and Sacha often joined us. Byron posed for the first of many portraits.

My dream of a house in the south of France became a possibility with the Ingram-Merrill grant. Byron and I decided to spend some time near Toulon. Pierrette recommended a house that she and Pierre had once rented in La Garonne, a seaside resort, empty at that time of year. We rented it for a spectacular month of April with daily visits to the beach. The house, garden and terrace were enclosed within walls, a barbeque installed on the terrace. We ate

With James in Delphi, 1961.

Solliès house in ruin, 1961.

fish soups, bouillabaisse, fish grilled, fish baked with wild fennel and white wine or raw with olive oil and lemon. Friends from Toulon, Sim Kass and Bob Ferec, came often to dinner. Sim's friend, Frank Pittaluga, then a bailiff's assistant (now "President des Huissiers du Var") led us to an abandoned property in the hills of Solliès-Toucas overlooking the valley of the Gapeau river. Cherry orchards transformed the valley into a blanket of white blossom in early April, the ground of the hillsides formed a tapestry of the blues and violets of flowering wild thyme, punctuated by bushes of wild rosemary, feathery shoots of wild fennel and the spring growth of oregano and winter savory—the poetry of Provence was in the air and tender tips of wild asparagus, invisible to the profane were breaking the ground everywhere. I fell in love.

The house, whose foundations bore a cornerstone dated 1859, rose sheerly from a high dry-stone wall grounded on a lower terrace; it was a shambles of rotted timbers, collapsed tile roofs and cracked walls. The property was an enclave, the only access from the road below, a precarious goat path bestowed with the oral tradition of a right of passage. A high wall, hewn from the natural rock, testimony to a former limestone quarry, rose to the first terrace above the house. Beyond, three hectares—about seven acres—of dry-stone terraces, built over the centuries, planted with olive trees that had been neglected for fifty years, reached to the summit of the hill.

Frank told me I could have the property for a million old francs (about two thousand dollars) but that it would take at least a year to gather together the heirs and get the papers together. I deposited half the price with him. Bernard joined us mid-month in La Garonne and, upon learning of the Solliès discovery, proclaimed that, since he had introduced me to Sim, he had a right to be co-proprietor.

At June's approach, Byron and I moved into Italy, pausing in Florence and Rome before continuing to Naples to board the *Nea Hellas*, on which James had booked passage from New York to Athens. In retrospect, my travels of the preceding ten years seem to have been a rehearsal for the couple of months that we were to spend delving into ancient Greece, Byzantium, and the Italian Renaissance wandering again on the Acropolis at the full moon, in the ruins of Delphi and in those of Agamemnon's palace in Mycenae, admiring the lovingly modeled testicles of a 5th century B.C. bull in Olympia, drinking too many dry martinis with Giovanna in Rome, settling into the Bartolini in Florence and visiting La Pietra, where Harold Acton's mother again shooed away the butler to prepare the martinis, herself. We spent a day on Capri, at the foot of a steep, rocky descent, which fell into the sea, the water crystalline, so limpid that one could see the bottom without fathoming its depth. Byron climbed to a high ledge of rock to dive and, pleased with the experience, climbed still higher for each new dive as James and I watched in trepidation. In Naples, we celebrated James's birthday, 12 July, in the same ambiance that Elizabeth and I had enjoyed five years earlier, with floating musicians playing and singing *Santa Lucia*. A shellfish concession served

With Byron, Paestum Greece, 1961.

With James, Florence, Italy, 1961.

Bernard and me at La Guingette, 1961.

up platters of raw bivalves, among which were exquisite, ten-inch long blue-black razor clams—I have never seen them since. And, of course, we did the Piero della Francesca tour, visited Assizi and Padua for the Giottos, Siena, Venice, Milan—Verona to eat at Dodici Apostoli.

Back in France, we stopped for a day in Burgundy to visit Charles Rousseau (Domaine Armand Rousseau) in Gevrey-Chambertin and to taste in his cellars. His son, Eric, who was about five years old, was a great fan of Steve McQueen and very excited by our visit, for he was convinced that Byron was the star in the flesh. Charles has vines in the first growth Gevrey-Chambertin appellations of les Cazetiers and the Clos Saint-Jacques and, in the Grand Cru appellations, Clos de la Roche, Mazy-Chambertin, Charmes-Chambertin, Ruchottes-Chambertin, Chambertin and Chambertin Clos de Bèze, which we tasted, in the 1960 vintage, from the barrels before uncorking a selection of older vintages. I had also made an appointment at the Domaine de la

Romanée-Conti, in Vosne-Romanée, where I knew no one; before leaving Charles Rousseau, we telephoned to confirm our arrival. The office manager, Mlle Clin, received us coolly with the observation that, if we were interested in tasting wine, there were large commercial establishments in Beaune that specialized in that sort of thing: fortunately, the cellar master, André Noblet, walked into the office at that moment and whisked us off to the cellars to taste Echézeaux, Grands Echézeaux, Richebourg, La Tâche and Romanée-Conti from the barrels.

The USSR's Kirov Ballet Company moved from full houses at the Opéra to the Palais des Sports at the Porte de Versailles, where we got tickets for the last evening's performance. The stage was a rickety affair, which seemed to have been hastily assembled from old packing crates, Rudolf Nureyev was twenty-three and his makeup was outrageous; he tripped on stage, fell on his behind and was in a rage—no one doubted his talent. The next day, at Orly

Byron, Pierrette, me and Bernard at la Guinguette, 1961.

*"Paintings by Richard Olney, Feb. 14 - Mar. 4, 1961.
Robert Isaacson Gallery, 22 East 66th Street, NY 21, NY"*

airport, having been ordered back to the USSR, he defected, under protection of the French police, to begin his spectacular career in the West.

Byron returned to settle in Baltimore and begin medical studies at Johns Hopkins. Sacha was going south to Magagnosc, but he had just bought an old farmhouse, surrounded by vines, in the Touraine, outside of Athée-sur-Cher, near Amboise, and wanted me to see it. James and I spent a few days there, getting to know Sacha's neighbours, cooking in the fireplace and bicycling around to the Loire Valley châteaux. I applied my recently acquired false marble artisan's skills to the decoration of the fireplace mantels. We walked down to the Cher one day with a tin can and a bucket. The riverbed was covered with flat stones; each time one was lifted, a crayfish scuttled into the tin can and was emptied into the bucket. We drank the local white wine from Montlouis with crayfish à la nage.

Madeleine Decure with Curnonsky, 1955.

Bernard had found work as an extra in a movie to be filmed in Rome, with Elizabeth Taylor in the role of Cleopatra; he moved into Giovanna's flat in Rome. Inez returned to Paris, came into the Flore, asking for Bernard, and found James and me. Back from Magagnosc, Sacha reported that Lili was not well, that Philippe was in the hospital, had been operated on twice for cancer of the colon, and had a private room where he received friends for regular opium-smoking sessions, which the hospital staff pretended to ignore.

In 1961, except for professional organs, *Cuisine et Vins de France* was the only food and wine magazine in France. *La Revue du Vin de France,* the wine review founded in 1927 by Raymond Baudouin and edited from 1956 to 1959 by J.R. Roger, had just been rescued from oblivion by Madeleine Decure; the two reviews shared the same roof and policies. *CVF* was founded in 1947, with Marcel Honoré's backing, by Madeleine Decure and Curnonsky. Madeleine then in her twenties, was Monsieur Honoré's mistress. (No one, including Madeleine, addressed him as "Marcel" and his family life was kept rigidly separate from his business and social life.) Curnonsky, né Maurice Sailland, elected "prince des gastronomes" in the 1920's by a group of journalists, whose fame in France was initially essential to the magazine's success, was mainly a figurehead; until his death in 1956, he wrote a brief monthly editorial, setting down (his) gastronomic laws and cursing those who broke them. *CVF* was Madeleine's creation. It was operated on a shoestring, circulation was small, Madeleine refused to advertise products of which she didn't approve (margarine, for instance), and, at that time, it was not available at newsstands, but most of the restaurateurs and winegrowers in France were loyal friends. Subscribers were members of a club called "Les Amités Gastronomiques Internationales," which organized monthly meals in Parisian restaurants, special "theme" dinners, for which evening dress was obligatory, in grand establishments like Lasserre, Lucas-Carton, Taillevent and the original Prunier, in the rue Duphot, annual three-day visits to the Bordelais vineyards and irregular two or three day visits to the vineyards of the Touraine, Alsace, Champagne, the Côte d'Or, Beaujolais, the Côtes-du-Rhône, and

Provence. Monsieur Honoré was president of "Les Amitiés Gastronomiques Internationales." Monsieur Honoré, who was a legal consultant, had spacious and elegant offices on the first floor of a building in the place Beauvau, the *CVF* offices were on the top floor and he housed Madeleine in a tiny, airless flat in the same building, whose only window was in the "cuisinette."

I had subscribed for a number of years to *Cuisine et Vins de France* but had never assisted at the organized meals or vineyard

With easel, "Breakfast in Clarmart," 1961.

trips. James and I joined *CVF* for the Bordeaux trip, late September 1961 during the grape harvest. It was an overwhelming experience. Year after year, the formula was the same: a Thursday evening buffet-reception in the city of Bordeaux with hundreds of wines to taste, at which the proprietors of all the principal Bordelais vineyards were present. Each succeeding morning, a bus picked us up in Bordeaux to visit Graves and Sauternes; the Médoc; and Saint-Emilion and Pomerol, not necessarily in that order. The first vineyard visited each morning served an abundant "cassecroûte," sausages or steaks grilled over vine embers, charcuterie and cheeses. Three properties were visited each morning; at morning's end a "commanderie" chapter (Le Bontemps du Médoc et des Graves, Le Bontemps de Sauternes et Barsac, Les Hospitaliers de Pomerol, La Jurade de Saint-Emilion) was held, with the dignitaries done up in their grand, psuedo-medieval robes, at which several members of the tour were ritually enthroned, lunch was catered at a château, proceeded by an aperitif of white Graves or Champagne and accompanied by three or four wines, the last of which was always an old vintage of the receiving château. There were three afternoon visits and the first two evenings were free for groups of friends to check out the restaurants of Bordeaux; Sunday evenings, we had dinner at a château, the tour winding up after midnight. Because the vendanges coincide with the cèpes season in Bordeaux, a meal without cèpes à la Bordelaise was a rarity.

The first day of the 1961 tour was devoted to Graves and Sauternes. The weather was glorious and, for lunch at Château Haut-Brion, round tables, each for six or eight, were set up on the lawn beneath shade trees. (Thirty years later, Jean Delmas, director of Haut-Brion, told me that they had never, before or since received large groups for lunch at Haut-Brion and that he and his assistant cherished sentimental memories of that day.) James and I were seated at table with Michel Lemonnier, who wrote monthly articles for *CVF*, and was then on the staff of *Finance* magazine and, under a pseudonym, wrote regular gastronomic articles for the same review. We instantly became friends and he hastened to sing praise of me to Madeleine and her assistant editor, Odette Kahn. We dined that evening—and the next—with Madeleine, Odette, Michel, and Monsieur Honoré, finishing the first evening with a Château Margaux 1928 and, the following, with a Latour 1929.

A few days later, Michel came to dinner in Clamart. He had suggested a pot-au-feu, the symbol of ultimate gastronomic simplicity. I prepared an oxtail pot-au-feu, discarded the vegetables and bouquet-garni, put the oxtail aside for a future meal and, with the broth, prepared a pot-au-feu with boned, tied-up beef shank, and another bouquet, adding little carrots, turnips and potatoes toward the end; a quartered, blanched cabbage was braised apart in some of the broth. The bouquets were bundles of leek, celery stalk, fresh thyme and bay leaf. Michel wrote an article for *Finance* about the most fantastic pot-au-feu of his life, which was quoted in *CVF*, and my pot-au-feu became famous in French gastronomic circles.

Jimmy Baldwin was back in town with his sister, Paula, and a shifty hophead, named Jimmy Smith (who willingly permitted people to believe that he was a famous jazz musician of the same name), whom Jimmy designated as "a sort of secretary." Jimmy (Baldwin) told me that Beauford was in the American Hospital. James and I collected Beauford's mail from Clamart and went to the hospital, only to learn that he had checked out that day. I forwarded the mail to his friends, the Boggs's and left for England with James, spending some time in London, then Oxford, where James settled in for his research. Back in Clamart, an urgent message from Charlie Boggs awaited me—Beauford wanted to see me immediately. I went around. Beauford did not want to see me in the presence of anyone else (possibly because the Boggs's refused to let him drink alcohol) and insisted that we go to a café, where we had a cognac while he recounted a horror tale. He was cross with friends who told him that it was only his imagination. He had taken trains, with several changes from Paris to Brindisi to board a boat for Athens. A "gang" followed him, changing trains when he did; he heard them cursing "niggers and queers," saying they were going to kill him. He thought maybe they were members of the Mafia or, perhaps, of some undefined police force. In Brindisi, he tried to give them the slip before sneaking onto the boat but, after it set sail, there they were. They began to chase him, shouting obscenities, and Beauford jumped overboard. By miracle, he was saved and delivered to a hospital in Athens, where he continued to hear voices and slashed his wrists with a razorblade. (An instinct for self-preservation saved him—he slashed on top instead of beneath his wrists.) He was sent to a hospital in Paris, where he was recuperated by the Boggs's. Beauford desperately wanted me to believe in the evil gang, which was so terrifyingly real to him; I saw no

Photo from "Cuisine et Vins de France," 1962.
Odette and I devour our menus to stave off hunger.

reason to disappoint him and join the rest of his friends in the dog-house. He returned to Clamart. He had always slept behind a locked door and tightly closed shutters but, finally, he could no longer stand to be alone at night and began coming upstairs to sleep in my flat. (Mlle Marty was no help—she had discovered that, if she crept into the garden in the middle of the night and made scratching sounds on Beauford's shutters, he would go wild, which, in her childish way, she found very amusing.) A couple of months later, one of his benefactors offered Beauford an artist's studio in rue Vercingétorix, beyond Montparnasse. I worried about his being alone there but, when I visited, he seemed to be pretty well in control.

I have saved the *CVF* menu of a dinner organized at Lasserre, 23 November 1961, the theme of which was "What to drink with Canard à l'Orange." (I noted rather smugly, in a letter to Byron, "I borrowed Sacha's tuxedo, which dates from 1910 but was recut in the '20's. Naturally, I looked very fine as it has much more style than modern evening dress and, also, I had not had a haircut in three months.") A roast or braised duck with bitter orange added to the roasting or braising juices is delicious, but these ducks were drowned in a sticky mess of boiled orange juice, sugar and alcohol; I thought that the Champigny suffered less than the half-dozen other wines served at the same time. Seated next to me was Simon Arbellot, director of the Kléber-Colombes gastronomic guide (Michelin's competition at that time) and monthly contributor to *CVF*. He was an old-fashioned charmer, with a monocle that tumbled regularly from his eye and a wealth of anecdotes; before the evening was over, he had invited himself to lunch in Clamart, promising to bring along the first course. A few days later, Simon arrived bearing a terrine of foie gras, a bottle of white Clos des Mouches 1952, a bottle of Château d'Yquem 1954 and a bottle of cognac 1914. I prepared a pheasant salmis (rare roast pheasant hen, cut up, skinned, smothered with thickly sliced black truffles, a few drops of cognac and a game bird velouté) and the same old apple pie that I had been making since childhood; served the Clos des Mouches with the foie gras, Ducru-Beaucaillou 1947 with the Salmis and the cheeses and the Yquem with apple pie. Simon devoted one of his monthly *CVF* articles to the lunch in Clamart, making it sound very grand.

Madeleine began to gather me into all the functions organized for the staff of *CVF.* She, Odette, Michel and I traveled to Burgundy for a vertical tasting of La Tâche at the Domaine de la Romanée-Conti. We were received by Aubert de Villaine, then twenty-two and seductive by virtue of a combined shyness, intelligence and respectful courtesy, Simone ("Simca") Beck, who was a loyal member of "Les Amitiés Gastronomiques Internationales," invited us to a reception to celebrate the publication of *Mastering the Art of French Cooking*. Nearly everyone present was American; I remember meeting James Beard.

My sister, Frances, was married. Bernard wrote bitter letters from Rome. He didn't like Italian food, he hated Rome, he hated the film: "There are eight of us who are 'butterflies,' ridiculously costumed with wings that are killing in the procession. The costumes are so complicated that they cannot be taken off so we have to stand in them for the whole day. Impossible to sit...." and so on.

(Byron later saw the film and assured me that I would do well not to see it.) Mary Painter could support Washington no longer. She resigned from her plush job and returned to Paris to work for the O.E.C.D. (Organization for Economic Cooperation and Development) at a much lower salary, with no PX privileges. She settled into a small flat in the rue de Sèvres.

Michel Lemonnier had recommended Chez Garin, a restaurant just opened at 9, rue Lagrange by Georges Garin, former hotel-restaurant owner in Nuits-Saint-Georges and caterer for the Confrérie des Chevaliers du Tastevin banquets at the Château du Clos de Vougeot. I invited Mary to dinner at Chez Garin. The food was wonderful but the dining room was nearly empty. (A year later it was thought by many to be the best restaurant in Paris, said to be the most expensive and one had to reserve far in advance.) After dinner, Garin offered us drinks and we sat far into the night talking about food.

15 December 1961, I wrote Byron that I was working on another portrait of Mlle Marty, "the best of the three," I had been to Solliès-Toucas, where the house was in a continuing state of disintegration, Frank Pittaluga had still not managed to gather together procurations from all the heirs for the sale of the property, I was expecting James in Clamart, 19 December, and Madeleine and M. Honoré were invited to dinner that evening.

4 January 1962. Bernard was back from Rome with vague plans to return there. Mary was to begin work at the O.E.C.D. in a week's time. She, Bernard, James and I had dinner at Calvet on Boulevard Saint-Germain, went to a Catherine Sauvage concert at the Théatre du Vieux-Colombier and finished the evening at the Blue Note, where Inez was singing.

6 January 1962. (James to Byron, from Oxford) "Richard had a recently completed large portrait of Mlle Marty which I had simply to buy while I was there—a very beautiful painting. So last night I wrote a rather careful letter home about money matters the beauty of art, etc. (. . .) Bernard is to go off to Rome shortly—but as with most of his arrangements the date is rather indefinite. I think the setting of the date has to do with the arrival of Richard's check."

Mary began an affair with Jimmy's "sort of secretary" Jimmy Smith. Jimmy Baldwin was living—no one knew why—at the Lutétia, a stuffy, expensive hotel on the Boulevard Raspail. Mary and I had dinner with him several times in the hotel's pretentious restaurant not because the food was remarkable but because the winelist revealed a Latour 1945 of breathtaking beauty.

Jimmy said he had a surprise for us and asked Bernard and me to meet him at Le Fiacre, a bar whose cruising territory was so packed that elbow movement was impractical. When we arrived, he announced his surprise: "I'm in love again!" He showed us a fan letter, posed glamour photo enclosed, from a boy in Australia, who simply adored Jimmy's homosexual novel, *Giovanni's Room*. Jimmy had sent him a plane ticket and he was due to arrive the next day. We never met the new love: he refused to share a room with Jimmy, was given a room apart at the Lutétia, and we all hoped that he was left to pay his own way back to Australia. Jimmy never mentioned him again.

The papers for the property in Solliès-Toucas were finally in order and Bernard renewed the pressure to be named co-proprietor. To avoid trouble, I accepted, we went south, signed the papers—and that was the beginning of trouble.

I began a portrait of Simon Arbellot, working two or three days a week at his place in Paris. Mornings, things went smoothly but he always profited from my presence to escape from his wife and take me out to lunch, alone or with friends, after which he fell asleep while posing, when lunch didn't continue until evening.

Bernard returned to Rome the first of February, stopped en route to visit in Magagnosc and wired me that, while he was there, Lili had fallen down the stairs and died of a concussion. Sacha and I went south for the funeral. (Sacha planted a mimosa (acacia) tree on Lili's grave and, until his death, twenty-four years later, he visited Magagnosc twice a year to tend the grave.) I saw Philippe, too weak to leave his bed, no flesh left on his body, the skin of his face like dried yellow parchment pulled tightly over the skull; he was smoking opium with two lady friends who had been in the Resistance during the war. He died a few weeks later.

I spent the month of February in Solliès-Toucas. The house was uninhabitable in winter; I took a room and my meals at l'Auberge de l'Escapade, near the village, dug the garden, pruned olive trees and planted magnolias, rose bushes and seeds. In 1955, I had met Lucien Peyraud proprietor of Domaine Tempier, a Bandol vineyard, when he was presenting his wines in Paris at the Salon des Arts Ménagers. I bought a couple of cases of 1953 and, since then, had ordered each succeeding vintage. A year earlier, Sim Kass, Byron and I had visited the Peyraud family, Lucien, his wife, Lulu (née Tempier), their young sons, Jean-Marie and François, and several daughters, of whom the youngest, Véronique, was then six years old. Lulu loves to receive and I became a frequent guest at Domaine Tempier. Because I don't drive, someone always came to pick me up and, if the invitation was for dinner, I stayed the night. The meals were sumptuous and Lucien loved to present a half-dozen vintages of Domaine Tempier at table.

In March, James and I explored England, visiting Eda and Sybille in their country retreat and spent several days with Peter Price in Tibberton, near Gloucester, where his father owned a large dairy farm. Peter had joined the family business in a role that he aptly described as "gentleman farmer," for I never saw him in the presence of a cow. He always had a good selection of white Burgundies and clarets and an endless supply of single malt whisky; he had invited film-maker friends up from London to impress them with my cooking talents.

In 1962, *CVF* organized winetasting tours both in Beaujolais and in Provence. From the Beaujolais tour, I remember Paul Bocuse's Volaille Renaissance en Vessie—a boned Bresse chicken stuffed with a mousseline forcemeat incorporating diced truffle and petits pois, enclosed in a pig's bladder and poached—and our reception at Château Thivin (Côte de Brouilly) by Mme Geoffray, known affectionately to everyone as "Tante Yvonne" (today, she is replaced by her nephew, Vincent Geoffray). From the Provence tour, I remember dinner in Avignon, Chez Hiély (then called Chez Lucullus), with Madeleine, Odette and Michel (the Hiélys, father and son, became good friends and it has ever since been one of my favorite restaurants, for the cleanliness of its cui-

Fireplace at Solliès.

sine, the honesty of its prices and the wealth of its wine cellar), our reception at Château Simone (Palette, near Aix-en-Provence) by the Rougier family, and our visit to Domaine Tempier, where Madeleine, Odette and Michel met the Peyrauds for the first time and Lulu prepared a spectacular array of Provençal dishes.

I spent most of the spring 1962 in Solliès-Toucas, found a mason, who accepted to work on the house on condition that I first carry all the cement, sand and gravel up the footpath on my back, and a plumber, who accepted to bring water up to the main terrace on condition that I dig a deep trench the length of the footpath. These chores wreaked havoc with my back, but I began to learn about masoning. I met James, mid June in Paris and we returned to Solliès for peace, quiet, good food and good wine until Bernard unexpectedly arrived back from Italy on James's birthday, July 12. The battles began immediately. Bernard hated everything I was doing on the property, he wanted to tear the house down and start all over again, he didn't want to be co-proprietor, he wanted all the property in his name, and so forth. His method of expressing his frustration consisted in battering at me with his fists. James and I left. We stopped in Saulieu to repair shattered nerves and make up for a ruined birthday dinner. It was Bastille day, Dumaine prepared a perfect meal, we drank another bottle of La Tâche 1951, among others, and, after dinner, wandered into the streets to discover a municipal hall where the local population, including all of the restaurant staff, was dancing the Java to an old-fashioned orchestra—they had never heard of jitterbug and rock-and-roll had not yet been invented.

In Clamart, a commercial artist friend of Bernard's, Jimmy Guibez, and his French lover, Robert, were moving into Beauford's vacated rooms. We visited Beauford in his studio, rue Vercingétorix, who seemed all right but melancholy. John commissioned a portrait of James. Mary, James and I had dinner Chez Garin and I invited Garin and Mme Garin to join us on their closing day, Sunday, for lunch in Clamart. James records that we had artichoke bottoms stuffed with a mousse of chicken livers on a bed of tomato mousse (the next week, artichoke bottoms stuffed with tomato mousse appeared on the menu Chez Garin), sautéed ortolans, cheeses, fresh almonds and cherries ("simple French food"). Garin invited us to Chez Garin. James to Byron: "Apéritif Veuve-Clicquot 1952; Jambon de Parme, Gratin de Homard on a bed of puréed mushrooms masked with sauce Américaine (Clos Blanc de Vougeot 1949); braised duckling in a heavenly sauce, on toast covered with a layer of foie gras (Nuits-Saint-Georges 1949), salad, cheeses (Corton Clos du Roi 1947), a cleansing lemon sorbet, coffee and 1904 cognac."

Bernard, who couldn't stand to be alone, returned to Clamart. (He had "sold" the flat in Montmartre that didn't belong to him.) 6 September 1962. (Me to Byron) "Bernard is back. Lucia and Ernst are here until the weekend. Jimmy Baldwin and his sister are here until tomorrow. I had a sort of buffet dinner party last night for the aforementioned plus Mary and others. Things were rather drunken. Buses were missed and a great deal of makeshift arrangement for sleeping everybody was finally necessary."

Mary and Bernard wanted to join James and me on the *CVF* Bordeaux wine tour. Neither of them spit while tasting or made any attempt to control the quantity of wine absorbed. I wrote Byron, "Mary is not really strong enough to support ten hours daily traveling and wine tasting and Bernard becomes—to use his expression—evil after a certain amount of consumption. He felt it necessary to quarrel with and insult some of the other members of the tour. In the future, I shall make such tours only with members of the family." Bernard returned to Rome.

James and I went to see Piaf, who was back at the Olympia in late September, this time with her latest lover and husband to be, Théo Sarapo. They sang a duet, *A Quoi Ça Sert l'Amour*. She was astounding as ever, a crazy miracle; Théo's strained, tinny voice and self-conscious movements were embarrassing. James returned to London in early October.

I continued to exchange dinners with Madeleine and Odette, at which Michel Lemonnier and M. Honoré were usually present. The Garins and Mary came often to Clamart for Sunday lunch; Michel joined us a couple of times. Once I prepared a boned and stuffed poached chicken, glazed in its jelly. It was very good, but Garin rather slyly asked me if I had ever thought to bone a bird simply by turning it inside-out, without slitting the skin at any point except for the back of the neck. (In France, birds are bled by the beak and the intestines removed by winding them out through the anus—the skin is cut at no point.) I had followed the only instructions to be found in cookbooks, where the bird is slit down the back, opened out to be boned, stuffed and sewn up; that was the last time I slit a bird to bone it. Garin subsequently introduced me to his colleagues as an adept of la Grande Cuisine; he never mentioned my amateurish method of boning. He asked me to hang paintings in the restaurant. I was told later that, when clients asked about them, he said they were not for sale—at first, I preferred not to believe it.

Garin was sentimental, irascible, jealous, possessive, generous, unprincipled and devious. When not being obsequious with the Duke and Duchess of Windsor (who usually came with Chanel and wanted a bottle of Johnny Walker black label and a bucket of ice cubes at table when they arrived), Dietrich (who stayed late to gossip with the master about pot-au-feu variations) or a celebrated prince consort (who, when asked in the third person if his highness preferred his steak rare or à point, answered, "Je m'en fous"), his manner was gruff. The restaurant kitchen was a visible and audible extension of the dining room where Garin's voice, snarling unprintable obscenities at the kitchen staff, soared loud and clear, silencing all conversation. When I told him he should take care, he said, "The clients love it." The clientèle ate late Chez Garin and there was no turnover. Lunch service began at 1 but the dining room was rarely full before 2 and often not empty until 5. Dinner service began at 8, the last customers were usually seated by 9:30 and some lingered until 2 a.m. Garin tasted every wine before it was poured, regular customers habitually asked him to join them after their meal for Champagne, cognac or whisky and, when the evening's last customers left, he needed first a whisky, then a change of scene to relax. We went often to les Halles (which was at its most active and colourful between 2 and 6 a.m.) where he ordered merchandise to be delivered to the restaurant and gossiped with colleagues in the bistrots, while we washed down tripe with Beaujolais. At other times, he liked going to a club called Castel or, if the restaurant closed early, we went to Montparnasse to eat oysters at the Coupole. He was always in the restaurant by 8 a.m. and after a night of "relaxation" he needed several glasses of pastis to pull himself together.

December 1962. (Me to Byron) "Received a check from Robert Isaacson—the gallery is closing. Garin bought a portrait of James, head thrown back, emptying a cognac glass. Rec'd confirmation of the Ingram-Merrill renewal, which will permit me to finish paying for the property before the January '63 deadline. And a letter, with "yours truly" replaced by "s'long and good luck," from the Washington art dealer with whom Dwight (Frances's husband) has been in contact—he wants to give me a show the end of January. Garin has asked me to organize an invitation dinner at the restaurant for Madeleine Decure, Odette Kahn, Simon Arbellot, Michel Lemonnier and M. Honoré. Everyone is agreed for a date in January—I have put it in Madeleine's hands. Bernard is back, his nerves in a disastrous state."

James had arranged with John and Byron to share the expense of a case of Château Bouscaut (Graves) blanc 1959 and a case of Château Beauregard (Pomerol) 1955, wines which we had particularly admired on the '61 and '62 Bordeaux tours, to be sent to me for Christmas. They and he arrived simultaneously.

January 1963. Garin's dinner for *CVF* was a great success. I remember partridge consommé garnished with little partridge quenelles, lobster soufflés and braised whole calf's liver with truffles, the liver pink and firm throughout, sliced almost paper thin. Garin always carved at table, with a dexterity that many still recall. With the cheeses, he served a decanted wine, unannounced; Madeleine tasted, discussed it with everyone at table, and said, finally, "We think it is a Château Margaux 1928." It was. Garin was not altogether pleased, for the main purpose of serving a wine blindly is to expose one's guests' weaknesses. With dessert, Simon dozed. He awoke to tamp his pipe with tobacco and mumbled, "Tu veu une pipe, Richard?" The others howled with laughter ("pipe" is slang for "blow job"). He may not have been quite awake, but he smiled shyly at his wit. The *CVF* dinners Chez Garin became an annual tradition.

James's thesis was finished, he accepted a teaching job at Drake University in Des Moines for the fall semester and spent the first week of February in Clamart before sailing to spend six months visiting the rest of the family. My show at the Agra gallery in Washington, D.C. must have been postponed from late January to February or March because James sent me photos of himself, posing with Washington hostesses at the opening.

Madeleine asked me to a reception at Ledoyen, a fancy restaurant in the gardeny part of the Champs-Elysées. I think it was to celebrate a change of management. The restaurant was closed for the reception and hundreds of people were milling around while waiters circulated with trays of elegant finger food and bottles of Champagne. Late in the evening, Pierre Troisgros, Gaston Lenôtre and I decided that it was time to find some solid food and good red wine. We took a taxi to Garin's, early clients had just liberated a table and we feasted on truffled duck terrine bound with foie gras, coq-au-vin and Chambertin. Garin joined us for drinks and I listened while they gossiped about "le métier."

"La Paulée" is a traditional late November dinner organized by the vignerons of Meursault, at which each offers his new wine. In the early 1950s, Raymond Baudouin, founder of *La Revue du Vin de France*, created, in collaboration with André Vrinat, proprietor of the elegant Parisian restaurant, Le Taillevent, "La Paulée de Paris," an annual dinner held in early March to celebrate the wines of the most recent vintage from all the French wine regions. Madeleine and André Vrinat continued this tradition; 6 March 1963, fourteen wines were presented at the Paulée—in the years to follow, there were twenty or more, nearly all from friends encountered during the *CVF* winetasting tours.

Financially, neither *CVF* nor *RVF* broke even, but M. Honoré made up the deficit and Madeleine was having a very good time. The restaurateurs loved these organized dinners and the vineyard proprietors, at a time when even the most celebrated were unable to make ends meet, were grateful and enthusiastic supporters of the two reviews and willingly offered their wines. (Today, they all cherish sentimental memories of "the time of Madeleine Decure and Odette Kahn.") Fifteen days after the Paulée, 21 March, *CVF* organized a "Diner Travesti 1900" at Lucas-Carton. I contented myself with renting a turn-of-the-century formal costume and sticking a false moustache to my upper lip. Some of the costumes were extraordinary. M. Vieilleville, a normally sedate and distinguished old gentleman, appeared in a flaming red wig, rouged and lipsticked, busted and bustled, as a mad duchess; Madeleine was a cameo from *A l'Ombre des Jeunes Filles en Fleurs* and Odette was a very grand demi-mondaine. Two weeks later, 4 April, again at Lucas-Carton, *RVF* organized its first "Diner-Dégustation," a comparative tasting of 1952 and 1953 Saint-Juliens—Châteaux Ducru-Beaucaillou, Beychevelle, the Léovilles and others. The proprietors of Lucas-Carton, Alex and Andrée Allégrier (née Carton) and their daughter, Monique, became good friends.

An aging bachelor, assiduous patron of these dinners, M. Mouquet, then president of the "Club des Cent," an exclusive gastronomic brotherhood limited to one hundred members from the social galaxy, asked my *CVF* friends and me to dinner. The meal was catered by Le Taillevent. The service was formal, elegant and white-gloved. Our host immediately directed the conversation to my pot-au-feu, of which he had read the eulogies. I invited everyone at table (plus two other members of the Club des Cent, at M. Mouquet's request) to a pot-au-feu the following week. Except when going out, I dressed in rags and received in rags. My studio-dining room was a shabby little affair from which the lingering scents of turpentine and oil paints were never absent. It was a mystery to me how people from worlds so foreign to mine could be so charmed. The pot-au-feu was a great success. A few days later, Garin reported that M. Mouquet had eaten at the restaurant and queried him at length about my antecedents, my bank account and so forth, hoping that I might be elected a member of the Club des Cent. Garin said, "Richard?... Ridiculous! He's nothing but a penniless painter." Of course, he was right but I would have preferred to answer for myself.

Jimmy Baldwin asked me a couple of times to join him for dinner with the writer, James Jones, and his wife, in a grand flat on the Ile Saint-Louis, which I recognized to be the same in which my friend, Tony Bower, had lived a few years earlier. The first time, we were received by a stylish butler and there was a heavy consumption of alcohol before we went to table, where the butler oversaw the white-gloved service of a catered meal, while several of the guests hurled insults at one another, after which the evening rapidly disintegrated into a drunken, pot-smoking brawl. Except for a new butler, who obviously detested his employers and their guests as much as had his predecessor, the second time was a repeat performance. On both occasions, our hosts begged Jimmy to do his "pulpit act," parodying an evangelistic brimstone and hell's fire sermon. I especially disliked watching him play the clown at what seemed to me his own expense. I told him I wouldn't be returning to the Jones's. On a personal level, with his friends, Jimmy remained unchanged. At the same time, his writing was becoming more polemical and, in larger groups, he was sometimes transported by the force of doomsayer's rhetoric to express attitudes which were not his own. Once, I mumbled, "Oh, Jimmy, stop talking shit." His eyes blazed, then he laughed: "You're right," glasses clinked and he said, "Cheers, baby!"

James Merrill (another "Jimmy") and his friend, David Jackson, came to Paris for a week. I had known Jimmy in New York during the late forties, had seen him and Robert Isaacson several times in Rome and Florence in the Spring of 1952, but had not seen him since. He gave a reception at his hotel for friends and recipients of the Ingram-Merrill foundation fellowship. I asked him and David to dinner in Clamart. Bernard was behaving that evening and we had a wonderful time. I remembered that Jimmy had a thing about (very) dry martinis (he believed in moistening a spoon with vermouth before stirring the gin and the ice) so we relaxed with martinis. We drank Bouscaut blanc '59 with scallops sautéed in a garlic persillade, Beauregard '55 with a guinea fowl "grand-mère" en cocotte, Ducru-Beaucaillou '47 with the cheeses and Yquem '50 with sautéed apples rolled and glazed in crepês. When they left, we promised to see each other again, soon and often. I never saw Jimmy again (he died in February 1995); our friendship consisted in brief notes over the years, promising to get together soon.

In May, I went south and spent three relaxed months masoning and gardening, punctuated by visits from Peter Price, Lucia and Julius Goldstein. Mary planned to drive down in August to spend her vacation and Beauford wrote that he would be "motoring down" with her. They arrived with Bernard, who immediately began to quarrel; he wanted the property in his name, he hated everything I was doing in the house and in the garden—the same old saw. I was so disgusted that I asked the notaire to draw up papers to transfer the property. Bernard was radiant with joy until I told him that, as soon as the papers were signed, I would leave Solliès for good and that I did not expect to see him in Clamart. He refused to sign the papers but did not stop quarreling. I took the night train to Paris.

10 October 1963, Edith Piaf died in Plascassier, a village near Grasse, within walking distance of Magagnosc. Her entourage considered it essential to the Piaf legend that she die in Paris and the body was hastened there by ambulance. 11 October, Jean Cocteau announced Edith Piaf's death in Paris on the morning radio; he died a few hours later of a heart attack.

Mary commissioned me to paint a portrait of Jimmy Smith. I don't like painting portraits of people I don't like. It revealed too much of the personality to please either Mary or the subject. In the background was a bouquet; he said, "I hate flowers." After dinner in Clamart one Sunday, Garin drove Mary home and spent the night. Jimmy Smith arrived late to pound on the door, Garin answered and invited him to disappear. When Mary began sleeping with Garin, she conveniently forgot that she had commissioned Jimmy Smith's portrait. She rather coyly asked me if I felt like a pimp. I wondered if she knew what a pimp was. In fact, I felt neither like pimp nor like cupid. Whoever sleeps with whomever is none of my business and I don't like being involved or held responsible. Mary and Garin failed to see things in that light; I was a participant in—and often a victim of—their adventure from then on. Garin launched into the first of many intrigues by claiming to his wife that Mary and I were lovers, which he figured would justify her frequent presence at the restaurant. Mary commissioned a portrait of her with Caesar the cat but "couldn't find the time to pose."

Robert Isaacson was in Paris with his mother, whose portrait he commissioned. We were all pleased with the result and celebrated with a meal Chez Garin. (Me to James) "Simple menu: foie gras, bécasses and sorbets—Fixin 1959, Grands Echézeaux Domaine de la Romanée-Conti 1953." Robert pleaded, unsuccessfully, with his mother to give more thought to the wine she was drinking and, with me, to move back to New York to become a successful painter.

18 February 1964. (Me to James) "Mary has become jealous and possessive about her lover. I don't think he realizes what is happening and is offended not to find me at the restaurant more often for a drink after work. And even when she comes to dinner in Clamart, instead of letting him come to pick her up as he wants to do, she eats hurriedly in silence (except for a few criticisms of the food—I have been replaced by a greater god as cooks go) and leaves early to be chez elle when HE arrives "

Bernard returned to Clamart, I escaped to the south, settled into l'Escapade and worked days on the hillside. Masons returned to repair the roofs. The main beam of the largest room in the house, hewn from a seven-metre long tree trunk and supported in the middle by a square pillar (since covered, several layers thick, with memorable wine labels), had to be replaced; the ends were rotten. I put it aside to use the central, healthy section as a fireplace mantel and bought all the books I could find on fireplace construction.

Byron and Marilynn, a fellow medical student, were planning marriage and they were plotting with James to sail in June to spend the summer in Solliès.

To the west side of the large terrace in front of the house, a sheer, natural rock wall rises to another terrace high above. Behind the house, stone steps and a winding path lead up the hillside. To the far side of the terrace above the rock wall is a huge basin, built into another steep rock wall, originally destined to collect winter rain waters for irrigation during the dry summer months. A long stretch of flat rock, leading from an intermediate terrace to the shallow end of the basin, seems designed for sunning bathers. I patched up the ancient basin, gave it a couple of coats of a magical modern, resistant paint and left it to be filled when the family arrived.

I went to Paris to meet Byron, Marilynn, and James. We had dinner with Mary at Chez Garin, drove south, stopping in Burgundy to visit vineyards and spent a night in Avignon to eat at

Chez Hiély. We more or less camped out in Solliès. The house was full of beds, I had not yet brought water from the far end of the terrace to the house, toilet duties were performed on the hillside; cooking was done on a single gas ring attached to a bottle of butane gas, meats were grilled over bonfire embers and one bathed out of doors with a hose. With a system of hoses, we filled the pool on the upper terrace (which required four days and four nights); it was a great success. All of our meals were taken out of doors on a raised cement-floored terrace in front of the house (which I later covered with antique floor tiles). Garin sent his wife off to visit family in Auvergne; he and Mary arrived to spend the month of August with us. That summer, Byron, James and I built the great corner fireplace which dominates the kitchen. At the southwestern corner of the terrace, sheltered from the southern and western sun by rock walls, Garin, with a dramatic gesture, swung a pickax, pierced the earth and decreed, "Your wine cellar will be here." I began digging, often breaking rock with a sledgehammer; as the cavity deepened, I built brick steps down from the future cellar's entrance to permit me to haul up the earth and broken rock in pails. (Nearly six years later, it was finished: where the walls were not natural rock, I built stone walls, poured a reinforced concrete beam against the widest natural rock wall; between it and the opposite wall, at an incline, I installed prefabricated reinforced concrete beams into which were fitted cement blocks; to cover the cellar, poured concrete over the top and coated it with tar; a vent high on the northern wall and a narrow chimney at the southwestern corner, reaching down to within a foot of the beaten earth floor, provide permanent air circulation. The top of the cellar is covered with a three-foot depth of earth, planted to wide-leafed saxifrage, which completely masks the surface; within, three walls of bins are built with sides of narrow cement blocks fitted with reinforced concrete shelves; the fourth wall is lined with metal racks. The temperature and humidity are perfect the year round.)

It was a wonderful and constructive summer. By a miracle, Bernard didn't arrive for the annual brawl until September, when everyone had left. He hated the fireplace and was going to tear it down; he didn't want a wine cellar. I returned to Clamart. Within a week's time, he was back in Clamart. I was preparing to leave a week later for the *CVF* Bordeaux tour and had planned, on condition that Bernard was not there, to go directly from Bordeaux to Solliès; he told me that he was going south with Beauford at the same time I left for Bordeaux so I changed my plans.

After the Bordeaux tour, I stayed an extra day to visit vineyards with Madeleine and Odette. Château Bouscaut had burned the year before and the proprietors, Robert and Ninette Place, had a flat in Bordeaux where we were invited to dinner. For the cheeses, Robert decanted bottles of Bouscaut 1929 and 1926, both intricate medleys of autumn scents. (He must have been touched by my awe for, a few weeks later, I received, unannounced, a case containing bottles of Bouscaut rouge 1959, 1953, 1929, and 1926.)

October 1964. (Me to Byron) "The morning I returned from Bordeaux to Clamart, Bernard was still here but planning to leave with Beauford that night. A hysterical 3-hour scene followed—screams and threats, never in life would he allow me or any member of the Olney family to set foot on his property again, he was taking me to court to get his property out of my hands, he was going to tear down the fireplace, the doors, everything that had my touch on it, etc. He finally lost his voice, fell asleep exhausted from his effort and woke up several hours later all sweetness and light, begging me to come south with him and promising never to quarrel again. (He did, however, want me to understand that the quarrels were all my fault for 'failing to take him in hand.') Since then, a couple of letters saying how wonderful the fireplace is and when am I coming south."

Madeleine, Odette, Michel, M. Honoré and M. Mouquet were coming to dinner again. I had decided to amuse them with something less rustic than a pot-au-feu. Our menu was:

Reflexions

Turban de Filets de Sole et de Saumon aux Ecrevisses
Château Bouscaut blanc 1959
§
Poularde en Gelée
Pernand-Ile des Vergelesses 1960
§
Cèpes à la Bordelaise
Château Grand Mayne 1955
§
Fromages
Clos de la Roche 1955
§
Beignets d'Ananas à la Frangipane
Château Rieussec 1947
§§§

The turban was prepared in a buttered savarin mould, lined with overlapping sole fillets and slices of raw salmon, packed with pike mousseline forcemeat, speckled with chopped black truffle and green pistachios, the tips of the fillets folded over the forcemeat, poached in a bain-marie, drained and unmoulded. The well of the turban was filled with a ragoût of truffled crayfish tails and the turban was surrounded with forcemeat-stuffed crayfish shells, warmed in the oven. The poule au pot en gelée was the same that I had served Garin a couple of years earlier, but this time the chicken was correctly boned.

We drank Champagne before the meal and Madeleine asked me if I would accept to write a monthly article for *CVF*—she had obviously discussed this with the others, for they were hanging on every word. She wanted the rubric to be entitled "Un Américain (Gourmand) à Paris: Le Menu de Richard Olney." She wanted a photo and, without knowing what that evening's menu was, suggested that it would be a good start for the first article. I accepted, convinced that the work would amuse me for a couple of months before being shelved and forgotten (the rubric continued for more than ten years until I finally begged off).

Madeleine invited. I assisted in the kitchen where skewers of lamb tenderloin and baby zucchini were waiting to be grilled. She closed the door to the dining room, opened the kitchen window wide, prepared a bed of charcoal embers in a little grilling apparatus and placed on top a bundle of dried grapevine prunings which burst into flame, clouds of smoke billowing into the place Beauvau while alarmed neighbours rang the fire department. When the firemen arrived, we were at table and there was no more smoke.

I spent the first three months of 1965 visiting family and painting portraits—another of James, nieces and nephews in St. Louis and Washington and, in New York, new portraits of Robert Isaacson and Bernie Winebaum. Robert asked me to gather together as many recent paintings as possible to place on view for a reception at his flat. It was a good party but not a stepping stone to success. Byron and Marilynn were in their last semester of medical school before moving to St. Louis in July to begin residencies. They asked several fellow medical students to dinner, for which Byron and I shopped in Baltimore's open market. Many stands displayed rows of freshly skinned, bloody creatures labeled "marsh rabbit." I asked a vendor what they were and how one prepared them. He said, "Muscrats—boil'm to get rid of the taste and fry'm like chicken." We decided to treat them with more respect: I cut them up, immersed them overnight in red wine with herbs, aromatic vegetables, a drizzle of olive oil and prepared them like a coq-au-vin. The flavour was delicately gamey, the sauce the colour of bitter chocolate, glossy with a velvet texture. Everyone loved it until, as cheeses were served, Byron announced that we had been eating muscrat; two guests turned green and fled to the bathroom.

I returned to Clamart to discover that the Franco-German couple on the first floor had left (taking much of Mlle Marty's furniture with them), Jimmy Guibez and Robert had moved from Beauford's old flat to the rooms upstairs, Bernard had moved a French photographer into the ground floor flat "for a fee," broken the lock on my wine cellar, drunk or sold the wine, and "sold" the cellar to the photographer to be used as a darkroom. I had no more wine, but I was cross; I put the photographer's equipment out, replaced the lock and invited Bernard to move out of Clamart to the clamour of screams and insults. He stayed. I went south.

Ireland was celebrating the centennial of W.B. Yeats's birth. James and I toured the country, visiting Yeats's tower and other pertinent memorials. The only decent food was in a seaside hotel on the far northwest coast where we were served a large, freshly fished, poached sea trout for breakfast. We were unused to that kind of breakfast so decided to order a bottle of white Burgundy and treat it like lunch. An old priest approached us in a graveyard and solicited our impressions of Ireland. We spoke of our disappointment with the food and said that we had hoped at least to find somewhere an honest Irish stew. He was horrified. "No self-respecting Irishman," he said, "would ever serve Irish stew to a foreigner."

We spent the summer in Solliès. Mary and Garin joined us for the month of August. "Richard," whined Mary, "why do you always call Georges 'Garin'? His name is Georges." I didn't bother to answer. Garin said, "Shut up Mary, Richard calls me 'Garin' out of respect for who I am—I am GARIN."

I received a sad letter from Lucia; she and Ernst were separating. She wanted desperately to have a child and was then at the age limit. Ernst loved Lucia and was very protective of her but he refused to cooperate, claiming that she was tempermentally unsuited to being a mother. (They were divorced and remained intimate friends. Ernst retired early with heart problems, moved to Florence where he bought a house and, at his death, left everything to Lucia.)

Bernard had shifted into his violent phase. Robert Isaacson was in town and we had arranged to meet at the flat of our friend, John Hohnsbeen. Bernard must have followed me for I had just arrived when there was a knock on the door. John opened it and Bernard burst in, flailing his fists at me. Robert and John were stunned; I had no idea what the problem was but I left with him to escape further embarrassment. He was irate because he wanted money, had checked my wallet earlier, then searched the flat in Clamart and found nothing. I told him that, if he wanted to sell me his part of the property, I would find the money and pay him the same sum that I had originally paid for both our parts. That enraged him but, after refusals, threats and reversals, he finally agreed. I opened a bank account, Mary agreed to lend me the money and Garin recommended a notaire, one of his clients, who placed our transaction in the hands of his assistant. The papers were drawn up and a rendezvous made to sign them and pass the money. I went to the bank to deposit Mary's check, Bernard followed to see where I was going and was outraged to discover that I had opened an account—he didn't want a check, he wanted cash; when he saw Mary's check, he was furious with her for lending me the money. We signed the papers, I wrote the check, passed it to the notaire's assistant, who confirmed the correct sum and passed it to Bernard. That should have solved all problems.

The rest of the story is a surrealist nightmare. The notaire informed me that his assistant had "absconded" with the papers of all the transactions that were in his hands. Bernard denied having sold me his share of the property. I hired a lawyer, Bernard was uncooperative, refused to appear in court, and the court decision was in my favour.

The house in Solliès was finally in a state to be inhabited the year round. I told Mlle Marty that I would be leaving the flat in Clamart to settle in the south. She broke down in tears, begged me not to leave and assured me that, if only I would keep the flat, I would have no rent to pay. I was embarrassed and promised to keep the flat; I continued to pay the rent and Bernard continued to live there. Life was not amusing for Mlle Marty then. I was rarely there and no longer gave parties, which she had adored. Jimmy Guibez's friend, Robert, was constantly fighting with her, about nothing, his voice rising hysterically to shrieks. When I was in Paris I often stayed with Mary to avoid scenes with Bernard.

Michel Lemonnier moved south to an old farmhouse outside of Egalières, near Avignon. For years we exchanged visits. Michel wrote a series of articlcs in *CVF* about Solliès, my "hermitage," my "jardin de curé" with intermingling flowers and kitchen herbs, meals cooked in the fireplace, the carnival atmosphere of dinners on the terrace lighted by strings of coloured bulbs, the great toad, named Victor, who noisily descended the steps at the side of the house to observe the terrace activity, and so forth.

Eda Lord and Sybille Bedford moved from England to the ground floor (and garden) of a house which belonged to Sybille's friend, Allanah Harper, in La Roquette-sur-Siagne, between Cannes and Grasse. Eda came often to Solliès to spend a few days, sometimes Sacha joined us. (Sybille was at first intimidated by the goatpath up the hillside—it would be another five years before a road led to the property.) Eda was enchanted by everything. She loved the rustic swimming pool, she adored my loin lamb chops (cut three inches thick, skin and fat removed, aprons rolled up and skewered to the chop with a sharpened rosemary branch, rubbed with olive oil, herbs, salt and pepper, grilled over fruitwood embers three or four minutes to a side—when that thick, there are five sides—until pink throughout) and the garden. In the morning, we drank bowls of black coffee on the terrace and she asked why I was staring so intently into my bowl. At first I couldn't answer because it was an unconscious thing—finally, I explained that all the vineleaves and skyscape were so beautifully reflected in dark light on the surface of my coffee, a sort of distillation of memory and eternity—she never again drank coffee on the terrace without admiring the clear, dark image on its surface.

A couple of days before the annual Bordeaux trip I had dinner at Mary's. The blood-temperature bottle of old Beaujolais was turning to vinegar. We agreed that it was bad. I suggested we open another and put it in an ice bucket; it was dull but I said nothing. The next evening she had promised Garin that, after dinner in Clamart, we would come by the restaurant for drinks. She was nervous. En route, she finally screwed up the courage to say, "I suppose I should warn you—Georges is very angry because you didn't like the Beaujolais." When we arrived, it was obvious that he had been rehearsing his temper tantrum for he immediately lashed out at me, screaming inanities; the message seemed to be that it is unforgivable to criticize wine when one is a guest. Mary cringed and wailed, over and over again, "Ohh...Georges must have misunderstood me." I could not know what she had told him but I knew he had not misunderstood. I informed them that I would no longer be interested in sharing the tables of idiots with whom one could not discuss wine and left. It took me a long time to understand—and I was never able to accept—that for Garin, violent, irrational quarrels were an essential element in a bosom friendship.

In Bordeaux, the Places had separated. Robert was camping out at Bouscaut while the château was being rebuilt. Ninette was convinced that the place was jinxed and refused ever to move back. (Robert later sold Chateau Bouscaut to an American group and disappeared into the Alpes Maritimes, where he lost contact with all his friends.)

Over the bar Chez Garin was hung a large after-dinner still life—a blue and white checked tablecloth with a few plates of fruit debris, a lingering cheese platter and a large array of wine bottles, carafes and glasses at various levels of emptiness. Bernie Winebaum's brother and sister-in-law, Sumner and Helen, wanted to buy it. Garin told them it was not for sale. I had steered clear of Mary and Garin since the Beaujolais incident but, instead of creating a scandal, I decided to organize a Sunday dinner party for them (Mme Garin had been shipped off to Auvergne) and the Winebaums to discuss the sale over a series of fine wines. It was like pulling teeth but Garin finally accepted to let "his" painting go. For the main course, I prepared "Les Oreilles de Veau farcies à la Lucien Tendret," as described in Dumaine's favorite book (and which, many years later, became a specialty at Alain Chapel's La Mère Charles, in Mionnay), calves' ears, bound in muslin to hold their shape, poached in stock and white wine, stuffed with diced sautéed chicken breast, braised sweetbreads and fresh truffles, chilled, rolled twice in lightly beaten eggwhite and fresh breadcrumbs, fried in clarified butter and accompanied by a sauce béarnaise. It was transcendental. Mary who, in Bernard's parlance, "didn't have a tastebud in her ass," always watched Garin to know what to do at table. When the master refused the sauce, she announced that it was obviously a mistake to serve a sauce with such a dish. Garin said shut up; it was not a mistake but that he, personally, could not digest sauces based on eggyolk emulsion and would have preferred a mustard sauce. When they left, Mary had revised her opinion; she said, "...of course I would have preferred a strong-flavoured sauce with the calves' ears." A few months later, Sacha wanted to buy a painting. Again Garin refused to let it go and again I had to insist. Paintings that were sold I always replaced; those that were not sold I never recuperated.

December 1965. An American woman and a small child climbed up the hillside in Solliès. Bernard had told her that he owned a "château" with central heating in the south of France and had accepted 150,000 francs rent from her for the winter months. I was helpless to quell the flood of tears when she realized that there was no château, no comfort and the primitive structure before her was not Bernard's.

January 1966. Simon Arbellot died. Pierre and Pierrette sold the Guinguette and moved to a far edge of Paris. Sacha wanted me to meet his old friend, Marie Ricard, then in her eighties, who lived in a wing of the house that belonged to her son, Jacques, on a vast, wooded property, Les Plaines, outside of Salon-de-Provence. At the turn of the century, Salon was the center of the Provençal olive oil commcrce and Marie's father, M. Fournier, had been the city's most important olive oil merchant. Sacha had met Marie at the beginning of World War II in her clandestine role of falsifier of identity papers; it was she who transformed him from Albrecht Niederstein into Sacha Neuville. Marie was angular, wiry and active. Her nose was an admirable and prominent beak and her head seemed chipped out of stone. (I regret not having painted her—she bought several of my paintings, all still-lives.) She was hard of hearing and spoke loudly. We exchanged visits for many years. She often drove to lunch in Solliès, with or without Sacha, when I would return to Salon for two or three days. She was a terrifying driver (in Salon, it was all right—everyone knew her and kept out of her way). Once, when Marie and Sacha had gossiped happily during a harrowing drive back to Salon, I asked Sacha (who didn't drive) if he wasn't nervous with Marie at the wheel; no, he said, he assumed that she was a good driver. Another time, when Marie and I were alone, we sailed from a side road onto the old National 6, with trucks screeching to a halt, the drivers cursing loudly, while Marie, unconcerned or unaware, continued weaving along the highway. I said nothing but held tightly to my seat.

When we arrived, she said, off handedly, "...gave you a little scare, didn't I?"

Garin claimed to be suffering a nervous breakdown, closed the restaurant for the month of February, headed south and rented a car. Mary's work prevented her from accompanying him. He came panting up the hillside quite early in the morning, trembling and complaining of thirst and hunger. I poured white wine, prepared a potato paillasson on my single gas ring, grilled andouillettes in the fireplace and opened a bottle of Domaine Tempier. The shakes disappeared and he was in fine form from then on. Except for the shocking absence of a serious cookstove, my kitchen was well furnished. Garin loved working there and, in particular, cooking in the fireplace. We roasted guinea fowl and legs of lamb on spits before the flames, grilled fish, steaks and chops over embers and baked potatoes in smouldering ashes. Lulu invited us to Domaine Tempier for a bouillabaisse prepared over a wood fire in her antique copper cauldron. Garin wanted to visit his truffle merchant, Jean-Marie Valayer, in Richerenches, a tiny village near Valréas in the northern Vaucluse. En route we stopped to have lunch with Jacques, his companion, Rosette, and Marie Ricard. On the property was a medieval monastery, l'Abbaye de Sainte-Croix, abandoned at the time of the Revolution, which Jacques had spent years restoring. Garin was fascinated and Jacques hoped that he would buy it and create a restaurant there (it was finally sold to a group that transformed it into a luxury hotel and restaurant). We spent the night in Avignon and dined Chez Hiély. Garin complained that they had no right to practice such low prices—it was bad for the profession. André Hiély was then in the dining room and his son, Pierre, was chef de cuisine. (Later, Pierre sent his sous-chef to Paris for a year in Garin's kitchen before returning to Avignon to become chef Chez Hiély.) Monsieur and Madame Valayer were old-fashioned peasants. We were led to a formal parlour which was obviously never used except to receive the rare client, and served sweet cordials in miniscule glasses reserved for such an occasion. I asked Mme Valayer how she liked to prepare truffles. "Oh," she said, "truffles are much too expensive to eat on weekdays but, in season, I often cook a batch in a bottle of Châteauneuf-du-Pape for Sunday dinner (by which she meant the mid-day meal)." We returned to Solliès with two kilos of truffles, prepared a truffle stew and, in the days to come, ate them in scrambled eggs, omelets, pig's trotter crépinettes and hot potato salad, I sterilized some and deep-froze the others. For ten years, each February when they are ripest and richest, I ordered two kilos of truffles from M. Valayer. The last time I rang him he had retired and recommended a large commercial firm, where I placed an order, was disappointed and fell out of the habit of living with truffles.

Sybille screwed up her courage and drove to lunch one day with Eda. She was seduced by the atmosphere, the wines and the simplicity of the food. We ate in front of the fireplace where I grilled Eda's favorite chops. We began with creamy scrambled eggs and truffles, with the chops I served a salad of garden lettuces spiced with a few salt anchovy fillets and chopped hyssop and finished with a platter of cheeses. Sybille loved my vinegar and the local olive oil. In her autobiographical novels (*A Legacy*, *A Favorite of the Gods*, *A Compass Error*, *Jigsaw*), a passion for the table, for freshly plucked or dug vegetables and creatures pulled from the sea the moment before being eaten alive, grilled or sautéed, is woven through the treacherous tales of imperfect love, heartbreak and desolation, a steadying and voluptuous thread of joy. The ritual litanies of classified Médocs, noble Burgundies or friendly little Italian wines that don't mind being warmed up on a trip to the beach and cooled down with an ice cube, are marvelous.

The local olive oil came from a mill owned by an eighty-year-old lady, Mme (Rose) Gerfroit, "la grande dame du pays," famous in the region for her ability to pinpoint the village origin of Provençal olive oils when tasting them. We became good friends and often exchanged lunches. She invited more often than I because of the precarious goat path leading to my house. Her housekeeper-cook, Blanche, worshipped her and prepared simple roasts to perfection. Mme Gerfroit liked receiving during the game season, when we ate roast thrush or partridge (three thrush or one partridge per person), often preceded by Mediterranean rock lobsters (langoustes), in court-bouillon or grilled. The wines were always Burgundies. In December, when most of the olives arrived, a fireplace in the mill was permanently ablaze, beside which slices of rough country bread, a bowl of chopped salt anchovies and a pitcher of new olive oil awaited the truckdrivers, who warmed their hands before the fire, then speared slices of bread with long-handled forks, spread them with anchovies, dribbled over oil and grilled them in front of the flames. In early January, with a pitcher of thick, murky, newly pressed olive oil, Mme Gerfroit's lunches opened with hot chick peas, accompanied by dishes of finely chopped garlic, onions and parsley, to be transformed into a salad at table. Sacha had met Mme Gerfroit and wanted to bring her and Marie together. She invited us to lunch. Mme Gerfroit wore a hearing aid that led a life of its own, often emitting disconcerting electrical complaints. She and Marie conversed loudly and passionately about olive oil but it was only with coffee that the light dawned and she exclaimed. "But you must be the Fournier girl!" ("Mais vous êtes, donc, la fille Fournier!")

Paris, 23 March 1966. David Leeming (*James Baldwin*) records that Bernard was out of town but that I had drinks with him and Jimmy before they left the following day for Istanbul. I don't know where Bernard was but he was blessedly absent from Clamart for the rest of the year.

I received an invitation to "exchange" lunches from a man in Toulon named Rougié Rebstock author, under the pen name Jean-Noël Escudier, of *La Véritable Cuisine Provençale et Niçoise*, a collection of recipes culled from local restaurants, amateur cooks, gazettes and books, whose great success owes something to the genial coupling of a poetic forename with the alliterative association of Escudier and Escoffier. M. Rebstock had been disappointed in the slight success of his earlier literary efforts—pornographic books disguised as medical sex manuals bearing the signatures of fictitious doctors—and decided to switch from sex to cuisine, with which he admitted to a limited acquaintance. His wife stewed sausage-stuffed squid in tomato sauce and we drank noncommittal wine. In Solliès they were enraptured by a first course of scrambled eggs and truffles; I was bemused to learn that the author of a cookbook which contained a number of truffle recipes (as well as the indignant claim that "so many truffles said to be from Périgord come from the Vaucluse") had never tasted a truffle. Communication was tangential and I imagined our exchange program to be at an end but I soon received an urgent invitation to lunch for "a special occasion," which turned out to be the fortuitous absence of Mme Rebstock, who was visiting family in Alsace. My host asked me to cook the steak. He explained that he had never grilled meat and didn't know how to prepare the garden charcoal grill. We began with an hors d'oeuvre that he described as his personal invention, small squares of sandwich bread, on each of which was a dab of tomato paste squeezed from a tube and a tinned rolled anchovy fillet. As we finished the steak, he said he had to take a siesta and would like me to lie down beside him. I excused myself and fled.

Madeleine, Odette, M. Honoré and I spent several days in Banyuls at the invitation of Dr. André Parcé, vineyard proprietor, a loyal participant in the *CVF* Bordeaux tours, Grand Maître of the Banyuls wine confraternity, indefatigable advocate for noble, natural wines whose distinctions are allied to their origins, a big man with a voluptuous Catalan accent, a devouring passion for the table and the soul of a crusader. (Today he is president of l'Académie du Vin de France, as well as president and prime mover of l'Académie Internationale du Vin.) André had asked his chef to create dishes using Banyuls in their confection or to be accompanied by Banyuls. We ate and drank sumptuously. (Another time, on a *CVF* organized tour of French Catalan country, buckets of live garden snails were plugged with pinches of sausage meat, grilled over grape vine embers and washed down with the cool, young red wine of Collioure.) André liked to serve his friends contraband Spanish absinthe (illegal in France), ritually dribbled into the glass over a perforated spoon containing a lump of sugar, while explaining that smuggling is an ancient and admired Catalan profession.

23 July 1966. (James to Byron, from Solliès) "Spent about a week in Paris—an evening with Mlle Marty, an evening Chez Maxim's, an evening in Champagne and—the greatest, on my birthday—an evening Chez Garin. Drove south, astonishing meal in Roanne—we were served all the specialties of the house, liberally wined and boozed and the next morning M. Troisgros père refused

to give us a bill for anything but our hotel rooms. Spent a night in Avignon, ate at Hiély." During the mid-sixties, when James was in town, we always made a point of having a meal Chez Maxim's with Mary and Garin. The art nouveau décor and the schmaltzy violins were other-worldly. Louis Vaudable was patron and Alex Humbert was chef. (I cherished the memory of very fresh scallops with coral tongues of roe in creamy saffron sauce, accompanied by a 1937 Meursault, at Le Caneton, Humbert's restaurant, rue de la Bourse, before he moved to the kitchens Chez Maxim's in 1955.) The food was very good, the service attentive and the wine list was spectacular, with '28 and '29 first growth Bordeaux at affordable prices. The sommelier was genuinely excited to have clients who loved wine; the beautiful people drank mostly Champagne and the tourists drank rosé de Provence.

Lucia spent a couple of weeks in Solliès, went on to Rome, felt sentimental about Solliès and returned. Lucia's nerves were fragile and she could not support everyone's company. I had imagined that the absence of a telephone would protect my privacy; on the contrary, it encouraged friends from Toulon and Marseille to arrive unannounced, laden with market produce for me to transform into a meal. On these occasions, Lucia more than once kept to her room, refusing to come to table. When we were alone she was relaxed and adorable.

2 November 1966. (Me to James) "Mary and Garin are in Solliès for All Saints—stuffing ourselves with woodcooks, gigots, moussaka à la française, cèpes and other wild mushrooms, pieds et paquets.... Garin insists that all menus be written down "for posterity's sake." I may take Raffaello from Cannes 24 November." p.s. from Mary: "Richard is going to do a portrait of G. and me, we all hope, if we ever stop eating. Tomorrow we lunch with Mme Gerfroit on langoustes and thrush." (It was not until late the following summer that we "stopped eating" long enough to begin the portrait. Each day, after a quarter of an hour's work, Garin announccd, "Time for a Champagne break!" Several bottles of Champagne disappeared daily, the weather turned bad and the portrait was never finished.)

18 November 1966. (Me to James) "…just finished dinner (grilled kidneys, grilled wild mushrooms, potatoes sous la cendre), leave tomorrow for dégustations in Beaune, return Monday, lunch Tuesday chez Mme Gerfroit, dine Wednesday in Cannes with Eda and Sybille, sail the next day. Raffaello cancelled—it will be my first time to travel American." It was not a civilized crossing.

Sybille was not the first friend to suggest that I write a cookbook. I had never taken the idea seriously but Sybille did. She asked me to contact her friend, Evelyn Gendel (to whom *A Legacy* is dedicated), at Simon & Schuster. Evelyn introduced me to the food editor, Pat Read, who seemed interested. Sybille must have paved the way for I had nothing to show except some articles in French which no one could read. Pat asked me to bring in some sample material before returning to France.

In Des Moines, James received me with an admirable hochepot, a pot-au-feu of oxtail, pigs' ears and trotters. His companion, Judy, was there. James and I went to Marathon for Christmas and to Saint Louis to celebrate the New Year with John, Byron and families.

Four

1967-1973
French Menu Cookbook. Liberia.
Summer Cooking Classes, Avignon.

Our aunt Florine, Father's youngest sister, was approaching her eightieth birthday and mourned a little dog, recently defunct from old age. John, James, Byron and I were of one mind: Florine needed a monkey. We found a seductive baby capuchin in a Saint Louis pet shop, named him Sebastian. James, Sebastian and I returned to Des Moines, where I spent many hours teasing the monkey out of his shyness while James taught his classes, and the three of us drove to Marathon for Florine's birthday, covered the cage and presented it. "A dog? a cat? a parrot?" she guessed. When the cloth was lifted, she was ecstatic. "Ever since I was a little girl," she said, "I've wanted a monkey more than anything in the world." Florine and Sebastian spent many happy years together (Florine died recently on the eve of her 108th birthday).

My articles for *CVF* were handwritten; I saw no reason for a painter to master the typewriter. S & S didn't agree. I spent a couple of weeks with Margaret and Elizabeth in the suburbs of Washington writing sample copy, typed by Elizabeth, which I carried to New York and presented to Pat Read, who was pleased. We had lunch at the Lutèce. She had invited an agent to join us because, she said, I would need one. I didn't know why. John Schaffner, whom I had known twenty years earlier, joined us. It was agreed that John would be my agent and that a contract would be prepared and sent to me in Solliès. I sailed, 9 March, on *Le France*, bought a typewriter in Toulon and learned how to poke at a French keyboard. For the rest of the year the flow of visitors was relentless. I went to Paris in May to paint a portrait of Sumner and Helen Winebaum's two boys. Mary thought it would be nice if I would stay on to help her entertain her mother, a thirteen year old niece and a ten year old nephew who were due to arrive; I couldn't spare the time so she sent them to Solliès where I painted a portrait of the children.

Byron and Marilynn, with a baby boy named James, moved to Palo Alto for residencies. Brother James had accepted a teaching position at Cuttington College in Liberia beginning in July. He and Judy spent a month in Solliès and Paris before continuing to Liberia. (Mother and Father were frustrated—there had been whispered rumours in the family of a forthcoming marriage. James and Judy had visited Marathon and, when questioned, James claimed to know nothing of such a project. The parents wondered if I knew anything about this irregular arrangement—I knew nothing. Father said he had heard of "common law marriage" and presumed it was just as sacred as any other kind.)

Julius and his friend Gertrude Buckman arrived, spent a few days and escaped, burdened with guilt, from the pleasures of the table. 27 July 1967. (Me to James) "I have always known that Julius considered good food immoral—Gertrude is even worse—of course each evening as hunger strengthened, the sense of sin diminished only to flow back multifold as the stomach filled. I trust they are enjoying ham sandwiches and mineral water somewhere at this moment."

Mary and Garin settled in for the month of August. 19 August 1967. (Me to James) "Carol Terrell, on vacation from United Nations, arrives this evening from Jerusalem. Michel Lemonnier arrives with friend day after tomorrow. I finally received the contract—they want the finished manuscript 1 December." (I learned later that publishers habitually impose impossible deadlines, mainly in the interest of torturing authors.) 2 September. (Me to James) "Garin went winetasting in Burgundy and returned to Paris a few days earlier than planned, Mary became hysterical at the idea of his being in Paris two or three days without her, couldn't change her auto-couchette reservation which was for 3 Sept., so she conned Carol into driving her to Paris. Carol didn't want to but Mary (incapable of driving alone, of course) insisted and Carol, out of politeness, couldn't refuse. To ease tensions, I accepted to travel as far as Avignon with them, we stopped first at Michel's for apéritif, ate you know where and stayed overnight at the Crillon. Carol will be back here before returning to Israel.

28 October 1967. (Me to James) "Finally rec'd advance from S & S, used it to buy a small professional cookstove—La Cornue. It was delivered yesterday by four men who worked very hard all afternoon long getting it up the mountainside." Madeleine and Michel spent two days with me. Madeleine attempted unsuccessfully to convince me that I was the property of *CVF* and had no moral right to publish a cookbook that was not signed by her. I returned with them to Michel's where the conversation continued. I suggested that I take a few months off from *CVF* to work on my book and was told that such a possibility was out of the question. I accepted to continue writing the monthly articles and there was no more discussion of cosigning the book. We sealed our friendship

Richard Olney, Portrait of James, c. 1970. Oil on canvas.

with a dinner Chez Hiély where we finished with a bottle of Romanée-St.-Vivant Les Quatre Journaux 1961, whose label bearing our signatures faces me from the great pillar as I write. Madeleine was suffering from back problems, subsequently diagnosed as cancer.

I wrote James, late November, that I thought the manuscript was half finished. In Liberia, the three-month academic vacation was December through February. James and Judy spent most of December in Solliès, a few days in Paris for gastronomic splurges and, early January 1968, I flew with them to Monrovia, stopping for a couple of days in Madrid. We were stunned by the Velasquez and Goya paintings in the Prado and ate in a restaurant recommended by Garin where dinner began with elvers—transparent eel fry gently warmed with a crushed garlic clove and a pod of cayenne, in a bath of olive oil until they turned opaque.

Except for trimming and rewriting, *The French Menu Cookbook* was finished in Liberia. Judy visited her parents while James and I drove into the Ivory Coast. Crossing borders was dramatic; officials claimed that our papers were not in order, that the borders were closed, or both. We were too innocent to understand that a tip (in Liberia called a "dash") was required and, once that was made clear, that a fraction of the sum suggested would have served. It took us a day and a half to get out of Liberia and into the Ivory Coast, at which point we were issued into the presence of the chief border authority, wondering if we might be headed for jail; instead, he graciously invited us to join him and his family for lunch—it was a command. Four generations of the family sat at a long table, many highly seasoned stews were served—our host explained that, in deference to foreign palates, they were underseasoned—with little side dishes of cayenne for the family. In our honour several French wines were poured; everyone was in high spirits when we left.

Michelin's road map to the Ivory Coast had the same reassuring look of authority, of infinite detail and absolute precision, as their French regional maps. In fact, we followed some roads that were not indicated while others had been devoured by the jungle or destroyed by erosion. We had driven for hours on a progressively narrowing road, without seeing another car or any signs of habitation, when it abruptly ended at a river. It was about 6 o'clock when, near the equator, day turns to night with practically no transition. To retrace our steps at night with the possibility of running out of gas was implausible and we couldn't cross the river. It seemed hopeless. Distant flickering lights from the other side of the river became identifiable as a car's headlights; they approached the river bank, two men got out and a Frenchman called out, wondering if we needed help. His chauffeur waded across, spent some time collecting odd boards, probably the debris of a wooden bridge, long since collapsed, and constructed two precarious tracks of overlapping boards across the river, supported here and there by surfacing rocks. He explained that he would have to drive the car while we waded. The crossing was spectacular—he sped across on the

Byron's son, James, with Harriet in Marathon, 1969.

tracks as the boards were flung high behind him, leaving no trace of the construction. The Frenchman was an old-fashioned dedicated doctor who had for many years operated a small hospital in the bush. He asked us to share dinner with him and his wife and to spend the night. Soon we were sunk into worn easy chairs with welcome glasses of whisky before sitting down to soup, roast pork, potato gratin, cheeses, red wine and fruit—we might have been in Auvergne.

Before I left Liberia, Harry Gillmore, a wild animal man, keeper of President Tubman's private zoo, arrived with a baby female spot-nosed monkey for James and Judy. She was named Harriet, after Harry, and was a cherished member of the family for years, until her jealous affection for James turned her aggressive toward Judy and other females, when she had to be confided to a zoo.

I returned to Solliès mid-March. The end room of the house had collapsed. I received a note from Robert, Jimmy Guibez's friend, in Clamart, saying Mlle Marty was dead and what did I want to do with the things in my studio. I mailed the finished manuscript to S & S, took a train to Paris and headed for Clamart, stopping at the café-tabac at the Place Marquis. The proprietors told me there was something suspicious about Mlle Marty's death, that Robert had arrived at the café saying he had found her dead in her apartment and asked them to telephone the police—he wanted to be left out of it. They knew that Mlle Marty lived behind locked doors and that no one ever entered her rooms before she unlocked the door. At the house, Robert met me with a flood of gibberish, words and phrases garbled and tripping over one another, in an attempt to explain the impossible—that he had simply walked into Mlle Marty's and found her dead. I assumed that her heart had failed during one of his lunatic, screaming tirades. There was nothing to say. Jimmy Guibez told me that Bernard had moved out of my studio, taking "what belonged to him." I went upstairs. All the paintings were gone. I left without saying goodbye and never returned to Clamart.

The year to come was spent rebuilding the collapsed room. 30 April 1968. (Me to James) "I have a mason to help me every

Saturday—spend a great part of each week hauling up enough cement, sand, gravel, concrete blocks and iron bars to be used up in a day." It was donkey's work, punctuated by visits from everyone I knew. Madeleine's back cancer was worse; Odette, alone, was responsible for holding *CVF* and *RVF* together. I went to Paris for gastronomic jury duty (a *CVF* recipe contest). The chosen recipes were prepared in Prunier's kitchens. Jean Barnagaud, Prunier proprietor, Odette and Michel were the other jury members.

Madeleine joined us later for lunch at Pierre Traiteur. I had dinner with Eda and Sybille and met Pat Read and a friend in Auribeau, near Cannes. Pat and friend returned with me to Solliès for three days; there was no problem about the manuscript except that S & S found it too impersonal (I had conscientiously avoided the use of the first person)—they wanted anecdotes, prejudices and personal opinions. Eda and Sybille came to lunch, curious about my progress with S & S—they were more excited than I about the forthcoming book.

In July, Mme Garin, momentarily exiled to Auvergne, died of a cerebral hemorrhage. Mary was ecstatic with joy and immediately began plans for marriage. Garin was in less of a hurry but accepted (after a respectable five months of mourning) to exchange vows in December.

Ninette Place spent a few days with me the end of July, Lucia came for two weeks in August, Mary and Garin for the entire month. Garin bought an hectare of terraced hillside across the valley from me on which to build their dream house "for the day of his retirement." He and Mary wanted their house "to be exactly like mine"—except, of course, that they wanted several bathrooms and all the other comforts and luxuries that mine lacked. Meanwhile I was charged with finding workers to build a road up to the property and with overseeing the clearing of the land and pruning the olive trees.

John arrived in Solliès mid-September, we met Michel in Avignon for dinner Chez Hiély (two years earlier, Pierre Hiély had commissioned a portrait of his father, which I had repeatedly postponed—I promised to return in a month), and drove the following day to Bordeaux for the annual *CVF* tour. I had arranged to have

John enthroned in the Commanderie du Bontemps de Médoc et des Graves. We dined Chez Garin the 24th, John flew to Liberia the 25th and, three days later, Mary and I, sponsored by Garin, were enthroned in the Confrérie des Chevaliers du Tastevin; Sacha joined us for the banquet at the Château de Vougeot.

Madeleine died the first week of October. I went to Paris for services and we drove to the family tomb in Houdan, sixty kilometers from Paris. Odette had not slept for days, was distraught and collapsed as the coffin was lowered into the vault. Back in Paris, Odette, M. Honoré, Michel and I were received by Alex, Andrée and Monique Allégrier at l'Hôtel de Lapérouse, a luxury pensioners' hotel owned by the family and managed by Monique. It was a private and soothing moment.

Until Madeleine's death, Odette and M. Honoré had entertained a superficially cordial relationship. Now there was open hostility. M. Honoré didn't want Odette to replace Madeleine as directrice of *CVF* and *RVF*. No one else was qualified and Odette wanted to buy the two reviews. M. Honoré was anti-Semitic though he would never have expressed himself so indelicately. Long experience, he claimed, had taught him that people of different races and religions should not mix. He finally accepted to sell, for an exorbitant price considering that neither review had ever been out of the red, a portion of the sum due immediately, the remainder in a year's time or the properties would revert to him. Odette was convinced that he was depending on her being unable to pay. (She managed to borrow the money at the last minute and the two magazines became her property the day before the deadline.)

26 October 1968. (Me to James) "Just returned from Avignon where I spent a week painting the portrait of Hiély père—the result pleased everyone. Garin and Mary arriving for All Saints', foie gras and thrush chez Mme Gerfroit."

A propos of my *CVF* articles, I received an effusive letter of praise from Claude Peyrot, a young chef who had recently opened his restaurant, Le Vivarois, in Paris. Sacha and I held a table there and had an astonishing meal of great purity—I remember the truffled pâté de lapin (a multi-textured mosaic of different colours and separate flavours, bound with a limpid jelly, enclosed in buttery puff pastry) and braised oxtail, sprinkled with crumbs and lightly grilled, accompanied by fresh egg noodles and the reduced braising juices, cleansed of all fat. Sacha began with a lovely still life of little vegetables à la grecque. Claude joined us after the service and began quoting by memory passages from my articles. He was impassioned by his métier, nervous and full of tics; he had worked in the kitchens of Fernand Point, in Vienne, and Raymond Thuilier at Baumanière and had no respect for either. ("He was crazy," said Thuilier, "when he left me he went into a monastery.") His two great idols were Alexandre Dumaine and Georges Garin. Garin was not pleased by my praise of Claude's table; "He's nothing but a pastry cook," he grumbled.

James and Judy came to Paris for the 20 December marriage celebration—lunch and a day-long party Chez Garin. Most of the guests were chefs of Garin's generation, then in their late fifties. To those I didn't know I was introduced as being solely responsible for his and Mary's bonheur; I was embarrassed (and, in my secret thoughts, unconvinced of the bonheur's durability). When the last guests left we went to the Tour d'Argent for dinner.

Mary liked to remind herself and others that "Georges is the greatest chef in France." She was proud to be married to this phenomenon but had not realized that, in the role of Mme Garin, she was "la patronne" Chez Garin and would be expected to receive all guests graciously, to keep smiling, to watch the till, write out the bills and keep an eye on the service. She hated it—she couldn't keep smiling and knew nothing about service. Marie-Madeleine, the hostess, who was efficient and professional, assumed all of Mary's duties except for sitting at the till. At the restaurant, Garin never sat down before the service, he paced back and forth between the kitchen and the dining room to check details, nibbling odds and ends and chasing them with wine. Mary never ate with the help. A table was reserved for her in the dining room where she ordered from the menu; when I was in Paris, I was expected to keep her company at table. Although Garin tasted all wines before they were served, one of his waiters, Raymond, wore a black sommelier's apron and poured at table. Habitually, Raymond was obsequious and correct, his face a blank. One evening, Mary and I were changing wines; my glass had been replaced but Raymond began to pour the new bottle into Mary's unemptied glass. I snapped, "Raymond, change Mme Garin's glass!" A sneer illuminated his vapid expression; he said, "She doesn't know the difference." He replaced the glass. Mary sat silent, apparently unaware of this exchange, but Raymond was dismissed the next day. The maître d'hôtel was the next to disappear for showing lack of respect to Mme Garin.

Garin's reputation had soared in the eight years since he had created Chez Garin in Paris; he was, professionally, at the height of his glory. Mary immediately launched a campaign to sell the restaurant and move to Solliès-Toucas. It cannot have been her conscious goal, but it seemed, not only to me, as if she were deliberately trying to destroy Garin. L'Escapade, the roadside inn where I had taken winter room and board before building the fireplace, was for sale. Garin didn't want it. Mary, despite her newfound hatred for the restaurant business, insisted on buying it; the responsibility of overseeing the renovation, of finding masons, blacksmiths, painters, electricians and plumbers, fell to me (and lasted four years).

My dream of a hillside retreat where I could receive friends but live and work in solitude became an increasingly distant gleam of salvation. My house and I were treated as the Garins' property, to use as they chose. When they were not in residence, Garin sometimes sent apprentice cooks to stay with me. After a week's visit from one seventeen year-old, a number of irreplaceable old cookbooks were missing. I rang Garin from the post office. "Oh yes," he said, "the boy is known to be a kleptomaniac." When he next came to Solliès, he proudly handed over several books (three were missing), saying, "I gave him a stern lecture and he returned the books." (Several years after Garin's death, Mary pulled out his collection of old cookbooks to ask me what they were worth; I discovered my three missing volumes and removed them before referring her to a specialist).

A belly in the high dry-stone wall, which rose from a terrace below to support one end of the house, worried me. The natives scoffed. "That wall has stood for a century and a half," they said, "it's good for another century." but I was convinced the belly was swelling. I began to collect rocks on the lower terrace and dug trenches in which to pour a reinforced concrete foundation for a buttress. To build a road for the delivery of building materials, the steepness of the hillside imposed a zigzag, serpentine route cutting through the properties of three owners, from each of whom I had to buy a right-of-way. One, a dedicated enemy of "progress" and the modern world, balked. After visiting me, reassured by the presence of a fireplace and the absence of central heating, telephone, radio and television, he finally accepted. (Seven years later, he refused to permit telephone poles to be placed on his property because, he said, "I thought you were honest and now you want a telephone!")

Henri Caméra owned a building materials business, a delivery truck and a small bulldozer with which he gouged out rocky hillside roads in the region. Together, we built the road, he bulldozing while I followed with sledgehammer and pickax, breaking up and leveling stubborn areas of bedrock. As we were finishing, torrential March rains set in for two weeks; I visited the wall daily, helpless as the bulge swelled. At dawn the day following Henri's deliveries of cement, sand, and gravel, I was beside the wall mixing concrete when the belly opened, stones hurtled down and a groaning complaint was wrenched from the newly rebuilt room above. I began mindlessly to heave rocks and shovels of concrete at the gaping wound until debris stopped falling; I continued to build from the inside out, instead of from the still unpoured foundations inward. Months later, the buttress was finished.

Henri, who was very taken with the hillside property and with the lunches I prepared while we were building the road, proposed to come for a day's work from time to time. (A few years later, he sold his business and suggested we make it one day a week, then it became two days a week.)

A young man, Michel Comte, who recognized me from photos in *CVF*, introduced himself and asked me to join him and his wife, Monique, for dinner. During the few years that they remained in Solliès-Toucas, I saw them and their three small boys often. Both were from the Ardèche and had sentimental memories of a dish prepared by their mothers and grandmothers called la bombine, which they hoped I could recreate but neither was clear about the ingredients. They gathered together a half dozen Ardèchois friends for a group revival of bombine souvenirs: all remembered finding pettitoes' bones (with which French children play tiddlywinks) in their plates; black olives, potatoes, tripe, garlic and bay leaves surfaced—no one recalled onions. I assembled these things with a split pig's foot in an earthenware pot, moistened them with pot-au-feu broth, heated and sealed the pot and put it into a cool oven for five or six hours. Monique and Michel loved it but were not convinced it was the bombine of their childhood. Another Ardèchois reunion was organized, this time including a lady of their mothers' generation who assured me that the dish I had prepared was authentically Ardèchois but that its name was "pot-au-four." ("But, 'pot-au-four' and 'toupine' are the same thing," said someone.) Except for the presence of green olives, la bombine, as she described it, was an Irish stew. I published a recipe for pot-au-four in *CVF*, with an introduction describing our bombine research. In the months to come, a number of bombine recipes sent in by Ardèchois readers, all very different, were published in *CVF*. Bombine and toupine are, in fact, simply local terms for a traditional, pot-bellied earthenware vessel, like the Provençal daubière, which lends its name to the stews, similar but variable from one family tradition to another, that are prepared in it.

In June, Pat Read visited "to work on the book." The book was already in copyeditors' hands—there was no work to be done. We ate, drank, and gossiped.

James was leaving Liberia the first of July to spend a month in France—his birthday dinner Chez Garin, the remainder in Solliès—and the rest of the year in London to work on a book, before beginning teaching duties in February 1970 at North Carolina Central University in Durham. Harriet was shipped to Marathon with messages attached to her cage concerning her needs, her desires and her affectionate nature.

Byron, with Marilynn, their son, James, and a new daughter, Elizabeth, was sent to Vicenza, between Venice and Verona, for three years military service beginning September 1969.

Margaret, Tom and their two oldest children, Matthew, 15, and Libby, 13, were planning a whirlwind tour of Europe during the Christmas-New Year season. Judy was insisting that she and James return to the United States before Christmas. Michel Lemonnier was driving to Paris. (We stopped in Burgundy for dinner with Charles and Jacqueline Rousseau, drank Ponsot's lovely white Morey-Saint-Denis Monts Luisants 1961, great Chambertin 1961 and breath-taking Chambertin 1933.) The McBrides arrived in London 18 December, flew to Paris 22 December, where we had dinner with Mary Chez Garin, James and Judy left London 23 December, Tom rented a car and we drove to Avignon 24 December, Hiély was closed Christmas eve, we attended a midnight mass, drove to Solliès Christmas morning, turned a spitted leg of lamb in the fireplace for Christmas dinner, flew the next day from Nice to Milan where Byron met us, drove to Vicenza and spent three days visiting Venice, Verona, Urbino, Ravenna and Padua. The McBrides continued to Florence (couldn't see the Masaccios because the church was in restoration), Arezzo (mass was being held New Year's day morning, they had lunch and returned to San Francesco, whose portals were then locked), Rome and Amsterdam. I returned from Vicenza to Solliès, promising a more leisurely visit in March.

Alexandre Dumaine had sold l'Hôtel de la Cote d'Or in 1964 and retired a year later to his home town, Digoin. Mme Dumaine died shortly after. Dumaine was a lonely old man, living with memories of glory. He took under his wing the young chef at l'Hôtel de la Gare in Digoin, Jean-Pierre Billoux (now established in Dijon), with whom he organized conversational sessions divulging his culinary philosophy, techniques and souvenirs, moments that brightened his last years and dazzled Jean-Pierre. In early February 1970, Garin organized a dinner in homage to Dumaine. Odette, Michel, a half dozen gastronomic chroniclers, most of whom I didn't know and I were invited. On the menu was a terrine of woodcock, truffles and foie gras, a salmon turban enclosing truffled lobster mousseline, and whole braised calf's liver. Bâtard-Montrachet 1961 was poured with the terrine and the turban, Musigny 1937 with the liver,

Elizabeth on the terrace at Solliès.

La Tâche 1929 with cheese and, after the "Poires Belle Hélène," a white rum 1878. Dumaine's face was radiant, moist with tears of emotion. That was the last time I saw him.

In Vicenza, I painted portraits of Byron with young James, of James alone and of Marilynn, we experimented daily with their magical new pasta machine and I bought one to carry back to Solliès. Mother wrote that she and Father might like to visit Europe. She dreamed of visiting the great museums and the cities in which Leonardo and Michelangelo had worked but, for Father, it was a dramatic decision; the contemplation of art treasures was not high on his list of essentials and vacations had no place in his vision of a life's structure—for fifty years, he had never been absent from the bank except for the rare business trip of a day or two and a few honeymoon days in 1924.

Garin was back and forth between Paris and Solliès, often leaving Mary, to her consternation, at her post in the restaurant, Chez Garin. He was fortunate in having a talented, well organized and fiercely loyal young chef, Gérard Besson, in the kitchen.

Mid-April, Sybille wrote that she and Eda would like to see me and wondered if they could come to dinner and spend the night. A couple of days earlier Garin arrived, unannounced. 22 April 1970. (Me to James) "As the dinner coincided with Garin's stay, things were a bit confused but I managed to find time to shop and prepare dinner—quite good:

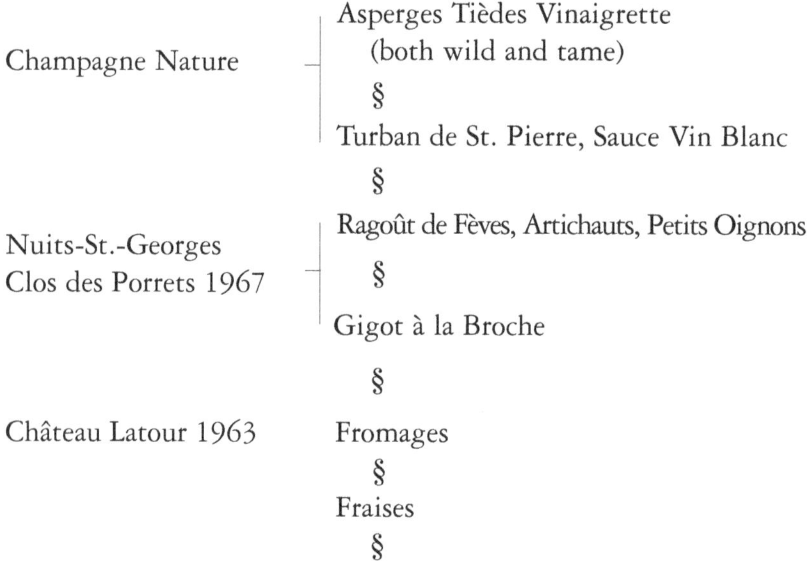

Champagne Nature	Asperges Tièdes Vinaigrette (both wild and tame) § Turban de St. Pierre, Sauce Vin Blanc §
Nuits-St.-Georges Clos des Porrets 1967	Ragoût de Fèves, Artichauts, Petits Oignons § Gigot à la Broche §
Château Latour 1963	Fromages § Fraises §

Neither Eda nor Sybille had lunched (preparing for dinner). Sybille and I drank quite a lot of white wine before dinner. Garin had promised to be back by 6:30—he was still not here at 9 so we sat down and he arrived in time for the turban." This was before still white wine from the region of Champagne could not be labeled "Champagne." 1963 was the first vintage after the British took possession of Château Latour. It was said (but not confirmed) that, to make it worthy of the new proprietorship, a certain amount of 1961 and 1962 had been assembled with the otherwise pathetic vintage; it was, in any case, easily the best of the red Bordeaux that year.

The parents were having second thoughts about their European venture. They worried about Frances, whose health was

Richard Olney. Portrait of Byron and James 1970. Oil on canvas.

progressively declining, and they were nervous about traveling alone. When James offered to accompany them and help plan the trip, they accepted but Father wrote, "Don't prolong things unnecessarily; we don't need to see everything." They opted for the first half of June.

Simca (Simone Beck) and her husband, Jean Fischbacher, had an old country house, Le Mas Vieux, outside of Plascassier on a large hillside property, "Bramafam," which belonged to Jean's relatives but which, in return for restoring the house, was theirs for the duration of their lives. Julia and Paul Child contracted to build a house on the property (baptised "La Pitchoune") which, by a similar arrangement, would be theirs during Jean's and Simca's lifetimes.

In early May, Simca wrote inviting me to spend a week during the first half of June at Bramafam. Impossible, I answered. A second letter informed me that she could not accept "no" as an answer; Julia would be at La Pitchoune and wanted to meet me. I apologized, explaining that James and I would be accompanying our parents on their European tour. Simca responded that she and Julia would be ravished to meet our parents, that there was plenty of room to put everyone up for as long as we would like to stay and that she would be expecting us. I figured that partying with food celebrities would not be Mother's and Father's dish of tea and refused again.

James and the parents were to arrive in Paris the morning of June 3rd. Garin was planning a grand dinner to welcome them. He and Mary were in Solliès the last week of May; I returned with them to Paris where I had a dinner date with Odette at the Cochon d'Or, an old-fashioned bistrot in the slaughterhouse district, celebrated for the quality of its beef. It had been her father's favorite restaurant, she said. We ate calf's head, vinaigrette, and grilled onglet (hanger steak) smothered in butter-stewed shallots; I remember a Ducru-Beaucaillou 1961 with the cheeses. Odette knew that I wanted to stop writing the monthly articles. We agreed that I could abandon the menu formula and I promised to write a series of articles on kitchen herbs, illustrated with pen and ink wash drawings.

I had held rooms at the Lutétia. Mother and Father arrived exhausted and wanted to lie down for a couple of hours. James and I went by the restaurant to greet Garin, who demanded that we fetch the parents for lunch. We insisted that they would not be able to deal with two haute cuisine meals in one day. He said, "But they have to nourish themselves," and promised that lunch would be starkly simple—a mere snack. It began promisingly—James and I were served the house apéritif, a glass of Champagne coloured with a few drops of raspberry liqueur; Mother and Father passed. A bottle of mineral water was placed at table with a dish of radishes, bread and butter. Father liked the radishes. Garin sent me to the cellar to choose the wine. Out of imbecile curiosity, I brought up a sample bottle of Beaujolais rosé, left there by a representative; it was thin and acidic. Father observed that what I had written about wine made it sound interesting; he thought he might like to taste it. He took a sip and made a retching sound of disgust. Slabs of duck terrine, spliced with foie gras and truffles, were served; he pronounced the mysterious flavours to be "highly unusual." Mother was enjoying herself but Father was becoming fidgety. He didn't like being waited on and he was unnerved by the smooth, gliding, tuxedo-clad maître d'hôtel, who persisted in addressing him in a language he didn't understand. The table was cleared, he assumed the meal was finished and was prepared to leave when a waiter arrived with a vast platter, on which was artfully laid out with its bed of court-bouillon vegetables, a 30-inch sea trout (fished that morning by a friend of his, Garin explained), two dozen crayfish à la nage scattered round, and a sauceboat of beurre blanc. Father said he had never eaten lobster but he supposed it was never too late to try. We drank a lovely Nuits-Saint-Georges Clos de la Maréchale with the cheeses but he declined to renew the winetasting experience. Both he and Mother were more at home with the biscuit glacé, a frozen genoise and ice cream confection with raspberry coulis poured round.

Mary and Sacha planned to join us for the grand dinner. Mother was looking forward to it as were James and I. Father announced that he had no intention of setting foot in that restaurant again. It was decided that I would stay with him until after dinner when James delivered Mother back to the hotel and we would return to Chez Garin for a drink. There was a gloomy bar-brasserie with booths and naked tabletops in a different wing of the hotel from their chic "gastronomic" restaurant. It had nothing to recommend it except for perfunctory and anonymous service, which I hoped might be less distressing to Father than that of a luxury restaurant. He wanted a well-done steak. I warned him that it would be tough but he was thinking of Mother's well-done steaks that were first floured and fried dry before being "tenderized" in a pressure cooker. He nibbled at a piece of steak, poked at it for a while, said it was too chewy for his taste and suggested that we take a walk. He was intimidated by city traffic and didn't trust the green lights, we crossed a street and crossed back, which he considered to be a harrowing experience so we walked a couple of times around the hotel block without crossing streets and settled into the hotel room to wait for Mother and James. They arrived just after 1 a.m., proof that the dinner had been a great success; James and I returned to the restaurant. The next morning Father decreed that, for the duration of the trip, we would partake of no more meals in restaurants. When our first room service of tepid hotel food

With Mother, Father and Byron in Venice, 1970.

beneath silverplate bells was trolleyed into the parents' room and we sat around, hands folded and heads bowed, while Father intoned, "Accept our thanks, heavenly Father, for the blessings of this hour. Help us to partake of this meal with thankful hearts. Sanctify the food unto our use and thus unto thy service. Guide and direct us, now and always. Amen." It struck me that the abhorrence of food consumption in public places was rooted mainly in the pilgrim instinct to pray at table.

We visited the Louvre. Father said it was very interesting but he thought one museum would be enough. Mother wanted to see the impressionist collection, which was then housed in the Jeu de Paume; James accompanied her while Father and I wandered in the Jardins des Tuileries.

On the secluded hillside in Solliès, surrounded only by family, Father was relaxed and happy for the first time. The weather was beautiful, he puttered in the garden and we ate out of doors, grills from the fireplace and salads of freshly plucked green things. Father studied a fragment of purslane in his plate and said, "Why, that's just a common weed." "But," I said, "it's good isn't it?" He concurred. There was no question of leaving the hillside to visit cities, sites, markets or monuments; James and I went down to shop.

From Vicenza, Byron drove us on day trips to Venice and Florence. We packed lunches to avoid restaurants. Venice was painless because there was no traffic but, in beautiful Florence, traffic and traffic racket were overwhelming and there was no centrally located park in which to wander; Father and I clung to the Piazza della Signoria while Mother, James and Byron visited the Uffizi, the Bargello and the Duomo.

We flew to Rome. Our taxi driver from the airport amused himself by screeching to a halt well into each intersection as crossing traffic swerved to avoid collision. Mother was oblivious but Father's nerves were in shreds before we reached the hotel. The driver asked for three times the sum on the meter, I called the hotel concierge to straighten things out, paid the correct price and refused to tip. He was screaming insults and babbling about how he had a family to feed when we finally escaped into the hotel. The rooms overlooked the Villa Borghese gardens, which was a bonus, but the hotel was not equipped for serious room service. Our meals were delivered on trays and the rooms contained no tables large enough to set out a meal. We built a precarious structure of suitcases around which to sit while eating after prayer. (Before each meal, so as not to rock the boat, James and I had whiskies delivered discreetly to our room in preparation for abstemiously sipping wine at the suitcases.) The pattern was set: Father and I roamed the gardens while Mother and James visited the Sistine Chapel, museums, churches and ancient monuments; in London, it was Kensington Gardens for us, the National Gallery and the Tate for them.

Father had not divulged his plan before arriving in England, when it became clear that, for him, the raison d'être of the European tour was to visit a village named Olney. He had a genealogy tracing the American branch of the family from Thomas Olney's arrival in Rhode Island in 1635. He hoped and believed that he would find traces of Olneys, past and present, in this village. In the ancient church graveyard, no stone bore the name; the local rector told us there were no records of Olneys having lived there—he thought there was a family by that name in a town some distance away.

Solliès-Toucas, 22 June 1970. (Me to Byron) "Traveling is over—put Mother and Father on a plane the 18th and returned here the following day. Visited Olney, which may have been the high spot of the trip, although Father was bitterly disappointed at the lack of interest the Olney residents exhibited in our name and perturbed to discover that no one by that name lived in Olney nor was even buried in the churchyard. Excepting one time—a village near Olney where we past the night—where there was no question of room service, Father absolutely refused to eat "in public" so all our meals in Rome and London were brought up, balanced on suitcases, etc. and, of course, blessed—the prayer in no way improved the quality of the food. The morning following the meal eaten in the hotel dining room near Olney, Father said if breakfast were not served in the room he would have none, so I rounded up cornflakes, sent a waiter out to find stewed prunes and served it myself in their room." (Father always ate three stewed prunes for breakfast.

Margaret once made the mistake of serving him four—he ate three and remarked that he had never like prunes.) James was staying on until mid-July to celebrate his traditional birthday dinner Chez Garin. From Marathon, Father wrote that Mother and he had had a wonderful trip and thanked us for taking such good care of them.

Byron and family planned to drive to Solliès to spend the last half of July. To Byron, Father wrote, "When we were at Richard's place he informed us that his roadway was impassable when it was wet and rainy. It was not rainy when we were there but, in my judgment, the road seemed almost impassable. I would be afraid to risk the lives of wife and children on that roadway—and the matter of welfare of wife and children would appear to me to be very uncertain with the present facilities to say nothing of the sudden and precipitous drop-offs here and there."

A letter from Simca awaited James's and my return to Solliès with the message that Julia was still there, we must come. Judy arrived and was "dying to meet Julia." We joined Simca near Plascassier in an auberge which had been allocated for a day's photography to illustrate an American magazine article dedicated to Simca, "co-author of *Mastering the Art*...." It was a confusing day; photographers, assistants, food stylists, restaurant proprietors and staff milled around with platters of food sprayed with glistening fixative while the author, a good-natured, stylish young man named Patrick O'Higgins officiated. Simca was distraught because Julia hadn't turned up. Patrick said he wanted photos of Simca and Julia together but that Julia had taken a dislike to him, he didn't know why. Simca's gardener and her housekeeper, Jeanne, were throwing down red wine and roaring with laughter at the bizarre scene. At day's end, Patrick returned with us to Simca's where we found a note from Julia, pointedly inviting only James, Judy and me to La Pitchoune for a drink. She gave us a tour of the house: in the kitchen, beneath each hook, was a pen-drawn outline of the utensil that belonged there; in the bedroom two framed *Time Magazine* cover formats were hung, on one of which was imposed a photo of Julia, on the other of Paul. We sat down for our drink, Paul was silent, Julia announced that Patrick was detestable, we enjoyed a few minutes of desultory conversation, she asked if she and Paul could come to Solliès for lunch, I said we'd be in touch and we escaped to dinner with Simca, Jean and Patrick where, after a plate of Jeanne's potato and leek soup, she served a plump, sparkling cold chicken which Simca innocently asked me to carve. The bird, a remnant of the photographic shoot, was stuffed with rumpled newspaper, fixed to the platter with globs of gum and coated with a film of rubbery gloss. From the kitchen door, Jeanne watched, fascinated, as I removed the skin and manipulated the platter while carving to keep the newspaper stuffing out of sight; I signaled to Jeanne, who hastily withdrew the infamous carcass.

(Me to Byron) "In honour of James's birthday (12 July) Garin did up some salmon and lobster mousselines flanked by poached sole fillets, sauce Nantua, braised whole veal liver garnished with sorrel and veal kidney pastries, Montrachet, Gevrey-Chambertin and Chambertin, all 1945, Yquem 1953, and so forth." Byron, Marilynn and children spent the last half of July on the hillside with none of the tragic mishaps which Father had forecast. Marilynn especially admired everything dipped in batter and deep-fried. The Childs came to lunch. The Garins settled in for the month of August. I received an advance copy of *The French Menu Cookbook*, which I offered to Garin, to whom it was dedicated. (Me to James) "As for the dedication, Garin pretended to be very surprised and kept saying, 'Mais, je ne savais pas!' Mary kept interrupting, saying, 'Mais, je te l'ai dit chéri.' He said, 'Shut up!' so she repeated, 'But I told you tu ne m'écoute jamais chéri,' so he said, 'That's right I never listen to you, shut up,' then assured me he had no idea. Mary said once more, 'Mais je te l'ai dit chéri,' was sent to bed and we had a sentimental hour of drinks, thank yous, tearful embraces and promises that he had no idea the book was dedicated to him." Mary pronounced the French "r" like a "w"; chéri sounded like "chez-oui."

Garin planned an experimental opening of the new restaurant. The former Escapade was in the "quartier des Lingoustes." "Lingousto" is Provençal for langouste (rock lobster), a word composed of "tongue" and "taste." Garin said it meant the tongue that tastes. He named the restaurant Le Lingousto.

October. I received a wire from Simon & Schuster. Urgent. Craig Claiborne to be in Paris to interview me for the *New York Times*. I didn't understand why he couldn't come south, but I traveled obediently to Paris to meet C.C. He was with a friend, we spent the day together, lunching at Michel Guérard's Pot-au-Feu in Asnières and drinking away the afternoon. It may not have been a meeting of souls but I thought we got along in a civilized way. The *Times* article was stiff. Like an anonymous member of a company board, I was designated throughout as "the gentleman." Silly but harmless, I thought. (It may not have been his intention to be harmless for, when I next saw Claiborne, sixteen years and thirty books later at an assembly of food people in New York, he feigned not to recognize me and refused to shake my hand.)

Eda wrote that her old college friend, M.F.K. Fisher, was renting a house in La Roquette and wanted to meet me. She wondered if she, Sybille and M.F. could come to dinner—M.F. would have a driver. (Raymond Gatti, a Cannes taxidriver, who lived in Plascassier, often hired out his Mercedes and chauffeur services and was familiar with the road to my house.) I published the menu in *CVF*:

Apéritif: Morey-Saint-Denis "Monts Luisants" blanc 1966

§

Artichauts Poivrade

§

Roulade de Filets de Sole à la Mousseline d'Oursins en Gelée

Château Filhot 1962

§

Daube à la Provençale, Macaronade

Château Carbonnieux 1966

§

Salade de Roquette

§

Fromages

Vieux Château Certan 1964

§

Sorbet de Framboises

§§§

Twenty years later, I read a letter, difficult to understand, written by M.F.K. Fisher to James Beard (published in Evan Jones's *Epicurean Delight*):

"The more I think of doing one of the climbs without a flashlight in pitch dark, the more I wonder how. The road was impassable, except to herds of sheep and Sybille Bedford and me. Richard and Eda Lord pranced up and down through the abandoned quarry, but once was enough for me.... I am not good at heights and depths, and more, especially without lights, air, guard rails, even steps....

"Of course, dinner was superb. Endless. The wines were very good indeed, and also endless. The talk, which with Sybille racing a hundred words a minute, was mostly about those two subjects, wine and food, it was endless...."

No one climbed the hillside, they were driven up in broad daylight. There were no herds of sheep and, except when comfortably settled in a chauffeured car, M.F. glimpsed no heights or depths. Nor did Eda and I "prance up and down in the abandoned quarry"—we passed the evening at table in front of the fireplace. When Raymond returned at midnight, everyone was amply lighted, on level ground, from the house to the car. M.F.'s letter continues, "We reached the bottom of the cliff at a very early hour, barely predawn, and Sybille stopped at every fountain in the village to judge the waters." A very unlikely story.

26 November 1970. (Me to James) "The Garins were here, decided Solliès was too hectic and left to spend a few days relaxing in a pension near Saint-Paul-de-Vence, which was not hectic enough so they insisted that I join them. Jimmy Baldwin was there, planning to spend a month "working in peace." And his editor was there. Everyone came back here and I am just recovering from a two-day crise de foie.... Promised Eda to spend a couple of days in La Roquette after a trip to Paris—M.F. wants to produce a dinner for me with her, Eda and Sybille each preparing a course.... My editor writes that she has learned from John Schaffner that Julia Child has promised James Beard to entice me to Bramafam for New Year's—I will be in Vicenza."

18 December 1970. (Me to James) "Just returned from my week's outing—Paris and La Roquette. The *CVF* meal at Lucas-Carton was sublime, wine-wise (Petit Village '64, Mouton '59, Margaux '53, Yquem '62—preceded, of course, by Champagne-Grand Siècle) and, food-wise, too complicated—crème de faisan, whole roast partridges, lièvre à la royale, sorbet au cumin, pâté de bécasse, salade Rachel, fromages, pêches flambées.... Spent three days with Eda and Sybille, Eda having arranged ahead of time meetings with the Childs and James Beard, who was already in residence. He is a huge, gentle and benign creature—touching, sad and very ill—poor circulation, bad heart—being treated in a nearby clinic with salt-free, alcohol-free, starch-free, food-free diet, after a year of which the doctor plans to give him a series of shock treatments to disgust him with food and wine for life. He plans to see other doctors and, after he escapes from this nuthouse, to eat and drink a little, all the same. Julia's message to me was how 'lucky' I was to have received a good review in the *New York Times* (I hadn't seen it.) from Nika Hazelton 'who is a nasty, vicious old cow.' (It was four years later that I met Nika—I found her to be honest, solid and generous, a fiercely loyal friend.) As for M.F.K. Fisher, she remains sweet but is essentially empty-headed, has no palate (eats practically nothing and drinks tumblers-full of sweet vermouth all day) and her writing is silly, pretentious drivel. I had never read her until these last days when Eda piled the books in my arms before going to bed each night. She had already asked me several times what I thought of M.F.—who is, after all, her old school chum and friend of fifty years. I kept saying, 'very nice, ever so sweet, I like her very much....' Eda insisted on knowing what I thought of the books. I mumbled a few embarassed inanities before blurting out that they were trash. She breathed a sigh of relief (as if to say, 'It's about time!'). 'I'm glad you feel that way,' she said, 'Of course, I agree.'

"For the collaboration dinner in La Roquette, M.F. prepared cold shrimp tails in paper cases set in their congealed cooking butter, Eda produced an admirable navarin and Sybille, a macédoine of fresh fruits sprinkled with kirsch. Sybille spent the days immersed in her biography of Aldous Huxley, only coming up for air in the evening at the apéritif hour. Eda and I passed an afternoon with M.F., who launched into an interminable and pointless tale about an 'institution' near her California home where 'deviates' were kept under guard, whether in the interest of straightening out the road or of keeping them out of circulation was unclear. She said she felt sorry for the poor things and regularly visited the place to offer them boxes of candy and bouquets of flowers. Eda appeared to be dreaming but, whenever there was a pause in the monologue that required recognition or response, she would murmur, 'Really,' or 'Not really?' Later, I asked her if she had understood. She said, 'Of course not, darling, I wasn't listening.' I repeated some of the more fanciful details. 'Oh dear,' said Eda, 'We won't tell Sybille will we? She doesn't like that word.'"

M.F. asked to see me privately. "Sybille," she confided, "is very bad for Eda. We must work together to separate them." I told her I was not into breaking up friends' love relationships. She was not pleased.

(Me to James, same letter as above). "I had a couple of evening sessions with Sybille—critical, negative, destructive judgments about everything and everyone—the terrible thing is that we agreed about everything.... Returned here to find a letter from my agent (John Schaffner): 'I have the exciting news that M.F.K. Fisher is writing about you! Now there is a stylist for you! I have adored her writing for many years—utterly enchanting.' (The 'exciting news' had been distributed before M. F. and I met.)... Am flying Nice-Venice the 21st—called Byron to warn him."

Alitalia, the rudest and most incompetent of national airlines, typically and without warning, deposited me in Genoa to fend for myself. I rang Vicenza, Marilynn told me that Byron was on his way to Venice to meet me. I took a train and arrived the next day. It was good to be with family. White truffles were still in season and it was a dream to walk into a local shop and find a pile of bumpy, greyish-white, stone-like objects which, when cut into, presented a pearly flesh veined with feathers of faded lilac; the perfume was explosive. Byron and Marilynn may have been the only residents of the American army base to use native produce. Byron noted in a letter to James that "We (the army) were so threatened by using local foodstuffs that we began daily airlifts of lettuce from the good old U.S.A." James wrote that he had arranged with Paul Urbani to ship fresh black truffles to Margaret, Elizabeth, Frances, John and himself for Christmas. In February 1971, Marilynn gave birth to a boy named Christopher.

Princeton University Press was enthusiastic about James's manuscript, *Metaphors of Self*, to be published in 1972. Eda and Sacha spent a few days with me. Eda's (and Sybille's) editor, Bob Gottlieb, had visited La Roquette, confiscated the long-overdue manuscript of *Extenuating Circumstances*, told her it was finished and would be published in the autumn.

The Garins had rented a house in the village which they didn't like so they continued to stay with me when in Solliès. My friends, the Comtes, moved and Garin rented the spacious house and property that they had vacated. The place could have been idyllic—a stream separated the road from the property and one crossed a bridge to gates which opened onto the garden. (They moved trunks and crates of books into the empty rooms, lived there for eight years and never unpacked.) For the first time in years, I thought, I could relax and work chez moi.

Jim Beard was frequently a guest at Simca's. Raymond Gatti was his chauffeur and he always came to Solliès, sometimes for a meal, often to spend two or three days, and insisted that I return with him, which permitted me, at the same time, to gather in visits with Eda and Sybille. That summer, a Peruvian Adonis, Felipe Rojas-Lombardi, laureate of Jim's New York cooking classes, visited Plascassier with his friend, Tim Johnson, smart and hip, a retired child movie star, who was grooming Felipe to become a food star.

Lucia loved the terraced hillside, the scents and the remoteness of my place and planned to relax with me for three weeks in July. Giovanna, whom we both loved, arrived with a new lover, then others arrived, unannounced. Giovanna's friend, who was all thumbs, wanted to be helpful. I had dug a deep trench the length of a lower terrace in which the plumber had laid waterpipes, but the earth laid up to the side remained to be shoveled back over—I told him he could start shoveling if he wanted to. Ten minutes later, he came up to ask if I had a bandaid.... 'No,' he said, he hadn't cut himself, it was nothing really—there was a little leak in the water pipe. I went down to check. Why he had been using a pickax in the bottom of the trench remained a mystery but he had managed to split the pipe and a geyser was flooding the terrace. From the post office I telephoned the water company. They cut off the water supply but the plumber couldn't come immediately. Our water had to be carried up in pails from a village fountain. Lucia had locked herself in her room and refused to see anyone except Giovanna and me. On the pretext that we had no water, I put everyone out, except Lucia, who was then able to relax for a week before I accompanied her to the Nice airport, with a pause in Antibes for the Picasso museum and lunch.

James had the month of August free; Byron had only a week. I met James in Paris, we flew to Milan where Byron collected

With Elizabeth, Vizenza, 1971.

us, we spent a few days in Vicenza and drove to Solliès. Late August, Odette asked James and me to lunch at l'Auberge de l'Ill in Alsace. A couple of days earlier, a history professor and his wife, friends of Frances and Dwight, came to lunch in Solliès. (We began with a roulade of sole fillets embracing a truffled and pistachioed angler-fish and sea urchin mousseline—I asked the professor why he was so carefully prying the sole fillets loose from the farce and pushing them aside; he said he didn't like fat.) They wanted to invite us to dinner at "the most expensive restaurant in Paris" the same day as our lunch in Illhaeusern. I suggested Maxim's. Much of the day was spent on highways and in the air. One always had a good time with Odette—she thought it would be nice to drink a Latour 1945 with the cheeses; it was more than nice. In Paris, we took a taxi directly from the airport to Maxim's. Our host was waiting for us with a bottle of Champagne. His wife, he said, was "feeling under the weather." We ordered a Chevalier-Montrachet, Château Latour 1928 and Château Filhot 1924. After a swallow of Latour, the professor turned green and fled to the gents. An hour later, when he returned, no Latour remained. He thought he shouldn't taste the burnished gold Filhot; it was not wasted.

At the Médoc lunch, during our annual *CVF* Bordeaux tour, I shared a table with Philippe Cottin, director of La Bergerie, Baron Philippe de Rothschild's wine firm. Our conversation turned around the dinners given at Château Mouton-Rothschild by Baron Philippe for his celebrity friends, the great and ancient wines lovingly served and thoughtlessly guzzled. He wanted to organize a lunch at Mouton-Rothschild for a few Americans who understood wine and asked me to choose the other guests from the present group. John Rolfson, Jack Shaw and Jon Winroth were chosen; a date was to be set in June 1972.

15 November 1971. (Me to James) "Received wire from Byron: 'Paris plans. Please phone.' Met him and Marilynn late the 9th, 10th Jeu de Paume, 11th a holiday, Louvre closed, they left the 12th—dinner Chez Garin should have been better.... Received Eda's new book, *Extenuating Circumstances*, simple, lovely, pure.... John Rolfson turned up unannounced with ABC television crew—they filmed and recorded for two days.... Sent outline for a new

Sybille Bedford, 1970s. Photo from the jacket cover of "Jigsaw," Knopf. Photo by Jerry Bauer.

book to be called *Simple French Food* to Schaffner...have accepted to teach a three-week, 'French Culinary Arts' course in Avignon July 23 to August 13.... Received letter from James Beard asking if he could come to Solliès some time after 10 December and could I spend some time in Plascassier.... Garins will be here for the holidays but I plan to spend them in Vicenza."

24 November 1971. (Me to James) "Had a letter from Eda—very depressed at the lack of reaction to her book. Later on the telephone she was feeling better because an English publisher had decided to buy it. Sybille, she writes, is unliveable with because of her intense involvement in the Huxley book, 'bursting from her workroom to prowl and growl like a bear with a sore head.' Eda is coming here for a couple of days.... Hiély père was killed a week ago in an auto accident." 17 December. (Me to James) "Jim Beard was to lunch yesterday. He had written that his diet precluded olive oil but that mostly it was a question of watching calories closely and that he was allowed a small quantity of wine. So I eliminated salad and dessert because of olive oil and calories. We had your favorite cold roulade of sole fillets and sea urchin mousseline, vegetable stew, pheasant roast in front of the fireplace, potato paillasson and cheese. A half bottle of Filhot '67 as apéritif, white Morey-St.-Denis '64 with the fish, Vieux Château Certan '67 and Ducru-Beaucaillou '61. When I saw the quantity of food and wine that Jim was consuming, I apologized for not having prepared a dessert and offered to fetch a bottle of Sauternes—which he found to be a splendid idea—so we drank a bottle of Suduiraut '61.... Leaving tomorrow for La Roquette and Plascassier, will continue to Vicenza."

In mid-January, Byron and I repeated the Piero della Francesca tour of eleven years earlier. Paul Urbani, New Jersey truffle purveyor, had arranged with his aunt and uncle and two cousins in Scheggino (near Spoleto) to receive us. In the canning factory several large vats were filled with black truffles boiling in blackened water; distant memories of tins of tasteless truffles were revived. At lunch every dish contained a mishmash of black truffles (the season for white truffles was past), treated with no respect. We asked if we could buy a kilo of fresh truffles—later, when we examined our purchase, we thought the cousin must have taken the truffles from a bin of rejects.

In Florence, we had our old room in the Bartolini. I knew from friends that Harold Acton's mother had died and that he had recently been very ill. I rang him to ask if he would join us for dinner at Sabatini; he seemed overjoyed. He arrived in sparkling fine form, with a carefree lilt that I had not seen since the days I had known him in New York. I imagined that his duties as caretaker of his father's art collection and host at La Pietra, however impeccably performed, must weigh heavily and that to be guest instead of host was a rarity and a relief. We drank a local white wine and I ordered a Ducru-Beaucaillou 1962. Harold upbraided me for ordering a French wine in Italy (it isn't done) and for my choice of restaurant (not typically Florentine). He nonetheless enjoyed the wine and we were comfortable in Sabatini's spacious old-fashioned dining room, where "Signor Acton" was received and treated like royalty; he didn't mind that. The next day Byron and I had a good, typically Florentine meal in the glaringly lit, crowded and noisy atmosphere of Cammillo.

In Solliès, I found a letter from John Schaffner: Pat Knopf (Atheneum) would take *Simple French Food* but wanted more information about length and number of recipes before drawing up a contract. (I have read that Jim Beard took credit for placing the book with Pat Knopf—as far as I know, he knew nothing of the project until after the contract was signed.) Also a letter from the Garins—they were arriving two days later, would I please heat the house for them and have lunch ready at my place? They were theoretically "on the wagon" except, of course, for red wine. I wrote Byron, "The Garins did their best to leave all my time to work, which meant arriving at 10:30 for white wine and a slice of sausage, returning at 12:30 for apéritif and lunch, leaving around 4 and returning for apéritif and dinner. An added complication: since drinking is being cut down on, there is neither whisky nor white wine at the restaurant so Garin had to sneak up here to snatch a whisky from time to time.... Had friends of Loren MacIver to lunch, used them as guinea pigs for a couple of 'simple food' recipes—chicken split down the back, flattened, skin loosened,

Eda Lord. Photo from the book jacket of "Childsplay," Knopf, 1971. Photo by Jerry Bauer.

stuffed between skin and flesh with a buttered mushroom purée mixture, rubbed with herbs and olive oil and grilled over hot coals. Do forgive my lack of modesty—it was a masterpiece (of simplicity). And the dessert (rather eccentric but delicious with a Sauternes)—dried figs stewed with fresh thyme, red wine and honey. They left in a vapour of ecstasy."

Garin had for the past year been informing his Parisian clientèle that he would soon close Chez Garin and open a restaurant in the south of France. Now, he summoned all the leading gastronomic journalists to lunch to announce that he would not close. Articles appeared in newspapers and reviews. He continued to announce the imminent opening of Le Lingousto in Solliès; many locals read Parisian newspapers, which led to a certain confusion. In Paris, he fired most of the dining room staff and hired a new maître d'hôtel, Alain Delaveyne. With Gérard Besson in charge of the kitchen and Alain and Marie-Madeleine overlooking the dining room, he and Mary were more and more frequently absent; they took off to spend a couple of weeks in Minneapolis.

Jimmy and Tania Stern were old friends of Eda, who had known Tania forty years earlier in Berlin. They lived in Wiltshire and vacationed Bandol. Jimmy wanted to see a British edition of *The French Menu Cookbook* and had asked for the name of Schaffner's contact agent in London. 13 March 1972. (Me to James) "Finally, after a year's time and after having asked for it repeatedly, Schaffner sent me the name of the London agent, which I promptly sent on to Jimmy Stern. The agent had never heard of me or my book— 'Oh yes,' he knew Schaffner, 'charming person, quite a good cook but, as an agent, a bit of a, shall we say, dilettante.'" (Collins later published the book.)

Jim Beard lived with a former lover and failed architect, Gino Cofacci, from whom he tried whenever possible to distance himself. To get him out of New York in autumn 1971, he enrolled Gino at the Cordon Bleu cooking school in Paris. In March 1972, he proposed that Gino be my assistant in the Avignon classes; to prepare him for this, Gino would stay with me in Solliès from April 5th until May 9th to receive private cooking lessons! Remuneration was not mentioned nor was my agreement solicited. I didn't want an assistant in Avignon and I certainly did not want to be locked up with anyone to dispense private cooking lessons. But Gino was not just anyone.... My perception that Jim's selfishness and his willingness to use friends dishonestly knew no bounds and prompted no remorse took a leap.

Gino was a blockhead. He possessed no semblance of that which, in human terms, one associates with a mind. Like a parrot, he could imitate sounds, even memorize long phrases, but he didn't know what the words meant. He was stubborn, petulant and perpetually discontent, outraged at having to share a bathroom and hated having to take a bus to market—he regarded my refusal to buy a car and learn to drive as a personal affront. If I had tried to explain that he was a non-paying guest, he wouldn't have understood—he had never paid his way. He had five toes on each hand and never learned to use a knife, but that was of no importance because he was not interested in learning to cook; he only wanted "recipes"—and he wanted them typed out "like at the Cordon Bleu." To me, alone, it seemed like a luxury to live without a telephone but, cut off from the outside world with Gino on the inside was an inferno—and he wanted no one to shatter our solitude. Three weeks into my calvary, I had spent the afternoon demonstrating how to bone a chicken by turning it inside-out, prepared a truffled mousseline with other chicken breasts and stock with the carcasses. The bird was stuffed, trussed and put to poach when a knock came at the door. Gino said, loudly and urgently, "Don't let 'em in—don't let 'em in!" I opened the door to find Aubert and Pamela de Villaine and two friends, apologizing profusely that they could not warn me by telephone of their arrival. I was so overcome with relief, they may have thought me demented. I begged them to stay for dinner and hastened to the cellar to fetch some bottles. Gino sat sullen and silent until I brought out the cheese platter, when he ordered, with sudden authority, "Put that back—you can't serve that!" (The cheeses had been cut into.) With the cheeses, I served a magnum of Domaine Tempier 1966. (Aubert and Pamela have often reminded me of the haute cuisine meal on the lonely hillside with the wonderful Tempier.) One of my most glorious memories is putting Gino on the bus and waving good-bye after five tortuous weeks. He returned to New York to await the beginning of the Avignon class and Jim left for Plascassier.

May was a mess. I was trying to write a cookbook and to organize cooking classes, had to travel several times to Avignon, Jim Beard was in Plascassier until July and wanted to visit, Simca and Jean wanted to come to lunch, the Childs wanted to come to lunch—I had the lot of them together. 2 June 1972. (Me to James) "Garins are still here—he has been on the rampage for three solid weeks, bellowing, screaming, insulting everyone in sight. When he gets bored with cringing and submission, he starts picking at me and when he touches a raw spot, he works hard until I finally explode. Then he is happy—but only for a moment. Had to go to Nice the other day, lunched with Childs and Beard "Aux Oliviers." Quite bad. Spent the night with them—Eda and Sybille came to dinner—I took off at dawn for Avignon to examine new quarters for summer class—a good experience: in the heart of town, large, professional kitchen laden with copper, installed in very pretty 18th century townhouse with attractive garden and pleasant dining room. It is a school (closed in summer) for professional formation operated by the Avignon Chamber of Commerce—the chef wants to attend the classes…(days later) Jon Winroth, the Peyrauds and Garins were to lunch Monday, later, intensive winetasting at Domaine Tempier. The Peyrauds drove me back Tuesday, Eda arrived that evening, picked up Jimmy and Tania Stern Wednesday and brought them to lunch. (She wanted them to admire the rustic swimming pool. Jimmy was terrified of heights, crawled to the upper terrace on his hands and knees, then crawled down backward; he visited the wine cellar, crawled in backward and crawled out head first.) We drove back to Bandol together, dined in Sterns' hotel, Garin left Wednesday, Eda Thursday, Mary Friday—I leave for Mouton lunch Monday."

9 June 1972. (Me to Byron) "Just returned from Bordeaux. Mouton lunch divine, morning tastings of '70s and '71s in the cellars of Mouton-Baron-Philippe and Mouton-Rothschild, very pretty Henriot Champagne '66 as apéritif. Simple menu: truffle omelette, roast duckling, asparagus tips and green beans, cheeses, strawberry ice cream (which I didn't taste for fear of interfering with the wine): Mouton-Baron-Philippe 1961, Pichon-Longueville 1929, Latour 1926, Margaux 1924, La Lagune 1900, Mouton 1899, Mouton 1895, Mouton 1878, Yquem 1921…1848 Grande Champagne with coffee." Same day (Me to James). "…so many stars but perhaps La Lagune will linger longest in memory…

With Julia Child at Solliès, 1972. Photo taken by Paul Child.

Mouton 1878 was perfection, stubborn old Latour 1926, although uncorked four hours ahead and decanted two hours earlier, only began to expand with the last drops, Margaux delicate and complicated...so many memories...Mouton 1899 not ready to drink, 1895 slightly on the decline...Yquem 1921 must be the greatest living white wine. We were six at table.... Hansons arrive last week of June, then Beard."

Sacha was planning a trip to the Alpes-Maritimes to tend Lili's grave and visit Eda. He wanted to meet James Beard. I answered that perhaps he didn't want to but he insisted. We met at a café in Cannes. It was hate at first sight. Jim held forth with banal pronouncements and clichés. He had arrived at the oracular period in his career when he expected listeners to bow in silence to his superior wisdom. I bowed in silence to nonsense as long as it

With Simca at Solliès, 1972. Photo taken by Paul Child.

did not touch me, personally. Sacha was not of the same bent; he was meticulous in his speech and in his judgments—he thought Jim was a pompous buffoon. Jim labeled Sacha a pernickety old queen.

The Garins were back in Solliès. Buck (Bernard) Hanson, my friend from Iowa City and Greenwich Village days, and his wife, Anne, arrived with a young art historian, John Clarke, whom Anne introduced as her star pupil at Yale. Garin asked us to the Lingousto for dinner. Buck and John dressed for dinner—in discreet drag. Buck wore a long gown (from a bargain basement on 14th Street, he said) with sandals and a very wide leather belt slung low over his hips. With his full white (once red) beard and long, flowing white locks (once short and brown), he resembled a William Blake vision of Jehova. My, my, I thought.

The Childs and Jim came to lunch. Jim stayed. Garin asked us to lunch. Jim wanted to see me split chickens and stuff them beneath the skin (reported to him by Gino), so it was I who cooked at the Lingousto. To prepare the stuffings, I used Garin's "robot-coupe," a large, professional version of the food processor, which Carl Sontheimer subsequently imported and commercialized under the "Cuisinarts" trademark. Jim was mesmerized by the machine.

James had received a grant, which freed him from teaching to work on another book. He planned to settle in London for a year and a half. Byron was to be released from military service in August. James and Judy, Byron, Marilynn and family planned to pass the month of August in Solliès. The Avignon classes would keep me busy until August 12th.

I knew nothing about cooking schools, as a matter of principle did not believe in them and, at first, rejected the Luberon College proposal. When, finally, I accepted, it was not for gain (they were offering $500 to teach for three weeks) but because a sudden conceit tempted me to imagine that perhaps I could teach something deeper than boring recipes. Lubéron College was a droll, fly-by-night outfit, the brainchild of Herbert Maza, who was also president of the American University in Aix-en-Provence. Norma Benney was registrar and director. Small ads, inserted in the back of *The New Yorker*, were designed to attract college students who wanted a cheap summer vacation—the tuition was not high and included inexpensive housing with French families. The class was supposed to be limited to thirty. To lend the project an air of seriousness, applicants were required to submit a photo and to fill out a form with birth date, educational history and culinary experience. By the first of April, thirty-two applicants had been accepted—I told Norma to stop. No college students had applied; the average age was forty-five. The mix included professional cooks and cooking school owners, food journalists, school teachers, retired industrialists and two ladies, Janina Bowey and Sue Florsheim, from the *Chicago Tribune's* society pages. Few of the students were interested in cheap housing. Janina and Sue settled into the Auberge de Noves, the plushest hostelry of the region, and hired a chauffeured limousine to drive them to and from classes. Others stayed at l'Hôtel de l'Europe, whose courtyard terrace attracted class members each evening at the cocktail hour. Norma showed me a late application with a sinister photo that looked like a police mugshot. The applicant, Joe Ansel, had years of restaurant experience and operated a catering service in New York City. "Let him in," I said. Madeleine Kamman was enrolled and a sudden inspiration told me that Joe might balance the scales. I think his initial motive in applying was to have a little fun being disruptive, for he viewed cooking schools with contempt; when he discovered that I had something to teach, we became friends and Joe was my champion.

The proposed formula was simplistic: three 8:30-12:30 participation classes a week, in each of which we were to prepare a specialty from a Michelin-starred restaurant, where lunch would be organized the following day. I had filled in the restaurant day programs with vineyard visits and receptions by the Châteauneuf-du-Pape and Tavel wine confréries and the CIVCR (Comité Interprofessionnel des Vins des Côtes du Rhône), whose seat was in Avignon. For use in the classes and to place on the restaurant menus, vigneron friends had offered wines and the CIVCR had provided cases of the principal Côtes du Rhône appellations—Châteauneuf-du-Pape, Tavel, Lirac, Gigondas, Hermitage, Côte-Rôtie.... At 12:30 on class days, we tasted and discussed wines before dishing up lunch. Most of the students were reveling in new experience, Gino spent much of his time gossiping and giggling with a few of the less serious girls and didn't get in my way, but I didn't feel right about the class; we were wasting time.

Joe had made friends with other professionals in the class. After a couple of sessions, he asked me to have a drink with them. The message was loud and clear: they'd had enough of the piddling participation nonsense; they were there to learn as much as I could teach and they wanted straight demonstration. I was pleased and determined to waste no more time—from then on, I bought everything that caught my eye in the early morning wholesale market and began to demonstrate, with no preconceived idea, inventing, recalling and shuffling around classical procedures, often surprising myself. I boned, stuffed, trussed, barded, larded, poached, roasted, braised and glazed, sautéed, sweated, fried and baked, whisked, pounded, moulded and unmoulded and the dishes accumulated. (Many of the preparations from those classes appeared two years later in *Simple French Food*, reappeared in the Time-Life *Good Cook* collection, were purloined by the Scotto sisters for publication in *Marie-Claire* and *Cuisine et Vins de France* and, more than ten years later, were discovered in *Richard Nelson's American Cooking*.) Naturally, I presented the split chicken stuffed beneath the skin, this time with a spinach-ricotta stuffing. (One of my students later published it with illustrations and no attribution in the *New York Times*—other students wrote indignant letters to the editor.)

Garin was cross that I had already scheduled our last restaurant meal to be held at Raymond Thuilier's Oustaù de Baumanière in Les Baux-de-Provence, but decided, nonetheless, to open the Lingousto for one day to receive us. He wanted to serve pieds et paquets as a main course and I agreed enthusiastically. A sous-chef and a young waiter, Dominique, from Chez Garin in Paris came down to help out (Dominique stayed on in Solliès). I received the group on the hillside for Champagne before moving on to the restaurant; Janina bought two paintings. How I could have forgotten—or not known—about Americans and innards, I'll never understand; the meal was beautiful but most of the pieds et paquets were returned to the kitchen untouched.

The classes had worn me out but I was pleased with the experience; I had been able to teach cooking as I understood it. A half dozen professionals in the class were enthusiastic, Janina and Sue were enraptured but, on the whole, the class was not a success. The promotional brochure had promised that printed recipes would be passed out at the beginning of each class session; many students were bitter that none had been produced and some claimed that, even after I had described a preparation verbally, I proceeded to demonstrate something completely different. Despite the negative reactions, Herbert Maza was determined to repeat the experience in 1973. I said no. He and Norma stormed me for two months until I said, all right, but: I wanted the classes to be held earlier in the season; no more beginners; the class must be limited to twenty experienced cooks and cut from three to two weeks with four working sessions each week instead of three; there would be no question of passing out printed recipes; tuition would have to be doubled to permit me to meet expenses and I would receive $5,000 (instead of $500). They hedged but agreed.

11 September 1972. (Me to James) "The shit continues—Mary went to Paris a week ago, G. got drunk and tearful, said we had to be 'like before'—brothers with no troubles between us and that the reason things have been so difficult in the last couple of years is that Mary keeps telling him that she bought my cookstove for me and doesn't understand how I can be so dishonest as to have written in my book that I paid for it with my first advance!! Also he confided that whenever she 'had a drink,' she accuses him of loving me more than her—how dumb can you be—so she returned last Wednesday; he obviously repeated our conversations, told her I was angry about her pretending to have bought the stove—and I saw nothing of them until last night when he came up and insisted that I come down for dinner—so I said to Mary, 'What is this shit?' she started quavering and finally whimpered, 'Well, I thought maybe I loaned you the money'—we ate in grim silence while Garin picked mercilessly on Dominique—joyful time."

James planned to join me in late September for the *CVF* Bordeaux tour. Janina was in Paris and wrote that Don (her husband) had told her she could join us in Bordeaux "if it was very important." She showered me with smart couturier bow ties. From Bordeaux, I returned to London with James. Eda's book had just been published in England; she and Sybille were in London. They were long-time friends of Elizabeth David. James had met Elizabeth and was enchanted. She had received *The French Menu Cookbook* (I suspected Eda, but never knew if she, Sybille or Jim Beard had sent it.) and wrote, asking me to look her up if I was in London. I went around to see her. As she was pouring glasses of white wine, she said, "I suppose you disapprove of putting ice into wine—I always do." "And, do you enjoy ice cubes in your Montrachet?" I asked. She admitted she would not go that far. I was subjected to a hilarious inquisition: "Of course, your food is much too grand for the likes of me.... I see that you like savory with broad beans—I detest savory with broad beans...and you like basil—I have no use for it...." I pronounced basil in the American manner with a broad "a"—she was beside herself: "You don't r-e-a-l-l-y pronounce it that way, do you?" Our interview continued in much the same way. I tried desperately to maintain a serious contenance but, finally, was helpless with laughter; by the time she had stopped roughing me up, we were great friends.

Simply being in Elizabeth's presence was magical. She was witty and literate. Her observations about people were often scathing, but only because they were so devastatingly accurate—they were funny, never cruel. She was generous and kind. In a letter to Byron, James wrote, "Elizabeth David is a very good person and she likes (though not necessarily in this order) to eat, to drink and to laugh."

When Jim Beard learned that I was working on a new book, he insisted that he must write a foreword and that, to do so, he should receive the manuscript, chapter by chapter, as I worked. Pat Knopf didn't want a foreword—nor did I, but I preferred not to offend Jim. I began to receive edited copy. My copy editor worked on the assumption that writers can't write and readers can't read. I wrote Pat that I didn't want my sentences chopped up—he gave the manuscript to Harry Ford, Atheneum's poetry editor, who promised that nothing would be changed.

Frances gave birth to a girl named Dianne. Dwight thought they needed an English nanny, a rarity on the Iowa plains; that dream faded.

Margaret's oldest son, Matthew, traveling with a family, one of whose boys was a former classmate, planned to spend the first days of the New Year in Paris. The Garins were in Minneapolis again, but I had the keys to their Paris flat and settled in for the time that Matthew would be in Paris. The family's interests didn't encompass grand restaurants but one evening Matthew accompanied Sacha and me to the Vivarois. Claude joined us after the service, marveled at Matthew's good looks and pretended that we looked exactly alike; it was not true but the flattery had the desired effect. The Finkenstaedts, assiduous clients of starred restaurants, reported to Garin that we had eaten at the Vivarois while he and Mary were in Minnesota.

23 January 1973. (Me to James) "Garin turned up. (He had told Mary that she was not feeling well, that she needed rest and solitude, so he kindly came down here for a few days to permit her to recover.) He was angry: 'How dare you eat chez Claude and not even set foot Chez Garin?'—got that straightened out after a few drinks. Norma Benney arrived the next morning on the pretext of organizing the summer course, Garin came to lunch and asked us to the Lingousto for dinner. Norma passed out at table, combination of fatigue and booze, Garin was drunk, drove us up the hillside and announced that he didn't trust himself to drive back down—'Don't worry about Norma,' he said, 'I'll take care of her.' He left before breakfast. Norma said that Garin was 'really quite beautiful,' didn't I think—'of course it's not the Greek ideal—another kind of beauty.' 'Unh, less idealized,' I mumbled. Garin cornered me alone: 'She has such beautiful eyes, don't you think?' I said, 'unh.' 'Quite a beautiful body, such a gamine!—and so innocent—not the slightest idea about the techniques of love-making....' I said, 'Please don't try to use me as a go-between.' Garin: 'You know that I have all the respect in the world for Mary...but I can't help it—simply can't get it up with her anymore.' So there you are. The old satyr is on the prowl again. He now feels that it is more imperative than ever to move to the south of France as soon as possible and telephoned Mary this morning that he had decided the restaurant in Paris could be sold more cheaply than he had originally thought.... So far all the applicants for the summer course are 'professionals'—they all write cookbooks. Felipe, the beautiful and pampered Peruvian boy who has been assisting Jim Beard and sending Gino into rages of jealousy, is signed up, also Julie Dannenbaum, who runs a cooking school in Philadelphia."

9 February 1973. (Me to Byron) "...A note written by Pat Knopf to Schaffner was forwarded to me—he 'expects *SFF* to be the best book yet published in America on French cuisine.'"

16 February 1973. (Me to James) "The Garins have been here for the last week fucking up my work and offering neither pleasure nor détente in compensation—sullen with each other and sullen with me, but too jealous of my solitude to leave me alone. Mary arrived at lunchtime two days before Garin. The refrigerator

contained a slice of veal liver, some parboiled spinach and a truffle, so I sliced the truffle and warmed it in a few drops of cognac and butter, sliced the liver, sautéed it rare and made a pink liver-truffle-spinach flat omelette—heaven beyond description. She opened her mouth, kept it open and pushed the stuff down in dull and unresponsive silence. I asked if she wanted cheese, she shook her head so, in exasperation, I mumbled, 'It was really quite good don't you think?' She emitted a dead sort of whine that could neither be translated as yes or no and asked for coffee, said she didn't like to cook on the restaurant stove so would I come down and cook her dinner. I said I preferred cooking here so she came back for dinner—poached, sliced calf's brain in cold cream, mustard, lemon, fines-herbes sauce, grilled lamb chops, carrot, navet, onion, garlic, artichoke stew—same dead response. Next day I gave her a slice of cold ham and a piece of cheese for lunch. She said she didn't like driving up here at night, would I please cook at the restaurant that night and, since I had to pass through the village to get there, would I pick up some meat—picked up lamb's heart and liver, forgot to bring parsley from the garden and discovered there was no garlic at the restaurant anyway (although the place was full of meats and vegetables—she said I'm saving all that for Georges tomorrow) so I sliced and sautéed the heart and liver, deglazed with white wine and made a sauce with preserved garlic purée and glace de viande from the chambre froide—very good it was and we ate in the same grim silence. Upon arriving the next day, Garin's first question as usual was, 'What did you have for dinner last night.' Mary said, 'I don't know. What was it Richard?' I said, 'heart and liver,' and she said, 'Not as good as your's Chéwi.' I begged off eating with them that night since she had someone to cook for her; G mumbled out of the side of his mouth that Norma was coming for the weekend. The next morning Norma arrived with her idiot husband, Frank, who started throwing down stiff whiskeys, carrying on confusedly about dikes, the joy of pornographic movies and God knows what. Garin arrived, he immediately attacked saying what did they know about dikes, lesbians, sex in general. Mary sat tight mouthed, nostrils taut, G said, 'We will have dinner at the restaurant and lunch here tomorrow, Richard,' and they left. And Frank got wilder, finally screaming at me that I'd better take 'Normy' out and fuck her because she needed it so I told him he'd better straighten up fast or get out very fast—he decided to get out, saying that 'Normy' could hitchhike or get back to Aix however the fuck she liked. She explained that she had been entertaining a girl friend a few evenings earlier, Frank had made a scene so she and the lady took off and spent the night in a hotel room. We hiked down the hillside to our Lingousto rendezvous, ate dried-out veal roast and drank too much in gloomy silence, come midnight G said, 'Don't buy anything for lunch, I put some front quarters of rabbit to marinate yesterday—we'll bring up the hind quarters tomorrow.' They drove us up the hillside, staggered in, threw down some whiskeys in gloom and left. I decided I'd better have a drink to relax. Norma was KO but accepted a cognac, then came a thunderous banging at the door and Frank came in looking sheepish—been to Aix, had a hamburger and decided that 'Normy' might need transportation home. I put them into their conjugal bed and died. The next morning I gave no one drinks 'til noon, Garins arrived, he gave me the hind quarters and said Roast them, don't do any cuisine, I'm hungry! I said it would be faster to sauté them. While they were cooking, I went out to pick some parsley and, when I returned, he bellowed, 'What are you doing now? I told you I was hungry.' I said, 'Relax the quarters aren't cooked yet anyway.' There was nothing in the house so they were only sautéed with onions, white wine and herbs, I messed together some cream and mustard to finish the sauce and threw a pile of butter-stewed, parsleyed potatoes into the thing. M and G shoved down vast quantities in resentful silence and both looked 10 degrees meaner each time Norma or Frank exclaimed how wonderful and unique the dish was, I went out to pee and when I returned, G was standing in the middle of the room in a rage bellowing, 'Merde, j'en ai marre, nom de chien, I came here to relax, not to be emmerdé,' then he crashed across the room, grabbed Norma, whirled her around roughly and let her go while Mary kept quacking over and over again, 'Oui Chéwi.' They started out and Mary said, 'Chéwi, Frank wants to see Teektay,' so G invited them to stop for a drink and see Teektay—the cat, you know. And they crashed out. Norma insisted that I go down with her and Frank, I said, 'Certainly not, I don't like shit,' so we had a couple of drinks and they took off to see the cat and continue to Aix. I had a quiet piece of bread and cheese for lunch. 'The next day, G arrived mid-afternoon saying, 'We waited lunch for you.' I said, 'Why did you leave in a temper yesterday?' He: 'Must have had too much to drink—I'll have a whisky now—we'll be expecting you for dinner!' The dinner consisted of the rabbit removed from its 3-day marinade, covered with thick strips of salt pork and roasted to death, with a lingering putrid acid taste from the marinade. The sauce was served apart in a terrine: lungs, heart, liver and blood whirled to a purée in the robot-coupe, mixed with the red wine from the marinade and boiled for ten minutes. It looked and tasted like vomit. Throughout the entire meal, he kept making sucking sounds, chomping and smacking his lips, exclaiming, 'Ça c'est bon! Ça, alors, ça c'est la vraie cuisine!! Ça c'est vraiment bon!' Then there were intermittent moments of conversation that went like this: 'C'est ça la cuisine! Have some more Richard,' 'Haven't finished what I have.' 'Smack, smack have some more Mary,' 'Haven't finished what I have Chéwi,' 'What's the matter, don't you like it?' 'C'est twès bon Chéwi,' 'Have some more then,' 'Mais j'peu pas Chéwi,' 'I SAID HAVE SOME MORE, IT'S GOOD,' 'Oui Chéwi,' 'Ça c'est la vraie cuisine...c'est vraiment très très bon—have some more Richard.... 'What's the matter, don't you like it?' 'Too long in the marinade maybe....' 'NON!...I can tell you one thing, this is really good and it's going to pass like that—I know that I am not going to be sick this night and that is more than I can say for la cuisine des autres....' And so it went—speaking for myself, I was up half a dozen times that night and the time spent in bed was all in twisting and moaning. The following day, I told them that I absolutely had to get some work done and holed up here. All of which is to say that I am sick to death of crazy people...."

26 February 1973. (Me to James) "Maza is trying to get me to teach a second class this summer—said no. Also has arrangements to make package deal with PanAm to fly over students for next Christmas and Easter if I will teach—said no."

The *Michelin Guide's* inspectors operate anonymously and the annual "star" situation is theoretically never divulged before the publication of the guide. Garin claimed this was not true in his case. He said that, months in advance, "le Grand Patron" had informed him that Chez Garin was slated to receive its third star in 1973 and that he had later invited the Michelin boss to lunch to renounce his third star and announce the restaurant's closing. Chez Garin closed two months after the 1973 Michelin guide appeared. In Paris, Le Taillevent and Le Vivarois received third stars. (The still unopened Lingousto was granted one star—Garin was not happy about Claude's third star.) Garin's chef, Gérard Besson, and Alain Delaveyne moved first to Jamin (which, twenty years earlier, Mary and I had frequented at the ortolan season) before Gérard opened the restaurant that bears his name in rue Coq Héron. Alain is still his maître d'hôtel. Garin's other maître d'hôtel, Roland, moved to Alain Senderens's l'Archéstrate and is still with Senderens at Lucas-Carton. They all cherish sentimental memories of "Le Grand Garin."

The book on which James was working, *The Rhizome and the Flower*, an examination of "The Perennial Philosophy" and of the mystic, philosophical systems of C.G. Jung and W.B. Yeats, had brought him into contact with the poet, Kathleen Raine, who introduced him to Anne Yeats, daughter of W.B. Yeats and keeper of his library. James had visited Anne Yeats in Dublin and had arranged with Franz Jung, the psychiatrist's son, to study his father's library in Zurich.

22 March 1973. (Me to Byron, from London) "...three-week visit to London winding up.... Elizabeth David coming to dinner Friday, Kathleen Raine, Saturday, Judy flies to U.S. to visit family Sunday, James and I to Zurich, where he will examine Jung's library and return to Solliès with me.... Mid-April will see James Beard, who is taking *Le France* to Cannes to eat and drink for a week cross-ocean and will fly back almost immediately."

Simca and I met *Le France* in Cannes. The first passenger to debark was Salvador Dali, twirling his silly, wild mustaches, rolling his eyes and swinging his cane, led by an ocelot, straining at the leash. Jim arrived with José (pronounced Josie) Wilson, a young

English woman, former food editor of *House and Garden*, who had been collaborating with him since the late '60s. José and I became friends immediately. She had a brittle, sometimes acerbic wit and a raucous laugh that was infectious. (In the years to come, she regularly visited Solliès and we prepared many a grand meal together—the Peyrauds were often guests.) When she learned that Jim was receiving my manuscript, chapter by chapter, she was appalled and begged me to stop sending it to him—she insisted that he only wanted it to use in his summer classes before the book was published. I attributed that notion to irrational cynicism and shrugged it off.

I received a letter from Julia Child, which I sent on to James to discover if he agreed with her judgment of "our kind of writing": "...Nobody ever thinks, as I was just writing Elizabeth David, that our kind of writing is even worth serious consideration—but it seems to me ours is much the most difficult of all. Not only must it be original, literate and stylish, it must be fully researched and accurate. Eh bien."

30 April 1973. (Me to James) "Garin is opening the Lingousto in May—Gault et Millau have ordered a meal in the course of which they plan to award him a 'gold key.'"

Enclosed in this letter, one from Sybille, dated "Good Friday 1973": "...Last summer the editors (of the *Sunday Times Colour Magazine*) talked to me—just in general conversation—about one day doing a series written by the best amateur-author cooks; and raved about Julia and M.F.K. I said, 'Yes, yes,' but there were better hands in the kitchen, and talked about you. A few days ago one of the editors rang me up to say that they were getting nearer to planning such a series and hadn't I talked of a rare bird, an American artist in France, etc., etc., who was the rarest of them all—and what had I said was his name? I gave the name, and cracked you up a bit more; saying darkly that you were very busy, very sought after, and not had for the asking."

Elizabeth David met Kathleen Raine and Valerie (Mrs T.S.) Eliot at a dinner party given by James and Judy. Her thank you note is dated 6 May 1973: "...Friday evening was sheer joy to me, from the taxi-ride to Addison gardens and seeing London's trees in such lovely, heavy blossom, right through your perfectly delicious dinner—that omelette confection is a triumph and the scents of the daube were still in my nose as I went to sleep—to the return journey and Kathleen Raine in her charming black cloak saying goodnight. She is an impressive figure.

"And you know, Judy, I don't think you could really call the evening genteel, not given those devastating comments delivered with such faultless timing in her clear gentle voice by Kathleen Raine—'You can't call a grown woman Babs'—'a drawing room Buddhist'—and there were several more which I shall treasure.

"Incidentally it was poor Babs who was the recipient of the Brian Howard barb which I recounted to Richard and James the night they were here: 'I know what's wrong with you, you have to earn your own living.'

"I loved meeting Mrs. Eliot and really took to her. She is a nice, good person. Thank you both for inviting me to meet such unusual and memorable company...."

So many details of that evening are stamped in my memory (a transferal, no doubt, from James's memory) that I have difficulty in convincing myself that I was not present. In any case, the night at Elizabeth's, which she mentions in her letter, had to have been in late March, after Judy left for the U.S. and before James and I flew to Zurich. She asked us to dinner, apologizing that she hadn't received in years and never really cooked anymore except to bake bread. When we arrived, she was trying to line a large tart mould by flinging dabs of sticky, batter-like dough at it. Most of the dough clung to her fingers. She said it was a new kind of pastry which she wanted to try. When the mould was finally coated with blobs, she poured in a mixture of cream, eggs and roquefort and put the tart to bake. We drank some white wine while she explained that a wine merchant had sent her a couple of cases of different Beaujolais growths—Brouilly, Morgon, Chiroubles, etc.—for her evaluation—with the food, we would taste our way through the different Beaujolais. The tart was out of the oven, swelled, golden and beautiful. She served out slices, poked at hers and said, "This is awful, I can't let you eat this," swept the plates away and put out some charcuterie and a platter of cheeses. There were several breads, which she had baked, all very good. We began to taste the Beaujolais; Elizabeth judged each to be bad, terrible, trash or awful. She said, "You want a drink, don't you?" She poured two tumblers of whisky, saying how much she envied us, being able to drink whisky—her doctors had forbidden it. For herself, she poured Cherry Heering. This continued for hours; conversation never lagged but James and I began to feel guilty about staying so late—after each drink, she would say, "Just one more and then I'll let you go." We left at about 5 a.m., with Elizabeth on her doorstep, wreathed in smiles and blowing kisses, an adorable little girl.

Sam Aaron, owner of Sherry Wines and Spirits, wrote, at Jim Beard's instigation, that he and his wife, Florence, would be traveling in Europe and would like to visit me. I invited them to dinner. It fell the same day as the Gault-Millau lunch and presentation of their clef d'Or at the Lingousto. Garin insisted that I bring my guests to the restaurant for drinks; that was impossible but I told him that he and Mary would be welcome to join us for dinner. Absolutely not, he said, out of the question. 14 May 1973 (Me to James). "...So I prepared my dinner and my wine for three: Asperges Vinaigrette, Raviolis aux Cuisses de Grenouilles, Famous Split, stuffed Chicken, this time with a farce based on fresh morels, wild salad, Cheeses, Strawberries with Raspberry purée; Laurent-Perrier Cuvée Grand Siècle, Morey-St.-Denis Pinot Blanc '64, Ch. Dauzac '66, Ch. Latour '63, Ch. Filhot '62. Well, you will be happy to know that G has now found a new trick for putting down my cooking. They arrived at 9:30—I was serving out the salad, the remainder of chicken still at table; Mary went directly to the cupboard and put out two more plates, G plopped a pot of vegetables left over from their lunch on the table and immediately without asking anyone served gargantuesque portions onto all plates (except mine—I made it clear that I wanted none). Mary said she was hungry so I served her some chicken—G said he wanted none of that, only vegs for him, so she didn't touch her chicken—then he kept asking the Aarons what was the matter, why didn't they eat their vegs, weren't they good? He complained several times that the Latour was acid (not true) and told me what a great mistake I had made to serve strawberries with the Sauternes which was killed by them (not true)—left in the middle of dessert and, a quarter of an hour later, as we were beginning to relax, they were back—couldn't find the keys to the house so spent the night here...."

Didier Marsauche came from a Parisian family of pastry cooks. His parents were separated but both operated pastry shops. His sister was married to a pastry cook. They wanted Didier to apprentice to Garin and become a real chef de cuisine. He was probably 16, but seemed younger. Garin took him on, mistreated him in the grand old tradition of master to apprentice, and gave him an attic room in their house in which to sleep. When the Garins came up the hillside, he came with them. When they did not, he climbed up alone of a late afternoon. Didier developed a crush on me. One day, he rather timidly asked me if I would teach him how men made love. I suppose I was embarrassed but I laughed and told him that it would be much more fun if he were to find someone his own age and they could learn together. (He didn't take my advice and I became, instead of lover, his confessor.)

Garin was acting crazier and crazier. He had inexperienced cooks in the kitchen—Didier was only an apprentice, peeling vegetables and scrubbing the floors. G and Mary were out front drinking. Simca, Julia and Paul wanted to invite me to lunch at the Lingousto with a journalist lady, who would, presumably, write up the restaurant—I was delighted as it meant that I wouldn't have to cook for a change. 2 June 1973. (Me to James) "...started out with soggy old waffles smeared with tapénade, then soggy waffles smeared with garlic purée, then pancakes smeared with eggplant purée—God knows what he thinks he is about—sweet-acid sorbet au cassis with marc de Provence poured over it after the fish, which very successfully kills the appetite—just as well perhaps as four of us had ordered roast lamb—Julia had ordered chicken with morels. The waiter arrived with a tiny overcooked saddle of lamb, said he was sorry, there was no more chicken, and served out grey slivers of lamb to everyone. Ten minutes later he returned to the table and said that the patron had decided to go to the kitchen and prepare an order of chicken for Madame. I went to the kitchen and told him the meal was over and to stop the preparation; he screamed that it was started and we had better eat it, etc., etc. Finally, we got up here and relaxed a bit with some Champagne—the Garins came up and things unrelaxed again...oh, well...." A few days later, I had a nearly identical experience, when Alex and Andrée Allégrier, proprietors of Lucas-Carton, asked me to join them with their daughter, Monique, her husband, Jacques Becquaert, their year-old son and Léon Beyer for lunch at the Lingousto. The baby adored the limp waffles with the Provençal spreads but no one else was ravished. Again, we repaired to the hillside for Champagne and again the Garins followed us up.

The 1973 Avignon program was ambitious. My assistants were Gary Harrell, California cooking teacher, alumnus of the 1972 class, and Judy. I had no intention of repeating the impromptu performance of the preceding year. There would be no specific recipes; invention could still dictate seasoning, forcemeat compositions and so forth. I wanted to teach kitchen mechanics, the principles of basic cooking methods, and taste, specifically food and wine alliances. Burgundy, Bordeaux and Champagne joined the list of donors. I visited restaurants to organize our menus and the wine service. I wanted the red wines served at cellar temperature and was surprised to discover that Baumanière stored their wines in a non-insulated shed (they have since installed an air-conditioned cellar)—they surrounded our cases of wines with tubs of ice three days in advance to be able to serve them at a correct temperature.

13 June 1973. (Me to James) "...Domaine de la Romanée-Conti is offering 18 bottles of La Tâche 1967, '66, '65, '63, '59 and '57 for an organized vertical tasting in the classroom...spent a couple of days working up an extremely detailed schedule of the program, dish by dish, step by step, wine by wine, etc.—filled five pages, asked Norma to run them off in multiplicate for the students so they may know ahead of time what to expect—also prepared two pages to be run off for La Tâche tasting notes...am much too nervous as this thing crashes down upon me—more upset even than last year if that is possible."

The official program was Thursday 28 June - Wednesday 11 July. The first case of Champagne—Philipponnat Clos des Goisses 1966—was poured at a reception the day before the first class; 12 July, the group was invited to lunch on the hillside in Solliès.

Class days were Monday, Tuesday, Thursday and Friday, restaurant days, Wednesday and Saturday. Consecutive class days permitted us to prepare certain dishes that required more time than a single session. On class days, several wines were served with lunch and discussed; an oenologist, associated with the CIVCR, gave late afternoon winetasting classes in their winetasting laboratory. The school had no decent cellar. On the morning of the La Tâche tasting, I nursed the bottles for hours, moving them in and out of the cold room, to be certain they were served at a perfect temperature. Michel Lemonnier and a couple of CIVCR officials were invited to join us. Norma's brainless husband, Frank, who had not been invited, was chain-smoking and swilling the wine; I put him out. The class had prepared gougères for the tasting and our guests remained for a lunch of Daube à la Provençale, fresh noodles and Château Thivin (Côte de Brouilly) 1972, green and cool. Thierry Manoncourt had offered a case of Château Figeac (Saint-Emilion) 1964, with specific instructions that it be decanted two hours in advance. We drank it on the last class day with a rare-roast fillet of beef that had been studded with truffles the preceding day.

I still wince at the memory of our first restaurant lunch. The Hostellerie de la Fuste had been chosen for the beauty of its pastoral situation, its vast, luxuriant garden terrace, the profusion of flowers and the gentle play of light through the shade of ancient plane trees. The chef had insisted on serving, without a pre-tasting, two specialties of which he was particularly proud: the rissole turned out to be crayfish tails and truffle pieces bound in a glue of tomato paste and enclosed in a voluminous envelope of half-baked vegetable shortening pastry; the duck was boiled to death in a grey gravy. (But, the cold ham that opened the meal was delicious and the barely sweetened quince tart etched in relief the vibrance, the almond and fresh peach overtones of the lovely Château Filhot.) On the duck I was to place a Beaune-Grèves 1970, exhuberant with the fresh fruit of youth; Romanée-Saint-Vivant 1966, one of the greatest red wines of Burgundy from a celebrated vintage, was to escort the cheeses. A week earlier, I had, myself, installed the wines in the coolest corner of the cellar, each bottle placed upright, and had insisted that notes be taken on their service, the salient points of which were: (1) They must not be disturbed until the day of the luncheon; (2) Each of the reds should be uncorked an hour before its service, but; (3) The bottles must remain in the cellar until the moment of serving.

My first vision, upon entering the gate, was that of a handsomely decorated, long table in the torrid illumination of the noonday sun; proudly lined up were all the magnums of Beaune-Grèves and all the bottles of Romanée-Saint-Vivant. They were sent back to the cellar and the instructions were repeated. After a glass of Champagne and a turn in the garden, I returned to the scene of the crime. In unbelief I saw again, like a recurrent nightmare, the military alignment of the precious bottles. Back they went again. Things were going badly....

I waited tensely until the second course was finished and asked to be served a bit of each red wine. Both were hot and new instructions were issued. The maître d'hôtel repeated them after me: the first wine was to be plunged into ice buckets and rapidly cooled for no more than five to ten minutes before being served; at the same time, the bottles of Saint-Vivant were to be placed in buckets of cool water, a handful of ice cubes added to each, and left in the cellar until the cheese service. Some of the Beaune-Grèves was served too warm, some too cool—under the circumstances, that was inevitable and I began to relax.

And then the glorious Romanée-Saint-Vivant was served: It had been packed in ice; it was iced; it had sunk to within a few degrees of freezing! In our glasses was only a mute reproach for mindless stupidity. (Two months later a bottle of the same wine was opened for me in the cellars of the Domaine de la Romanée-Conti. Its eloquence was heartbreaking, the more so because the pain, the helpless rage, the dumb despair of that summer day were so vividly still with me.)

Wednesday, the 4th of July, was a celebration day. In the morning, we visited the Domaine de Mont-Redon in Châteauneuf-du-Pape, where the proprietor, M. Fabre, fired by our enthusiasm, opened bottle after bottle, receding through the years. He and

Mme Fabre accompanied us to Château Malijay, where M. Nativelle received us for a buffet-lunch, the dishes of which had been prepared by the students during the two preceding class sessions. That evening was the Gala Dinner at Baumanière.

Fieldwork for our dinner at l'Oustaù de Baumanière began months earlier. I tasted most of the preparations on the regular menu and discussed repeatedly with Raymond Thuilier the finer details of our own menu, finally choosing for the main course something that was not on the menu: a plain roast baron of lamb accompanied by fresh little vegetables, its simplicity designed to enhance a suave Ducru-Beaucaillou 1964 and a muscular Mouton-Rothschild 1962. The cheeses were carefully selected so that none might offend the Château Margaux 1959, a wine whose shimmering, melting beauty brought tears to my eyes. (Monsieur Boxberger, the chief wine steward, had told me, "It is criminal to place that wine on a menu—it should be savoured alone.") Our Margaux 1959 brought a rush of memories of all the Margaux I had ever tasted, but two, in particular, stayed with me: the gentler 1953 and the scintillating, filigree-structured 1924. It reminded me of both—perhaps it was less perfect than either. I don't know. But I do know that that wine, alone, could have justified my summer. The dessert, too, was chosen with care to honour a sumptuous, amber-edged Yquem 1955. The service of the wines, from one end of the evening to the other, was perfect. During the preceding months, I had suspected Messieurs Thuilier and Boxberger of being irritated with me for being so picky about every detail. Later, they were both very proud of that meal—and, in retrospect, I am not a little proud, myself. It was a very beautiful evening.

Perfect meals are hard to come by: Charles Bérot's bouillabaisse and the New York's bourride were, each, the best of its kind that I have ever known in a restaurant. Charles Bérot, chef and proprietor of l'Escale, in Carry-le-Rouet, a seaside resort town near Marseille, never accepted large groups in his restaurant; he claimed that it was impossible to cook impeccable food under those conditions. As a personal favour, he accepted us, refused everyone else—and did the impossible. Only bouillabaisse was prepared in his kitchen that day and we saw the live fish being delivered by a local fisherman as we arrived. (Mme Bérot was worried—she confided to me that the shepherd who furnished all their fresh goat cheeses had promised delivery that morning and had not shown up; the shepherd's wife arrived during the service of the bouillabaisse, laden with cheeses, and honour was saved.)

Bouillabaisse is an exciting and genial dish, but it is a wine-killer. The Marseillais drink the white wine of Cassis with it, but I thought that a tannic young red wine with an adolescent edge of sparkle could better support the alliaceous, cayenne, saffron and acid-sweet tomato onslaught. I had often drunk just such a wine at Domaine Tempier. Charles Bérot's enthusiasm was immediate. There were problems: officially, red wine bearing the Bandol appellation may only be bottled and commercialized after 18 months in the wood (I rationalized that it was not being commercialized); Lucien Peyraud feared that his wine, tasted in an unfinished state, might not be understood by a group of neophyte Americans and preferred to offer a mature vintage; his son, Jean-Marie, was tempted by my suggestion and offered the obvious solution—the young wine would accompany the bouillabaisse and the last remaining bottles of 1969 in their cellar would be offered for the cheeses so that the comparison could be made.

Now the young wine had to be chosen (before bottling, it is raised in huge wooden vats, each containing a wine made mainly from the same proportions of grape varieties and vinified in the same way, but picked on different sections of the property and, as always happens, the wine in each vat was taking on a life of its own, developing in its own way) and a luncheon date was set: six numbered flasks were brought up from the cellar as we sat down. Six glasses were at each setting and a pact was made to remain silent until, after repeated tastings, each of us had made his choice; we frowned and side-glanced our ways to a single cuvée, to everyone's delight. The chosen cuvée was drawn immediately into bottles and, the following morning, the wines were delivered to repose in Charles Bérot's cellars for the couple of months preceding the sacrifice.

Lulu Peyraud and Michel Lemonnier joined us at the bouillabaisse lunch. The attention to detail was beautiful to watch. The day was hot and the tables were set on a high open terrace juttied above the Mediterranean. As the cellar-cool wine was brought up in relays, the bottles were immediately placed in buckets of cool water with a handful of ice cubes added. Mme Bérot kept a sharp eye on the buckets and, as ice cubes began to disappear, she would order another handful to be added. Throughout the bouillabaisse service, the untamed red Tempier, still slightly prickly from its young residue of carbon dioxide, flowed at a constant 50°F.... It was the kind of day that assumes greater importance in retrospect, memory distilling the limpid blue sky, the intermingled scents of the sea air, the bouillabaisse, and the cool fruit of the wine into a crystalized symbol of well being. Lulu was ravished. With her next bouillabaisse, she insisted that Jean-Marie serve cooled red Tempier from the most recent vintage. The entire family was seduced by the alliance of the cool wine's wild fruit, the saffrony bouillabaisse and the garlicky rouille.

The New York-Vieux Port restaurant (a name dating from a period when it was fashionable for restaurants, bars and night clubs to assume names like "Le Hollywood," "Le Miami," or "Le New York"), facing the old port in Marseille, was then a serious restaurant and bourride, a velvety fish stew bound with aïoli, was one of its specialties. That morning we had visited, near Aix, the 16th century cellars of Château Simone and tasted the young wines. M. and Mme Rougier, the proprietors, joined us at the bourride lunch, for which they had offered a selection of their wines. From Marseille, Judy, Gary and I went on to Solliès to begin preparations for the next day.

The day in Solliès-Toucas is a kaleidoscope of incoherent souvenirs. The Garins, Didier and several members of the Peyraud family joined us; strains of Damia, Fréhel, Lys Gauty and Piaf were punctuated by the muffled explosions of Champagne corks and Lucien Peyraud danced La Java with all the ladies. The atmosphere was euphoric; beneath the grapevine arbour, the dance of light on the moving figures reflected Renoir and Monet. We made no attempt to produce a serious lunch. A crate of sardines, stiff-arched and bright with the steel-blue reflexions of the morning's catch, were wrapped in vine leaves and grilled over olive wood embers; legs of lamb and veal kidneys had been cut up and marinated with herbs and olive oil—they were skewered with fresh bay leaves onto rosemary branches and grilled over the same coals; cheeses and a crate of fresh figs. With the sardines, a Bordeaux de Monbousquet 1972, supple and cool; Château Monbousquet 1970 with the brochettes. For the cheeses—the last wine of our last day together—I had reserved one especially beloved: a Charmes-Chambertin 1970, offered by Charles Rousseau.

A few of my guests had climbed to an upper terrace to admire the rustic swimming pool. I heard screams and raced up to find simple Frank Benney in paroxysms of demonic laughter; he was drunk and had thought it would be fun to push a couple of fully dressed ladies into the swimming pool.... It was time to say goodbye.

Richard Olney

Déjeuner du 30 Juin, 1973 à l'Hostellerie de la Fuste
"Les Arts Culinaires," Lubéron Collège

Les Vins:	Les Mets:
à l'apéritif: Champagne Vve. Clicquot, Carte d'Or, 1966	
Riesling Réserve, 1971 (Léon Beyer)	Jambon des Alpes au Pebre d'Ail et Romarin
	Rissole Nantua
Beaune Grèves, 1970, en magnum (Joseph Drouhin)	Caneton de Pays au Sang
	Salade
Romanée-Saint-Vivant, Domaine Marey-Monge, 1966 (Récolte du Domaine de la Romanée-Conti)	Fromages
Château Filhot, 1970	Tarte Chaude aux Coings
Eau de Vie de Poire (Manguin)	Café

Reflexions

Diner du 4 Juillet, 1973 à l'Oustaù de Baumanière
"Les Arts Culinaires," Lubéron Collège

Les Vins:	Les Mets:
à l'apéritif: Champagne Laurent-Perrier, Cuvée "Grand Siècle"	
	Foie-Gras Frais
Puligny-Montrachet, clos du Cailleret, 1970 (Joseph Drouhin)	Turbot au Chablis
Château Ducru-Beaucaillou, 1964	
	Baron d'Agneau Renaissance
Château Mouton-Rothschild, 1962	
Château Margaux, 1959	Fromages
Château d'Yquem, 1955	Tarte Tatin
	Mille Feuilles
Grande Champagne, Réserve Spéciale (Marcel Ragnaud)	Café

Richard Olney

Déjeuner du 7 Juillet 1973 à l'Escale (Carry-le-Rouet)
"Les Arts Culinaires," Lubéron Collège

Les Vins:	Les Mets:
à l'apéritif: Champagne Perrier-Jouët, 1966	
Vin Rouge de Bandol 1972, tiré sur fût, offert par le Domaine Tempier	Poutargue aux Petits Oignons Bouillabaisse
Domaine Tempier 1969	Fromages de la Région du Rove
	Sorbet à la Purée de Framboises
Chartreuse VEP	Café

Déjeuner du 11 Juillet 1973 au Vieux Port–New York, Marseille
"Les Arts Culinaires," Lubéron Collège

Les Vins:	Les Mets:
à l'apéritif: Champagne Bollinger, 1966	
Château Simone (blanc) 1969 (La Palette, Jean Rougier)	Melon de Cavaillon au Jambon de Parme
Château Simone (blanc) 1966 Château Simone (blanc) 1965	Bourride Provençale
Château Simone (rouge) 1964	Banons à l'Huile d'Olive
	Sorbet à l'Abricot, Mignardises
Grande Champagne, Réserve Spéciale (Marcel Ragnaud)	Moka

The next day, James, who had been communing with Yeats and Jung in Solliès during our gastronomic adventure, Judy, Gary and I drove to Avignon to gather together my coppers, mortars, the remaining bottles of wine that had been offered for the class, and our suitcases. We stopped first at the kitchen, the dishwasher was busy packing up the wine to carry away—some had already disappeared. I told him to cool it. We took what was left and continued to the flat to pack suitcases. Norma and Maza arrived: he handed me a check for $1,000. "What is this for?" I asked. He said, "You are an associate of Lubéron College, not an employee," (that was news to me) "and you must share our losses; we have lost money because of the exchange—we expected five francs to the dollar and only received four...and, besides, you have spent too much money." As far as I was concerned, the exchange was none of my business and I had not spent too much money. In answer to everything I said, he announced, "I take issue." I told him to keep the check, we would go to court.

James and Judy returned to London, Felipe decided to spend a few days in Solliès, Susan Raven, from the *London Sunday Times Magazine*, who had contacted me in Avignon (thanks to Sybille's efforts) arrived with a photographer to follow me through the Toulon Market and shoot a how-to spread in the kitchen...and Maza bombarded me with letters and telegrams, demanding that I telephone him (fortunately, I still had no telephone).

20 July 1973. (Me to James) "Received a slimy, dishonest letter from Maza, written after a telephonic contact, in which he managed to write all that I did not permit him to say on the telephone. He seems particularly pleased with his gift for ironic wit. Following some of the prize passages: 'I have been thinking of the unpleasant development and I think I have a solution which, not satisfactory to everyone, might be considered fair all around...I feel that our basic calculations were correct...but the real root of the disaster is that we got only 4 francs to the dollar instead of 5 as calculated. That means for every thousand dollars (per student), we only got 4,000 francs instead of 5,000. The total loss is about $5,000 from the budget.... It seems disgraceful to me that the remainder would only be $500 a week for you (note irony). The

only solution that I can see is that I would hope that the resulting publicity—which should be considerable and worth at least 5-10 thousand dollars, will help to (here he wrote 'console,' then crossed it out, apparently sensing that it might be the wrong choice of word) sell your new book and place you in a position of recognized pre-eminence...I would urge that what is past be past. We are victims of a financial disaster similar to an earthquake, explosion or flood and we are lucky to come out as we did.' The next morning received an urgent 'appel téléphonique' in the name of Mme Denis. I spent an hour and a half at the post office getting through the appel to Mme Denis and there was the familiar, soft, oily voice saying, 'Why, hello Richard.' I said, 'Who is Mme Denis?' 'Why, I don't know, Richard, why do you ask?' 'I've read your letter, Herbert. I don't like it.' 'You must absolutely come to Aix today, Richard—it will be so good for us all to get together again.' 'There is no question of my coming to Aix, but....' 'You say you can't come? Why, that's too bad.' 'Don't interrupt me—I want a check for $5,000 and I want it sent immediately.' 'You say you want your thousand dollars? Why, of course, Richard, we will send it along any time you feel that you need it.' 'I did not say one thousand dollars, I said five thousand dollars—one, two, three, four, five thousand dollars and you heard me.' 'Oh, I see—well, I am afraid, Richard, that in view of such a strange request, you would have to write us a letter....' That was when I slammed down the receiver."

Maza was strong on "letting bygones be bygones." There were more letters suggesting that he always had my welfare at heart and that I should consider teaching more cooking classes for Lubéron; I wondered how he had managed for so long to evade the loony bin. (As a matter of principle, I took him to court; the French judge decided we should split our differences—Herbert had to reach into his pocket for $2,500.)

12 September 1973. "Returned this morning from Burgundy—Lalou Bize tasting '50 Years of Vosne-Romanée,' 44 wines beginning with Romanée-Conti '70, finishing with same 1919, yesterday morning visited the Domaine to taste the young wines, had lunch with Aubert and Pamela de Villaine, Aligoté and Grands Echézeaux '63, Aubert deposited me with Charles

Rousseau, tasted a dozen '72s and Charles put me on a train in Dijon.... Garins have been in Paris for some time, he worried about his health (nerves and booze)—Lingousto closed indefinitely."

29 October 1973 (Me to James). "John Rolfson died of leukemia.... The book continues to be torture but I think it is winding up.... Garins planning big anniversary meal this week. What anniversary? I asked. OUR TENTH, of course, he said. (I finally realized that it must be a celebration of the first time they slept together.)"

Late November, a year overdue, I mailed the last chapters of *Simple French Food* to Atheneum. James and Judy were preparing to leave London. Michel Lemonnier had for long been trying to lend me his house in Marrakesh. We spent the first two weeks of December there before James and Judy returned to Durham.

Simca and Jean still kept their flat in Paris but always spent the Christmas and New Year's holidays in Plascassier and insisted that I join them.

Five

1974-1976
Simple French Food. New York, Berkeley, San Francisco. French Wine Tour. Cooking Classes, Venice.

1 January 1974. (Me to James) "Returned day before yesterday from Simca's—made certain to get out before their New Year's Eve party—spent all my time cooking, of course—just as well as it keeps me out of the social teas and apéritifs—had told Simca that I would spend a few days there only if there were no other guests—there were three others—she explained that they didn't count since I had already met two of them. Dined one evening with Eda and Sybille, who are back in La Roquette, Sybille until March, Eda

until autumn. Confided that I had broken down and accepted, at Atheneum's insistance, to subject myself to a PR tour when the book is published. Sybille was horrified, assured me that it would be very wrong, very destructive to me and would not sell any more books. (Eda: 'But, darling, you give interviews and sign books.' Sybille: 'That is different.')"

19 January 1974. (Me to James) "Julie (Dannenbaum) is mad—she will be in Paris, 8-15 February and wants me to pick out a pile of restaurants to eat in—also invites Michel and proposes to put us up at the Ritz.... Poor old legs are so bad I can hardly limp around—Garin calls it sciatica and says white wine is very bad for it—but he gave me a rotten bécasse the other evening that went, in part, straight to the legs, (the rest stayed, unhappily—and painfully—in the gut for one excruciating night and all the following day) raw it was too and I really ate very little (saw him the next day and he asked rather gruffly how I felt, just fine I groaned, so maybe he suffered too).... Sacha arrives for a few days end of month—we will go to Cannes for lunch with Eda and to Salon to see Marie Ricard."

Julie's gastronomic week in Paris was fantastic—and exhausting. We had twelve meals in eleven restaurants (for the two most elaborate dinner menus, we skipped lunch). I went around ahead of time to Prunier-Duphot and to the Vivarois to organize the menus ("Leave it to me," said Claude). Jean Barnagaud, proprietor of Prunier, was organizing, the day after Julie's arrival, an invitation "Pot-au-Feu Dodin-Bouffant" dinner for some thirty guests to which he invited us, as well as reserving a private salon for lunch later in the week. The "pot-au-feu Dodin-Bouffant," an assemblage of tarragon-flavoured beef and thyme-flavoured pork and veal sausage poached together, chicken poached in a different broth and whole foie gras poached in Chambertin, accompanied by onion purée (Soubise), was a literary fantasy (*La Vie et La Passion de Dodin Bouffant*, by Marcel Rouff, 1924) long before it became a culinary reality. Jean Barnagaud enjoyed teasing me by presenting mystery dishes or wines. Between the seafood fritters and the pot-au-feu, he served little sea urchin crêpes (not on the menu), the puréed corals incorporated into the batter, and asked if I could guess what they were. The flavour of sea urchins is unique and unmistakable, but he was delighted that I had found it. For lunch, later in the week, we drank Pouilly-Fuissé with oysters, praires and palourdes (clam-like bi-valves), followed by lambs' trotters in poulette sauce. Before the cheeses, the sommelier arrived with a bottle carefully wrapped from the base to the lip in a napkin. No sooner had I tasted the wine than M. Barnagaud asked, "Well, what do you think?" "Maybe a Mission Haut-Brion 1961," I ventured. "How did you guess? There must have been something to give it away!" I admitted that I had glimpsed a sliver of blue and silver capsule at the lip of the bottle which I associated with La Mission—most Bordeaux have red capsules; as for the vintage, at that time, among the red Bordeaux, only 1961 had that quality of power, density and fruit.

(Me to James). "We had good meals at Lucas-Carton, Taillevent, La Marée and Lous Landès, not so good at the Pot-au-Feu, l'Archestrate and Coconnas. Michel joined us at the Tour d'Argent (indifferent food, pleasant service, marvelous wines—finished with Château Margaux 1934) and at Le Vivarois. Of course, the mad meal of genius was Claude Peyrot's—it would have been a disaster in anyone else's hands but was, in fact, sublime."

Maison Prunier Menu -- 9 Fevrier 1974

BISQUE DE CRUSTACES

Accompagnee de Beignets aux Fruits de Mer

***

LE POT-AU-FEU DODIN-BOUFFANT

d'apres Marcel Rouff

Pare de ses Legumes

PUREE SOUBISE

***

FROMAGES AFFINES

***

MOUSSE GLACEE AU KUMMEL

Les Friandises

***

CORBEILLES de FRUITS

PULIGNY-MONTRACHET 1970 CHATEAU HAUT-BRION1953

CHATEAU RICAUD 1929

Le Vivarois. Diner du 12 Février 1974

Les Vins:	Les Mets:
	Consommée d'un Jardin de Curé
Bienvenues-Bâtard-Montrachet (Ramonet-Prudhon) 1969	Turban de Sole et de Saumon avec son Ragoût d'Ecrevisses
	Queue de Boeuf en Braisage de Moutarde
Volnay, Clos de la Bousse d'Or, 1969	Chartreuse de Primeurs et Truffes aux Ris de Veau
	Foie d'Oie en Poularde avec ses Fruits au Gingembre
	Asperges à l'Orange
Clos Saint-Denis, Domaine Dujac, 1969	Fromages
Château La Tour Blanche, 1957	Arlequinade de Bananes au Coulis de Framboises

Claude paced around our table, hands clenched behind his back, and said, finally, "You see, Richard, the turban is really yours—I took it from your book.... But I put the crayfish tails inside instead of out!" (He was mainly inspired by an introductory paragraph in the S & S edition of *FMC*, which was eliminated in the revised edition.) When the swelled turban arrived, pink and white striped, flawlessly unmoulded but trembling, the entire dining room gasped at the beauty of the thing. In cross-section, the sole and salmon fillets encircled two layers of pistachio-flecked mousseline, between which lay a bed of crayfish tails; a Nantua sauce made from the crayfish carapaces was served apart. The sections of braised oxtail were melting, the chartreuse was another beautiful geometric structure of little green vegetables, carrots, truffles and sweetbreads and the foie d'oie en poularde was exactly that: a boned Bresse chicken stuffed with a whole, two-pound fresh truffled goose foie gras, poached in a rich stock and served cold in its jelly. (Claude abides by the 19th century principle that truffles are the only element which may appear more than once on a menu.) The asparagus spears were served hot, enclosed in a napkin, accompanied by Hollandaise sauce containing threads of orange zest, and the arlequinade was an unmoulded architecture of banana slices and red fruits, bound in a Bavarian cream, with raspberry purée served apart. We rose from table in a dream, light in body and in spirit.

23 February 1974. (Me to James) "Garin is playing games again—angry about something, God knows what; they were up Sunday, said a friend was coming to visit on Wednesday and could they borrow bedcovers, I said of course, then G said they would be up to dinner the next evening, Monday, I said okay I would expect them but I had no meat and the butcher is closed on Monday—he said they would bring the meat. Today is Friday and have had no word since. Waited until 11 pm Monday and finally ate, expected them to pick up bed clothes on Tuesday—no one. You know that I am not going to the restaurant to discover what insanity is brewing now—if scenes are to be made, he will have to come up here to make them. They used my place while I was in Paris with Julie, two plats à gratin are missing, my omelette pans are scraped deeply with knife cuts and the stove was swiped with a wet sponge, leaving it red with rust when I returned—maybe he is angry because I mentioned none of these things. He does not treat his own kitchen equipment with such contempt." 6 March 1974. (Me to James) "The Garins finally turned up after two weeks' angry absence—seems they were mortally offended because, when they invited

themselves to dinner, I noted that the butchers are closed on Mondays. Jesus. (The real offense may be that Julie, Michel and I dined at Claude's.)"

Sacha's brother, Werner Niederstein, wanted to spend a couple of weeks each spring on the Côte d'Azur. Sacha asked if I could recommend a comfortable hotel in quiet surroundings with discreet but attentive service. I thought La Réserve in Beaulieu, on the coast between Nice and Monte Carlo, was the answer. In late March, they asked me to join them there for a few days. Werner arrived by plane, his chauffeur drove from Germany to meet him. The time was spent searching out restaurants in the region for lunch and dining at La Réserve, whose restaurant, overlooking the sea, with a pianist tinkling old-fashioned tunes, had a nostalgic shipboard atmosphere. The maître d'hotel and the sommelier were my friends and the wonderful short, thick-speared Niçoise asparagus with dark purple tips was in season. It was cooked to order, kept firm and served hot; I have never seen it outside of that region. For ten years to come, I spent a few days each spring with Sacha and his brother at La Réserve.

Julie was avid for new experience. She was returning in June and asked if I could arrange to have her enthroned in the Commanderie du Bontemps de Médoc et des Graves, in Bordeaux, and in the Confrérie des Chevaliers du Tastevin in Burgundy, following which we would eat our way south and collapse for a few days' relaxation at La Réserve. Afterward, she hoped that I would give summer cooking classes in Solliès for a small group—she had contacted Judy, Gary, Jane Salzfass and Janina. It didn't seem to be coming together.

20 May 1974. (Me to Judy and James) "...saw Eda the other day—doctor told her if she didn't stop smoking her toes would fall off, I said why, she said extremities, tobacco very bad for circulation—I now smoke one or two less cigarettes per day.... I don't mind if the summer cooking thing falls through—and, in any case, Julie will be rich in new experiences by the time our whirl through Bordeaux and Burgundy is finished, so she should not regret too much the other thing. And, really, I don't know what people think they can learn from me—I'm certain it's all better said

in the new book than I could teach it—so shall teach a bit about drinking (which, I have a feeling, although am not certain, is good for the circulation)."

Byron spent the month of June settling the family in Rochester, Minnesota, where he is still with the Mayo Clinic. 10 June, I met Julie in Bordeaux.

3 July 1974. (Me to James) "Passed a busy two weeks with Julie—tasted a dozen vintages of Bouscaut and as many of Haut-Brion first day, had dinner with Jean Delmas and his wife—next day Margaux and Mouton—next day Fête de la Fleur banquet at Latour—Julie was very pleased to be enthroned with Prince Philip, finished with Latour 1949, beautiful, and Jean-Eugène Borie invited us to a picnic-supper in the gardens of Ducru-Beaucaillou, which began 6-ish with Champagne, finished with Ducru '67 at 2 am. (Here I met Martin Bamford, director of International Distillers and Vintners, France, who received at Château Loudenne, Médoc, and became a close friend.)...Flew to Lyon, Julie decided she could drive no longer, hired a car with chauffeur, stopped en route to Beaune at La Mère Blanc (Georges Blanc), Vonnas, extraordinarily good—sommelier-maître d'hôtel (Antoine) asked if I was me, I said yes, he wanted my autograph. Dinner in Beaune with the Drouhins—lovely Clos de la Roche '47 to finish—next morning visit to Domaine, another La Tâche tasting—'72, '71, '70, '69, '65, '63, '62, finishing with Montrachet '70—went to lunch with Aubert who carried several bottles of La Tâche to the restaurant, raced to Beaune to dress for the evening circus before visiting Charles Rousseau to taste his '62s—he drove us to the Château de Vougeot and Julie, to her ravishment, was the first to be enthroned—next day collapsed. Chauffeur picked us up Monday morning, stopped in Beaujolais to visit Mme Geoffray (Château Thivin), dined Chez Bocuse. He imposed the menu—5 dishes plus cheese and dessert, 4 wines, no bill. Flew next morning to Nice and flopped for three days at La Réserve swimming pool, where Michel joined us. Had daily lunches near-naked at the pool terrace restaurant, more serious evening meals. M. Potfer, the director, was absent until the last day when Julie left. She said it was the cheapest place she'd ever been in so I examined the note—our drinks for

three days had been on the house, 30% reduction on rooms and 10% restaurant reduction. M. Potfer asked Michel and me to join him for lunch, Léon Beyer arrived and we were four."

James had accepted a post as visiting professor at Northwestern University for the fall semester. 16 September would be our parents' fiftieth wedding anniversary; the eight offspring planned to descend, without warning, on Marathon. I had promised Atheneum to do a book promotion tour, but no one knew when *Simple French Food* would appear; printing had been postponed for a month. Jim Beard wanted to organize a book-launching party on the official day of publication and had also asked me to teach a week of classes at his house on West 12th Street; Julie had booked me for the first week of December at her school in Philadelphia. La Transat—The French Line—was about to pass into oblivion: *Le France's* last west-bound voyage was 30 August. I booked passage.

10 August 1974. (Me to James) "Classes in New York scheduled for the week before Thanksgiving—5 morning classes limited to twenty, demonstration only; 5 evening participation (in part) classes limited, I hope, to eight but Jane Salzfass (from Avignon class), who will assist me and is taking care of registration, thinks I should accept ten.... Spent a couple of days in Plascassier with Jim and others last week—he wanted to come here, but can hardly get around so I discouraged it, promised to return (today, Saturday) and shall put him on a plane for London, Tuesday—he should go home and go to bed, but won't.... Peyrauds to lunch, brought their last case of '67 magnums—I told them they were crazy. Bill Rice, Odette, Felipe arriving later in the month...."

Simca wanted me to prepare lunch for Jim before his departure; the Childs were invited. She had written that friends in the southwest were sending two large farm ducks—canards de Barbarie—and wanted a shopping list of what I needed. (I never knew what I needed, a source of great frustration for Simca.) I answered not to worry, I would see what I found in the larder and the garden. In the fridge I found brousse (ewes' milk ricotta) and, in the garden, beautiful Swiss chard. I boned the ducks, prepared a dense stock with the carcasses and a stuffing of parboiled, squeezed and chopped chard, brousse, diced and sautéed giblets, a chopped, sautéed onion, garden herbs, eggs, grated Parmesan and semi-fresh breadcrumbs. The birds were half roasted to rid them of excess fat, braised in stock and glazed, constantly basted with a reduction of degreased braising liquid, until glistening bronze. Blanched green olives were simmered briefly in the remaining reduction. The presentation was glorious and, of course, carving a nearly boneless bird at table is childsplay. I was pleased but remained silent—the others were sufficiently loquacious.

4 September, Lucia met the boat in New York. She had recently moved from Waverly Place to less cramped quarters and wanted to lend me the Waverly Place studio, across the street from Leon Lianides' Coach House restaurant, for the duration of my on and off stay in New York. It was a life-saver, a small, square room with bathroom, kitchenette and tall French windows overlooking interior gardens; street noises were muted or inaudible. I loved it. Jim had insisted that I come by as soon as I arrived. I found him in the 12th Street kitchen surrounded by a crowd of ladies. José and Julie were there; the others probably included Cecily Brownstone, Nika Hazelton, Helen McCully, Doris Tobias...none of whom I knew at that time. Another lady was demonstrating how to fry pieces of meat on the newly installed electric surfaces offered by Corning; she was clearly disgruntled at my inopportune arrival. Conversation turned from the fried meat to my passage on *Le France*—Jim was shocked that I had travelled tourist class. ("If things are done right, one never pays one's way and one always goes first class.")

Jim had just moved into the 12th Street house. Clayton (Clay) Triplette, who always addressed him as "Mister B," was housekeeper, dresser, shopper, cook and sometimes butler; he had a fine sense of style. The third floor had been transformed into a pastry kitchen for Gino, who spent all his time there, keeping out of people's hair while assembling dacquoises from disks of nutty meringue and butter cream.

Felipe, who had had himself fitted by a couturier for a seductively cut chef's costume in which to appear for cooking demonstrations (with Tim as his publicity manager), had offended the master by permitting himself to be described in a Chicago newspaper as "Prince of the Blood, heir apparent to the throne of King James" (or words very similar in a royal declension). Jim was outraged: "They're stepping on my toes," he said. He had a new assistant, a young taxi driver, Carl Jerome, who abandoned his taxi and moved into the 4th floor flat. Carl immediately became (self-appointed, according to José and Clay) "Director of the James Beard Cooking School." Jim asked me "as a special favour" to give Carl lessons in boning a chicken. "Of course, I would teach him, myself," he said, "but my hands are too big." (Why are my hands not too big to bone a quail, I wondered.) We each had a chicken and a small, sharply pointed knife. I explained that the purpose of the exercise was to turn the bird inside-out, working delicately with fingertips and knife-tip, to remove a clean rib structure, breastbone and backbone without damaging skin or flesh, and asked him to follow me, step by step. It was not possible to teach Carl anything—he tore away at his chicken, the flesh was in shreds and he was very pleased with the result. I left it at that.

I joined Margaret and Elizabeth in Washington, we collected John and James en route to Rochester and continued with Byron to Marathon. Frances was there; Norris lived there. Mother and Father pretended, unconvincingly, to be surprised at our arrival. In early October, I was in Evanston with James and Judy. Janina threw a grand party and organized a few private cooking classes in her kitchen; Sue and Harold Florsheim asked us to dinner—we drank Romanée-Conti 1959 which, said Sue, had been waiting years for the right occasion.

Simple French Food appeared in early November. For the launching party, Jim wanted caillettes—garlicky, caul-wrapped parcels of chopped pork and innards, spinach and chard. I devoted the preceding day, arms elbow-deep in a tub, to mixing, moulding, wrapping and baking several hundred caillettes. A caterer furnished the rest. Of the party, I retain only a blurred memory of a crowd of strangers.

Nika Hazelton reviewed *Simple French Food* in terms so glowing that I would blush to quote. Lucia, who lived a few steps from Lydie and Wayne Marshall, had seen my book in the window of Lydie's cooking school, A La Bonne Cocotte, and introduced herself. Lydie's friend, Cecily Brownstone, Associated Press food editor, invited Lucia and me to dinner; Lydie brought a leek gratin and Wayne grilled skirt steak in the fireplace. Cecily never missed an opportunity to write about me, endearingly and possessively, in her AP columns. One article was entitled, "French Cooks Revere Our Richard." After claiming that I had a reputation for being difficult, she wrote, "At a late evening meeting at my house, when neither of us had time to eat dinner, Richard was suddenly and ravenously hungry. To meet the emergency without interrupting our conversation, I phoned for the speediest nearby possibility—second-rate Chinese food. He downed it with the utmost amiability. I suspect that Richard's temper waxes and wanes with the company he keeps." (In fact, the meeting was late afternoon. Cecily is a slight little lady with a mountain of will and resistance and could, at that time anyway, drink anyone under the table without blinking an eye or slurring a syllable; it was midnight when hunger pangs imposed a call for Chinese food.) Nika and Cecily both asked if they might visit the morning demonstration classes; I was delighted.

Carl had relieved Jim's secretary, Emily Gilder, of the financial responsibilities relating to the school; he controlled incoming fees and outgoing expenses. The kitchen countertops were too high for me to work at ease during demonstrations. I asked him to have a couple of planks nailed to 2x4 crossbars to lift me a few inches from the ground.

Jane was largely responsible for the registration of the evening class. José registered. (I told her she was mad, she could cook with me any time in Solliès without paying a small fortune—but she wanted to be in on the fun.) Irena Chalmers may have registered on her own initiative. Gael Greene was a close friend of Jane's, the others were friends or cousins, world travelers and habitués of France's three-star restaurants; they were there to have a good time and we drank rather grand wines, including those from the Domaine de la Romanée-Conti, Château Figeac 1964, Ducru-Beaucaillou '66 and '64 and Margaux 1953, several first growth Sauternes, and Château d'Yquem 1967. The morning classes were less expensive and we drank simpler wines, but the members were there to learn; because I wanted to teach, it was my favorite class.

In the evening classes, there were roasts, stews, truffled scrambled eggs, pastries, fresh pasta, crêpes, granités, and so forth, to keep the group busy participating. Most of the demonstrations from the morning classes I also demonstrated in the evening. I was very taken with the ducks that I had prepared at Simca's that summer and incorporated them into my "show-off" repertory. The day preceding the opening classes, I boned, stuffed and trussed ducks (to be cooked in class while demonstrating boning, etc.), prepared a sole fillet roulade in aspic (to be eaten Monday morning after demonstrating another to be eaten Tuesday evening after demonstrating another…) and a truffled rabbit terrine, which needed to ripen for a couple of days (to be eaten Tuesday morning after demonstrating another to be eaten Friday evening)….

Felipe wanted to be my assistant. Okay for morning, I told him, but Jane was my assistant for the evening classes. He was a conscientious and adulatory assistant, but he was also a spoiled baby and didn't want any other assistants in his face. He turned up in his glamorous chef's costume for the first evening class and began rather aggressively to assist. I had to explain forceably that only one assistant was possible in each class. He pouted but bore no grudge. (My real assistant in the classes was Clay, who helped me to shop, performed endless kitchen chores and kept things running smoothly with charm and jokes.)

Nika joined us for the first morning class session. I was in the midst of boning a duck (she was mesmerized) when Carl stalked in and announced loudly that I owed ten dollars for the "platform" (on which I was standing) and wanted the debt settled immediately. The classroom was stunned and it took me a moment to register the message before telling him to get out fast and never set foot in the kitchen again while I was teaching. That made Clay's day and he saw to it that my order was respected for the rest of the week. Jim never entered the kitchen during classes but he received an instantaneous running commentary about everything that was happening. In the morning, Clay and Felipe (who was back in Jim's good graces) reported; in the evening, Clay, José and

Jane. I had drinks with Jim every afternoon before the evening classes; we talked about nothing but food. One morning, Clay reported to him that I had just made "the most wonderful pastry and it's so easy—-nothing to it." Jim couldn't wait until our afternoon session—he wanted to see me immediately. "What's the secret of your pastry?" he asked. No secret: "Lots of butter, very cold, diced; cross two knives, like our grandmothers, to cut it into the flour, work fast, don't overwork, keep it cold. Wrap in plastic and refrigerate for an hour before rolling it out, give it a turn and roll out again. If you want puff pastry, use at least as much butter as flour by weight (4 oz. to 1 cup) and give it several turns with refrigerated rests between turns."

After the last evening class, José, Irena Chalmers and I had drinks in the Waverly Place studio while I unwound. A couple of years ago, I was upset to read, in Evan Jones's biography of James Beard, *Epicurean Delight*: "When he arrived in Jim's tension-ridden forum, Olney was faced with José, who was drinking more heavily than usual because of the obvious friction. In response to her distaste for Jerome, she threw herself (while Jim sat by in agony and concern for her) at the wrong person." This is all nonsense: José and I were friends, she was not drinking heavily and she did not throw herself at me. If Jim pretended to others that he was "sitting by in agony and concern" for José, that was merely part of his established pattern of trying to create intrigue where there was none; he enjoyed stirring things up.

In Philadephia, Julie threw another great party. Classes—morning demonstration only—began the first Monday in December and ran through the week. The classroom was a small auditorium, a stage at front with countertop, burners and an overhead mirror, stoves and ovens behind. Julie was determined that I was going to make money on these classes; she was registrar and assistant. I never knew how many students were registered—fifty or more, at a guess; that week paid for all my expenses during the seven months I spent in the United States.

In January 1975, James and Judy were back in Durham. Beni Hargrove, in charge of promotion for Atheneum, arranged my schedule around family and friends whenever possible. Many of the television appearances were five-minute spots following a newscast or ten to fifteen-minute spots on talk shows—no time to be serious. I bought a large, ugly frying pan with rounded transition from bottom to sharply slanted sides, permitting me to sauté with ease, tossing foodstuffs high in the air and retrieving them in the pan. I emptied out family's and friends' refrigerators of odds and ends—a chicken breast or slice of ham, zucchini, green onions, a couple of artichokes if I had time to turn them—anything that could be finely sliced raw and sautéed in a couple of minutes' time, parsley, garlic and lemon. A hot pan with a splash of olive oil: slice, add, toss, talk, slice, toss, grind over pepper and salt, toss, chop and add parsley and garlic, talk, toss, squeeze over lemon and it was done. My first experience was a national morning talk show broadcast from New York. I arrived with chopping board, knives and whatnot, assuming they would have a heat source—they thought not, but finally discovered an antique hot plate with a wire electric coil and a single low heat setting. I couldn't get the pan hot enough for the vegetables to slide easily and fly into the air; I muddled the stuff around with a wooden spoon—it made no difference. A hot plate was added to my luggage.

For Boston events, I stayed with the Childs in Cambridge, in Philadelphia with Julie, in Detroit with Lester Gruber, owner of the London Chop House, and his wife, Cleo, in Tulsa with Ailene Martin, alumnus of the Avignon classes. (At the Tulsa ladies' club, after having demonstrated an almond and pistachio soufflé pudding, samples were passed around to be tasted; "how unusual," "how interesting," "how extraordinary," the ladies exclaimed. I tasted—the pudding was "sweetened" with a bowl of salt instead of the sugar measured out ahead of time.)

Margaret found herself receiving in Chevy Chase at a Washington buffet-cocktail, book-signing event; Bill Rice, food editor of the *Washington Post*, and Robert Shoffner, about to become food editor for the *Washingtonian*, collaborated to organize demonstrations, book signings and dinner parties. On a T.V. talk show in Saint Louis, a comic, left over from the preceding act, thought he would like to continue being funny by poking his fingers in the food while I was demonstrating—poor thing suffered a nervous breakdown when he discovered that his fingers smelled like garlic.

Only in Dallas, where I demonstrated at Nieman-Marcus, and in Beverly Hills was I obliged to stay in hotels. The streets of Dallas by night were empty and sinister; for blocks around the hotel I found no sign of a restaurant. I returned to check the hotel's dining room, a Hollywood reproduction of a wild west saloon with cowgirls serving. I locked myself in my room and had something sent up. In Beverly Hills, the police stopped me while walking to a radio station five minutes from the Beverly-Hilton hotel—anyone not in a car is suspicious.

José was in San Francisco when I arrived. We both stayed with Gerald Asher, a wine merchant whom I had first met at Domaine Tempier with the Peyrauds and later known in London before he moved to New York and then to San Francisco. With José, I met Dick Graff, creator of Chalone Vineyard, whom she was interviewing for an article. José insisted—and I was grateful—on lending moral support by accompanying me and helping to drag along the culinary paraphernalia to TV studios. We were waiting to be received by a local TV personality, widow of a famous movie star, when a lavishly ermined lady sailed past us into the studio and asked, "Darling, who're you interviewing today?" The answer came listless but clear; "Oh, another one of those dumb food people." I could hardly take umbrage, for the words described exactly the way I felt. But I was sick of playing the circus clown; when she began messing around with a wooden spoon and asking silly questions, I told her sharply to leave the food alone and be serious. She became quite friendly and human.

José knew everyone in the Bay Area; to me, it was a blank slate. She introduced me to Chuck Williams, creator of the Williams-Sonoma kitchen equipment shops, where I was scheduled to give demonstrations in San Francisco, Palo Alto and Beverly Hills. I liked Chuck's gentle, self-effacing style and fine intelligence. Janina, who had left Don on a quest for new experience, had settled in Santa Barbara. She drove to San Francisco, walked into Williams-Sonoma and announced that she wanted a front row seat for the demonstration. When told that none were left, she wandered around the shop, bought a couple of thousand dollars worth of merchandise and said, "Now, can I have a front row seat?" She got it.

The flyers had announced that I would present a boned, stuffed sea bass, wrapped in lettuce leaves and braised in white wine, accompanied by a beurre blanc made from the reduced braising juices. I had no idea that all sea bass came from the East Coast; there was neither sea bass on the market nor any other fish of the right size, shape and quality. Instead, I settled on presenting the split chicken stuffed beneath the skin. It was raining. I explained the change of program. A man in the front row exploded. (I was later told that he published a restaurant review newsletter.) He had left his comfortable home and driven through blinding rain, he said, to see me prepare beurre blanc and he intended to see it done!! The pre-prepared chickens were in the oven, I finished my demonstration with another bird and whisked up a beurre blanc (an emulsion of butter, mounted with a reduction of shallots, wine and vinegar or, in the case of a braised fish, with the reduced braising juices—its success depends on low heat; there is no binding agent). The indignant gent admitted grudgingly that it was "quite" good...and confessed that he had never seen a beurre blanc prepared without a thickener.

After wine and chicken tastings, Alice Waters and Jeremiah Tower introduced themselves. Four years earlier in Berkeley, Alice had opened Chez Panisse, named in homage to the Pagnol film trilogy. Jeremiah had studied architecture at Harvard, but the kitchen was his passion. Alice and Jeremiah alternated weeks as chef in the Chez Panisse kitchens. Alice must have checked with Gerald—she knew that I was free for dinner, and knew that Kenneth Anger and I were old friends (I didn't know Kenneth was in San Francisco) and had arranged with Kenneth to call for me at Gerald's and continue to Chez Panisse. Jeremiah was in the kitchen, Alice had a date but promised to return to the restaurant before we left. I hadn't seen Kenneth in twenty years and I suddenly had two new friends.

The next day I demonstrated at Williams-Sonoma, Palo Alto. Janina had her front row seat. A young man, Mark Miller, who worked at the shop, was extremely attentive, anxious to run errands and to assist in any way possible; Chuck murmured, "You are Mark's idol." (Mark visited me later that year in Solliès, offered a beautiful copper gratin dish in souvenir of his visit, left Williams-Sonoma for Chez Panisse, opened his own restaurant in Berkeley, created the Coyote Café in Santa Fe, and has since soared to restaurant stardom.)

Two days later, I was to appear at Williams-Sonoma, Beverly Hills. Janina said, "Forget about your plane ticket, I will drive you." She had a station wagon, crammed to the hilt with the merchandise that had assured her of a front row seat in San Francisco. I rang up Sarah Boutelle, Mary Holmes's sister, in Santa Cruz. Mary lived on a secluded mountainside nearby. I had seen neither of them since the late 1940s. Sarah asked us to lunch. Mary arrived, accompanied by a young man (she was always accompanied by young men), carrying a saucepan of soup which, because of a rough drive down the mountain, had slopped all over her. Sarah screamed, laughing, "Why, you crazy old thing, you!" Mary held out the saucepan and said to me, "You'll never guess what this is!" I said, "It looks like sorrel soup." She was momentarily crestfallen. Sarah had prepared a huge salad of wild greens, avocado, green beans, hard boiled eggs, grilled peppers, anchovy fillets—a near replica of the salads with which I nourish myself in Solliès. In Iowa City, Mary and Buck Hanson had been close friends; I related Buck's visit to Solliès and the drag outfits at Garin's dinner. Janina, in her little girl, wide-eyed innocent style, asked, "Do you think that your friend is...homo...sex...ual?" I tried to maintain a serious countenance as I answered, "I don't know, people are complicated."

I was back in New York in early March. Nika said she and Harold wanted to know my "real friends, not those from the food world." She asked me to invite some friends to the Hazelton home and to prepare the dinner. I asked Robert Isaacson and Jimmy Draper, curator at the Metropolitan Museum. Nika asked Jill Norman, her English editor, who was passing through New York. I never visited Nika when she did not shower me with gifts—first editions of old French cookbooks were high on the list.

Paul Kovi and Tom Margittai, proprietors of The Four Seasons and the now defunct Forum of the Twelve Caesars, planned a two-week *Simple French Food* festival at the Forum. The Italian Line was about to dissolve; I had booked passage on the *Michelangelo* for its last voyage, halfway through the festival. I spent evenings in the dining room the first week. Tom wanted to introduce me to all the celebrity clients, most of whose names were unknown to me. I remember the old world charm of Virgil Thomson and the new world beauty of the young composers who surrounded him. Danny Kaye astounded me as he began to recite by heart long passages from *The French Menu Cookbook*; when his memory failed, he sent a busboy out to buy a copy of the book. We went on to The Four Seasons for supper.

José threw a going-away party, for which she borrowed a very grand mid-town apartment from friends. The next morning, my brothers and sisters, José, Lucia and Nika joined me in my cabin for Champagne. On the quay, before boarding, we passed Hermione Gingold, swamped in luggage and surrounded by friends, trying to hail a porter. I ran into Jimmy Villas, food editor for *Town and Country*, who had just seen the dining room steward. He apologized for taking a table to himself, said he had to be alone to appreciate and analyze food correctly. I went to see the steward, he said, "Oh yes, you are at the Captain's table." (He made it sound like an honour—it was the largest table in the dining room.) I asked if Miss Gingold had been assigned to a table. Not yet, he said. We will have a table for two, I said.

Hermione scanned the dining room; her gaze settled on Jimmy Villas. "Your young friend over there looks lonely," she said, "Why don't you ask him to join us?" I did and he was ravished. (There was, in any case, no food worthy of being analyzed—the menu was hopelessly banal and the only dish that could be specially ordered was spaghetti alla puttanesca, the Neopolitan prostitutes' speciality.) Hermione's wig was habitually askew and her false eyelashes came unstuck at the outer edges. Throughout the crossing, she clung to Jimmy and me to protect here from the vultures; one got hold of her and whined fawningly, "Oh, Miss Gingold, you must have been beautiful when you were young." It ruined her day.

1 April 1975. (Me to James) "The crossing was quite funny and relaxing. Miss Gingold was my table partner (she often made grotesque animal sounds to express her displeasure with the food) and we eventually enticed James Villas to join us. She occasionally did her Queen Victoria act at table, to the horror of the waiters. It is an apoplectic version of W.C. Field's, a menu or any other object that takes her fancy perched atop her wig, those tubular paper doilies intended to garnish mutton chops stuck on her fingers which she raises in majestic command (accompanied by grotesque Italian). Half-chewed food flies in all directions as she talks and smears magenta lipstick across that animated facescape. (We debarked at Cannes and I installed Hermione in the Carlton, where Simca picked me up; the two ladies bristled at the sight of each

With Hermione Gingold and James Villas, 1975.

other.)… The Garins are closing the restaurant (for good) in ten days' time! Lucien Peyraud recovering from heart attack, Lulu broke both legs in auto accident driving to hospital to see him. Claude Peyrot in hospital from ski accident, Odette in hospital to have something removed from her neck…."

The Collins' edition of *The French Menu Cookbook* appeared in Britain at the same time as *Simple French Food* in America. Susan Raven's *Cooking For Love* article in the *London Sunday Times*—three pages of colour photos—appeared in February 1975. She wrote an awestruck text, Barry Lategan's photos were beautiful and my "sponsor," Sybille, wrote, "I remember one time we met at Julia Child's, and Richard created a quite magical soufflé out of whatever he could find in the larder and the garden, and a handful of mangetout peas I'd brought. It was exquisite." One of the letters awaiting my return was from Dale Brown, London-based European editor of Time-Life Books. Time-Life was considering a new "how-to" cooking series, he wrote, and my name kept cropping up. He wondered if I would be interested in a consultantship. I rarely analyze my motives for a decision: certainly, I was suspicious of Time-Life; perhaps, also, I was intimidated by the potential vastness of such a project. I answered politely that I was not interested.

Another letter was from Hyman Charniak, Canterbury Travel, Kent, Connecticut. The agency wanted to organize a 16-day gastronomic vineyard tour of major French wine regions in May 1976. Sam Aaron had suggested that I should organize the tour and be "tour leader." I accepted.

The Garins preferred my house to theirs. During my absence, they had moved in, leaving Didier in the big house in the valley. I had bought a case of Chambertin 1972 from Jean-Marie Ponsot, bottled in the spring of 1974, and tucked the bottles into a corner of the cellar to grow up, with the intention of tasting the first four or five years hence. When I returned, the Chambertin had disappeared. It was a deliberate insult, another invitation to a lunatic brawl, which Garin hoped would end up in a tearful reunion with renewed promises of eternal brothership. I said nothing. After a couple of weeks, he could no longer contain himself; à propos of nothing, he snarled, "Ton Chambertin, c'est de la

MERDE!" I mumbled, "It wasn't ready." He screamed, "Je te dis, c'est de la MERDE!" I remained silent. He was evil. He may also have been cross about a recent profile of me by Naomi Barry in *The International Herald Tribune*, the last line of which read, "For some fun cooking, he would like to try his hand with Claude Peyrot of the Vivarois in Paris."

4 May 1975. (Me to James) "*Simple French Food* receiving 'Best Cookbook of Year' Tastemaker Award—ceremony tomorrow, told them I couldn't assist...letter from José, who is busy 'hand-picking' the participants of next year's wine tour...letter from Julie D. inviting me to La Réserve next month."

Mr. Charniak and I didn't share the same wavelength. He wanted the group to eat in three-star restaurants, but he proposed to choose prix-fixe menus with cheap wines. I assured him that the restaurateurs and the vineyard proprietors were friends: we would

Lucia, 1975.

be given sumptuous meals at reduced prices and the vineyards would offer all the wines. He wanted to know how much the "offered" wines would cost and noted that, in the U.S., "corkage" was so expensive that it was often cheaper to drink a house wine than to bring one's own. I thought it would be easier on Mr. Charniak's nerves—and on mine—if I were to organize the tour without divulging the details. I had already discussed our gala dinner at the Taillevent with Jean-Claude Vrinat and reserved a private dining room. To assure their being in perfect condition, Jean-Claude wanted to receive and lay down the wines six months ahead of time. I planned to visit all the wine regions and restaurants before the end of the year. Aubert and Pamela de Villaine invited me to Burgundy. (M. and Mme Menneveau, proprietors of La Rôtisserie du Chambertin, spent their August vacations on the Ile du Levant, a nudist island not far from the coast near Solliès. "Come to the island," they said, "we'll organize the menu there." That was the only menu for which I had to strip.) Aubert wanted me to meet his friend, Hubert de Montille, proprietor of a number of first growths in Volnay and Pommard (Champans and Taillepieds in Volnay, Rugiens and Pèzerolles in Pommard, among others), who had law offices in Dijon and spent weekends at the family home in Volnay. Hubert asked us to taste in his cellars Sunday morning and stay to lunch. He was sorry that we couldn't return to the cellars after lunch but he and his wife, Christiane, were expected in Alsace, a four-hour drive, that afternoon.

10 July 1975. (Me to James) "Had a fantastic dégustation at Hubert de Montille's, vintages going back to 1947 (Hubert's first vinification, under his father's tutelage), dozens of bottles, lasted from 11:00 a.m. until 1:30 a.m.... He had told Aubert that he could receive us for a couple of hours but that he and his wife were expected in the north of France for dinner. By 4:00 p.m. in the afternoon, he was having such a good time that he told Christiane she could go north if she liked but he was not budging (then uncorked another bottle). She was very upset and finally did take off—but returned half an hour later, saying she wouldn't be able to find her way alone. So another bottle was uncorked. Astounding wines, old-fashioned vinification, as much structure and muscle as

any Côte de Nuits with no loss of delicacy.... Philippe Cottin has offered Mouton-Rothschild '67 for the cheeses at l'Auberge de l'Ill; Yquem '67 offered for Taillevent meal."

Alice Waters arrived in Solliès. I had spoken to the Peyrauds of her and of Chez Panisse, where Domaine Tempier (then imported by Gerald Asher) was a favorite wine. Lulu invited us to dinner, but we were to taste in the cellars in the afternoon. After sampling all the new wines in the wood, we moved back through vintage after vintage. Alice and I danced (that is to say, we whirled with wild abandon—Alice assured me that we were dancing the tango) until we collapsed on the cellar floor. Alice fell in love with the Peyraud family. In her foreword to *Lulu's Provençal Table*, she wrote, "I felt as if I had walked into a Marcel Pagnol film come to life. Lucien and Lulu's warmhearted enthusiasm for life, their love for the pleasures of the table, their deep connection to the beautiful earth of the south of France—these were things I had seen in the movies. But this was for real. I felt immediately as if I had come home to a second family."

1 August 1975. (Me to James) "Simca, Jean and Michael James came yesterday to lunch, quite good I thought: grilled pepper salad, zucchini fans, braised lambs' shanks and garlic, potato-sorrel gratin (mandoline-sliced potatoes, unrinsed, and finely sliced onions, brought to a boil in less than enough salted water to cover, poured into a buttered gratin dish, shredded, butter-stewed sorrel mixed with cream, brought to a boil, spread over the surface, baked forty minutes), cheeses, peaches; Perrier-Jouët '66, St.-Véran '74, Beaune-Grèves '70, Corton-Bressandes '59, Filhot '67. Simca threw caution to the winds and suffered for it later." Simca and Michael were wild about the potato-sorrel gratin, had never tasted anything like it, they said—nor, I admitted, had I. (Michael, whom I had met in New York, was organizing cooking classes at Robert Mondavi's winery in Napa Valley, wanted me to teach; I declined.)

13 August 1975, Judy gave birth to a boy named Nathan.

The Gritti Palace Hotel in Venice organized tourist season "Gourmet Cooking Classes." Jim Beard and Carl were scheduled to teach during the last half of August, then planned to pass a week at Simca's before packing in all the three-star restaurants between the

Côte d'Azur and Paris (with Raymond Gatti as chauffeur)—Jim wanted me to join them, I couldn't face it. Simca, who didn't like Carl, begged me to spend the week at Bramafam. Impossible, John and Elfriede were visiting during the first week of September, but I promised to come for three days. Jim fell ill in Venice and had to return to New York, but Simca held me to my three-day promise. She wanted to create a cooking school and was building a new house on the property in which to teach and put up the students. Gossip had it that my classes were The Most Expensive; she pumped me mercilessly about prices. I knew nothing. "Could I charge $100 a day?" she asked. Not enough, I said. She hastily agreed. (A few days later I received from Julie a glossy brochure, jointly produced by Air France and a New York travel agent, proposing "Going Gourmet with Simone Beck," transportation from and to New York, 25 October-2 November, five days of classes, room and board at "Domaine de Bramafam," two days in Paris, hotel, bateau mouche, etc.: $898. Julie had scribbled across the bottom, "It is impossible for Simca to make money on this!!")

4 September 1975. (Me to James) "Five minutes after returning from Simca's yesterday afternoon—it was raining, the place was cold, gloomy, humid, I was undressing—two strangers drove up the hillside, said they had been given directions at a sordid, unclean-looking restaurant by a slovenly lady who was apparently a compatriot of mine—turned out to be the director of Cheval Blanc (Jacques Hébrard, whom I had never met) and a friend. Despite the reception they were given, he has accepted to receive our group at the château and to offer a case of 1964 magnums for the cheeses at Taillevent. (I was later offered Lafite-Rothschild 1961, on condition that it be placed on the cheese course at Taillevent—Cheval Blanc was moved to the duck.)...Went by the Lingousto later, found Finkenstaedts and Garins, everyone potted—Garin a grotesque, muddling caricature of a former self."

19 September 1975. (Me to James) "Returned yesterday from Champagne. Gérard Boyer will receive us on a Sunday, the restaurant's closing day, Veuve-Clicquot offering all the wines (to finish with magnums of 1947, disgorged a week earlier). Rémi

Krug inviting to lunch and offering magnums of '66 for Taillevent. Jean Dargent (Comité Interprofessionnel des Vins de Champagne-CIVC) offering different Champagnes for each of the other restaurant meals. Moët et Chandon, lunch, Claude Taittinger reception at his home in Reims and dinner at Comtes de Champagne vineyard, Laurent-Perrier, etc.... Your book jacket design is finished. (I had been working for a couple of years on a painting-illustration of W.B. Yeats's zodiacal-mystical system of intertwining gyres, as explained in *A Vision*, for the jacket of *The Rhizome and the Flower*.) See you in London 5 October."

We were together for a few days in London before James continued to Ireland for more research on his book. Valerie Eliot asked us to dinner at a plush, old-fashioned restaurant, The Empress ("Tom's favorite restaurant," she explained—it later became a private club), where we had a perfect meal of smoked Irish salmon, pinkly roast grouse and bread sauce, beautiful wines. Valerie was a favorite client and we were pampered. James invited Valerie, Eda, Sybille, a lady colleague from Northwestern and me to the Gavroche. The cuisine was not memorable, but the company was and we drank good wines. After dinner, Valerie asked us for drinks in Eliot's study, surveyed from above the mantel by the poet's portrait, where we passed several magical hours with photo albums recording Eliot's life from early childhood on—the five-year-old child bore a striking resemblance to the mature poet.

During the month of July, Julie had taught at the Gritti Palace and loved it. She wanted me to teach with her in July 1976. Natale Rusconi, the director, and I agreed.

28 October 1975. (Me to James) "Just returned from Vonnas 'Mère Blanc'—perfect meal, Michel Lemonnier drove, spent the night there, lunch the following day Chez Bocuse. Two more menus together for May next." 19 November (Me to James). "*CVF* game dinner in Madeleine Decure's memory: Lanson 1969, Domaine de Chevalier '66, Latour '64, Clos des Porrets '52, Château Gilette '54. After dinner had drinks with Claude Ricard (Domaine de Chevalier) and got things together for next spring's meal at Dubern—he will present a 1961 on the cheeses (Filhot '71, Malartic-Lagravière '66, Haut-Bailly '66 leading up to it)...."

29 November 1975. (Me to James) "Dumb old Canterbury complained that I was creating 'unexpected expenses.' I had told them in July that they should base the price of the Illhaeusern meal on that quoted by Bocuse—200 fr. including service; Jean-Pierre proposed a menu at 120 fr. plus service, which brings the total to 138 fr.—I told him that, since the price was so extraordinarily reasonable, the agency should foot the bill for printing our menus—and wrote the agency that they should count a total of 150 fr. per head (50 fr. less than they were planning on). I seethed with rage for a couple of days, then popped off a letter, explaining in detail, that I had saved them $13,000 worth of wine, invited meals, etc. and was, furthermore, giving them a year of my life and spending more than my own fee on the organization of the thing.... I was beginning to feel relieved at hearing nothing from Time-Life—thought that the project had fallen through—but received yesterday a letter enclosing a prospectus completely redone in accordance with the suggestions I had made last summer and a note from Dale Brown saying that he had been given the 'go-ahead' from American Time-Life to launch 'a test.' (Which means, apparently, that they mail out a million brochures in several languages to test the public response.) Dale is 'flying to Amsterdam Monday to talk about revamping it with colleagues there' and wants me to telephone him in London Tuesday. So now I am nervous again. I suppose I should be happy as it is something, unlike all my other projects, that promises to make me some money." My feelings about the Time-Life business, if no longer completely negative, remained equivocal. I applied for a telephone, which suggests (to me) that I wanted to make communications easier.

For a year or more, Dale and I played a cat and mouse game. After my initial letter of rejection, he wrote that he understood how I felt and of course they would find another consultant, but perhaps I could help him out, eventually, by spending a week in London to create test brochures. I began, despite myself, to dream of action photos of the preparation of real food with no artifice or maquillage, of white plates, sober traditional cooking vessels and unencumbered work surfaces, where no frivolous detail could distract the eye from the food and the hands that manipulated it.

I didn't know that because a tentative food series, with James Beard and John Clancy as consultants, had tested negatively a couple of years earlier in America, the American Time-Life Books editors, who were Dale's superiors, were opposed to a new food series, or that an aura of jealousy reigned between the American staff and the European staff. I came to understand that Dale's project was his private brainchild, he had to answer to his superiors in America but he wanted the American editors to know as little as possible about it and was determined, should he receive the go-ahead, not to let the Americans snatch the package.

Dale returned from Amsterdam with plenty of suggestions, wrote a long letter in which he enclosed the two-year-old Beard-Clancy prospectus, asking for criticism—it was awful. (Me to James) "Big colour photos of Jim and Clancy, both done up in multi-coloured vaudeville costumes, Jim in yellow and red striped shirt, shocking pink bow tie and blinding yellow leather waistcoat, Clancy in flaming red apron, striped red shirt, matching wide red tie with four-in-hand knot the size of two fists—two very unconvincing but very broad shit-eating grins—horrible photos of incorrectly carved meats, nasty, unimaginative foods on trashy dime-store glassware, etc.") I answered in eight pages, with no attempt to sugarcoat the pill, and, to James, I wrote, "I have successfully just burned another bridge behind me." Dale answered, "I want to give you an instant reaction to your letter (essay?). Marvelous. Now I will read it again, slowly, and ponder. But before I do, let me say that you've displayed your credentials to full effect, and as far as I'm concerned you're my top contender for that not-so-enviable position of overall consultant, when or if we do the series. Your intelligent response and the mastery of the subject give me plenty of ammunition to use on New York in the battle that will determine which group wins the series."

Christmas Day. (Me to James) "Have had quantities of visitors—one, whom I like very much, named Jeremiah Tower, chef at Chez Panisse in Berkeley—quite mad, he is—his gods are Escoffier, Ali Bab, Elizabeth David and me—but he is not so simple as all that and will certainly be a star in the food world before too many years have passed. A couple of young men who have cooking classes in Princeton came by (one, a recent Catholic convert, burst into tears when he thought I had spoken irreverently of the Virgin Mary)—had a letter of introduction to Julia and wanted me to accompany them to meet her, drove to Plascassier for the day. The Childs appear to be more bitter, more destructive and more irrationally anti-French than ever—"only Americans (guess who) understand French cooking." Very bitchy about Odette—seems she has not been enthusiastic about the new cooking school (La Varenne) in which Julia, Simca and Jim have all invested a pile of loot."

2 January 1976. (Me to James) "Received a telephone number in today's mail—no sign of telephone poles, wires or instrument.... Went by the Mouton sisters (local butchers) to pick up a scrap of meat, the old one said she had saved an oxtail for me, knew I liked it, so I got a bag of bones, marrow, hocks, etc., picked up a pile of chard—madness overtook me—have spent the afternoon preparing stocks, bonding, stuffing, tying tail to be braised tomorrow.... 4 January: oxtail delicious—idiotic preparing things like that for oneself alone."

14 February 1976. (Me to James) "Spent several days in Plascassier—don't know why I do it except that Simca keeps insisting. Am sick to death by now of Julia's sugarcoated barbed tongue. Most of the barbs are directed (although with careful indirection) at me. Too boring.... Simca was quite funny—just before I left, she sat me down, attacked head on, 'Now tell me Richard, very frankly, WHAT do you think of Julia's book?' 'Very frankly,' said I, 'it is without interest.' 'Yes,' she said, 'I think so too—and those cartoons; SUCH bad taste!' I said 'flied lice,' 'rooti-ti-tout,' and 'cookery bookery'"were also in questionable taste—too quackery-wackery. She didn't know what I was talking about but agreed...."

21 February 1976. (Me to Byron) "Telephone being installed.... Dale Brown wants to come here with a Time-Life promotion man from Amsterdam to 'spend a couple of days watching me cook and discussing plans for the series.'"

The Gritti Palace promotion brochure listed: Simone Beck & Michael James, May 30-June 12; Julia Child & Anne Willan, June 14-July 2; Julie Dannenbaum & Richard Olney, July 5-July

30. I received an outraged letter from Julia asking me to join in a boycott against the Gritti. (Me to James): "We all signed agreements that we would be guest stars treated to room and board and wine at table, excluding bar and laundry bills and that the cooks from the Gritti kitchens would double as our assistants. Simca has managed to get star billing for her assistant, Michael, so he is in free, but Anne Willan is shipping in another assistant from La Varenne, who will spend the entire month and assist Simca and Michael as well as her and Julia and Julia is bringing along Rosie Manell, who works with her in the States; both Simca and Julia are bringing their husbands. Soooo...they were told that the fee for husbands would be 25,000 lire per day and that extra assistants would be given a reduced rate and be put up in maids' rooms." I offered perfunctory sympathy but, as I had neither spouse nor assistants, thought it was none of my business.

Dale and the promotion man came to Solliès. I demonstrated the boned, stuffed, braised duck, an omelette and some simple sautés, we drank wonderful wines and Dale was ecstatic; he asked me to come to London for the week of 28 March-3 April to prepare photos for the test brochures.

8 April 1976. (Me to James) "London. Sybille had written that Eda had an 'ulcer' in her throat, was going into the hospital for a biopsy. They operated while I was there, it was diagnosed as cancer—Sybille won't pronounce the word (Eda 'trying to smoke as much as possible,' but it hurts her throat).... I was put up in Brown's Hotel, very nice, adored the ancient, bed-size bathtub.... Two days in conferences with promotion people from Amsterdam, Dale, myself and a staff of terrified youngsters (who eventually calmed down and will be very easy to work with if anything comes of the project—mostly English in their early twenties, ragged jeans and other more bizarre costumes, but serious, hard-working, no pretentions, generally anti-Time-Life in spirit—they just work in their funny little old house doing their thing, called Time-Life International Books.... I was surprised to find that I was by far the oldest person around—Dale, who is daddy to everyone, is years younger than I...four days spent in food photographers' studios. I kept everyone late, averaged 12 hours daily, cooked non-stop while

the kids from the staff asked non-stop questions with a tape recorder turning. (One of the photographers, Alan Duns, was wonderful to work with, several of the photos from that week's session were evenutually used for book covers in the series; we worked together for the next seven years.)...Sacha met me at the Nice airport, had dinner with him and his brother at La Réserve and returned to Solliès the next day."

The following weeks were ugly and sordid. 10 April. (Me to James) "Great stupid scene with Garin—he claims that Mme Clos-Jouve, whom I do not know (don't know her husband either—gastronomic journalist), reported that I had told her Garin used to be a great chef but that the Lingousto was a bad restaurant. Tears, anger, insults, Jesus—whatever I think, I would never say that to anyone less intimate than, for instance, you." I asked Odette for Clos-Jouve's address and wrote the lady: "I don't know you. You pretend, apparently, that I have been spreading tales about Garin: I do not traffic in gossip; if I have anything to say on the subject of Garin, I will address him and not strangers." I sent a copy of the letter to Garin. And then the shit began to fly. I received a very nasty letter from Clos-Jouve, copies of which he addressed to Garin, Odette and Michel Lemonnier. (Odette and Michel begged me to make up with him, said he was a viper, very vindictive and dangerous.) Garin rang up from the restaurant, in a state of shock, said it was all a mistake, he had only mentioned Mme Clos-Jouve to "protect Fink." Me to James: "I roughed Mary up rather badly on the phone to extract the truth from her—she sobbed it all out and has now, I understand, gone to bed sick...." In a nutshell, Finkenstaedt had been present at the Prunier Dodin-Bouffant meal two years earlier to which Julie and I had been invited. He reported to Mary that he had overheard me saying something negative about Garin ("nul," he thought). Ever since, whenever the Finkenstaedts and Mary were together, they had dwelt on this shocking betrayal and discussed endlessly whether they should remain silent about my infidelity, lest it wound the master, or whether, in the interest of justice, they should expose it. Justice won out.

20 April 1976. (Me to Finkenstaedt) "Garin has explained that you relate your gossip to an evening Chez Prunier two years

ago, at which time you claim to have wagged a warning finger at me à propos of things you pretend me to have said concerning Garin. That is all one big pile of shit. My memory of that evening is crystalline: My entire evening was spent discussing food, wine and, above all, wine temperatures; at one point, Jean Didier (director of the Kléber-Colombes gastronomic guide), who was seated beyond the lady to my left, and you, who were across the table from him, tried to bring me into a discussion concerning the merits of Garin. My response was a succinct two words: 'connais pas.' To anyone of intelligence, those two words could only be taken to mean, 'I prefer not to join the discussion.' Didier understood.... Personally, the whole lot of you disgust me—most particularly you with that tongue that has been flapping around in the pretended interest of exposing 'disloyalty' among friends—and Mary, who has accepted to sit around with you dabbling in a pot of festering puss for the last two years." A copy was sent to the Garins.

26 April 1976. (Me to James) "I believe that the break is definitive and am relieved—feel liberated. It has been too much, scene after scene over the years, mostly growing out of Mary's jealousy and deviousness. Garin rang up the other day to scream MERDE and broke my eardrums hanging up, then called Michel to tell him that he would see to it that my 'reputation' would be destroyed in France and that I would never again be received in gastronomic circles or in restaurants—and Michel called last night to read me a horrendous letter that Mary had written him (copies to Odette and Clos-Jouve)—must have been pages long as it took Michel at least ten minutes of rapid reading to get through it—all about how they have known for years that I am a traitor but, for human reasons have continued to see me and to constantly render me services...carries on at length about 'close friends and colleagues in Paris' (the Peyrots, obviously), who are au courant and who, although they hate me, have, for the Garins' sake, accepted to receive me at the restaurant...but will no longer do so. Oof."

The agency claimed they would make no money on the wine tour and could afford no personnel; I became tour courier, in charge of luggage, plane tickets, confirmations, buses, hotel registrations, tips and so forth. Time-Life wanted to be able to contact me at every moment; I prepared a 16-day timetable of hotel, restaurant and vineyard telephone numbers. I met the late plane from New York, settled everyone in an airport hotel, had a drink with José and Jeremiah and, the next morning, we were packed into a small propeller plane for Colmar. Our first visit was with Léon Beyer, in Eguisheim, where we tasted twenty-three wines, while Léon gave a running commentary and I translated. The following day, after morning vineyard visits, lunch at l'Auberge de l'Ill lasted all afternoon: the frog mousselines and the feuilleté de bécasse—woodcock, foie gras and truffles baked in puff pastry—were transcendental. From Strasbourg we flew to Bordeaux and, four days later, from Bordeaux to Lyon. For the rest of the tour—Beaujolais, Burgundy, Champagne, Paris—we traveled by bus with the same driver. James, Judy and Nathan (for whom the hotels provided babysitters) joined us in Reims.

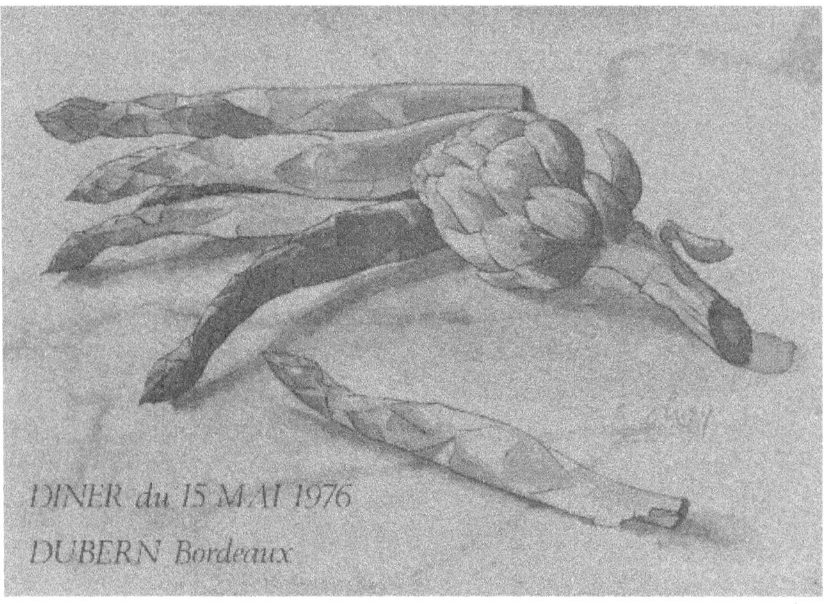

DUBERN, Bordeaux
Diner du 15 Mai 1976

à l'apéritif: Champagne Henriot brut 1970

§

Terrine de foie-gras frais
Château Filhot 1971

§

Petit ragoût de ris de veau Pierre Bugat
Château Malartic-Lagravière 1966

§

Roti de baron d'agneau médocain
Printanière de légumes
Chateau Haut-Bailly 1966

§

Fromages de France
Domaine de Chevalier 1961

§

Cocktail de sorbets et de fruits

§

Moka

The restaurateurs competed to produce the most Lucullean meals and, from feathery beds of black mould, the vignerons pulled bottles undisturbed for decades.

After delivering the group, exhausted but starry-eyed, to the airport for their return trip, I wrote Mr. Charniak, "Too many high points to describe the entire tour—everything was a high point. A glorious, liquourous 1937 caramel coloured Bouscaut blanc as apéritif before luncheon there, at Loudenne, Martin Bamford received us in the Salle des Vendangeurs, with legs of lamb, hung from twisted cords, slowly winding and unwinding before the fireplace blaze, at Monbousquet, a family poule-au-pot in the kitchen that finished with 1900 Grand Champagne; everyone adored the sarment-grilled steaks at our Haut-Brion breakfast;

members of the group were enthroned at special chapters of La Jurade de Saint-Emilion and La Commanderie du Bontemps des Graves et du Médoc. Our tasting at Charles Rousseau's finished with Clos de la Roche 1937 and Chambertin 1934 and, at the Domaine de la Romanée-Conti with Romanée-Conti 1959. The Veuve-Clicquot Champagnes that had been tasted for us and recently disgorged were spectacular (and, perhaps, despite so many glorious meals, Gérard Boyer's dinner was the purest of all); everyone was impressed by our receptions and meals at Krug and Moët & Chandon, one a family meal, the other in the grand tradition with liveried service. The food, the elegance and the service at Taillevent matched the wines—the Krug magnums of '66 are as great as a Champagne can be; I doubt if many members of the group had tasted a wine as sublime as the Lafite 1961—or as the Yquem 1967, both still in their infancy."

Le Taillevent, Paris
The Joys of Wine
Diner d'adieu du 27 Mai 1976

Ce diner est placé sous le patronage de la *Revue des Vins de France*
avec la collaboration de Monsieur Sam Aaron
Président de SHERRY-LEHMANN Inc.

La Menu a été conçu par
Richard Olney
et Réalisé par
CLAUDE DELIGNE

Consommé aux Ecrevisses en Gelée
Champagne Krug 1966 en Magnum

§

Cervelas de Fruits de Mer aux Pistaches
Beaune Clos des Mouches 1973 Domaine
Joseph Drouhin

§

Truffe sous pâte Taillevent
Château Haut-Batailley Pauillac 1971

§

Aiguillettes de Caneton au vin de Saint-Emilion
Château Cheval Blanc Saint-Emilion 1964 en Magnum

§

Fromages de France
Château Lafite-Rothschild Pauillac 1961

§

Crêpes Soufflées aux Amandes
Château d'Yquem Sauternes 1967

§

Café
Liqueurs de France

I cherish so many memories, perhaps meaningless to a reader, of lunches at Ducru-Beaucaillou, Figeac, with Robert Drouhin in Beaune and Jacques Seysses at Domaine Dujac, of dinner Chez Bocuse, where Lalou Bize joined us, and at Georges Blanc's, where we inaugurated a new dining room, dominated by a fireplace aglow, and were enchanted by the melodic conversation of nightingales through an open window. In Beaujolais, at Château Thivin, Mme Geoffray invited a folklorique group from Fleurie to dance before serving a rustic lunch of charcuterie and coq-au-vin; in Bouzeron, Aubert de Villaine prepared a tasting of 1973 Côte Chalonnaise wines before we sat down to a garden lunch, prepared by Pamela, their friend, Becky Wasserman, and Aubert's cellarmaster, Valentin, who grilled spatchcock "beggars' chicken" in memory of his native Portugal; Lalou Bize cooked dinner for us at her country home near Meursault, where Jean Troisgros joined us with terrines of thrush pâté. When we arrived at La Maison des Comtes de Champagne for dinner, a helicopter was spraying the vineyard, climbing high in the sky, then plunging so low, it seemed, to sweep the vines with spray, as to graze them. José wanted desperately to go up in the crazy machine; the gallant pilot complied. She debarked in high elation, clasped hands reaching for the sky and pumping the air like a victorious prizefighter. (I was reminded of Noah Greenberg, at the YMHA in New York, after the first performance of Pro Musica Antiqua.) Rémi Krug joined us at Taillevent; I invited Odette and Naomi Barry, who wrote a funny and very good article in the *Herald Tribune*, about the dinner and her companions at table, entitled: "Americans and the Great Wine Temperature Controversy."

James, Judy, Nathan and I collapsed in Solliès for the month of June, they drove me to Venice and returned to Solliès. The classes at the Gritti were straight demonstration and painless, but there was little excitement; they were conceived mainly as a distraction for rich American ladies who didn't know what to do with their time.

The Gritti, even more than most of Venice, seemed to float outside of time, peopled with relics of outmoded eras. A number of the guests, as far as I could tell, were distinguished year-round freeloaders—deposed royalty or retired celebrities. In the latter category, Valentina, a dress designer who had arrived in New York with La Revue Russe in 1922 and enthralled the American fashion world for three decades, often joined Julie and me of an afternoon at the Lido and later, for drinks, on the Gritti terrace. She was comfortable company but she dwelt with ghosts; the marvelous moments she had shared with Greta Garbo and Gaylord Hauser dominated her conversation. Each evening I ate alone overlooking the Grand Canal, pampered by the sommelier who wanted me to taste all the wines of Italy. After dinner, on the terrace of a nearby café, I found John Hohnsbeen, who was then curator of Peggy Guggenheim's art collection. John kept me laughing but I longed to be back on the hillside in Solliès.

James and family left before I arrived back in Solliès. Eda had spent a week with them and awaited me alone. She was thin, tired easily, eerily more beautiful than ever—Eda's face, however animated, was always a mask of makeup, applied meticulously each morning before facing the world anew. She was in good spirits, but her thoughts were with eternity and the mystery of life. We were studying the world in bowls of black coffee. Abandoning for a moment the disassociated memories that populated her conversation, she asked, "Do you believe in World Knowledge?" I said I supposed I did and did she? "Well of course, it's obvious," and the conversation, memories and chain-smoking continued. She stayed for a week, I accompanied her to the Marseille airport and put her on a plane for London. We knew that we would never see each other again.

10 August 1976. (Me to James) "Simca called the day after my return from Venice to check up on the month and find out if I would be returning—said no, she said she would, 'she owed it to Michael,' and that Anne Willan wanted very much to also, but that Julia would not return; Julia called an hour later—indignant she was because she had spent $1,500, including taxis, etc.—very cheap, I thought, as $1,000 of that went for Raymond Gatti's fancy Mercedes taxi from Plascassier to Venice and she had a husband and an extra assistant—to have got by on so little, she must have tipped very badly. Received letters from both José and Jeremiah,

who had heard from Jim Beard that poor Julia had spent $3,000—impossible to know if that was what she reported to Jim or if he thought it best to double the sum for the sake of decent gossip."

Jimmy Baldwin bought a house near Saint Paul-de-Vence in 1971, where Bernard established himself as self-appointed overseer, majordomo and general director of Jimmy's affairs and love life. Because I didn't want to see Bernard, I never visited, but Jimmy came a couple of times to Solliès and I sometimes saw him in Paris. He told me of Beauford's visits to Saint-Paul, his loss of memory, failure to recognize friends, being picked up by the police, not knowing who he was or where he lived...and, always, the menacing gangs who were out to kill him. In April, 1975, Beauford was committed to Sainte-Anne, a Paris hospital for the insane. In August 1976, Jimmy came to see me, distraught, tortured, miserable...."Le Canard Enchainé," an unprincipled satirical weekly—intellectual tabloid, mainly political, but avid for scandal—had published a vicious article in its Bastille Day issue, 14 July 1976, with no indication of the source: "...The legal guardian of his (Beauford Delaney's) worldly goods—all his paintings are under seal—is James Baldwin, the black writer, who divides his time between New York and his villa in Saint-Paul-de-Vence. Apparently, he does not want Beauford to be freed. Neither does he want Beauford's friends to be able to visit him. What is his game?" Jimmy never knew who had passed this story to an irresponsible journalist—someone, obviously, who was determined to harm him and who did not know Beauford well. (Beauford died at Sainte-Anne in March 1979.)

In Burgundy, Aubert and I had another marathon tasting in Hubert's cellars—all day long with a break for lunch. At day's end, Hubert picked up a few bottles and said, "Let's have dinner at the Vieux Moulin in Bouilland." The patron-chef (the restaurant has since changed hands) joined us and began to gossip about the misfortunes of his colleagues. "And," he said, "the worst tragedy of all is Georges Garin, the greatest chef in France, who was lured into a trap in the south of France by a dirty little American and destroyed ('attiré dans un guet-apens dans le midi par un sale petit Américain et détruit')." Aubert and Hubert were suddenly all ears and wanted to hear more—and more. The idiot was delighted to embroider but couldn't understand why they were transported by gales of laughter as he unveiled the tragic tale. I was less amused. I thought that, if this blabbermouth, who had never met Garin, was spinning wild fantasies, he had certainly heard similar tales from others and it was probably common gossip among all the soup mongers—les maîtres-queux—of France. I interrupted his hallucinations to introduce myself...as the dirty little American in question. He left the table in a rage, convinced that we had been amusing ourselves at his expense.

11 September 1976. (Me to James) "Funny and touching letter from Eda saying 'how healing and pleasuring it was to stay on your mountain: in the house, in the garden, in the pool. Sitting with James on the terrace, playing with or watching Nathan. (James, himself, said, more than once, that it was the most wonderful place in the world.)...visited Mme Gerfroit in Solliès-Pont (olive mill closed, she is now deaf and blind, terrible for her—Blanche says that, as a result, she is sometimes difficult to live with)...found beautiful cèpes and a pretty little mallard. Nicholas Malgieri, a young American pastry cook, arrives tomorrow—will have pinkly roast duck with cèpes sautés à la Bordelaise.... Bordelais trip with *CVF* as usual, Sept. 23-27."

26 September 1976. (Sybille to James—I didn't see this letter until years later) "Another malignancy. On 28th September Eda will go into St. Thomas's Hospital for a very serious major operation. I think she is very ill...I am not writing to Richard (on reflection). He is alone and easily upset...."

14 October 1976. (Me to James) "Had to go to Paris to meet Dale Brown. Michel came to dinner here with a friend—drank white Morey-St.-Denis '61, Brane-Cantenac '65 and Mouton '53. And spent the next day lunching and tasting at the Peyrauds before Michel put me on the plane for Paris, so I was already in training.... Dale to be transferred to U.S. after Christmas, someone else will take his place—what a mess.... Had dinner with Odette at the Cochon d'Or and, with Dale, at Pierre Traiteur (foie gras and navarin), at Jamin, where Besson is now chef (St.-Jacques à la nage with dill, partridge) and at Vivarois (hot oysters with spinach and

curry sauce, truffle and foie gras beignets, hot pheasant and foie gras galantine)—no bill, Claude more intense than ever.... Finally only today wrote to Eda because I didn't know how to write—and ended up writing mostly about myself and about reflexions in a bowl of black coffee. Which is about all of us."

26 October 1976. (Me to James) "Eda's funeral tomorrow. Have had Sacha repeatedly on telephone, worried about what kind of flowers to send—he arranged to send flowers for me also and it took quite a lot of discussion to avoid chrysanthymums ('Why?' he asked. 'Because they are mournful and symbolize death,' I said. 'But that is what it is,' he said. 'Yes, I know,' I said. 'Oh, I understand,' he said.) and to settle on roses, but I didn't want white...and so forth—so coloured roses have been ordered with the express wish that they be scented. In any case, I have before me a large bouquet—all the roses left in the garden—which I picked for Eda. And they are all scented.... A post card from Elizabeth D. in Spain—everything beautiful, had just finished a glorious lunch with almond and garlic gaspachio. So the spirits seem to have taken an upward turn. Mine are low...but all things pass.... *WWD (Woman's Wear Daily)*, Paris office called yesterday—a young lady and a photographer will come here to interview me, a notion cooked up by Doris Tobias, I assume. A Christmas interview the girl said, ideas about receiving, Christmas menus, table settings, décor, etc. I told her she might be surprised at my table settings and décor. She assumed that I was a 'decorator'—didn't know who I was but had been told that I had a 'beautiful kitchen.' I suggested that it would facilitate the interview if she were to pick up my books at Brentano's and glance through them before coming down...."

29 October 1976. (James to Byron) "...Something beautiful and gracious is gone, never to be known again.... Strange, but I think of you in particular, because I told Eda last summer that you much admired her writing and would like to meet her; she was greatly pleased, but also said that she yearned to meet you because of all she had heard (from Richard) about you. Now that can never happen. She was one of the loveliest people I have ever known—and one of the most sensitive and funniest...."

The Time-Life project had not been okayed by U.S. Time-Life, but Dale asked me to begin collecting recipes for the anthologies. I spent several days in Paris at the Bibliothèque Nationale going through 17th, 18th and 19th century cookbooks and had begun to pick through the books in my library. He wanted me to "keep track of the hours" so that Time-Life could reimburse me—told him I couldn't count hours, I was working daily until I collapsed from fatigue, bleary-eyed. Dale's letters to me, destined to be read by his superiors in the U.S., were masterpieces of digression and subversion. He was determined not to let me off the hook but, at the same time, wanted me to understand that, if the project were approved, a mere "consultant" had no real power—I would not be "in charge" of the series. My own ideas were distinctly different but I decided that, for the time being, it would be politic to keep them to myself.

I received a letter from a California wine merchant, Kermit Lynch (soon to move from Albany to Berkeley), whose friends, Lydie and Wayne Marshall, had suggested that I might be useful to him (he needed an interpreter). In *Adventures on the Wine Route* (1988), Kermit wrote: "His name, Richard Olney, meant nothing to me, but when I mentioned him to Alice Waters...her mouth dropped open. 'Richard Olney! Don't even think about it. Pack your bags and get on the plane.' I remember waking up at Richard's hillside home in Provence the morning after my arrival.... Before his kitchen fireplace, we warmed ourselves with coffee and toast while a mistral tried to raise the roof. By the time we were prepared to leave for Châteauneuf-du-Pape it was 11:30 a.m., and Richard suggested we have a bite of cheese in order to avoid an immediate stop at a restaurant. He brought out a platter of cheeses on a bed of autumn-coloured grape leaves and uncorked a 1969 red from nearby Bandol. It sounds simple, but I was astonished by the marriage of wine and cheese (mostly mild chèvres of various ages). And by that wildly delicious red wine! What is a Bandol, I wondered. And when it was sipped with those cheeses, it became one of the most fantastically delicious wines I had ever tasted. Two lessons in one simple snack: you find gold kicking around in the unlikeliest places (Bandol, for example), and something can be created by matching food with wine that surpasses either of them standing alone. After one week, Richard had introduced me to Hermitage, Cornas, Côte-Rôtie, Condrieu, Muscat de Beaumes-de-Venise, Côte de Brouilly, and Mercurey, in addition to Bandol. Moreover, he changed the way I tasted, judged and selected wine. He did not instruct me. I observed him matching wine to food and food to wine in restaurants, listened to his appreciations in the cellars as he searched for whatever distinguished each wine. He did not taste with a fixed idea of 'the perfect wine' in mind. He valued finesse, balance, personality and originality. If a wine had something to say, he listened…." (The Bandol was Domaine Tempier. Today, Kermit imports more than a third of their entire production.)

24 November 1976. (Me to James) "My wine merchant left this morning…expecting, day after tomorrow, John Rolfson's son, now grown up, teaching in Paris and, at the same time, studying cooking, because he wants to return to Maine, where his mother and sister now live, and open a French restaurant. Then Alice Waters arrives. Received a Time-Life brochure, made up in U.S. for American consumption, presenting a totally different program from anything we had conceived in London—ghastly photo of me that I had never seen—I am described as a 'marvelous maverick,' ugh." 30 November. (Me to James) "Eric Rolfson has come and gone—nice boy—reported that his father, who had built up a spectacular wine cellar, said, upon learning that he had leukemia and only a short time to live, 'If I had only known, I would have drunk many more of the wines'—and his palate was affected by the disease, so he asked his son to drink a number of them and describe them to him…. Left no money and life insurance papers were not in order so the cellar had to be sold off at a fraction of its value. (Winroth took care of that and I remember when it happened—quite funny, during a *CVF* Bordeaux tour, John's replacement as ABC bureau chief was there, so was Winroth, the replacement was saying indignantly what a mistake John's wife had made to contact some dumb journalist who was obviously going to take her for a ride, etc., Winroth spluttered, I giggled….)"

12 December. (Me to James) "Just returned (10 p.m.) from lunch at the Peyrauds—picked up this morning and returned chez moi now by Alice Waters—and, after a day of many wines, am feeling at loose ends—will soon cook me up a plate of spaghetti as we ate very well of course, but not very starchily—vioulets, oursins, mussels, Château Chalon '59, Condrieu '73, rosé Tempier '75 to start, huge grilled dorade with saffron-fish sabayon and rosé '74 to continue, civet de lièvre, rouge magnums '67, then '63, then '61 with the cheeses, then the marc that you know with coffee, then a magnum of '71 for tasting...."

31 December 1976. (Me to James) "Simca called, said I absolutely had to come to Plascassier during the holidays, I asked if the house was full, she said no one, so decided to go for a couple of days the week preceding Christmas—the house was full and, day after day, she insisted that I must stay just one more day—it was the day following Christmas that I finally returned home—profited to go through her cookbook library as well as Julia's and take notes for Time-Life anthologies—so many people who never stopped talking that I took to staying up 'til 4 a.m. and staying in bed until 11 a.m.... A lot of confusion with London but, as of yesterday, it is settled that I should go there Sunday 9 January and that the 10th and 11th will be devoted to conferences. Will see Kenneth Anger, who is in London making a film. Have written Sybille asking if she is free for dinner on the Sunday of my arrival. Dale leaves 13 January for the States. I will return here by way of Paris to assist at a *CVF* dinner, Monday 17 (mostly because Lafite '53 is being served with the cheeses)."

Six

1977-1982
Solliès-Toucas, London: *The Good Cook.*

1977. American Time-Life Books had moved its headquarters from New York to Alexandria, Virginia, a suburb of Washington, D.C. In London, I was told that the brochures throughout America and Europe had tested "two, point, something positive." Grim news, I imagined. "You don't understand," they said, "two percent means a huge success." Alexandria had promised to make a decision in the week to come. Dale's replacement, George Constable, had arrived, fresh from Alexandria, and announced that he had no faith in the new food series (brainwashed by Alexandria, I thought); by week's end, he had experienced a complete reversal—his enthusiasm and that of Kit van Tulleken, assistant European editor, equalled Dale's. London was on my side. The conferences were mainly useful in helping us get to know each other; until Alexandria made its decision (three weeks later, they said "go ahead"), our hands were tied. I had lunches and dinners with Kit, George, Dale, Lou Klein, the design consultant, and Pam Marke, director of photography, attended a going away party for Dale and his wife, Liet, and never stopped talking about food and wine.

Alexandria, of course, had checked up on my reputation with the American food constellation. George passed along the letters. One, in particular, remains with me, from a lady whose name was unfamiliar, who, I was told, had worked on the 1960s *Foods of the World* project. I was described as "flaky and untrustworthy." I checked "flaky" in Webster's and read, "Slang: slightly eccentric: screwy." My friends were worried about my possible involvement with Time-Life. José, who had written a volume for *Foods of the*

World, said, they're cheap, they pay badly, they don't respect writers' work. Jimmy Stern, who had worked for *Time Magazine* during the '40s, likened the Time-Life machine to a vast meat grinder into which the editors packed the finest talents available before turning the crank and reducing them to anonymous mince. (I told him the machine would clog if they tried to crank me through.) Sybille: "Very dangerous."

Elizabeth David asked me to lunch at her favorite Indian restaurant. She had just read *The Taste of America*, by Karen and John Hess, a scorching indictment of the "American Food Community," designated as "collaborationist food writers and gourmet frauds." Julia's Francophobia was highlighted: "French women don't know a damn thing about French cooking although they pretend they know everything" and, speaking of the French nation and La Nouvelle Cuisine, "They've finally got it through their thick heads that there are some people who don't want to be stuffed full of fat and truffles." Jim was roughed up a bit also. Elizabeth was treated with reverence. She had obviously had a good giggle reading the book and noted that the authors were right in all their judgments, "but it was really not very correct of them to publish it." (Me to James) "Had a terrible case of heartburn after eating Indian food with Elizabeth (I think it is her favorite restaurant because everyone hovers constantly saying Oh Mrs David this and Oh Mrs David that and she eats nothing at all so never gets heartburn.) but I suppose one can put up with a ball of fire in one's gut for the rare pleasure of spending an afternoon with such a glamorous and adorable creature.... Well the heartburn was so dreadful that I wondered if it would be possible to have dinner at the Ritz with Sybille. Left Elizabeth 5ish, had to go back to Time-Life, threw down a whisky, returned to Browns, swallowed some bicarbonate, went early to the Ritz bar to await Sybille and drank a couple of medicinal Fernt-brancas—finally, when she arrived, was able to swallow with pleasure some Bollinger 1969...lovely dining room, same bad food as Brown's Hotel, but cheaper—a 1957 Margaux, quite cheap, made up for everything. Sybille worries terribly about enjoying herself and I have to reassure her that Eda would approve.... While choosing the wines, in the presence of the sommelier, there was question of the '64 Ducru, outrageously cheap, which S. and I referred to as an old friend, sommelier insisted that, if we knew it and liked it, we should certainly take it as the Margaux might be a little hard—that settled things—the Margaux was, indeed, firmly constructed."

20 January 1977. (Me to Byron) "Stayed with Naomi Barry, cooked for her and friends the day before the *CVF* meal. She sent me the proof for a *Herald-Tribune* article entitled 'Olney's Budget-Minded Guinea Fowl,' the first line of which read, 'America's leading food authority, Richard Olney, on a brief stopover in Paris, accepted to prepare a meal.' (The *Trib* editors cut the first four words.) The next evening, leaving Naomi's flat, the minuterie went off, I missed a step in the dark stairwell and badly sprained an ankle, managed to get a taxi to Chez les Anges and suffered excruciating pain throughout the meal, which was organized to celebrate the publication of a book by Robert Courtine. The Rothschilds were present. Courtine ostentatiously ordered a bottle of red Rully in an ice bucket for himself, didn't deign to taste the Lafite 1953 (exquisite), the Rothschilds got up in the middle of the meal and left without excusing themselves—loony. Don't know how I managed to crawl back up the steps to Naomi's, couldn't get out of bed the next morning—or the next, was pampered, then got myself wheeled around to and from airplanes, feeling quite silly—also because of overheated London hotel room contracted bad cold so returned here hopping, hooping, hacking, sniveling, dripping—total mess, but the sort of mess that clears itself up quickly...."

George rang to say that London had received the "go-ahead," Alexandria was working on my contract and that Jerry Korn, chief Time-Life Books editor in Alexandria, would be in London mid-February to meet me. He asked me to recommend consultants from various countries, whose principal duties would be to suggest published recipes for the anthologies. I named Michel Lemonnier for France and Elizabeth for England. George told me he had finally managed to fix a lunch date with her—very complicated, he said, as everything had to be arranged through an agent. Elizabeth had neither agent nor secretary. Her telephone was unlisted. She answered in a disguised voice, asked who was calling and, if she chose to communicate, the "secretary's" voice would murmur, "I'll see if Mrs David is available," and she would return to the phone with her normal voice; if the correspondent was a journalist, Mrs David was never available and she would have her unlisted number changed. I assume that the troublesome "agent" was Elizabeth's close friend and editor at Penguin, Jill Norman. She found George to be "a very pleasant young man" but was wary of Time-Life and declined the consultantship; Jane Grigson accepted. Elizabeth continued, nonetheless, to be assiduously courted by Kit and George. Champagne and flowers were delivered to her door with cards signed "The Editors of Time-Life Books"; she wrongly suspected me of being instrumental.

Uneasy, mutual suspicion reigned between Alexandria and London; I had reason to believe that Alexandria considered me a dangerous, uncontrollable element and I intended, on my first meeting with Jerry Korn, to leave a good impression. Kit, Pam Marke, George and Lou Klein were present. We had hardly begun to speak when Lou interrupted with a raucous, nasal "Nyaaa..." and continued, "You don'know nothin' but fancy French cooking": he was quite pleased with his wit. Only George's restraining hand prevented me from doing Lou bodily harm (another year would pass before Jerry Korn eyed me with less than profound distrust).

My stay in London was extended. I was still living at Brown's Hotel and we still had no studio-kitchen in which to cook and photograph. A researcher, a designer and I hauled food and equipment in taxis to Alan Duns's studio to get the *Poultry* volume underway. Time-Life leased from the City of London an old five-storied house at 42 Conduit Street, a few steps from the Time-Life Building. The top floor was being prepared as an apartment (which would become my home-away-from-home for six years to come). The first floor, one flight up, was destined to be the kitchen-studio. For the photography studio, Kit's husband, Tony, designed a series of tables on wheels, one with a gas-burner top, another with a marble top for pastry, and one with changeable work-surface tops; the kitchen was fitted with a large, professional cookstove, a grill, refrigerators (but no coldroom) and shelves everywhere—I caught the workers in time to prevent ghastly formica work surfaces from being installed. Kit and Tony foraged in out-of-town antique shops to find solid old-fashioned wooden tables. I brought over heavy restaurant copperware with a friendly used look, old marble mortars, antique moulds and other articles, difficult to find in London. Except for the lack of a fireplace, it began to resemble my kitchen in Solliès; it was a comfortable place in which to work and everyone was seduced by the atmosphere. Organization took time. We had no anthology editor, no translators and I was dumb—I thought I had to do everything. I wasted time translating French recipes into English for the anthologies and I needed an assistant, but didn't know how to use him. I sent for Jeremiah, who had just left the kitchens at Chez Panisse. He was delighted. Each volume had its editor and designer, but different researchers were sent in for each day's shoot, on the Time-Life mince-machine theory that an anonymous assemblage of material produced the best overall result. In fact, it only discouraged researchers from taking their work seriously, since they would receive no credit for their efforts. That changed. After the first two titles, I had a single researcher for each volume, who identified with the subject and whose studio notes were abundant and precise.

It was May before Alexandria's legal sharks proposed the promised contract. I had not expected an honest contract; neither had I imagined that they could be so vulgar and contemptuous. It specified that I could be dismissed at any time but, if I attempted to resign, I would be subject to court proceedings; American Time-Life would "adapt" the series but publish a photo and credit me as consultant; I would receive a flat fee per volume.

I rang my friend, Suzanne Wolfe, an international lawyer in Geneva, and asked if she could help me out. She arranged a conference with Kit, George and Time-Life's British lawyers. Over dinner, I explained to Suzanne that I didn't care about the possibility of Time-Life's dismissing me, but that I must also be able to resign, if necessary, and that, if the volumes were adapted for the U.S., my photo would have to carry a caption to the effect that I was not responsible for any adaptations. The conference began at 9 the next morning. I was working in the studio. When I locked up at 6:30 p.m. and wandered across the way to George's office, it was empty; half an hour later, Suzanne, Kit and George arrived, good friends but visibly exhausted. Apparently, Suzanne had worn everyone down by repeating, all day long, "Why, I just don't understand.... This is not a contract...I've never seen anything like this." The new clauses read: "Either party hereto shall have the right to terminate this agreement by giving to the other party not less than four months notice to that effect..." and "In the event that Time-Life International (TLI) does not ask you to consult with respect to changes, TLI shall cause an appropriate legend to be published in the volume as revised which accurately reflects that you were a consultant with respect to the original volume but that the revisions were not made in consultation with you." I signed. Alexandria was especially upset about my refusing to take credit for revisions. Jerry Korn wrote that the best solution would be to remove my photo and my consultant credit from the American volumes. I thought not. I received a not very polite letter from another official, demanding that I sign a document stating that I waived the disclaimer of responsibility for adaptations. It went the way of all trash. (One of Alexandria's most mysterious "adaptations" was that of the braised lambs' tongues with lentil purée in the *Offal* volume. I had been pleased with our photo of the finished dish: the purée was beige, supple and buttery, the glazed tongues glossy with amber highlights. Alexandria retained the eight "how-to" shots but replaced the presentation photo with one displaying a mass of granular, dark brown purée bearing deep spoon marks to emphasize its stiffness; to either side, lined up like soldiers, are a dozen unglazed, dull brown pigs' tongues, three times the size of lambs' tongues. A thumb and a forefinger enter the picture frame pinching a bouquet of curly parsley.)

The Severn flows out to sea at Gloucester. It is one of the principal European rivers to receive each spring billions of elvers, the tiny, transparent eel fry which, ten years earlier, had ravished me in Madrid. Eels spend most of their long lives in fresh water. They are said to battle their way across the Atlantic at life's end to spawn and perish in the Sargasso sea, between the Antilles and the Florida coast. The spawn is said to tangle itself by the millions into large balls and roll along the sea floor for three years before rolling up the mouths of the Severn, the Gironde, the Loire and other rivers, where they are netted in May. I spent a weekend in Tibberton near Gloucester with Peter Price and several of his cineaste friends. He had a dense bucketful of tangled live elvers and asked me to prepare them in as many ways as possible. I sautéed them with persillade, tossed them in flour and deep-fried them, made elver omelettes...but, the way I had eaten them in Madrid was most exciting—immersed in cold olive oil with a crushed garlic clove and a cayenne pepper pod per person and gently warmed until they turned milky and opaque. I returned to London with a bucket of elvers and asked Elizabeth to dinner; she adored them. The remainder I packed alive, by handfuls, in small freezer bags and deep froze. I unfroze them by soaking them in cold water—they had to be rinsed, in any case, to remove fragments of seaweed. The result was perfect—I thought then that the elvers I had eaten in January in Madrid must have been treated in this way. (For six years to come, Peter furnished me each spring with a bucket of elvers.)

I was spending too much time in London, but we had to get the project moving. I told George and Kit that July and August, the hot months without rain, were out of the question, my garden had to be watered daily. By the end of May, I needed a breather, went home for a week but promised to return for the month of June. We created a supple schedule—except for July and August, I would spend half my time in London, half in Solliès, in two or three week stints. They would send researchers to work with me in Solliès and install a telecopier, the ancestor of today's fax, a refrigerator-size monstrosity, which honked, hooted and grumbled in the middle of the night as the London night staff sent 80 to 100 pages at a time of copy to be corrected and returned the following evening. In London, I was cooking daily in the studio and I organized weekend lunches and work sessions at the Conduit Street flat with Pam, researchers and designers to plan future volumes—there was no time to read copy.

Jeremiah arrived in Solliès. Julia rang to ask us to a "luncheon party." We stayed with Simca. Julia wanted to start with soupe de poissons, asked Jeremiah and me to go into Grasse to shop and said, "Of course, you will prepare lunch, Richard." While shopping, I began to feel sick, probably at the idea of being so mercilessly used. I told Julia I wasn't feeling well and couldn't possibly prepare lunch. She said, "Jeremiah will cook." One of the guests was Carl Sontheimer. Sybille, who was visiting Allanah Harper in La Roquette, was invited, I forget the others, Simca and Jean were not present and no place was set for Jeremiah. His fish soup was perfect and the rouille, mounted with olive oil and pounded garlic, basil, grilled, peeled and seeded red pepper and fresh breadcrumbs, was exquisite. But for Sybille and me, the guests assumed he was hired help.

Jeremiah returned to London with me. Julia wrote a long, incoherent letter to "Time-Life Books, Food Series, Rockefeller Center." They forwarded it to Alexandria and it was telecopied to George, who handed it to me—all about metric equivalents and the danger of using milliliters with dozens of examples cited.... "And as for translating tablespoons into grams or milliliters, that is cumbersome and silly. I bring this up because it is a matter I feel very strongly about indeed, and have worked on for years. If we start out on the wrong foot in this matter there will be hell to pay later.... If you have someone in charge of this situation, I would very much like to discuss it—I know that Richard Olney doesn't agree with me at all, but I feel he is less in touch with American problems than I, since he is living in France and England." The purpose of the letter appeared to be to build straw men to knock down. No one is crazy enough to translate tablespoons into grams or milliliters and Julia had no way of knowing whether I agreed with her or not. In fact, precise measures bore me—I prefer pinches, suspicions, splashes and handfuls. I showed the letter to Elizabeth, who sighed long and deeply, then murmured, "Poor old Julia.... Now she is Minister of Measures."

I followed the wine auctions, buying both for myself and the studio, often rather grand wines for myself and, for the studio, good but inexpensive wines. José was in London. She initiated the tradition of my inviting visiting food luminaries to studio lunches. On those occasions, I was careful to organize the work so that we finished photographing something impressive to serve as the main course for lunch. We were eight or ten at table—researcher, designer, home economist, photographer and assistant, guest or guests, dishwasher.... When we were shooting food I thought would appeal to Elizabeth, I invited her—everyone was in awe and she loved the young people, admired their enthusiasm, and enjoyed their adulation.

Nureyev and Fonteyn were dancing. Jeremiah and I attended most of the performances, with Sybille, José or Time-Life friends. Some of the choreography was eccentric but the curtain calls were glorious. Suzanne was often in London. She, Jeremiah and I had dinner at the Ritz, I ordered a thick lamb chop grilled medium-rare, it arrived grey throughout and I asked the waiter to return it to the kitchen. Instead, he called the maître d'hôtel, who sneered, "If you think you can do better, go to the kitchen and do it." I got up and started for the kitchen. He grabbed a hold of me and tried, unsuccessfully, to force me back into my chair, screaming, "SIT DOWN. Don't you know where you are? THIS IS THE RITZ!" When he realized the entire dining room was enchanted by the entertainment, he snatched the chop and headed for the kitchen. The next chop was less overdone, but I never returned to the Ritz.

George received another long letter from Julia, laying down the law of metric equivalents, but she was barking up the wrong tree; European editions of *The Good Cook* were not concerned with American measures. Jeremiah returned to California to open a restaurant (he was back in London early 1978). Buck Hanson had recommended a young man, Glen Recchia, as a possible assistant in Solliès. I was worried about leaving the property unattended half the time and thought it a good idea to have someone to drive me to and from airports. I returned to Solliès mid-July, bought a car and Glen arrived. (He stayed 'til the following April but didn't enjoy being left alone on the hillside.) José spent a week with us the first half of August. I invited six Peyrauds for dinner, decided to begin with a variation on the theme of Paul Haeberlin's frog mousselines, lined dariole moulds with saffron-flavoured fish mousseline, filled them with small-cut squid à l'Américaine, drained of most of their sauce, and poached the moulds in a bain marie. We had picked up a bag of tellines, fingernail-size bi-valves, which I opened over high heat with a splash of white wine, as for mussels marinières. José spent most of the afternoon removing them from their shells, their cooking liquid was joined to the squids' sauce, reduced, and the tellines were added at the last minute to accompany the mousselines. Everyone pronounced the dish to be sublime. I incorporated it into the Time-Life *Fish* volume (without the tellines—too rare on the market).

I had a fuzzy souvenir of receiving Marion Cunningham, who was then working on the revised *Fanny Farmer Cookbook*, and Jim Beard, who had asked me to prepare "pieds et paquets." I asked Marion if she could refresh my memory. She copied a page from her diary: "August 23, 1977. James Beard and I are staying at Simca's. At 11:00 a.m. we are off to Solliès-Toucas to visit Richard Olney for the day...Jean (Simca's husband) drove...Simca, Ailene Martin, James and me.... Arrived at Richard's 1:00...he and his new assistant, Glen, met us...such a wonderful setting, garden, grape arbor with grapes hanging, tables inviting set and waiting, covered with a cloth and clean, large napkins (like dish cloths). Richard is truly an artist he created a perfect setting of French country life...he served a saffron mousseline with braised leeks and mussels in a broth...the main dish was pieds et paquets, lambs feet and stomach (tripe) filled with lean bacon, parsley and herbs, this is cooked in a daube with mirepoix, wine, broth and barely simmered for 15 hours...small potatoes were boiled and served with it...it was satisfying and delicious.... A salad of mildly bitter greens with a light olive oil dressing was served in our 'pieds et paquets' bowls, Richard ladled a little broth on top and it was good.... Next a wicker tray of handsome cheeses on grape leaves...the finale, blanc manger (almond Bavarian cream)...a memorable lunch." I don't remember the saffron mousseline with leeks and mussels, but it must have been an experimental variation on the squid mousselines that José and I had prepared ten days earlier.

Ursula Beary, researcher for the *Fish* and *Shellfish* volume, spent ten days in Solliès. (Me to James) "After a week of talking, fish-cooking and constantly repeating myself, the researcher kept saying how much work we had got done, I pray that she is right but kept feeling that nothing was getting done.... Never stopped eating fish—worked our way through grilled seabass with fennel, raw sardines you know how, star gazies, red mullets in grape leaves, fish soup, petite friture, suppions en beignets, turban with sea urchin mousseline, and I forget what else. Saturday, she announced that she could not be expected to work solidly through the weekend, so we went to Avignon, had lunch at Hiély, then dinner at Michel's."

9 September 1977. Frances died. She was forty years old.

I hadn't forseen any problem about recipe rights for the anthologies. All recipes were credited, Time-Life was offering an honest fee and I assumed that most living authors would be pleased to be included. In the U.S., Judith Jones, cookbook editor at Knopf, categorically refused permission for all of her authors (Julia, Simca, Jim, amongst others). She wrote Time-Life she was very pleased to report that "without any coercion on my part, Marcella (Hazan) and other writers unassociated with Knopf have agreed that it is not in their interest to be anthologized by Time-Life." Evan Jones, Judith's husband, wrote to editors of other publishing firms, asking them not to cooperate with Time-Life. Simca was cross—she wanted to be included in the anthologies, but there was nothing I could do. George received from Julia another interminable dissertation on metrics, which continued, "On another front, I have talked to Judith Jones about the business of not wanting to release any of her authors' recipes for your series, and I must say I agree with her, since I am interested in selling my books—not yours!" Jim Beard recounted to whomever would listen that I was "furious" with Judith Jones. I thought these people were crazy. (Privately, I doubted if being included in an anthology had any effect at all on the sales of a book; the effect, in any case, could not be negative.) American Time-Life was upset. To me, no particular writer was of any importance—there were plenty of cookbooks, in and out of copyright, from around the world and across the centuries. I chose recipes from as many contemporary sources as possible simply to please the authors, but the anthologies bored me. My secret intention was to teach the reader how to cook without recipes.

In England, the problem was different. No one refused but, because Jill Norman was Elizabeth David's editor, no one was willing to accept until Jill had made a decision. George, Kit and I organized a lunch in the Time-Life dining room, a fancy penthouse affair, in which *Time* and *Fortune* editors usually received. Time-Life must have scoured all of England to discover Mr Page, the perfect British novel prototype of butler. I organized the menu with the chef and Mr Page. We drank Champagne, white Burgundy, two clarets and a Sauternes. We were fifteen at table—Jill and eight other cookery editors and permissions people from major publishers, Kit, George, three other Time-Life editors and myself. Jill figured that each volume's anthology should be limited to four recipes per author. That was settled and I was delighted—it was the formula which I had respected from the beginning, without making it written law. Later, Elizabeth said, "I don't know why Jill wanted to impose that ridiculous restriction. I'm willing to sell Time-Life as many recipes as they like."

In France, only Flammarion balked: they didn't refuse; they simply didn't answer letters. They owned the rights to Escoffier, Ali Bab, Paul Bocuse, André Guillot, Fernand Point and others. I wrote to Bocuse, Guillot and Mme Point, all answered that they would like to be included in the anthologies and wrote to Ghislaine Bavoillot, director of Flammarion's Art de Vivre department. We received no word from Mme Bavoillot. I had a few bottles of Lafite-Rothschild 1961 left over from the wine tour lying in Taillevent's cellar. With Jean-Claude Vrinat, Kit and I organized a dinner (placing the Lafite '61 on the cheeses) to which Mme Bavoillot, Charles-Henri Flammarion and his wife, Michel Lemonnier, and several editors from the Paris offices of Time-Life were invited. The meal was flawless and the atmosphere relaxed. After dinner, Ghislaine (Gisou) Bavoillot and I took a taxi to the Left Bank to have a drink at Lipp. She told me that "le Grand Patron" (Charles-Henri's father) hated Time-Life for its unfair competition policies. She cited specifically the *Foods of the World* series, which had been unsuccessful in France, being hawked at cut-rate prices on Paris street corners. But, she said, never mind, we'll cooperate. (I checked with Alexandria about unfair competition, they assured me that

Time-Life always operated at a high moral level, I asked about hawking books on Paris street corners, they said, oh, that only happened once.)

Time-Life Flammarion Dinner
Jeudi, 17 Novembre 1977, Le Taillevent, Paris

Consommé Aux Queues D'Ecrevisses
Champagne de Krug 1969 en Magnum
§
Cervelas de Fruits de mer
Bâtard-Montrachet Domaine Delagrange-Bachelet 1973
§
Caneton de Challans au Citron
Château Ducru-Beaucaillou Saint-Julien 1966
§
Fromages de nos Provinces
Château Lafite-Rothschild Pauillac 1961
§
Blanc-Manger
Château Filhot Sauternes 1928
§
Cafe

Pierre Escoffier, the great chef's grandson, a retired industrial engineer, lived between London and the Côte d'Azur. He asked me to come around to see him in London, told me he understood that Time-Life had tried to railroad Flammarion into working with them by pouring Lafite '61 down their throats; he was going to see to it that Escoffier was not included in the anthologies. (I wondered if he resented not having Lafite poured down his throat.) I assured him that Time-Life offered Lafite to no one, that the Lafite was mine and explained that there was a difference between "railroading" and diplomacy. He was constipated by nature; I gave up on Escoffier. (As a matter of principle, I used a few Escoffier recipes from turn-of-the-century magazines in Elizabeth's collection, which had never appeared in books—Pierre Escoffier complained, so I abstained.)

Alexandria was up in arms. For a chicken pie in the *Poultry* volume, we had shot a spread on pastry using pure butter. Julia Child had apparently decreed that pastry must not be made with pure butter and American flour. An interminable and ludicrous correspondence by telephone and telecopier ensued. Alex: "Julia says it is impossible to make good pastry with American flour and pure butter." RO: "Don't worry about it. I've been making perfect pastry with American flour and pure butter since I was a child." Alex: "But JULIA says...." RO: "I don't care what she says, it's all nonsense." Alex: "But JULIA can't be wrong...." RO: "The fact that she's a television star doesn't mean she knows how to cook." Alex: "Julia is very firm.... SHE says...." RO: "I refuse to add vegetable shortening to my pastry." Alex: "Julia blah blah blah blah." I received by air express a carton containing fifty pounds of American all-purpose flour with orders to "experiment." I was disgusted but decided that, at least, it was an excuse to organize a party and drink some good wines. I invited Kit and Tony, George and his wife, Evelyn, Pam and a half dozen other *Good Cook* editors to a Sunday lunch in the studio kitchen. The two wooden tables joined to neatly accommodate twelve people. (This first extracurricular studio meal was the inspiration for many subsequent dinners organized for visiting American editors or other Time-Life officials, who were always seduced by the atmosphere, as they milled around drinking Champagne, while I was still working with the photographer to wind up the day's shoot—which would be our main course.) We nibbled at puff pastry whorls, twists, straws and butterflies with the apéritif, opened the meal with something quiche-inspired, continued with a giant deep-dish goose pie (most of a roast goose was left-over from the Friday shoot), blanketed in egg-glazed rough puff, and finished with apple pie. The judgment was unanimous: all the pastries were wonderful; I heard no more from Alexandria on that score.

Anton Mosimann was chef of the Dorchester kitchens. He was enthusiastic about *The Good Cook* and anxious to be useful in any way possible. If I needed a kitchen utensil that was missing from the studio, I sent to the Dorchester for it. In season, Anton furnished both Time-Life and me with fresh truffles and several times organized lunches for Elizabeth, Kit, Jeremiah and me in his private office overlooking the kitchens.

November 1977. Alice Water's most cherished dream was to meet Elizabeth David (in *Romanée-Conti*, I mistakenly placed this meeting in 1979). I asked Elizabeth to lunch one Sunday, the day Alice was arriving in London from Piedmont. A little truffle lunch, I thought, the kind of simplicity that both Elizabeth and Alice adored. Earlier that week, I had made truffled and pistachioed poaching sausages in the studio; they needed only to be poached in a white wine court-bouillon and served, sliced, with new potatoes boiled in their skins, a ladle of court-bouillon poured over. To begin, creamy scrambled eggs with thickly-sliced black truffles. Alice arrived with fresh white truffles and tender young Parmesan, with which I replaced my cheese platter. We drank Bollinger 1973, Montrachet 1975 with the eggs, Hubert de Montille's Volnay Champans 1974 with the sausage, then chipped away at Parmesan and white truffles and sipped Domaine de la Romanée-Conti Grands Echézeaux 1953 until nightfall.

In a picture meeting, before we began shooting the *Breads* volume, Lou announced that he wanted a professional baker to demonstrate shaping loaves of bread and intended to direct this session, himself. I concurred. The young baker arrived, confident in his mission, his hands were grimy, the fingernails torn jagged and black. Lou was transformed into an irate Caesar: "Scrub those hands! Trim those nails and see to it no dirt remains beneath them!" He lectured on the preeminence of Time-Life Books and declared that those hands would appear in millions of books in many languages. Lou had misjudged his quarry. The boy exploded. "Bugger off!" said he, "I'm a working class lad, I am—ain't no bloody movie star!" With gentle persuasion, I coerced him into washing his hands and trimming his nails. Lou bowed out and the session went smoothly.

Lou's contributions to picture meetings often had little to do with design: "I don't want to see any more damn artichokes in these books! May Lou (his wife) hates artichokes." "Goddamnit, I'm sick of seeing onions stuck with three cloves! Why can't you stick 'em with two or four sometimes?"

3 December 1977. (Me to James) "Just returned from visiting Elizabeth in the hospital where her good spirits continue (she was in a car accident with her nephew)—have established a same time each Saturday visiting schedule. Am sending, under separate cover, her bread book (which Judith Jones has refused to publish in U.S.!)—told her it would do her broken wrist good to inscribe it.... Sybille has decided to spend a few weeks in the south and, as she is terrified of airplanes, I am flying to Nice with her, Glen will meet us and we will deliver her to Allanah before going on to Solliès. She has been having conversations with Eda thanks to a medium that Rosamund Lehmann has put her onto. Her attitude toward that sort of thing remains, as she puts it, intellectually detached (but, I think, emotionally quite involved).... Sybille to dinner tonight, having lunch tomorrow with Jill Norman, who wants to publish *Simple French Food*."

20 December 1977. (Me to James) "Back in Solliès since Saturday eve, having accompanied Sybille to Nice, quite a project. She surreptitiously crossed herself several times before our "takeoff," then we rolled around the airfield for a while before stopping for the captain to announce that the skies were so full that we might have to wait some time before the real takeoff (gasps and more crossing)—I hardly knew whether to keep pretending to read *France Soir* and not to notice or to offer aggressive physical comforting—then the hostess started the business over the loudspeaker about making certain seatbelts were tightly fastened and seatbacks straight—Sybille listened intently to both English and French and at each suggestion reached for the seatbelt buckle to make certain it was very tight and for the back of her seat to be sure it was very straight.... Finally, after roaring down the field and screeching straight into the air, we were well above the clouds when she untwisted her hands, turned to me without looking out of the window and asked breathlessly, are we in the air? I decided on the direct approach, hugged her tightly, said yes and that we would continue to climb but that everything would be all right, we would level out, air pressure differences might make our fountain pens

leak but that once we had a drink things would look up—she was scarlet with terror, embarrassment and pleasure all at once, then the stewardess announced that due to catering strikes there would be no bar service (lunch, yes, but only orangeade to drink)—depression and terror struck again—one had been depending on the booze—finally got glasses of ice (for the orangeade) and slipped duty-free whisky into them—Sybille had brought along sandwiches, determined not to eat any of the poisonous airline food and ended up eating both, the trip was short and suddenly, after the drama of landing, we were in Nice and the sky was blue.... Elizabeth left the hospital Friday (quite frightened of going home, I think, having only for the first time, with several nurses standing around, managed to get into and out of a bathtub herself the day before....) Alice called from San Francisco this morning...she was with Jeremiah who told me he had just had dinner with James Beard and that the one subject Jim refused to discuss or comment on was me and Time-Life...."

1978, New Year's day, Byron telephoned. (Me to Byron) "It was good to hear your voice, ever so briefly, Byron—and I hasten to write the letter that I owe you.... The trouble is that all the details of my life seem so boring that I hardly know what to write. The details you know mostly, if not from me, from James—half my time spent in London, half here. Here I do not relax much as there is so much to do in the way of holding together the cookbook series that cannot be done while in London (mostly reading for anthologies, reading copy, etc.) that the much needed exercise in the garden never seems to happen. In London, four days a week are spent in the kitchen-photography studios—a 9 to 7 formula, and then I drink a bit too much and flop into bed—the extra 'work' day is spent in the Time-Life offices conferring with editors, writers, researchers and designers (a good bit more enervating than cooking all day long), and weekends are spent mostly in the Time-Life offices, the only time it is possible to get much work done there as one is nearly alone. I do see Sybille and Elizabeth, hardly anyone else—my flat is in the same building (top floor) as the photo-cuisine studio, so, certain days, I never leave the building; the Time-Life building is less than half a block away and that is about all I see of London (though I admit that I don't mind all that much). I suppose the series will be quite good, mostly because I spend all my time fighting. I must say that I do not find my position there particularly glamorous, but a number of other people apparently do, so much so that Julia Child and Jim Beard are doing their best to fuck up the works. Of course, they will not succeed and, despite the bad taste left in one's mouth, one's life is simplified by 'knowing who one's friends are.' (...) My assistant (Glen) is a good boy, posessed of most of the old-fashioned virtues—serious, honest, hard-working, clean and neat; he unfortunately at the moment has his friend visiting and the friend is precisely the other side of the coin, never stops talking in a ghastly whining lisp, never says anything, the subject of that nothing being always himself, a good bit of it having to do either with his waistline or with how much he is adored by his Sicilian parents; his two favorite words, repeated ad nauseum, are 'shit' and 'garbage'; I have taken it so far in silence with clenched teeth and trust that I shall continue to do so, thereby avoiding a sordid explosion—only a few days left before returning to London."

11 January 1978. (Me to James) "Have spent the last week reading for *Fish* and *Shellfish* anthology—350 recipes chosen from some 200 books and, of course, 150 will have to be removed. Starting to read for *Soups*, but a bit wearily. Meanwhile, back in London, they are still trying to wind up the writing for *Poultry*.... My assistant has announced his intention to leave—mostly loneliness, I think, although he is no doubt piqued at my cool reception of his friend (who, thank God, has returned home now). Evelyn Gendel died a couple of weeks ago after a series of operations, said to be 'nothing to worry about,' but I suppose it was the malignancy whose name Sybille never pronounces. Sybille returning to London on the 15th."

5 April 1978. (Me to James) "Return to London 10 April, Glen leaving a few days later so house will be abandoned.... Arranging a private tour of the Bordelais to have Sybille enthroned in the Médoc and Graves Commanderie. Jeremiah and Sybille's friend, Lesley Marple, will be along also—we are staying mostly at La Réserve in Pessac, but one night will be spent at Château

Loudenne—the Fête de la Fleur banquet is at Ducru-Beaucaillou this year and Jean-Eugène Borie will present Sybille.... All of this to take place June 6 through 10.... I am told (by Jeremiah, who asks me to bring over goat cheeses and fresh fèves for the occasion) that a 'surprise' birthday dinner is being organized at Lesley's flat upon my arrival back in London, the other parties to the surprise being Sybille and Elizabeth...." Jeremiah cooked, Sybille offered me six bottles of Lafite 1962 and Elizabeth, who lived surrounded by exquisite, ancient, artisanal kitchen and tableware, arrived with an antique porcelain platter with a faded burnt orange rim, a thread of the same colour running inside the rim. I gasped at its beauty and have rarely received since without using that platter; when it is not in use, it is always in view.

We were shooting *Fish* and *Shellfish*. Before photographing the skinning of an eel, I had cracked its head against a table edge to knock it unconscious. Ursula insisted it had to be dead; I complied by piercing the brain with a small, sharply pointed knife, but that didn't arrest the muscular spasms. I had slit the skin beneath the head, hung the eel from a cord in front of the camera and was perched on a ladder beginning to remove the skin with pliers, while the eel's body and tail lashed violently, wrapping itself around my arm. Alan Duns and the designer, Doug Whitworth, were green, Ursula fled to the loo to be sick, and Kit entered the studio with Henry Grunwald, editor-in-chief of Time, Inc., who surveyed the scene calmly for some time, then burst out laughing. The shot was never used.

Correcting copy was frustrating. Often I slashed through words, sentences, paragraphs, scribbling "Get rid of Time-Lifese," "Stop being cute," "Keep it simple" and so forth. Unfortunately, the writers loved reading my comments, in particular one, Norman Kolpas, who wrote more and more outrageously for the pleasure of savouring my reactions. Alan Lothian, editor of the *Vegetables* volume, received a letter from Jane Grigson: "April 23. You may well say that it is none of my business, but I feel the writers are often adopting an unfortunate tone. Too many adjectives, too many unnecesary words, the occasional howler such as the Carpaccio piece that five minutes with a reputable book on Italian painting would have avoided. It seems to me that Time-Life, in employing Richard and the style of photography I have seen, want a series that will be right outside the glossy trash that fills shelves in bookshops at the moment. A series of the highest integrity. At least that is the impression I get from your and Richard's work. The style should match this shouldn't it? Journalese, Americanese (flavourful, flavoursome), advertising titles (Story of the Sizzle, Firing with Finesse), over-wordiness that has a kind of buttonholing—I could put a ruder word—tone, are going to put serious people off. With a clear, classic style, the sparing use of adjectives, these books could be used for a lifetime. There are too many false notes in the text at the moment. I haven't seen one false note in the photographs or the actual cookery. Of course at this point you may well tell me to mind my own business, but I'm getting very fond of the series and would hate it to be let down by the text." (To me, Jane wrote, "A thought—keep the writers off the word melding, as it means what you might think it means in various Scotch dialects. A moist melding in one title sounds splendidly indecent.") At the far end of a very long day, Alan and I had a drink, he showed me Jane's letter, which I photocopied, and suggested we have dinner around the corner at a chic "French" restaurant, La Mirabelle. It was the sort of institution where the manager, the maître d'hôtel and the staff sniff at all the clients, their noses highly trained to sniff out money. The food pretended to be haute cuisine but was all masked in the same sauce. I found a Château Margaux 1953 on the wine list, asked the sommelier to bring up a bottle at cellar temperature and decant it. The wine was blood temperature. I asked for an ice bucket, he refused, said it was not done and that their respectable clients would be shocked if LA MIRABELLE were to place a great red wine in an ice bucket. I insisted. It was put into a bucket, kept out of sight—and out of my reach—until it was too cold. I told him to take it out of the bucket—and so it went. I recounted our Mirabelle experience to Elizabeth, who had a good laugh. She said, "I went there recently with friends who had held a table in their name. When we arrived, the manager met us and said to me, 'We know who you are and we don't want you here!'"

4 June 1978. (Me to James) "John left yesterday after a 3-day visit.... I'm off Tuesday for Bordeaux—the program: WED, Haut-Brion in the morning, lunch at Bouscaut; THURS, lunch at Yquem; FRI, morning tastings at Latour and Mouton, lunch at Lafite, dinner at Loudennne, where we spend the night; SAT, Sybille enthroned ('Do you think I'm worthy of such an honour?' she asks), banquet at Ducru-Beaucaillou; SUN, lunch at Domaine de Chevalier; MON, London...."

I asked Jane and Geoffrey Grigson, Sybille and Jeremiah to dinner. It was a pleasant evening of lively conversation. I knew that Geoffrey was a well-known literary critic but knew nothing of his bents and tastes. He had a fixation on the Sitwell family, couldn't keep off the subject all evening long. I had never read Osbert or Sacheverell, but I knew Edith's poetry, enjoyed its whimsical, lilting cadence and couldn't understand how it was possible to hate with such intensity something so innocent. Jane wrote, "We both loved Sybille—thank you for giving us the chance to get to know her a little."

James was working with a French colleague, who was vacationing in southwest France. Mid-July, he flew from Bordeaux, Margaret from Washington and I from London, we met in Nice and continued to Solliès by rented car. They left in early August, Margaret with enough paintings and sketches to organize an exhibition of "Small French and Other Paintings," James in time to move from Durham and settle in Amherst, where he was to be visiting professor for the 1978-79 academic year.

18 August... Kit gave birth to identical twins, Alexander and Christopher.

I'd never met André Guillot, a cult figure in the professional French food world. Fragile health had forced him to close l'Auberge du Vieux Marley in 1972. He lived most of the year in Menton and taught cooking classes for a couple of weeks each summer in Grimaud, near Saint-Tropez. Michel knew him, Flammarion published him, Gisou was his editor and I remembered Charles-Henri Flammarion, who had taken his classes, speaking of him with reverence. I thought the easiest way to make his acquaintance would be to enroll in his classes. I wrote him. He answered that he couldn't accept me because I was of a different caliber from his other students but, if I would be his guest for a day, to observe the classes and join him for lunch, he would send a chauffeur around to pick be up. One of his students was Louis Vaudable, proprietor of Chez Maxim's, most were sons of restaurateurs, who all ready had experience in their fathers' kitchens; André Daguin's son was there, I don't remember the others. In 1978, André Guillot was seventy years old. He was formal, somewhat old-fashioned, in his speech, of a gentleness and sweetness that was almost eerie—some would say "saintly"; he was unconditionally worshipped by his students. The day I visited his classes, the first volume of *The Good Cook* was about to be published. I brought along my books in English and dedicated them to him (until then, he had only known my articles in *CVF*. Each time a new volume of *The Gook Cook* appeared, I received a dithyrambic letter from André—"Magisterial.... Imperishable.... The master encyclopedic work of the century.... The Bible for future generations.... Merveilleux Monsieur Olney, merveilleux ami...." The dictates of formality and the longing for intimacy created a certain tension in the letters; they always opened, "Cher Monsieur Olney, Très cher ami"; eventually he came to address me by my first name. We corresponded for fifteen years, but only saw each other once again: He asked if he could visit me, came with his wife, driven by a young acolyte, Guy Gedda, who had a restaurant in Bormes-les-Mimosas. He insisted that they come for tea—his health didn't permit him to eat the kind of food he loved and he couldn't drink wine. We were seated on the terrace, but André couldn't keep out of the kitchen; he was enchanted by everything, called his wife in to admire the fireplace, the professional cookstove, the work surfaces—he was especially in awe of the long table, poured in reinforced concrete and faced with antique tiles, which joins an ancient marble sink—"One never sees things like this anymore!" (In the years to follow, I was told several times by restaurateurs, who had studied with him or were great admirers, that they had expressed an interest in meeting me. André invariably responded, "Monsieur Olney is a very private person. I would not dare send you to him.")

4 September. (Me to James) "Jeremiah is leaving Sunday and has organized a lunch Saturday for Elizabeth and Alice Waters, who is arriving at week's end—he asked if I could return Friday."

Paul Grimes stopped in London on his way to an intense restaurant experience in France. He had written me a year earlier to introduce himself (twenty-years-old, in his junior year at Kenyon College, formulating a Watson Foundation grant proposal, "The Aesthetics and Function of Kitchen Design," for autumn 1978) and seek advice. The best I could do was to give him a list of people to contact—Odette, Simca and a number of restaurateur friends. (He did stages at Taillevent, Troisgros, Auberge de l'Ill, Georges Blanc, Bocuse, Léon de Lyon, Nandron, La Bonne Auberge, Roger Vergé, Le Cerf in Marlenheim...and eventually became Simca's assistant, returning each year; they always celebrated the end of the classes with a lunch at Solliès.)

Byron telephoned. Father had instructed him to "inform the rest of us that he may not be around much longer." He was approaching his 93rd birthday and, except for a honeymoon and the brief visit to Europe in 1970, had never been absent from the bank, when cancer struck. The decline was rapid. He wanted to say goodbye to all his children, but he didn't want us all there at once, hanging around, waiting for the end. Byron was back and forth every week between Rochester and Marathon; the rest of us visited in relays. I met James in Rochester mid-October and we drove to Marathon; John was there. Father was too weak to leave the house and so thin that it was painful for him to sit in his straight-back chair at the dining room table. A week later, when Margaret and Elizabeth arrived, he could no longer leave his bed. I returned to London. Father died on the first day of November.

George was being shipped back to Alexandria to become assistant managing editor to Jerry Korn (an ally amongst the cowboys, I thought), Kit was named European editor. George had become a great wine enthusiast; I was his mentor. Kit asked me to organize a winetasting, in George's honour, for the European Time-Life Books' staff. A dining room and several hundred wine glasses were rented. Sybille was the only outsider. The researchers, writers and editors on the other series, few of whom took wine seriously or drank anything but plonk, thought the *Good Cook* people were a bit snobbish and la-di-da. I chose Graves as my theme—Haut-Brion, Domaine de Chevalier, Malartic-Lagravière, Haut-Bailly and Smith-Haut-Lafite, each in the same three vintages, for purposes of comparison. As we tasted, I lectured non-stop for two hours. I have no idea what I said, but George, Kit and Sybille were ravished and a number of the infidels, who for two years had been eyeing me suspiciously in the corridors of Time-Life, assured me that it had been a rewarding experience and that they'd no idea wine was so complex and fascinating.

After Father's death, I established an annual routine of visiting family over the Christmas and New Year period to accompany Mother on trips from one brother or sister to another.

1979. Since 1961, James, Byron and I had corresponded, sometimes daily, often weekly. In 1979, neither James nor Byron received a single letter from me to brighten my memory today. We were always shooting two volumes, I was correcting copy on volumes all ready shot and planning future titles. I was told that I was driving myself and the staff too hard, but the deadlines were merciless—a new volume had to appear every two months. As far as I know, the staff never complained—I often kept the researcher, the designer and the photographer in the studio until 2 or 3 a.m. (While shooting *Snacks* and *Canapés*, the photographer, John Elliott, once managed to keep the studio open until 5 a.m. As I was locking up, he said, proudly, "Now, I've beat the record, haven't I?") I was told I should "delegate." I never stopped hearing that word; I delegated, but only what I wanted to.

In February, the first issue of *Petits Propos Culinaires* appeared. A few months earlier, I had explained to Alan Davidson my problems with Alexandria. They insisted the step-by-step photography in the front of the books illustrate precisely published recipes from the anthology; they wanted to pretend we were producing a teaching series, but they didn't want to teach. I refused. I regularly gave the researchers several anthology references to illustrate different aspects of a preparation, but much of what appeared in photos had no equivalent in published form; the purpose of the books, in my view, was to teach how to cook, not how to follow a recipe. Alan suggested that we launch a little magazine to publish "back-up" recipes, since all recipes in the anthology had to come from an already published source. Because of our rule that no more than four recipes per author could be included in each volume, I had to use pseudonyms. The first issue contained recipes signed Nathan d'Aulnay and Tante Ursule; Jeremiah also contributed. The fictive names continued to appear in future issues and other recipes were attributed to series researchers or writers.

Kit asked me to organize a dinner party in the studio for Jerry Korn and his wife, Bobby. The menu has disappeared but I remember placing two 1976 Nuits-Saint-Georges (Clos des Porrets and Les Saint-Georges, neighbouring vineyards, same proprietor) on the main course to illustrate the mysterious influence of terroir on a wine. I think it was at this dinner that Jerry Korn began to understand what I was about and to become less wary of me.

I organized a Sunday truffle lunch in the studio, to which I invited Elizabeth, Sybille, Pam Marke, Kit and Tony. There may have been others.... Sybille was very excited and asked if she could come early to help me prepare the truffles; it was a great sensuous experience for her, simply to handle them—she caressed each truffle before cutting into it.

Patrick Woodcock, who is now retired from his London medical practice, preferred to treat artists. Sybille and Elizabeth were his patients and friends. David Hockney was his patient; when painters were patients, he preferred paintings to fees. A young friend, Patrick Allman-Ward, known as Patrick II, who was passionate about wine, rented rooms from him and often shared his table. Patrick Woodcock was a decent cook but he thought of wine as a mere necessity for washing down food. He wanted to present his friend, David Hockney, to Sybille and me and organized a dinner party. Sybille offered the red wines and respectfully stood them on end in the cellar a couple of days in advance. I went by her flat in Old Church Street to pick her up and assisted as she meticulously decanted a bottle of Haut-Brion 1959 and a Cos d'Estournel 1962. Each of us cradled a decanter between our knees in the taxi to avoid ruffling the wines and, upon arriving, Sybille asked Patrick to place the decanters in a cool corner until the wines were served. David Hockney, had not arrived and we settled down to a glass of Champagne with Patrick II while Patrick Woodcock proudly displayed a number of drawings and paintings by Hockney, who showed up quite late. When asked what he would like to drink, he answered, monosyllabically, "plonk," whereupon his host raced out and snatched the decanter of Haut-Brion, Sybille rose in horror, as if levitated, and wailed, "OH NOooo, not that!" Patrick sheepishly returned it and came back with the Cos d'Estournel. It was hopeless. Sybille and David Hockney detested each other at sight and he, in a misguided attempt to shock her, monopolized the conversation with a history of his sexual escapades. He and Patrick Woodcock swilled the wines while Sybille, Patrick II and I pointedly swirled, sniffed, sucked air through them and chewed them, as the evening went from bad to worse. Without addressing Sybille, David offered to drive me home. Sybille said, "Young man, you will drive me home first!" He decided to drop her at the corner of Old Church Street and she murmured through clenched teeth, "You will drive me to my door." After I had seen Sybille to her door and returned to the car, David said, "Who the fuck is that old bitch?" I tried to explain that she was a very distinguished writer but he had definitively pigeonholed her with the stuffy middle classes.

James, Judy and Nathan were with me in Solliès. Simca asked us to spend a couple of days in Plascassier. She knew that I was tired of Julia's interfering nonsense and had decided to keep my distance, but she believed in keeping up appearances. The morning after we arrived, she said, "Julia wants to see you. She and Paul are going out to lunch, so she is expecting you at 11." I said, "I won't see her." Judy, petulant and defiant, as if I had insulted her, announced, "Well, I want to see Julia!" That was none of my business. She saw her.

I was alone. Didier came up the hillside in a state of shock. Garin was dead. Didier had just been released from military service; he and the Garins had spent the evening with friends in a country auberge, drunk too much, Garin had fallen down a flight of stairs, had a concussion, a doctor was called, an ambulance had raced him to the hospital, but he had never regained consciousness. Didier pleaded with me to come down with him, said that Mary needed me. We went down, Mary's sister, Charlotte, was there, Mary said, "Oh, hullo Richard." No mention was made of the ugly past; henceforth, whenever I was in Solliès, Mary arrived every day for lunch and spent the day. She said Garin wanted his ashes spread on my property, brought them up in a miniature, sealed coffin and deposited them, explaining that it was perfectly illegal, that, except for special dispensation to very distinguished persons, who wanted their ashes scattered in the sea, ashes or bodies had to be buried in consecrated ground in France; she had told Garin's relatives that his ashes were buried in a cemetery. She asked if her ashes could be scattered on my property also. Since I spent half my time in London, she said she would have to have the keys to my mailbox and the house—one couldn't let mail collect. I acceded to all her wishes. When I returned from London, I often found tables and chairs overturned and there was always a heavy depletion of booze. I made a point, finally, of leaving no whiskey in the house and it was the stock of 1900 cognac which began to disappear.

Garin had sold the Lingousto in 1977. In 1979, a young Burgundian, Alain Ryon, became owner and Mary became an habituée.

Mary went to the pound for a dog. The wretched beast with which she returned had been chosen, I think, to prevent its destruction, for it could never have found a home elsewhere. She didn't like the name, Fifi, so she rebaptised it "Fife" which, to an old dog's ears, sounded the same. It was mangy. It peed everywhere. It never barked, howled, growled or lay silent like other dogs; when it didn't whine, it whimpered. Fife's presence unnerved me. I begged Mary not to bring the creature to lunch but she paid no heed; where Mary went, Fife went. When she moved in during my absences in London, I returned to the stench of Fife's pee. She was going to spend a week with friends in Paris and thought it would be nice if I would keep Fife.... NO, I said, I could not share my life with that beast! She deposited it with Alain. (For nine years, until he sold the premises in Solliès and moved with the name, Le Lingousto, to more luxurious quarters near Cuers, Alain was Fife's keeper whenever Mary chose to visit for a day, a week or a month with friends in Aix, Paris or America.)

Late September 1979 marked the last of the annual *CVF* Bordeaux wine tours. Odette lost *CVF* and *RVF*—needed money, sold 51% of the shares in both revues to a magazine conglomerate with the verbal agreement that she would remain editor-director. They promptly put her out and resold the two reviews separately ("Marie-Claire" bought *CVF*, which is now one of many glossy, banal and boring food magazines; *RVF* has since passed through several hands.)

Odette and Michel, who were members of l'Académie Internationale du Vin, proposed me for membership. I was received in December at the Academy's annual symposium in Geneva, where I learned that Odette and Michel had proposed me several years earlier but that Robert Courtine (who had since resigned for reasons of health) opposed my candidature.

1980. John Ronsheim, composer and professor of music at Antioch College, had a dream: he wanted to create a department of gastronomy at Antioch, which would incorporate vineyard and restaurant field trips to Europe into the program of studies and, of course, confer diplomas. He came to see me, wondering if I would be interested in directing such a program. His enthusiasm was contagious, we shared several meals and venerable bottles and were invited to Domaine Tempier to taste in the cellars and to partake of one of Lulu's meals, but "returning to my roots" had no place in my plans. As it happened, some of John's colleagues were opposed to the concept of elevating such frivolous bodily essentials as food and wine to the Elysian Fields of Academia; the project collapsed, to be taken up by others, in whose hands it became the American Institute of Wine and Food (AIWF).

In London, I was without an assistant again, received a letter from Richard Sax, who had restaurant experience and was then an editor for a food and wine publication. I suggested to Kit that Time-Life bring him over.

4 February. (Me to James) "...had dinner with Sybille and Richard Ollard in a Chinese restauant, was sick for two days, vomiting and cramps, thanks to MSG no doubt—Sybille rang, I asked

if she had suffered, she had not, said, 'My dear I had no idea you were allergic—always thought it was simply snobbism not wanting to go to Chinese restaurants.' Recovered sufficiently to receive Elizabeth for lunch today (Sunday). She came bearing homemade bread, goat cheeses and two bottles of wine, one with pale pinkish-violet capsule peering above the wrappings, I said could it be a Vieux Château Certan and she said 'Oh Richard!' Out came the bottle of '64 along with the story of how you had offered it to her and she really thought that better palates than hers should be permitted to appreciate it—I got back at her by serving a Lafite '48 with the cheese. Richard Sax was with us and I think he enjoyed himself although he was very silent throughout—the usual 1 to 7 lunch with little to eat—smoked salmon, scrambled eggs with asparagus, salad, cheeses, pears in red wine; Bollinger '73, Chassagne-Montrachet '75, Lafite '48, Rieussec '75—he was no doubt bemused by our cavalier treatment of the food world. (E.D., speaking of M.F.K., 'Of course I am not supposed to say this (muffled laughter) but I do find her writing to be TOooo detestable.')"

A researcher was responsible for organizing a book with me, for taking notes in the studio that would be passed on to writers, and for researching material outside the realm of cooking itself. The researchers' names were lost amongst the list of editors, writers, coordinators—some forty in all—listed in the front of the books; their salaries reflected their presumed inferiority to writers. The researcher was my closest collaborator. The quality of the text depended on the researcher's notes. Nearly all the reserachers were loyal, intelligent, and so enthusiastic as to cooperate with me in my occasional subversive activities à propos of Alexandria. A new researcher was hired for *Preserving*, after the volume was organized but before we had begun shooting. She dressed in the style of 1940s artists' wives, with sandals, black stockings, long billowing, multi-coloured skirts and carried a sort of carpetbag. In a picture meeting to review the book's organization, she screamed, "No, we can't have rhubarb!" Kit asked why, she said, "It contains oxalic acid." I exclaimed, "Ox—Alic—Acid?!!" She fled to the ladies'. She often fled to the ladies' and some of the other girls followed to find out what was up. She didn't go to pee, she tipped up a bottle from

Lunch, Wednesday, May 16, 1979

Apéritif: Bollinger, R.D., 1964

English Asparagus, Vinaigrette

-.-

Château Loudenne Blanc, 1977

-.-

Spring Saddle of Lamb
Mangetouts
Jersey Potatoes

-.-

Château Léoville Lascases en Magnum, 1971

-.-

Salade Verte

-.-

English Cheeses

-.-

Château Lafite-Rothschild, 1962

-.-

English Strawberries

-.-

Château d'Arche Lafaurie, 1971

Time-Life Menu from Lunch for Naomi Barry, 1979.

her carpetbag whenever she was upset. She was replaced by Nora Carey, until then Gregory Usher's assistant at the La Varenne Cooking School in Paris, a wonderful researcher with a quiet, understated wit, who became a great friend.

Nora's next volume was *Offal* (titled *Variety Meats* in the U.S.), part of which was shot during one of my absences in Solliès. I thought things were going well; Richard Sax conscientiously telephoned at the beginning of each studio session to discuss the preparations being photographed that day. Our communication was less satisfactory than I had imagined, for a number of things had to be re-shot. He was queasy about offal and refused to shoot the lambs' heads, which I subsequently prepared in his presence. He later confided to Nora that he'd been made sick at lunch that day watching me relish an eye and had hastened to the toilet to throw up. (Faulty memory or mere nonsense? The eyes had been removed and discarded before the heads were split and baked.) Another time I walked, unexpected, into a studio landscape of asparagus—crates of raw asparagus, platters of cooked asparagus, the staff was busy peeling asparagus and the photographer had nothing to do. The home economist said, "I thought it was very odd when he ordered all that asparagus, but you told us when you're absent, he's the boss." Richard explained, "I'm writing my own cookbook! I was so fascinated by the asparagus with Maltese sauce in the *Sauces* book, I just had to experiment!" I locked up the studio for the day.

Nico Ladenis was said to be irascible and difficult. His restaurant, Chez Nico, was then in Battersea, a vaguely sinister quarter of London; one had to ring a bell to be permitted entry. Kit asked Ellen Galford, *The Good Cook* text editor, to invite me to dinner at Chez Nico. Because Ellen's usual habit of dress leaned toward ragged jeans and farmers' work shirts, Kit tactfully explained that it was the kind of restaurant for which one had to dress. Ellen dressed in spanking new jeans and bright yellow walking shoes. We rang, Dinah-Jane, Nico's wife, cracked the door, eyed us warily and asked if we were sure we were at the right place. Yes, we said, Time-Life had held a table. As we were led to it, Nico was peeking through the window of the kitchen door, he recognized me from photos and arrived at the table before we were seated to introduce himself. It was a memorable evening, Nico joined us after the service, we talked endlessly about food and became fast friends. (Seven years later, in the foreword to *My Gastronomy*, Nico's book of memories, culinary philosophy and recipes, I wrote, "My first visit to Chez Nico, in 1980, is joined in my cast of sublime memories to the transcendental meals of my first visit to Alexandre Dumaine's l'Hôtel de la Côte d'Or in Saulieu in 1954 and of that to Chez Garin in Paris, just after he opened in 1961.") I hastened to invite Elizabeth, who loved Nico and his food; he was in heaven.

Château Loudenne, in the Médoc, is a comfortable country house, a château only in the sense that every vineyard in the Bordelais is called a château. It was the property of the Gilbey family who, with other firms, formed a company, International Distillers and Vintners (IDV) in the 1960's (which changed hands in the early '70s). Martin Bamford, at the age of 27, became director of IDV France in 1968, made Loudenne his home and its table came to be known as the best in Médoc. The house staff consisted of a "châtelaine," or hostess, Sylvain, the butler, his wife, Josette, who was the cook, and Albert, the chauffeur, who seconded Sylvain at the table service. Martin was a maniac about the perfection of details, form and service, he was crazy about the table and very excited about *The Good Cook*, to which he subscribed in French, for Josette, and in English, for the Loudenne library and the pleasure of his guests, British and American members of the wine trade and wine journalists. Guests began to arrive on Monday, some for a day or two, others to pass the week. The house was cleared out on Saturday; the staff had Sundays off. Martin had invited his friends, Jean-Michel Cazes, proprietor of Château Lynch-Bages, and his wife, Théréza, to dinner on a Sunday, he had a baron (hindquarters and saddle) of milk lamb and asked me to stay over to help prepare it (Albert sacrificed his Sunday evening to serve). We found elongated deep purple eggplant and out-of-season tomatoes in the larder, rubbed the baron with olive oil, herbs and salt, placed it on a scattering of sliced onions and garlic, pressed eggplant and tomato fans over the entire surface, scattered over more onions and garlic, dribbled over olive oil, added a splash of white wine to the baking dish, baked and basted for an hour and a half.... The striped red and purple form of the baron was startlingly beautiful. I asked Albert to present it in its baking dish; he carved and served masterfully, with all the fans intact.

In early June, we shot the boned, stuffed suckling pig coated with chaud-froid sauce—creamy, gelatinous velouté, which sets when chilled. It was the looniest of my Time-Life projects, not because it presented any technical difficulty but because the studio kitchen was not equipped to chill a whole pig, whose preparation required that it be poached for eight hours, chilled overnight, then repeatedly chilled between each application of chaud-froid.

Day 1. Paul Levy, food editor for *The Observer*, arrived with a photographer and assisted at the boning. His article was entitled, "What, No Spare Pig, Mr. Olney?" (The researcher, Tim Fraser, was quoted as saying, "Richard is the only cook in the world who would dare to work under these conditions with only one beast.") The boned pig was rubbed with herbs and coarse salt and left overnight.

Day 2. The pig was rinsed, dried, stuffed, trussed, wrapped mummy-like in cheesecloth, fitted to a trivet in a large fish kettle and poached. The bathtub in the flat, four flights up, was filled with cracked ice. At 2 a.m., I removed the pig on its trivet, emptied the kettle, replaced the pig and installed the kettle in the bathtub.

Day 3. We removed the mummy-cloth and all traces of fat. Since only one shot of painting the pig with chaud-froid was necessary, we photographed mostly other preparations. By the end of the day, after repeated trips between the bathtub and the studio, the pig, still on its trivet, was thickly coated in chaud-froid, but the ice was melting. I ordered more ice to be delivered the next morning and arranged with the chef of the Time-Life Building's restaurant kitchen to leave his cold room unlocked so I could deliver the pig there that night and pick it up in the morning. John Elliott and I slipped the trivet onto a solid board and headed for the Time-Life Building. We were accosted in Conduit Street by a drunk who wanted to know what the bloody hell we were doing with a bleedin' pig in the street. He pursued us, snarling obscenities; I worried, lest he take a swing at the pig, but we arrived, the night watchman opened the door and shooed off the drunk.

Day 4. The pig was back in the bathtub. James, Judy and Nathan were in town. Jim Beard was in town. (The grapevine informed me that he regarded *The Good Cook* with acid bad humour, but he couldn't keep out of the studio when he was in London.) I invited Elizabeth, Jill Norman and Jim to assist at the carving and photography of the pig and to join us for lunch. Judy was off shopping, James and Nathan left the studio on an errand, James was carrying Nathan, looked left instead of right before crossing Conduit Street, a motorbike ran into them, Nathan went flying, received a gash over one eye, James picked him up and took a taxi to the nearest hospital. Witnesses of the accident had seen James and Nathan leaving 42 Conduit Street; the police invaded the studio, wanted to know who was related to the child who'd had an accident, questioned me for an hour and left. James and Nathan returned, Nathan with a few stitches but in good spirits. He was fascinated by the pig. After carving, studio work was finished for the day. The guests stayed late and three-quarters of the pig returned to the bathtub. James and I had invited Sybille, Valerie Eliot and Kathleen Raine to dinner at the flat. Valerie was the first to arrive, Nathan was very excited about the pig in the tub, immediately took her hand and tried to lead her to the bathroom, she said, "No, dear, I don't have to go," but he insisted; she was properly impressed. Nathan loved red wine and his father allowed him an occasional sip from his glass. Sybille said, "My dear, when I was your age (Nathan was five), I was not permitted to drink wine unless I was able to recognize its origin after tasting it."

The next day I cut the remaining pig into sections and distributed them amongst the staff; Pam Marke saved the head to share with her father, whom she saw every Sunday, and reported that it was a great success. James and Nathan left for a month in Greece, Judy had other plans.

Simca rang, said she hadn't visited London in years and wanted to spend the last week of June there doing a bit of tourism. I insisted she come by the studio; Kit and I organized a lunch in her honour in the Time-Life dining room on the day the studio was closed. Theoretically, the studio opened at 9 when the photographer and the staff arrived, but I always opened early to prepare food so as not to waste the photographer's time. Simca was always there at eight and never left until I locked up the studio; if it was at an honest hour, we had dinner in the flat, if I kept the staff late, we dined in the studio. She was rhapsodic about everything that was happening in the studio, like a little girl thrust into a fairy-tale. Her week of tourism never strayed from Conduit Street and the Time-Life Building.

I have no records, but I think that Margaret, Byron and family, John, James and Nathan all visited Solliès in the summer of 1980. Elizabeth began to visit a few years later. My summers always gather in family, languorous lunches and dinners with an array of great wines—it is vacation for all of us.

Didier's new friend, Roger Chastel, was proprietor of a dreamy country auberge, l'Aiguebrun, with beautiful gardens and rooms for a dozen guests, near Bonnieux, in the Lubéron, north of Aix-en-Provence. Didier was chef de cuisine. He and Roger often invited Mary and me to spend time there. Mary drove a funny little plastic jeep, called a Méary (I think), which was fine for local shopping but very hard on the behind for a three-hour trip.

August. José committed suicide. I was told that she had tied weights to her body and thrown herself into a pond near her country house in Massachusetts.... Ugly, incomprehensible, heartbreaking....

To compensate for my absence at the Christmas and New Year's season, Simca decided that henceforth, I should prepare the pièce de résistance for Jean's birthday dinner, 29 October. She had been fascinated, a few years earlier, by the boned duck and wanted to watch me bone fowl but, for the stuffing, she didn't want to hear any more of the "never mind, we'll see what we find in the larder and the garden" nonsense. She rang up to say, "I have two farm guinea fowl and plenty of foie gras and truffles for the forcemeat—what else do you need?" I ordered a chicken, bards of pork fat, pistachios and crème fraîche. I removed the chicken breasts, made a rich stock with the boned guinea fowl carcasses and the rest of the chicken, mounted a mousseline forcemeat with the pounded and

Richard Olney

Lunch for Simone Beck, Tuesday, June 25, 1980

*

à l'Apéritif: Champagne Krug, 1971

*

Terrine de Foie-gras aux Truffes Montrachet
Domaine Jacques Prieur, 1975

*

Châteaubriand, Sauce Béarnaise
Pommes Nouvelles de Jersey Persillées
Château Cantemerle, 1973

*

Salade Verte

*

Plateau de Fromages
Château Latour en Magnum, 1963

*

Soufflé au Grand Marnier
Chateau Suduiraut, 1971

..ooOoo..

Lunch for Simone Beck, Tuesday, June 25, 1980 in the Time-Life dining room..

sieved chicken breasts and cream and incorporated hulled, chopped pistachios, diced truffle and cubes of foie gras. The birds were stuffed, trussed, barded, wrapped tightly in muslin, poached in the stock for an hour and a half, unwrapped, bards and strings removed, and accompanied by their reduced, degreased poaching liquid. Cameras clicked before I carved and Simca was enchanted. (Another time, I prepared a chartreuse of partridge and cabbage, surrounded by pinkly-roasted, split young partridges—I suppose I prepared a half dozen such dinners.)

1981. 3 February: Kit took a few days' maternity leave. The new boy was named Jonathon.

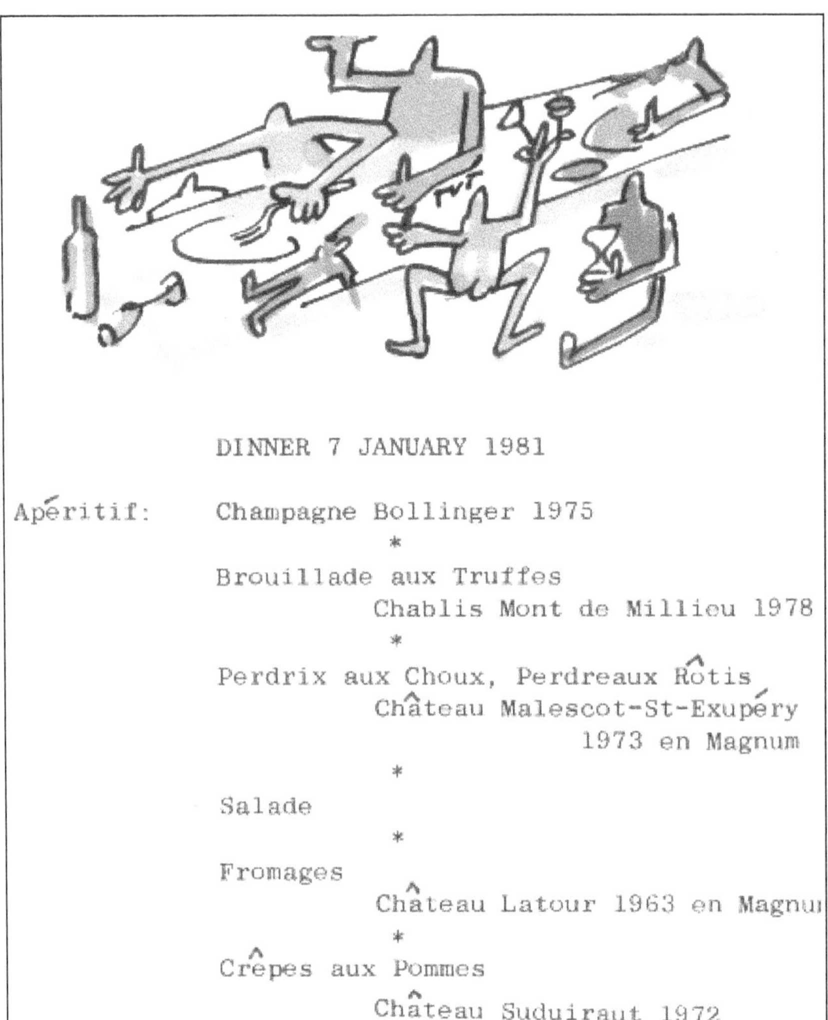

DINNER 7 JANUARY 1981

Apéritif: Champagne Bollinger 1975

*

Brouillade aux Truffes

Chablis Mont de Millieu 1978

*

Perdrix aux Choux, Perdreaux Rôtis

Château Malescot-St-Exupéry 1973 en Magnum

*

Salade

*

Fromages

Château Latour 1963 en Magnu

*

Crêpes aux Pommes

Château Suduiraut 1972

Studio Dinner, 7 January 1981.

Mary's landlord wanted to lodge his son and family in the house she was renting, but he offered her the smaller house from which the family was moving, better adapted to Mary's need's, surrounded by a typically Provençal terraced garden.

James's friend and colleague, Germaine Brée, a French literary scholar and Proustian authority, transplanted to the U.S. after her wartime adventures in the Resistance, had been invited to spend time at the Camargo Foundation in Cassis. I asked her to lunch. 7 March 1981. (Me to James) "Germaine Brée was to lunch today...settled on my usual menu (no imagination): scrambled eggs with truffles, vegetable ragoût before and with the grilled lamb chops, salad, cheeses (fruits were present but not eaten); Krug's new prestige bottle is lovely, Michel Niellon's 1978 Chevalier-Montrachet, a bit young but of great elegance, and a 1962 Mouton of green, chewy, leafy and fruity perfection. A very good, relaxing day of escape from Time-Life.... My latest problems have to do with the (Time-Life) Germans claiming that balls are illegal in Germany—so everyone wants to tear apart and destroy my beautiful *Offal* book to eliminate balls. I garnished the most spectacular number in the book (stuffed, braised and glazed honeycomb tripe) with little poached lambs' balls all around—everyone was so impressed that the same dish has been reshot for the cover (without balls)." I asked Sacha to find out if balls are really illegal in Germany—he didn't believe it possible. (In fact, the Hitler regime had apparently passed a law making it illegal to commercialize or to eat testicles; it was not my first problem with Germany—from the *Fish* and *Shellfish* volume, we had to discard a glorious shot of a couple of dozen crayfish, clinging to each other by their pincers, being spread dramatically into a hot sauté pan; the same regime had declared it illegal to represent pictorially the killing of animals.) Mary went to Paris with cat middle of last week.... Helen Avati called to say that Mary was in the hospital, worried that the Solliès landlord would backtrack if he knew she was hospitalized, so could I take care of having all her things moved into the house during her absence." (All of Mary's furniture had been in storage since she and Garin had moved to Solliès, the trunks in their house had never been unpacked.... I spent two weeks trying to get the

CHEZ · PANISSE RESTAURANT

For Lulu, Lucien, Jean-Marie & Richard

MENU

25 · JULY · 1981

Les Huîtres de «Pigeon Point»

Pigeon Point oysters on the half-shell

Mount Eden Vineyards Vin Mousseux

Escalope de saumon grillée, beurre de chardonnay

Charcoal-grilled salmon with a chardonnay butter

Stony Hill Chardonnay

Soupe de maïs et tomates jaunes

Corn and yellow tomato soup

Jambon de cochon de lait à la broche

Spit-roasted leg of suckling pig

Joseph Swan Zinfandel

Salade du jardin rouge et fromages

Red garden salad with cheeses

Ridge Zinfandel Langtry Road

Tarte aux prunes

Plum tart cooked in the brick oven

San Francisco, 25 July 1981, Alice organized a dinner at Chez Panisse "For Lulu, Lucien, Jean-Marie & Richard." Jean-Pierre Moullé, chef.

With Dick Graff, AIV reception at Chalone Vineyard, California, July 1981.

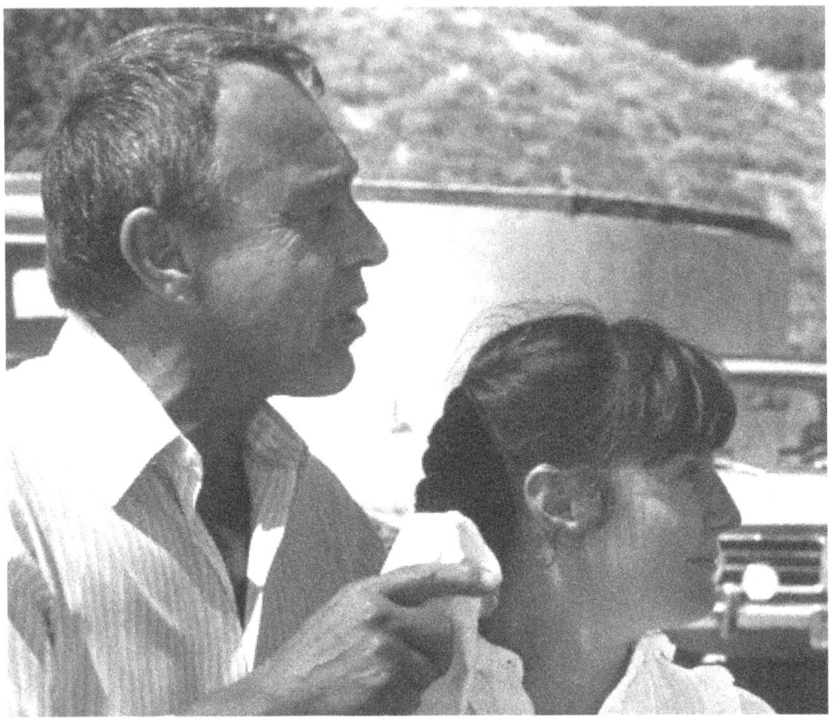

L'Académie International du Vin, California tour, with Alice Waters, Chalone Vineyard, July 1981.

new house in order, never knew why she had been hospitalized, but assumed that it was a combination of depression, excessive drinking and, perhaps, a disinclination to take charge of the moving, herself.)

I was biding my time. Alexandria didn't trust me and I knew that they didn't trust truffles. In *Poultry*, *Beef and Veal*, *Fish and Shellfish*, *Lamb*, there was not a trace of truffle. In *Vegetables*, a tiny box was devoted to the truffle, in *Eggs and Cheese*, not even a box, merely a suggestion that truffles could replace asparagus in scrambled eggs. In *Pork*, I slipped a truffle into a loin and into poaching sausages (visible in the photo but not mentioned in the text), in *Soups*, a few matchsticks of truffle garnished one of the consommés. When Alexandria realized that, despite their predictions, *The Good Cook* was a success, they let me out of the torture chamber and began begging for more volumes. (I had promised 15, with the understanding that I could resign with four months' notice if things didn't go my way; they wanted 17, then 20, then 24, then 26.... I cut off at 27.) The cover of *Terrines, Pâtés & Galantines* was a generously truffled pâté in aspic, enrobed in puff pastry; there were several other preparations using truffles, one of which, a foie gras terrine, was used as a full-page chapter opener. I wondered when I would receive the order from Alexandria to cool it on the truffles. It came while we were shooting *Offal*: "No More Truffles!" The next day, we shot braised sweetbreads smothered in slices of coal-black truffle, glistening beneath a film of demi-glace; it was so beautiful, it had to be a chapter opener. A week or so later, an ox tongue, studded with spikes of truffle, marinated, stuffed into a gut and braised with aromatics and veal stock, also became a chapter opener. I have never tasted anything so magical in a restaurant.

Alexandria wanted a volume called *Beverages*. I wanted a wine volume. They said I could include wine in *Beverages*; I said, "No, I could not." And, furthermore, I couldn't stand the idea of wasting my time shooting coffee, tea, cocoa, fruit juice and cocktails; I got my wine book and delegated *Beverages.* (George wanted a wine series, which never came to pass.)

In late July 1981, the Académie Internationale du Vin organized a tour of Northern California and Oregon vineyards. Lulu, Lucien and and Jean-Marie Peyraud (and I) were members of the group. The day of our arrival in San Francisco, 25 July, Alice organized a dinner at Chez Panisse "For Lulu, Lucien, Jean-Marie & Richard." Jean-Pierre Moullé was chef and many of the guests had been visitors to Domaine Tempier and to Solliès in previous years. The following day, Dick Graff received the Academy at Chalone Vineyard. The chefs were Alice, Mark Miller and Deborah Welch, who had also apprenticed at Chez Panisse and, at that time had her own restaurant in San Francisco. All the Academy members retain sentimental memories of that day and of the meal. Jeremiah was present both at Chez Panisse and Chalone. I remember a lovely, simple lunch, constructed around barbecued beef tenderloin, at Rutherford Hill Winery, a grand fancy affair at Domaine Chandon and a drole buffet luncheon at Sterling, where we were received by Coca Cola: from afar, the huge glass bowls that constituted the principal nourishment seemed to contain an appetizing salad of chunks of cervelas sausage in mayonnaise; on closer inspection, it turned out to be quartered, unpeeled red-skinned potatoes in miracle whip. The popular American sport of eating potato skins is incomprehensible to the French; I glanced around at the other tables and was delighted to see everyone assiduously scraping off the miricle whip and peeling the potato wedges.

In October, I organized a tour of the Bordelais with Krystyna Mayer, researcher for the *Wine* volume, and a French photographer, who had often worked for Time-Life. In the Médoc, we stayed at Château Loudenne, where we photographed in the cellars and the vineyard, had lunch at Lafite with Martin, photographed at Latour, Mouton, Palmer, Vieux Château Certan and Yquem, visited Figeac, Cheval Blanc, Malartic-Lagravière, Haut-Brion and had the traditional Sunday lunch of oysters, roast leg of lamb, white and red Domaine de Chevalier with Claude and Monic Ricard. The photos were important but, for me, the essential thing was to immerse Krystyna in wine; the researcher's passion and involvement was primordial to the success of a book.

Kit was scheduled to pass the first six months of 1982 in Alexandria. The staff and I organized a studio dinner for her, 12 December 1981. I dug into my collection of auction-acquired wines to make it as special as possible:

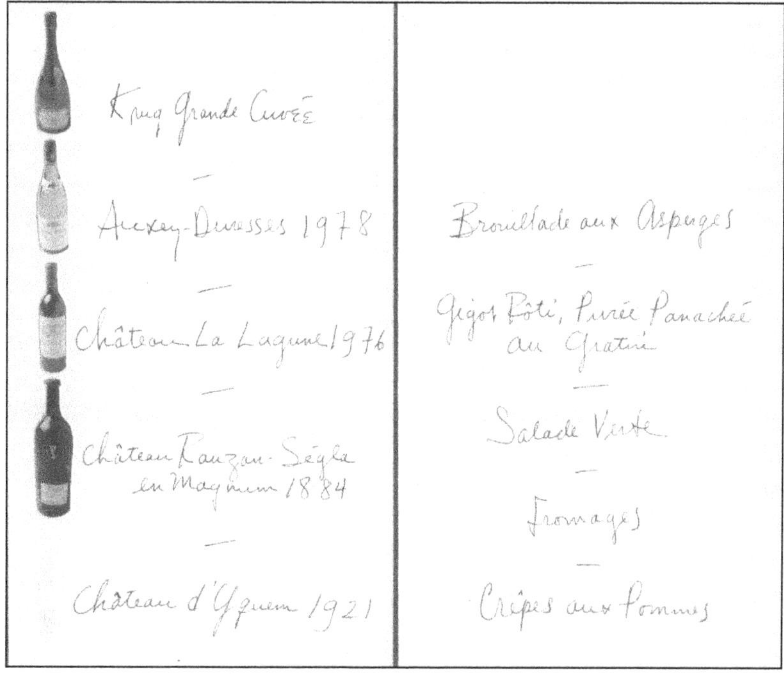

Kit's Studio Dinner, 12 December 1981.

1982. I was winding up my annual family visit with Margaret in Chevy Chase. Kit was established in Alexandria and asked us to join her, Henry Grunwald and several Alexandria editors for dinner at l'Auberge Chez François, in the Virginia countryside. For someone in his position of power, Henry Grunwald seemed to me very human and understated, sympathetic and without pretention. We had a good time.

John Porter had been sent from Alexandria to London to replace Kit during her six-month absence. I was working on the *Wine* volume. It was not possible to transmit all the technical aspects of viticulture and vinification or my personal and sometimes complex reasons for matching wine to food to the writers, whose knowledge of wine was superficial. Except for *The Guide to the World's Wines*, (for which we enlisted Sybille's help), I wrote most of the text. I tried to keep it simple and to avoid technical terminology. One of the aspects of vinification, which must be explained, is malolactic fermentation, a secondary fermentation, following but unrelated to the alcoholic fermentation, in which malic acid is broken down into lactic acid and carbon dioxide, at the same time lowering the wine's acid content and stabilizing it. John called me into the office. He said, "I just HATE that word, 'malolactic.' You've got to get rid of it!" I did my best to tone it down, but I couldn't get rid of it. Ellen was after me, also, to "simplify"—she wanted to get rid of "enzymes."

Nika Hazelton was in London. I asked her to assist at photography and to stay for a studio lunch. She said, "But these are your books—you're doing everything. They're a huge success in the U.S. and Time-Life America doesn't even mention your name in their magazine and TV promotion." I said, "I know." Nika wrote a furious letter to "Carl G. Jaeger, President, Time-Life Books" (I didn't even know there was a president—I thought that Jerry Korn was the boss) and sent me a copy. I decided, foolishly, to follow up. I wrote Mr. Jaeger, "Copies of promotional literature, carrying your signature, have been sent me by a number of friends—most recently Nika Hazelton—who are, justifiably, outraged that the only credit given is to "an international panel of leading food experts," all named, none of whom, in fact, have been of the least use to me in the creation of these books. My name is not mentioned. Everyone at Time-Life and most of the people in the food world are perfectly aware that, not only is the concept of the series mine, but that I have personally organized each book in every detail with the researcher and the designer, I have personally prepared most of the food for the photography and have remained in permanent contact with the kitchens when someone was replacing me, I have personally chosen all of the anthology selections—as many as possible from the material sent in by consultants from other countries, but more than half of the selections come either from my personal library or from my personal research at the Bibliothèque Nationale; I have checked all of the styling of the recipes, often being obliged to restyle them, and have corrected all the copy, often several times over. I have assisted at as many picture meetings as time permitted and have conferred with the designers through all stages of the layouts to be certain that every detail is correct at each step in a volume's development.... Time-Life's apparent willingness to ignore my association with these books is, commercially, a tactical error and morally irresponsible."

In response, I received a disgusting, slimy letter from a person, who signed, Paul R. Stewart, vice president, director of marketing: "On behalf of Carl Jaeger, please allow me to apologize for not including your name in proper recognition of your single contributions to *The Good Cook* series. As Jerry Korn has said, 'Mr. Olney made this series one of the greatest ever published....' Oddly enough, we are willing and happy to credit you properly. I don't know if you remember, but we did indeed submit a special letter for your signature. Undoubtedly, our proposed letter was not to your liking, since you objected most strenuously to it. When you objected, we lost the opportunity to include you in our launch. We were more than a little nervous about upsetting you.... We are most interested in using both your name and your likeness in our promotions. I might also add that the United States audiences are well pleased with *The Good Cook*.... I am and have been directly responsible for all of *The Good Cook* sales and promotions and I am looking forward to better promotions using both your name and likeness in association with *The Good Cook*." I regretted having written my letter and did not answer this trashy attempt at blackmail.

Jerry Korn was leaving Time-Life. George became managing editor. Jerry made a good-bye trip to London. He and Lou came to dinner in the Conduit Street flat. I was showered with compliments and we finished with a bottle of Yquem 1913. Lou was shipped to Alexandria.

Liz Timothy bore the title of series coordinator. Part of her job was to keep me happy. Whenever I was not working late in the studio or otherwise occupied, she invited me to dinner, often to The Ark, in Kensington, or to an Italian restaurant in Soho. We hatched the idea of her driving me from London to Solliès as a means of transporting some of the wines that I had been collecting at auctions. We stopped overnight in Reims, ate at Gérard Boyer's and spent the next night at Marc Meneau's l'Espérance, near Vézelay.

28 June. Pamela de Villaine's mother had rented a house in Saint-Rémy-de-Provence. I invited her, Pam and Aubert to dinner:

Apéritif: Champagne Krug 1973
§
Brouillade aux Truffes
Chevalier-Montrachet (Niéllon) 1978
§
Gigot aux Aulx, Sauce au Vin Rouge
Gratin Dauphinois
Domaine Tempier en Magnum 1964
§
Fromages
Château Rauzan-Ségla 1900
§
Monbazillac 1874

That was the night Aubert fell into the rose bushes with several glasses of Champagne. The Rauzan-Ségla was part of a lot containing Léoville-Poyferré and Rauzan-Ségla, 1899 and 1900, both great vintages, which had never left the Lawton cellars in Bordeaux until being sent to Christies. The Monbazillac was sweet; it had never been a great wine but it was still alive.

In July, Odette was operated on for cancer.

James, Judy and Nathan went to Greece in early summer, then came to Solliès. Jill Norman, her husband, Paul Breman, and their two girls, Sasha and Elinor, who was Nathan's age, rented an apartment, separated from the main house, at Domaine Tempier. They, the Peyrauds and the Olneys were back and forth almost daily between Tempier and Solliès. The girls and Nathan adored the swimming pool. Lulu cooked; I cooked. Those were my truffle years; out of season, the deep freeze was always well stocked. 27 July, I invited Jill, Paul, the girls and six Peyrauds to dinner. Except for the wines, the menu was the same that I had served a month earlier to the de Villaines. We drank Krug '75, Ducru-

Beaucaillou '76, Parempuyre '29, Léoville-Poyferré '18 Rauzan-Ségla 1900 and Rayne-Vigneau 1921.

27 September 1982. "Les Amis de Curnonsky" organized a banquet at Le Coq Hardy, in Bougival, outside of Paris. Nora was in Paris. I asked her to accompany me. Odette slipped up behind me and covered my eyes with her hands; I knew immediately who it was. She was sparkling with joy and high spirits; she looked wonderful. Nora said, "She really adores you, doesn't she?" Odette died a month later. She was 56 years old.

During the grape harvest, I received a phone call from Luce Naval, Château Loudenne's "châtelaine." Sylvain had brought Martin's breakfast up to his room and found him dead in bed. He was 41 years old. He was buried in the local cemetery of Saint-Yzans-de-Médoc. (A month later, I attended a memorial service in London—the entire British wine trade and all the wine journalists were present.)

Russell Hone, who shared with Jane Grigson the British consultantship on the *Wine* volume, drove me to Solliès in a stationwagon packed with wine. We stopped overnight in Burgundy with Pam and Aubert. I think it was on this trip that he met Becky Wasserman, to whom he is now married.

10 December. *The Good Cook* was winding up. The last volume appeared in 1983, but my work was finished in December. A staff party was planned. Kit received telexes from Alexandria, Amsterdam and New York with messages to be read aloud to me. Lou composed ten verses with instructions to Kit to sing them to the tune of "These are a Few of My Favorite Things" ("Saffron and Truffles/Preserving Anchovies/Skimming or Scumming/ Removing of Ovaries…"). Dale: "Please give Richard a hug for me. I remember being the first to lay eyes on him and lead him down off his hill—into temptation. But I am glad I did. The world now knows how to cook, and Richard, whether he cares about it or not, has won immortality. I salute our patron saint of the kitchen." George: "Not many people have the ability to change the world, much less the drive and tenacity to do so. You are one of those rare people.… When the history of the 20th century is writ, it shall be observed that the twin centers of Food and Wine were Solliès-Toucas and 42

Conduit Street, abodes of that grumpy saint known to posterity simply as R.O." The design department prepared a folder for staff autographs, with a rejected winetasting photo of me, looking as if I were about to retch; it was appropriately tinted a bilious green.

Kit did not willingly abandon *The Good Cook*. She obtained from Alexandria permission to film a test sequence for television. I've never seen myself on TV without wincing, but I wanted to please Kit. The producer was Barry Hanson, who was then working on a TV wine series with Jancis Robinson. The film-maker was Mike Adams, Nora was to act as my assistant in the film and Ellen was named, I think, "script editor" (there was no script). We did a lot of talking, eating and drinking while making plans to film in January.

Anne Balfour, a longtime friend of Eda's and Sybille's, organized a dinner to celebrate my winding up *The Good Cook*. (Fifteen years later, at lunch in the south of France, Anne produced a copy of *Simple French Food*, from which she extracted a folded sheet of paper, Sybille's notes, written after the party:

"AT ANNE'S Wednesday 15th December 1982

DINNER PARTY for RICHARD OLNEY

Richard—David Cossart Lesley—Sybille—Susan Raven

Apéritif	
Ruinart Brut Tradition	
White Rhônes	
Crozes-Hermitage (bland)	Smoked Salmon Mousse
Châteauneuf-du-Pape 1978 (well-balanced. slightly spicy, right age: entirely right against the potted shrimps)	Potted Shrimps Toast
Clarets	
Domaine de Chevalier 1966 (A Big Wine: but this bottle curiously unyielding—dumb—some of the quality came out later)	Brace of Roast Pheasants (Shot by A's brother Peter) Mashed Potatoes Bread Sauce
Château Mouton-Rothschild 1964 (Big Nose, Big Wine, Deep, Complex: Much Power and a good deal of Glory)	Brussels Sprouts
Château Pichon-Longueville-Lalande Comtesse 1961 (the best of the three: Subtle, the most complex taste: simply delicious yet not simple—light yet full authority: a joy to drink.)	Double Gloucester Jarlsberg Stilton
Sauternes	
Château Suduiraut 1967 (Beautiful colour: true luscious Sauternes)	Salad of Peaches & Currants Comice Pears & Coxes

Conversation not brilliant—Richard and David talk much shop.... Lesley's animation slightly dimmed by oncoming cold.... Susan napping carrément.... Anne had shouldered all the cookery work—Susan does not say much either: Table looked very fine: gleaming glasses, plate, proper white napkins.... Break up near 1 a.m.)"

Solliès, 29 December. André Parcé, his companion, Jacqueline Nogarede, and the Peyrauds came to lunch. The wines were noted but the menu is lost. I remember scrambled eggs finished with the roes of three dozen sea urchins. We drank Krug '75, Chevalier-Montrachet '78, Domaine de Chevalier '67, Mouton '62, Rauzan-Ségla 1899 and Suduiraut '29.

Seven

1983-1985

Yquem. Paris, Bordeaux.

1983. We shot the film, Mike and Barry said things were going swimmingly but, when it was shot, I was told my voice was too soft, that I would have to dub myself "in sync," which meant memorizing the words I had spoken extemporaneously and repeating them into a microphone while watching the film to synchronize the sound with the lip movements on the screen; it was a shattering experience. They assured me the result was perfect; to me, it seemed stilted and amateurish—I hoped they were better judges than I. Mike, Nora and Ellen came to Solliès a couple of times during the spring and summer. I suppose we were planning new films. American Time-Life killed the project. I was sorry to disappoint Kit but privately relieved to escape from a métier for which I was not intended.

15 August 1983. Fanny, whose name, like that of Chez Panisse, was inspired by the Pagnol trilogy, was born to Alice and Stephen Singer, a young San Francisco wine merchant.

29 August 1983. (Me to James) "The swimming pool missed Nathan this summer.... Spent a week in Burgundy with Aubert and Pam—tasted, amongst other glories, a 1966 Montrachet to break one's heart. Aubert asked if I would accept to write a book on Romanée-Conti (how could I not accept? I would

never have dared ask for the privilege)—the day after I left, hail struck the heart of Vosne-Romanée—the Romanée-Conti harvest was 80% destroyed, half of La Tâche and Richebourg, a good part of Romanée-Saint-Vivant and parts of Echézeaux and Grands Echézeaux.... The revision of *The French Menu Cookbook* is like writing a new book—something I did not want to do—long, slow, painful days of composing, destroying, etc.—first 100 pages thrown out, but have not finished rewriting to replace them...."

James was offered a professorship at Louisiana State University and became, at the same time, editor of *The Southern Review*, a literary quarterly published at the University. He, Nathan and Judy moved to Baton Rouge. Judy stayed a few weeks and returned to Durham.

When *The Good Cook* wound up, I figured I'd had about enough of the worldly life and it was time to reinforce the foundations of my Arcadian existence. I built a chicken yard the length of one side of the terrace, some twelve metres, an extension of an already existent shed, in which I installed roosts and nests. I ordered from a farm in Normandy eight pullets and a young cock of the temperamental, blue-footed Gauloise race. They were not especially good layers, but they had personality. The cock was named Jules, the brightest and most mischievous of the hens, Maude; the others, who cowered in Maude's presence, were nameless.

25 September. (Me to James) "I finally, after years of periodically broaching the subject, gently twisted Mary's arm the other day. ('Mary, it's such a beautiful day—we must profit from the good weather—I will bring down Georges's coffin immediately, unseal it and we will scatter the ashes.')—She was petrified, I worked rapidly, breaking the seal and unscrewing the coffin, poured the ashes into a plastic bag (so that we might not be surprised by a visitor in the illegal ceremony of moving around with this obviously funeral object)—Mary wanted me to scatter but I insisted that she must do it—there was a certain lack of flair and majesty in the act but now it is done and I believe it is a great relief to her—certainly to me."

9 November. (Me to James) "Off Sunday for a week of winetasting with Kermit, mostly in Piedmont (white truffle season), ending up in Hermitage, where Gérard Chave plans to cook us a meal after tasting in the cellars."

Judy Rogers, co-proprietor-chef of the Zuni Café in San Francisco, joined us. A few kilometers distant from his home and cellars in Mauve, in the hills of Saint-Joseph, Gérard has a rustic farmhouse with a fireplace dominating the kitchen-dining room; after tasting in Mauve, we settled in there. Gérard and Monique arrived late with a Japanese client, a case of oysters (to be drizzled with Champagne before being warmed over hot coals), a half dozen woodcock, a glorious selection of charcuterie and cheeses and a mixed case of white and red Hermitage in vintages reaching back to 1929. I don't know how long we stayed—I cooked lunch the next day.

18 November 1983. Robert Shoffner, food editor of the Washington, D.C., monthly magazine, the *Washingtonian*, rang to say that, while reading a review copy of *Richard Nelson's American Cooking*, just published by NAL (New American Library) with a glowing foreword by James Beard, he had discovered a number of recipes taken from *Simple French Food.* He read several to me; the wording was identical. In the week to follow, Suzanne Hamlin from the *New York Daily News*, Candy Sagon from the *Dallas Times Herald* and Liz Logan from the *Orlando Sentinel* called me. From then on, the calls multiplied. The first story appeared 7 December in the *Daily News.* When, asked what I intended to do about the plagiarism, I am quoted as saying, "I don't know whether I can go through all the legal hassle. Or if I can afford to pursue it. And then, what good would it do?"

I planned to pass the Christmas and New Year holidays with family and asked Byron to find me a copy of the Nelson book. When I settled down with both books, I found thirty-nine recipes, word for word as I had written them except for slight editorial changes—replacing a semicolon with a period, changing one-half hour to thirty minutes, gratin dish to baking dish, flame to heat.... It was a spooky experience. I rang Suzanne Wolfe in Geneva to ask her advice; she put me in touch with a friend and colleague in New

York, Joseph Santora, whom I visited in early January. He was not enthusiastic. There was no precedent for a case like this, he said, and many people considered recipes to be in the public domain. I handed him a copy of *Simple French Food* with a list of recipes and page numbers and began to read aloud from Nelson's book. Into the third recipe, he said, "OK, you can stop. We have a case." It was not a question of recipes but of language and style. He warned me that a law suit would be expensive, that it could drag on for two years or more and that NAL's first move would be to hire specialists to prove that I was a plagiarist. I told him to go ahead and left for Solliès the next day. 24 February 1984, Joe Santora filed suit against NAL and Nelson, charging copyright infringement and unfair competition.

Atheneum declined to cooperate. From 1977 to 1983, Marvin Brown, president of NAL, had been president of Atheneum, which had been absorbed by Scribners in 1978. Robert Shoffner sent a list of recipes and page numbers to Scribners (the following letters I saw six months later after Brown's deposition):

15 December 1983. (Providence Cicero, legal advisor and vice president of Scribners, to Marvin Brown) "I am afraid that it does appear that at least 33 of the recipes in your book are either identical with or sufficiently the same as *Simple French Food* to warrant considerable concern. I have attached a list of page numbers from Nelson and from Olney for your reference. I think that you will agree that we do have a problem."

19 December 1983. (Brown to Cicero) "Dear Provi: Thank you for your note of the 15th. I have not checked out your listing but I'm not sure that's altogether necessary. The Bally-Hoo (sic) around this book has surely given us all some food (no pun intended) for thought. What is it you have in mind? Most certainly we should avoid any precedent setting actions which in the long run would work to the detrement (sic) of all publishers.... If indeed the recent accusations surrounding this title and author are true, it does point out the vulnerability we publishers might have, especially those of us who from time to time publish cookbooks.... Merry Christmas." All wrapped up. Publishers know that authors can't

afford to sue; they're right but they forget that some authors are crazy.

Alan Kaufman, vice president and legal counsel for NAL (*Seattle Times*, 14 December 1983): "We do not anticipate any legal action. People don't usually sue for copyright infringement."

Jim Beard, in an attempt to distance himself from Nelson became more and more embroiled. Journalists suggested that he had not read the book for which he had written the splashy foreword.

Beard (*Daily News*, 7 December 1983): "This was a terrible and extremely stupid thing for Dick to do. Morally, it is a major thing, although I can tell you this kind of thing has been going on for years and it is time something was done to stop it.... Legally there is nothing I can do about this but I can tell you I feel personally transgressed."

Beard (*Seattle Times*, 14 December 1983): "(Nelson) pretends innocence but a lot of us know better. It was extremely foolish of him, especially since we were all on his side."

Nelson (*Seattle Times*, 14 December 1983): "That snake!"

Beard to Shoffner (*Washingtonian*, January 1984): "Well, my dear man, I have been looking forward to this manuscript because I was trying to figure out just how many other people's works were going to show up.... I hate to tell you this, but you missed quite a few of mine.... I'll be very frank with you in saying that I'm so sorry that I ever attempted to do this introduction.... I was in the vise, if you know what I mean."

The stars of the food world were interviewed. Most of them spouted imbecile drivel about there being nothing new under the sun, recipes belonging to no one and so forth, some claimed to be above caring whether they were plagiarized, a few offered advice about changing words or an ingredient in the text to avoid problems of copyright infringement. Irena Chalmers and Paula Wolfert concurred that "Olney's writing style is distinctly different from that of anyone else in the field." (Chalmers) and "Although Richard Olney is a wonderful wonderful cook, he didn't invent those French dishes. The point is that he wrote them in the style which is so uniquely Olney. Nobody else writes like that." (Wolfert) Julia

Child (*Orlando Sentinel*, 11 March 1984): "I'm very fond of Richard Nelson. I just think he got into a pickle."

Richard Nelson was out of his depth. He seemed to have no idea what was happening or why. He is quoted repeatedly: "Recipes don't belong to anyone.... There is no such thing as an original recipe.... All cooks get recipes the same way—they're passed around.... They all came from my files.... If I'd known they were Richard Olney's recipes I would never have used them...." He couldn't understand why the language was identical. In the original draft of a statement prepared for NAL, he writes, "Jim has always said that changing one ingredient or making some change in instructions is enough to make it 'your recipe.' I didn't even try to do that with what is in my book. If I liked a recipe that was given to me, I did not make any change." In guise of a manuscript, he had sent his files of some 800 recipes; his editor organized the book, discarding 300 recipes. (I wondered if as many of mine had been discarded as accepted.)

17 March 1984. (Me to Byron) "NAL tried to settle out of court with stupid offers that were insulting. (The first was that I should receive 7% of the royalties for Nelson's book, on the grounds that the lifted recipes represented only 7% of the total number in the book, that, in subsequent printings, I would be credited for my recipes—and that, finally, the settlement would have to remain 'confidential.' I said no, so they came back with the same 7% and the promise that my recipes would be removed from further editions—at this point, my lawyer told me that it was up to me to propose a settlement since neither of these was satisfactory, so I suggested they pay me $20,000 + lawyers' fees and take the book off the market. They were outraged but finally eame up with another offer—they would give me $7,500, remove my recipes from the book in further editions and the settlement still had to remain confidential. My lawyer said, 'May I tell them to go to Hell?' I said yes, so we are going to court.) I have come to a rather startling conclusion—which is simply that James Beard is sitting on a load of dynamite and is scared to death. In Shoffner's first interview with Nelson, after listing a number of recipes which appear identically in the two books, Nelson brushes it off, saying,

'Oh, those were all things I worked on with Beard in his West Coast classes in 1974.' José had warned me. At the time, I didn't take it seriously but, in the last few days, wheels have been turning fast in my slow head and everything fits into place. Details that made no sense before (the imbecility of copying word for word, Nelson's persistent denial that he had ever copied anything directly from a cookbook—he keeps saying, 'the recipes are all typed out on 8 1/2" x 11" paper in my files') fit perfectly if he thought the recipes he was lifting were Beard's. I now do not doubt that Jim xeroxed all my recipes, passed them out to his students without identifying the source and taught them in the summer of '74, several months before *SFF* was published, and that his assistant, Nelson, filed them away to be put into his own book. (One of Beard's quotes, 'How could Dick have been so stupid!' should translate, 'Doesn't he know that you have to rewrite and disguise the source?')"

Me (*Orlando Sentinel*, 11 March 1984): "I am at this point very cross with a lot of people and I think Jim Beard needs a spanking too."

When I finally understood that Jim was at the bottom of the whole bloody mess, I rang Joe Santora. He said, in effect, "For heaven's sake, keep quiet about it. Now, we have a neat case. We certainly don't want two guilty parties and two different misdemeanors to confuse the issue."

Jim rang Joe Santora to say that he wanted to "make a deposition" and fixed an appointment for a few days later at his house. A couple of hours before the meeting was to take place, he rang to say that he couldn't receive anyone—he was too ill. Ten days later, the identical scenario was reenacted. He never deposed.

By mid-April, NAL had raised its offer to $15,000. Joe said no. In late August 1984, I had stopped in London for a day, en route to New York to appear in court. Joe Santora rang me in London to say that I could return to Solliès—to avoid going to court, NAL had agreed, in extremis, to an acceptable settlement. The settlement agreement, signed by NAL, Nelson and me, forbids the disclosure of the terms and conditions. Journalists estimated

("It is rumoured that....") five or six figures. Joe Santora cut his fees in half to permit me to pay.

1984 opened with a party in Chevy Chase at Margaret's. James and Nathan were there. Although Judy was not living in Baton Rouge, she contrived to be at Margaret's, where she announced that she had the most wonderful idea for a new book, to be called "Olney's Herbal." I told her she'd better call it "Judith Olney's Herbal." (I never understood what made Judy tick. She decided to become an author of cookbooks, but she didn't like food or wine. At table, she ate nothing and drank nothing, but she kept stocks of supermarket ice cream in the deep freeze to dig at between meals and hid chocolate beneath her pillow to devour in bed. She decided to be a painter, removed all of Margaret's and my paintings from the walls in Durham, replaced them with frames containing virgin canvases and, in the space of an afternoon, filled them with hideous, garish still lives. Some years ago, a friend sent me a clipping of a weekly rubrique from a Washington, D.C., newspaper, property of the Moonie religious sect, a trashy mish-mash of snobbish celebrity gossip and restaurant-going, entitled "Olney in America." I have no idea what Judy's married name is at present, but I am told that "Olney in America" continues to appear.)

12 February 1984. Robert Isaacson was with me for a few days. We drank a bottle of 1927 Taylor's Port to celebrate our shared birthyear. I invited Pam and Aubert to dinner and to spend the night.

Solliès Toucas—12 February 1984
(Robert Isaacson, Aubert and Pamela de Villaine, Mary)

Apéritif: Krug 1976
§
Soupe de Baudroie au Safran
Anjou 1928
§
Gigot Rôti, Estouffade aux Truffes
Château Haut-Brion 1971
Château Mouton-Rothschild 1953
§
Fromages
Château Léoville-Poyferré 1900
§
Crêpes aux Pommes
Château d'Yquem 1937

The Anjou (which, today, would be called Coteaux du Layon) came from Prunier-Duphot, whose wines were sold at auction when Jean Barnagaud retired.

14 April. I no longer had any reason to visit London for professional reasons, but I had made friends and James often came for reasons of his own. I joined him there, we wanted to organize a special meal for friends and asked Nico to create the menu. He opened the restaurant on a closing day for the occasion. I furnished the wines. We ran into Gisou and her friend, Joe Fitchett, a journalist with the *Herald Tribune*, and asked them to join us. Other guests were Elizabeth, Valerie, Sybille, Lesley, Suzanne, Jill and Paul, Kit and Tony, Russell Hone.... We were seventeen in all. I seated Joe between two great ladies, Elizabeth and Valerie, he made the mistake of trying to defend the honour of journalism, a word that was anathema to his two neighbours. We passed, nonetheless, an unforgettable afternoon and Nico produced an exquisite meal:

Chez Nico, London, April, 1984

Apéritif: Champagne

§

Ballotine de Foie Gras avec sa
Petite Salade d'Artichauts
Anjou 1928

§

Délice de Barbue au Beurre de Morilles
Anjou 1928

§

Canette de Challans au Miel et au Poivre
avec sa Sauce au Fumet de Cèpes
Château Pichon-Longueville
Comtesse de Lalande 1962

§

Plateau de Fromages
Château Rauzan-Ségla 1928

§

Tartelette au Coulis de Pommes Caramélisées
Château Guiraud 1942

§

Café et Petits Fours

25 April 1984. Suzanne's youngest son, Charlie, was fourteen. I invited him and his mother to the Taillevent to celebrate his birthday. He loved the Champagne.

Suzanne wanted to eat chez Paul Bocuse. I booked a table, we met in Lyon and drove to Collonges. Bocuse told the maître d'hôtel that he would see to our menu and settled down to gossip about cuisine. Much of the conversation concerned salt. He said the only salt he used in his kitchen was coarse grey sea salt from the salt marshes of Guérande, on the southern coast of Brittany. Later, as we left the table, the maître d'hôtel asked me to stop at the checkroom, where a ten-kg bucket of Sel Gris de Guérande was handed to me, "compliments of Paul Bocuse." (Then, it was avail-

With Nico Ladenis, Chez Nico, April 14, 1984.

able only in specialty shops—today, both grey sea salt and "fleur de sel," the delicately flavoured, crumbly salt crystals culled from the water's surface, are in all supermarkets.)

Gisou told me she would like to publish *Romanée-Conti* but wondered if I would accept to first write *Yquem*. Henri Flammarion, she explained, had a particular passion for the wine of Château d'Yquem and wanted to publish a book to celebrate the bicentenary, in 1985, of the Lur-Saluces presence at Yquem. (In 1785, comte Louis-Amédée de Lur-Saluces married Françoise-Joséphine de Sauvage, only child of Laurent de Sauvage, whose family had controlled Yquem since 1593, originally on lease from the crown, later by purchase.) To illustrate the beauty of the project, Monsieur Flammarion had organized a dinner at which he served Château d'Yquem 1937. Yquem had remained in the same family for four

Valerie Eliot and James, Chez Nico, April 14, 1984.

centuries and Romanée-Conti offered eleven centuries of history for virgin exploration. My work was set out for years to come.

In May, Alexandre and Bérengère de Lur-Saluces organized a lunch at Château d'Yquem to discuss the book. Gisou, Joe Fitchett, Marc Walter, the designer, Michel Guillard, the photographer, and I were present. Gisou asked me if I could produce a finished manuscript by autumn of that year. We both knew that such a feat was humanly impossible; I said, "Oh, yes." (In the year to come, I traveled repeatedly to Yquem to work in the archives and with the photographer and to assist at the grape harvest and the vinification. I never met Henri Flammarion, the instigator of the project, who died in August 1985. His son, Charles-Henri, whom I had met seven years earlier at the Time-Life-Taillevent dinner, replaced him.) After lunch, Gisou, Joe and I drove to Auch to dine at André Daguin's Hôtel de France and pass the night.

Elizabeth David and Kit van Tulleken, Chez Nico, April 14, 1984.

Margaret, James and Nathan, Byron, Marilynn and the children, James, Elizabeth and Christopher, were in Solliès that summer. Mary asked the family to dinner. When we arrived, she was a bit unsteady, stumbled toward Elizabeth, age 14, hugged her and said, "How wonderful to see you, Marilynn" and, to me, "You cook, Richard." She had bought a leg of lamb, tomatoes, shell beans, green beans and cheeses. We shelled beans. I prepared a tomato salad, roasted the leg, cooked the white beans and the green beans separately, then tossed them together with butter and a persillade; it was a splendid meal. 12 July, we celebrated James's birthday:

Apéritif: Krug Rosé
§
Velouté de Baudroie
Puligny-Montrachet "Les Combettes" 1982
§
Epaule d'Agneau Farcie, Sauce Vin Rouge aux Aulx
Pommes Vapeur
Domaine Tempier 1975
Château Haut-Bailly 1964
§
Salade
§
Fromages
Château Lafite-Rothschild 1962
Château Léoville-Poyferré 1918
§
Pêches au Sauternes
Château Latour Blanche 1937

Gisou and Joe spent several days in Solliès. Mary joined us for lunch Chez Hiély, where we drank the last bottle of Yquem 1904 in the cellar. (At the publication of *Yquem*, the empty bottle appeared in a window display at the Flammarion bookshop in Paris.)

Michael James and a crowd of Americans celebrated Simca's 80th birthday at Bramafam. I offered her a wash drawing of the tied-up bundle of celery stalk and split leek, enclosing thyme, bay and parsley, which Jeanne had for years been presenting to Simca's classes as "le bouquet-garni de Monsieur Richard."

In September, after the NAL-Nelson lawsuit had been settled, Nora and Suzanne organized a Champagne press party in Paris. Nora spent two days preparing a glorious Boeuf Mode en Gelée. Gisou, Joe, Naomi, Susan Heller Anderson, Simca, Gregory Usher, Paul Levy, Robert Shoffner, Phyllis Richman and a bevy of journalists whom I didn't know were present.

Kermit emerging from cellar, 1984.

Judy filed for divorce, failed to pursue but preferred not to reintegrate herself into the family. (A year later, James relaunched divorce proceedings—the final decree was signed in March 1986.)

I was flying to the U.S. 15 December for my annual family visit. Two days earlier, Kermit arrived to spend a month in the house with his companion (subsequently his wife), Gail Skoff, who was scheduled to arrive after my departure.

From Kermit's journal: "13 December 1984. TGV, Paris-Toulon. Nothing but grey skies. Plucked a pheasant upon arrival chez Olney. Fresh egg noodles, sautéed snails, chanterelles and marjoram, truffled pheasant with wild rice, cheeses; '76 Krug, '82 Meursault 'Narvaux' from Michelot, '66 Dauzac, '53 Mouton, '49 Coutet. Duke Ellington, Billie Holiday. 14 December. Bright sky. A tour with Richard to prepare us for his quirky house. Lunch: Vioulets, white truffle risotto, cheeses; local white, '75 Monts

Luisants Ponsot, '82 Nuits Perrières Chevillon, 1900 Cognac. Dinner at Mme Garin's."

En route to Rochester, I stopped briefly in New York. Lydie Marshall bore a message from Jim Beard that he had to see me—it was very, very important. I went around to the house. We sat for ten minutes in excruciating silence, a silence shrill with pain; whatever Jim had so desperately wanted to say refused to be said. Gino entered the room, chose a small, straight-backed chair, sat rigidly erect with knees touching, toes pointed inward, hands clasped and head bowed. He frowned for some time while assembling his discourse, then began the recitation. Jim turned crimson with embarrassment and tried to stop him, but he had memorized it and was determined to follow through. The message was how bad the Time-Life *Good Cook* series was and the words were Jim's. Gino appeared to have no idea that his exposition was a direct attack on me. He lifted his eyes often, pleading for approbation—I said, "It's all right Gino, I understand." It was time for me to get out. I leaned over to give Jim the ritual peck on each cheek—he recoiled as if I were about to strike him. I left. (Jim died a month later, Gino five years later.)

31 December. I was at Margaret's. John telephoned. His oldest boy, Stephen, had just been killed in a car accident while driving through a blizzard. We all flew to Saint Louis.

In Provence, January 1985 was, depending on the recounter, either the coldest in memory or the coldest since 1956. Excerpts from Kermit's journal:

"The fire is so easy to start in his handmade fireplace—so easy to control for grilling. At night the walls shake to the sounds of James Brown, The Temptations, Smokey Robinson. I don't think this house ever heard these sounds before.... How can a great cook have such a terrible stove? Two burners, impossible to fine tune. He has thirty knives or more, thirty or more copper utensils, and only two uncontrollable burners.... The Kermit Lynch Three Egg Aïoli: One egg fails to hold, even in the marvelous marble mortier. Second egg, I break the yolk cracking the shell. Third egg, Voilà! Buster Keaton in Richard Olney's kitchen.... Débussy, Ravel, Satie. Little purple artichokes raw with vinaigrette.... Gail stays in bed. I go to the pharmacy. Once I get back, I go to bed too. Muscle aches, fever, cough, no appetite, headache.... This is no house to be sick in. To get to the bathroom you go through the unheated 'sun room.' Glass roof. Stone floor. The toilet seat like ice. From the bed, feverish, to the john, shivering. The skull on the pillar. This is no house to be sick in.... A shower would be good for my spirits, but it is too icy in there. How does Richard stand it...?

"2 Jan. Lunch at Tempier. Mistral, icy, dry. At night the wind howls. The house quakes and creaks. The wind roars. It slams into the house. Ferocious.

"3 Jan. No fresh fish because of the mistral.

"5 Jan. Still no fish. What is this weather? The air is brittle, the fish pond solid ice. We slide down the hill in our car. Five to six cm. of snow. We dine and sleep at Tempier. Rosé 1958, rouge 1955.

"6 Jan. Not enough traction in the slush to drive up Richard's hill. No running water. No shower, toilet, etc. Gail melts snow to make coffee and wash some potatoes. The heat works, there is light, the fireplace is cozy. French radio plays Hank Williams and Elvis.

"7 Jan. It snowed all night. We descend the treacherous stone steps to go into town for bottled water. Kids are out with sleds. In Provence! There is excitement in the air.... The stove again. You cannot light the oven without burning your fingers or dropping the matchstick in the little hole. And there is no temperature guage. You guess. And don't drip water on the stove's surface. The burners don't know 'low.' Is that why he has so many asbestos pads?

"8 Jan. Dinner at François Peyraud's. Warm chick peas with garlic. Aïoli with vegetables and a fabulous octopus stew. Minus 17° centigrade. Impossible to return to Solliès. Chains required to cross Toulon.

"9 Jan. At 4 p.m. the gas in the stove goes off. I switch on valves and knobs. Nothing. So I call Richard in the U.S. 'Oh yes, I forgot to tell you about the little switch above the stove. Turn it off, then on again.' He said, 'I heard about the cold spell.' Cold spell! In Florence, the Arno froze for the first time since 1929. Coldest day in Paris since 1956.

"10 Jan. Spent the night at Tempier. Had a bath.

"11 Jan. ...the fireplace is wonderful. But we read that certain sections of the countryside have lost electricity and Richard's house is heated by electricity. Mary Garin calls. Her water is off too. Her house is heated by hot water radiators. No mail for days. Everything is done with melted snow: cooking, cleaning, bathing, a bucket for flushing.

"12 Jan. Mary Garin calls. Can she move in? She's freezing with no heat. Richard's house a refuge! She brings a pork roast, but says she has no idea how to cook it. We make quite a dent in Richard's cellar.

"13 Jan. Rain, sleet, snow. Twice a day I go down to the fountain to fill plastic bottles with drinking water. The stone steps have a layer of slush with hard ice beneath that. For dining a brouillade aux truffes with Richard's handy frozen black truffles. The title comes to me as I cook: 'A California Yankee in King Richard's Kitchen.'

"14 Jan. All flights cancelled. I make a good casserole. Rub garlic on earthenware grating dish. Butter it. Add layer of thinly sliced onions, then sliced potatoes, then sliced truffles, more onion, more potato. Pour over white wine and crème fraîche. Dot with butter.

"15 Jan. Still frozen solid. The snow is granular, like salt. The airport is open. We slip and slide down the hill with (Gail's) suitcases.

"16 Jan. I awake to clear skies. Jean-Marie comes to lunch. He tries repeatedly to drive up the hill, but has to give up. Good. He has on the phone acted like I'm a baby complaining about the weather. After 3 p.m., the chill leaves the air. Richard is on his way. He calls. I tell him not to arrive after dark or we'll never get up the hill." (I feel that Kermit has dealt rather cavalierly with my cookstove, whose two burners, which I have always been able to regulate to a fine degree, are supplemented by a cast-iron plaque on which one may move pots and pans around to find the precise degree of heat necessary for slow-cooking stews or to keep dishes warm; I have never burnt a finger lighting the oven and the absence of a thermostat is deliberate—I don't trust them.)

The thaw set in shortly after I arrived; my pipes and water meter had burst, like hundreds of others in the region. I had to shut off the water for ten days until a plumber finally turned up.

30 March 1985. I don't remember the name of the man who invented a system of creating the infallible winetasting note. He organized, for about fifty sommeliers and journalists, a tasting of 15 or 20 vintages of Yquem at the château, to be followed by a lunch. Alexandre and Gisou decided that this manifestation would present ideal circumstances under which to photograph me for the dust jacket of Yquem.

The man's system, as I understood it, depended on professional palates, whose proprietors were informed that they must not attempt to guess vintages; the tasting was to be an exercise, not in identification, but in the definition of abstract quality—the vintages of the numbered bottles would be revealed after the results of the tasting were announced. We received a number of pages on which to mark numbers related to 100 (ultimate perfection) in endless categories—robe, nose, mouth, complexity, persistence, and I forget. These notes were then to be passed through a computer, the figures for each category added up and divided by the number of tasters to find the mean, then the computer added and divided the means to find the absolute, correct scientific note for each wine—and, of course, there was a winner, whose notes came closest to those of the computer. (The winner was Thierry Manoncourt, proprietor of Château Figeac, where the same circus was to be enacted the following day.)

The man was very suspicious of my presence. All the other guests were there at his behest, but he didn't know why I was there; it was his show and, yet, Michel Guillard spent all his time photographing me and no one else (with a half-dozen glasses in front of me, trying desperately to look serious). Before the notes were passed in, the man approached me and asked to see my notes. I had noted nothing—how one can decide that a nose or a mouth is worth precisely 87 or 93 points eludes me. He upbraided me crossly, said that my frivolity upset his system.... I suggested that my blank pages and I be eliminated from the computer—and so it was. Thierry asked me to spend the night at Figeac to assist at the next day's tasting. That evening, with Marie-France, we had a relaxed and civilized supper. The following morning, my notes were not sollicited.

Sacha and his brother were back for their annual sojourn at La Réserve. I spent three days with them. Sacha was moving more slowly, carefully advancing each foot as he walked. His speech was no less precise, but slower. The motor was wearing down. Sacha, in the thirty-four years that I had known him, had never mentioned his age; his brother's chauffeur told me he was 85. I thought, when we parted, that we would not see each other again.

I wrote *Yquem* in English, working closely with the translator on the translation. The manuscript was finished in May; for the six months to come, I spent more time in Paris than in Solliès, working with Gisou and Marc Walter, choosing photos, writing captions and cutting or expanding the text to fit the pages. I wrote in French—there was no longer time to wait for the translations. I was put up around the corner from Flammarion, in a hotel whose bar, from 6 p.m. on, was the daily meeting place for Flammarion editors and their authors. Françoise Verny, Flammarion's literary editor, a famous figure in the French world of letters, who nourished herself mainly on whisky, was there every evening. Once, I arrived early for a date with Gisou and settled at the table I had often shared with her and Françoise; the bartender apologized but, he said, "This table is always reserved for Madame Verny." I took another table until Gisou and Françoise arrived.

James planned to be in London. *Yquem* pressure didn't permit me to meet him there. He wanted to take Elizabeth David and Valerie Eliot to dinner and Nico was closed. I recommended 'Hilaire,' a restaurant in Old Brompton Road, opened in 1983 with Simon Hopkinson as chef, in which I had eaten very well with Paul Levy. James and Simon both have vivid memories of the dinner. James writes, "Simon was very embarrassed at having put us downstairs when he came to realize who the company was. In fact, we were happier because we were alone down there and didn't have the noise and distraction that would surely have been too much upstairs. When he discovered that Elizabeth and Valerie were in steerage, he proceeded to spend the rest of the evening there himself." (Simon and Elizabeth became great friends. In 1987, he moved to Bibendum as chef and co-proprietor. Bibendum became Elizabeth's favorite dining-out place.)

15 July 1985. When, at the age of nineteen, Bipin Desai arrived in the United States from India to continue his studies in nuclear physics, he was a teetotaler and vegetarian. Encounters with European colleagues at the Center for Nuclear Reaseach in Geneva opened his eyes to the magic of the table, he began to collect wines, organize winetastings and became a carnivore. Bipin was excited about my "work in progress" and asked me to organize, with Jean-Claude Vrinat, an "Yquem Dinner" at Taillevent.

"GRAND DINER YQUEM"

Organisé par Bipin R. DESAI et Richard OLNEY

INVITES D'HONNEUR

Comte Alexandre de LUR-SALUCES

Comtesse Alexandre de LUR-SALUCES

Madame Ghislaine BAVOILLOT

Monsieur Christian MILLAU

Monsieur Richard OLNEY

PARTICIPANTS

Monsieur et Madame Bipin R. DESAI

Monsieur Wolfgang GRUNEWALD

Monsieur et Madame Aziz KHAN

Monsieur et Madame Manuel KLAUSNER

Le Taillevent, Paris, 15 Juillet 1985

Consommé de Crustacés en Gelée
Krug Grande Cuvée
§
Turbot Braisé, Sauce au Sauternes
Château d'Yquem 1945
§
Ragoût de Ris de Veau, de Truffes, de Foie Gras et de Crêtes de Coq
Granité de Melon Charentais au Champagne
Château d'Yquem 1937
§
Caneton à l'Aigre-Doux
Château d'Yquem 1921
§
Fromages Persillés
Château d'Yquem 1980
§
Blanc-Manger
Château d'Yquem 1893
§
Krug 1979
Pour vous rafraichir le palais entre chaque plat

Nico, Dinah-Jane and two teenage daughters had a house near Le Luc, forty kilometres from Solliès, in which they passed summer vacations. They came to lunch. We ate boned, stuffed, braised oxtail, cold in its jelly, and finished with sliced peaches, macerated in1937 Château Latour Blanche (Sauternes).

October 1985. Alice and Stephen were married. To celebrate, they and Fanny rented a farmhouse in Tuscany, at the heart of the Chianti vineyards, and asked Lulu, Lucien, Jean-Marie and me to join them. We cooked in the ancient kitchen fireplace, local raw hams, from old-fashioned pigs, were cured on the bone and the countryside was beautiful. Driving on a winding country road, a wild boar mother with several babies in her train blocked our passage as they sauntered across....

The revised *French Menu Cookbook* appeared that fall. Nahum Waxman, proprietor of Kitchen Arts and Letters in New York, organized a reception, 19 December, to coincide with my annual family visit.

Yquem was running late. By the end of November, it was at the printers in Switzerland. The official publication date was 6 December. In Bordeaux, from the 6th to the 9th, a series of manifestations—colloquies, book-signings, TV and newspaper interviews, lunches and dinners, winding up with an evening reception at Château d'Yquem—was organized. Gisou spent the preceding week in Switzerland, tightening the screws to keep the printers under pressure. By the evening of 5 December, enough books were off the press to load a van, which drove through the night, delivering its cargo to Mollat, Bordeaux's principal bookstore, at 4 a.m. When I arrived four hours later to prepare for the first conference in the shop's auditorium, the display windows were all dressed with *Yquem* and the aisles were lined with stacks of *Yquem*. The reception at the château, fifty kilometres distant from the city of Bordeaux, was very grand; there were hundreds of guests, a *Who's Who* roster of Le Tout-Bordeaux. Champagne flowed, Yquem flowed and the caterers had worked wonders with foie gras, truffles, caviar and seafood. In black tie, men all look alike, but the ladies had outdone themselves; Bérengère was coiffed and dressed like a dream-princess. Eight year old Philippe, the youngest of the Lur-Saluces children, was unbridled with excitement and wanted everyone to sign his copy of *Yquem* over and over again. Had I not been the principal object of curiosity, I'd have been enchanted by the evening. The mayor of Bordeaux, Jacques Chaban-Delmas, gave a speech, Alexandre spoke and he wanted me to speak; he called out for me and looked for me, but I was hiding (not very nice, but I couldn't help it).

Bernard Pivot conducted a weekly, hour-long television program, Apostrophe, a sort of literary round-table of recently published authors, hugely popular with the entire French public, well-read or unread. Each year, on the Friday preceding Christmas, the program was dedicated to books on food and wine. Gisou rang to say I was booked on Apostrophe, 20 December. "Impossible," I said, "I'll be in New York." Gisou: "No one can refuse to appear on Apostrophe. It's the most important thing that can happen to an author or a publisher. Flammarion will fly you from New York on the 19th, we'll pick you up at the airport, you'll stay with me and we'll put you back on a plane the morning of the 21st." When Gisou's mind is made up, there's not much anyone can do about it. I received from Pivot books by the other authors on the program, requesting me to read them carefully and be prepared to discuss them.

In New York, I spent the afternoon of the 19th with Lucia and Elliott Stein; they accompanied me to Kitchen Arts and Letters, time to have a drink and apologize for having to leave the reception early. Gisou got through to me there with the information that ground crews were on strike and no planes were landing at Paris airports—my plane would land in Brussels, where a chauffeur would pick me up. I signed a pile of books and took a taxi to the airport, feeling very guilty, just as guests were beginning to arrive.

The plane landed, unexpectedly, in London, presumably to release the passengers who preferred not to end up in Brussels. Just before taking off, the pilot announced that we would, after all, land in Paris. I assumed that no one would be there to meet me, but Air France had been in touch with Flammarion and there was Brigitte Bendéritter, promotion director, with the perpetual filter cigarette clenched between her teeth. The metros were on strike. Circulation in Paris was paralyzed. The taxi-driver's radio announced that Fauchon, the fancy food establishment in the Place de la Madeleine, was burning and that fire trucks were unable to penetrate the frozen traffic. (The director and several of her employees died in the flames.) Gisou's flat was fortunately not in the heart of Paris; we arrived there a couple of hours later than normal traffic would have allowed. Brigitte deposited me, I soaked in a hot bath and flopped in bed.... When I awoke, Gisou and Brigitte were there with Maurice Bernachon, the Lyonnais chocolatier, who was also scheduled to appear on the Pivot show, and his daughter-in-law, Françoise, Paul Bocuse's daughter. The show was at 8. We were expected in the studio at least an hour in advance. Considering the traffic problem, Gisou figured we should leave at 4:30 (for a drive that, under normal conditions, demanded 20 minutes). Françoise went in Brigitte's car, Monsieur Bernachon and I in Gisou's. When we moved, it was because Gisou was driving on the sidewalks. It was an interesting adventure; I was relaxed for I told myself that I had done my part; if we failed to arrive at the studio, a TV appearance was hardly a matter of life or death.... M. Bernachon, on the other hand, was in torment, moaning, wringing his hands and exclaiming repeatedly, "Oh, poor Monsieur Olney, who has crossed the Atlantic for Pivot!" We arrived at 10 til 8 to find everyone in a state, Pivot was not there. Alexandre and Paul Bocuse were there. (Alexandre told us that grape-picking—the final "tri"—at Yquem had wound up the previous day, 19 December, the latest date on record.) Bernard Pivot arrived and installed himself on the set, at the head of a rectangular table with three chairs to each side. To his left were Martine Jolly, author of *Merci M. Parmentier*, a potato cookbook, I and, to my left, André Vedel, an INAO inspector, consultant for the first of the annual Hachette guides to "the 5000 best wines of France." To Pivot's right were Michel Serres, French philosophy professor at Stanford University in California, author of *Les Cinq Sens*, Maurice Bernachon, author of *La Passion du Chocolat*, and Pierre Escoffier, representing his grandfather for a book entitled *AUGUSTE ESCOFFIER Souvenirs Inédits*.

Pivot had brought a bottle of young Saumur-Champigny, one of the wines recommended in the Hachette guide, and a Château d'Yquem 1969. Alexandre had brought a bottle of Yquem 1967. Pivot questioned Mme Jolly about potato varieties, then asked, "How do you make mashed potatoes?" A pause.... She uttered a prolonged nasal sound, like a sheep bleating, "BAaaa.... You put them into a food mill and turn the handle." "Is that all?" he asked. There was anothor bleat.... "You add milk and butter and beat them." He asked, "Would you agree with that Monsieur Olney?" I choked a bit and mumbled, "Well, no, I would save the hot cooking liquid, push them through a sieve without turning the pestle and gently stir in butter and enough cooking liquid to render them supple." He began to question Vedel about wine. I asked if I might act as sommelier so that we could taste what was being discussed. I poured the Saumur-Champigny. Vedel ritualistically passed the glass beneath his nose and said "poivron vert" (green bell pepper). Pivot smelled and tasted (very good at his job) and exclaimed, "Fantastic! I think I can find that too—how did you recognize it so fast?" Vedel: "I knew ahead of time—they all smell alike." We moved into Yquem. I poured both vintages. Pivot again addressed Vedel, who did his sniffing trick with both glasses and pronounced: "Agrumes" (citrus fruit). Pivot: "What do you think, M. Olney?" In essence, I said it was too bad to discover nothing but grapefruit in sumptuous, complex wines that defied definition. Next on the list was Pierre Escoffier. I had enjoyed reading his grandfather's sketchy souvenirs of his life as a chef for generals during his military service, of his experiences as chef for the Ritz hotels, his friendships with celebrities, the dishes he created in their honour, and so forth. Pierre Escoffier, when questioned about the book, mumbled that it was really of no interest, nothing but an old man's boring memories. (Pierre was proud of being "educated"—he had a diploma in industrial engineering—and rather ashamed of his grandfather, who was nothing but a cook from a poor family, a member of the servant class.) By that time, I was beginning to feel sorry for Pivot, who didn't deserve to have so many jerks on his show; I wondered, audibly, why Pierre Escoffier had accepted to appear on the program. Maurice Bernachon was paralyzed; he was sweating and words stuck in his throat. Pivot took pity and asked him a few questions which could be answered with a nod, a yes or a no. Michel Serres's book was a bit obscure for my pragmatic mind, but I had no quarrel—he wrote wonderful things about Yquem and he spoke lucidly.

Gisou, Brigitte, Françoise, Alexandre, Paul Bocuse, Maurice Bernachon and I were going to Brasserie Lipp for supper after the show. Bocuse asked Pivot to join us. He declined, explaining that, as a matter of principle, he was never seen publicly with his television guests immediately after a show. A few minutes after we were seated, Pivot arrived and took a table, alone, adjoining ours.

Brigitte gleefully pulled from her sack two copies of a pornographic magazine, which she offered to Alexandre and me—the four middle pages, preceded by nuns having sex and followed by young women displaying themselves indiscreetly, were devoted to a spread on *Yquem*. We went to Gisou's to relax and watch the show, which had been taped on her TV. That morning, I flew to Rochester (Pivot's reputation was not exaggerated—*Yquem* was out of print by the new year.) I learned later that Didier was in a Paris hospital the day I was there. Mary had mentioned that he was having problems with muscular coordination, but I didn't know it was serious. I was told that he watched the Pivot program and wept with joy. He died of AIDS a week later.

Eight

1986-1991

U.S. *Yquem* tour. *Ten Vineyard Lunches*. *Romanée-Conti*.

1986. A letter from André Guillot, delighted with my "potato purée lesson." Jean-Eugene Borie: "Bravo! It was time that someone put Vedel in his place." While André Vedel was INAO inspector for the Côte d'Or, he encouraged growers to fertilize the vineyards with a chemical fertilizer, which culminated in the disastrous vintage of 1977. Charles Rousseau: "Il nous a foutu dans la merde, puis il a foutu le camp!" (loosely translated, "He dumped us in the shit, then he jumped ship!") In Solliès, where I had managed to remain anonymous for a quarter of a century, the local population was suddenly avid for news about my "copain, Bernard Pivot."

17 January. Kit rang. Pam Marke had been working late in the Time-Life offices, apparently fainted in the ladies' room and died of asphyxiation.

13 March. (Me to Byron) "Have to go to Paris next week to receive a prize for *Yquem*, given by an organization called 'Relais et Châteaux'—will lock myself up in the Bibliothèque Nationale for a couple of days to do some research on *Romanée-Conti*."

The Relais et Châteaux reception at the Hôtel Crillon was a Champagne-flowing affair catered by the kitchens of the Crillon. It seemed to me that most of the Michelin galaxy of chefs and restaurateurs were present. My prize consisted in a meal ticket for two at any or all of the members of the Relais et Châteaux chain for a period of one year. The promotion director was expected to make arrangements for each meal. That evening I asked Michel Lemonnier to join me at Michel Rostang, where we ate very well and drank some rather grand wines. (A year later, I asked Nora to a Paris Relais et Chateaux restaurant which neither of us knew. The promotion lady seemed quite hurt that, except for the first and last days of the year's duration, I had not profited from my prize. I couldn't explain that the proprietors of the restaurants that interested me most were friends, that I visited them rarely because I was embarrassed never to receive a bill and would consider it an insult to turn up with a free meal ticket. I mumbled something about not driving.)

The following evening was the private invitation opening of the annual French Book Fair, Le Salon du Livre, at the Grand Palais. Gisou asked me to be present and we planned to have a late supper at the Plaza-Athénée's Relais, a few steps away. As I began to wander, examining other publishers' stands, I was hailed from all sides—everyone had seen the Pivot show. I decided that I'd better hole up in the Flammarion complex until suppertime.

Nora was in Solliès for a few days at Easter time. Gisou joined us for the Easter weekend. Wild thyme was in flower everywhere and shoots of wild asparagus were pushing up daily on the hillside. We lunched on wild asparagus omelettes, swelled and golden, semi-liquid inside, and salads composed of tender garden lettuces, rocket, salt anchovies maison, grilled, peeled and seeded peppers, green sweet shallots, green beans.... Neither Gisou nor Nora had ever eaten wild asparagus; the omelettes were a great success.

Sacha died. Since I had seen him, a year earlier, he had grown progressively weaker and could no longer live alone. His family brought him back to Germany. Madame Gerfroit died, blind and deaf, with a broken hip.

Stephanie Alexander, restaurant owner and chef in Melbourne, Australia, writer and impassioned crusader for all things pure and fresh in the kitchen, arrived in Solliès from Burgundy, where she had eaten garden snails (petits gris) prepared in different ways. In *Stephanie's Feasts and Stories* (1988), she writes, after describing Bernard Loiseau's soup of snails and nettles, "I was becoming more and more excited by these snails. My enthusiasm was encouraged a week later when I spent an evening with Richard Olney in the south of France (...) The conversation turned to snails. Richard was up in a trice and returned with a large bucket. One glance was enough. These were the same as our snails! I was determined. We would start collecting. And we have." (From a later book, *Stephanie's Australia*, I learn that she now has a producer of garden snails, who furnishes the restaurant.... I was pleased also to find a chapter on Damien Pignolet, a Sydney restaurateur who, a few years before Stephanie's visit, had come to lunch with Simca and Jean.)

12 July. Suzanne and Laurent Martin, a Swiss banker, were married and organized a three-day celebration in Geneva and the Swiss countryside. I took a night train from Toulon to Geneva. Charlie, who was too young to drive, met me and we waited for Laurent's son to pick us up. Charlie had just discovered Proust and we had a long discussion about his merits. When we arrived at a country hotel, where I was put up, I found Jimmy Baldwin, whom I had not known to be a client and friend of Suzanne's. He was with a young Harlem friend and aspiring writer, who told me, "Jimmy is the grandaddy of us all!" Jimmy's eyes flared, then he relaxed and laughed. The second day was devoted to a train ride on an ancient, narrow-track line, which was only used to rent out, for special occasions, a train of antique coaches, drawn by a small, period-piece steam engine that hooted, screeched and belched smoke through the winding Alpine landscape. The head coach was the old dining car, stocked with picnic food, beer and wine. The train

stopped at a dozen villages, long enough for the guests to wander around and gather in the quaintness. At each stop, Jimmy and I, faithful to old habit, headed for the nearest bar to drink a whisky.

Late July, I met James in London. Judy was there with Nathan, whom she lent to his father for three days. We stayed with Jill and Paul: Valerie offered us tickets to *Cats*, which wowed Nathan and Elinor.

James and I continued to Solliès. Margaret, her youngest son, John McBride, John, Elfriede and their son, John ("Johnny" to the family) joined us. John McBride, a city-bred musician, was fascinated by the chickens and their habits; each time one proudly squawked, he hastened to collect the egg. Johnny was uncertain about his future. I thought he should spend a year in Europe but, to justify such an indulgence, "higher education" had to enter into the program. I suggested the American University in Aix (whose president was my old adversary, Herbert Maza), which was close to Solliès. We drove over and registered him for the following autumn.

8 August. (James to Byron) "Mary arrived last evening for dinner, a return invitation for one of the most bizarre dinners of my life...the hostess was far from sober, the silverware, the glasses and the plates were far from clean and the escalopes de veau were far from properly attended to. (Mary had a vague memory that breaded veal scallops required eggs, breadcrumbs and flour—she dumped them all into a mixing bowl, messed them around, emptied the contents into a pan of hot oil, stirred and served.) The hostess later apologized for being 'such a mess' but explained that she had got into the Scotch the day before and had stayed right in there until the unsuspecting guests arrived. Last night we had a better meal: marinated raw sardine fillets with a Château Simone Blanc 1982 and rabbit in a saffroned cream sauce with Domaine Tempier 1984. Today we are going to lunch with the Peyrauds at Domaine Tempier...."

When I began to raise incubator chicks, I built a right-angle, ten-metre extension at the end of the chicken yard to keep the young birds out of reach of their blood-thirsty elders. A young serin, wild cousin of the canary, insinuated its way through the chicken wire into the chicken yard and rapidly grew too large to get out again. He was very friendly and we called him "Little Yellow bird." He often escaped when I opened the door to the chicken yard, but always returned to be let in again. I installed high perches and bought a female canary; he was very excited, but she was too dumb to stay out of the chickens' way and I found her pecked to pieces. One day Little Yellow bird flew out the door and didn't return, but I retained a sentimental memory and began to think of an aviary.

Paula Wolfert and her husband, Bill Bayer, were on a bouillabaisse tour of the Mediterranean coast to prepare an article for *Connoisseur* (April 1987 issue). Alice had told them, "Lulu makes the best bouillabaisse I've ever eaten." The day before coming to lunch at Solliès, they had spend a long day at Domaine Tempier, beginning early in the morning with Lulu, meeting the fishing boats, back in the kitchen preparing the fish soup with which to moisten the bouillabaisse, putting the fish to marinate with saffron, garlic and olive oil and cooking it out-of-doors in Lulu's antique copper cauldron over a fire of vinestocks. I thought they should eat something else for the last day of their tour. My six-month-old cocks were becoming dangerously quarrelsome, so I sacrificed two of them to a coq-au-vin, the best I've ever eaten, thanks to the fine, firm, deep-flavored flesh of the Gauloise race. I was planning to spend several months in England and America to promote the English edition of *Yquem*, due to appear that autumn. I killed the four remaining rambunctious cocks, plucked and cleaned them and tucked them into the deep freeze, dreaming of coqs-au-vin to come.

The last time I had seen Marie Ricard, she was in her mid-nineties, deaf and blind, terrible for her and hopeless for her friends to be completely out of contact. Rosette had been twice operated on for breast cancer and no one had faith in its having been checked. I received from Michel Lemonnier a clipping from a Marseille newspaper: a fishing boat had been blown up at sea; the body of the owner was identified as Jacques Ricard from Salon-de-Provence. I thought it was the end of an epoch. (In January 1996, I received a phone call from an old friend of Jacques and Rosette, who told me that Rosette had tried several times, unsuccessfully, to phone me. Marie, she said, had died at the age of 99; the next morning, Jacques packed explosives into his fishing boat, went to sea and blew himself up. Rosette, who had lived with Jacques for fifty years, but never been married, lost Les Plaines to the French government and was living in a flat in Salon. A few minutes later, Rosette rang. "He shouldn't have done that to me," she said, "I loved him so...but, of course, he could never have supported to see me grow old.")

When I began work on *Yquem*, Gisou and I formulated a questionnaire (When do you serve Yquem? Greatest vintages in your cellar? Fondest memories? Anecdotes? etc.) which she sent to a number of Yquem connoisseurs and collectors, whose names were furnished by Alexandre. Hardy Rodenstock, who is said to own and to have tasted more Yquems than anyone in the world, responded that he, too, was working on a book on Yquem, encouraged by many German publishers. He enclosed published notes of all the Yquems he had tasted and a photo of him and Alexandre with his permission to publish it in our forthcoming book. At about this same time, his discovery, in an unidentified Parisian cellar, of bottles of Yquem and Lafite, embossed with Thomas Jefferson's initials and the date, 1787, created a spate of publicity. I used some of his notes of 19th century Yquems, credited, in the "Vintages" chapter of *Yquem*. Gisou told me he was influential in German publishing circles and wanted to co-sign the German edition of *Yquem*, with his name on the cover. I said no. (A Swiss firm later published it in German.)

30 September 1986. Hardy Rodenstock organized a banquet-winetasting event at Château d'Yquem. In addition to Bérengère, Alexandre and himself, there were forty guests, ten of whom were Alexandre's. England was represented by Jancis Robinson and Michael Broadbent. Bipin Desai was present, a Belgian journalist, a Dutch collector, a dozen Bordelais...the other guests were German. Bérengère and Jancis were the only women. We were requested to appear in black tie at 9:30 a.m., in the lobby of our Bordeaux hotel, where a bus would be waiting to drive us to Yquem. The day was beautiful; we drank Champagne in the courtyard where Jacques Hébrard introduced me to a member of the

group, explaining that, just as Hardy Rodenstock was known in Germany as "Monsieur Yquem," this man was known as "Monsieur Cheval Blanc." We went to table at about 11 a.m.; Jancis later wrote that we were thirteen hours at table—I counted fourteen.

Twelve courses and sixty-six wines were broken into four services with Champagne breaks in between. Jancis: "Three thousand, five hundred splinter-stemmed crystal glasses were, in sobering progression, cleaned, filled, emptied and cleaned again." I don't remember if all the glasses were the same; those in which the Yquems and the red wines were served (one of which was offered to each guest as a souvenir) contained 75 cl—the Yquem coat of arms was engraved on the bowl, Rodenstock's and Alexandre's signatures at the base. Rodenstock brought his chef and sommelier from Germany, the mineral water came from Belgium and the glasses from Austria. Alexandre was troubled because none of the service was French; he imposed Francis Garcia (then proprietor of Clavel in Bordeaux, now of Le Chapon Fin) for a couple of the courses and a Bordelais sommelier to assist at the wine service. (I joined Garcia during one of the intervals; he was in a gloomy mood—he and his staff had nothing to do and he didn't like the German's cuisine.) Toward the end of the first service, after a series of German reislings, another of white Burgundies, twenty vintages of "Ygrec" (the dry white wine produced in certain years at Yquem), and before drinking Yquem 1976 with sautéed foie gras and grapes, four Yquems were poured: 1858, 1847, 1811 and ca. 1750. They were all in perfect condition, the 1847 the most astonishing wine I have ever drunk, nervous, intense, vibrant, laced with chocolate, caramel and more mysterious, spicy memories which words cannot uncover. 1811 was "The Great Comet Year," the most famous vintage of the 19th century. By comparison to the 1847, it and the Louis XV vintage may have seemed a bit dusty, but I was awed to be dipping so deep into history, the one produced while Napoléon was wreaking havoc in Europe, the other while Mme de Pompadour was scandalizing the court at Versailles, before revolutions were dreamt of. The 18th century bottle was said to have been spirited out of the U.S.S.R., a remnant of the Russian Czars' cellars; the bottle was squat, deep blue, with enamel-painted white and yellow flowers scattered over its surface and bore the arms of the Sauvage family. (It now stands in a showcase at Château d'Yquem.)

The second service led into the red wines, all in large format—magnum, double magnum, jéroboam, impérial.... After a series of 1978s (California Mondavi Reserve and three Médocs) and four 1966 clarets, there was a pause in the food service to play a little guessing game: ten famous growths from venerated vintages, the youngest a Latour 1937, the oldest a Lafite 1848, were poured blindly and out of order, to be identified by the players. I don't like parlour games at table and I remember none of them. A Brane-Cantenac 1978 was then served with guinea fowl in elderberry sauce—the wine and the elderberries quarreled. Third service: Truffle flans, Brillat-Savarin and seven great clarets from celebrated vintages, finishing with Mouton 1929: the Germans exclaimed, "Stupendous," the Bordelais murmured, "Not authentic." I didn't know—by that time everything tasted the same. Fourth service: Two desserts, seven white wines; my palate was resuscitated by the two Yquems, 1937 and 1921. Antique alcohols were offered with coffee and, as the guests began to move around, another Champagne was poured. I stayed with the '21 Yquem.

Kermit and Gail bought property in the hills outside of Le Beausset, in Bandol vineyard country, a stone's throw from Domaine Tempier and a half-hour drive from Solliès. (They divide their time between Le Beausset and Berkeley, Kermit has planted vines, they've added new rooms to the house and built a swimming pool.)

Jean Fischbacher died.

Yquem appeared simultaneously in England, America, Denmark, Sweden and Japan. Jill, who had moved to Dorling-Kindersley, was my editor for the English language editions. In the U.S., it was published by David Godine. I stopped in London to promote and continued to New York, where a "Who's Who of Cooking in America" manifestation coincided with the *Yquem* promotion. It was at this reception that Craig Claiborne deigned not to shake my hand and Judith Jones hastened to apologize for her and her husband's subversive activities à propos of *The Good Cook*, saying it had nothing to do with me, it was only because they disliked Time-Life. Marion Cunningham and Alice Waters presented me for the award.

Alexandre joined me in New York for booksignings, dinners and interviews. The International Wine and Food Society gave a fine, splashy dinner in a mid-town restaurant (formerly Quo Vadis). The previous day, we spent several hours with the organizers signing copies of *Yquem* for a hundred and some members and guests. The French Culinary Institute, under the direction of Dorothy Cann, a captivatingly high-spirited young woman, organized a press dinner. Jim Peterson, who had visited me years earlier in Solliès, was the chef-professor in charge of a beautifully ordinated meal:

French Culinary Institute
Château d'Yquem Dinner
October 21, 1986

Aperitif: "Y"
§
Salade Françoise
Potato, Truffle, & Artichoke Salad
Flavored with Château de Fargues
Château de Fargues, 1981
§
Ragoût de Homard à la Crème d'Oursin
Lobster & Sea Urchin Ragout
Château d'Yquem, 1980
§
Epaule d'Agneau Braisée aux Cèpes
Shoulder of Lamb Braised with Cepes
Château Talbot, 1979
§
Crèpes aux Pommes
Hot Apple Crepes
Château d'Yquem, 1975

A promotion tour leaves little time for friends, I stayed with Lydie and Wayne Marshall. Lydie had received a fresh duck foie gras and asked me to cook it. I sautéed it pinkly, we shared it with Cecily Brownstone and accompanied it with mashed potatoes. I cooked once for Nika, who was permanently confined to a wheel chair. Robert Isaacson and I had dinner at Sally Darr's restaurant, La Tulipe, where we finished with hot apple pie and 1967 Yquem. He cooked for Lucia and me. Had dinner with Paula Wolfert and Bill Bayer; Paula invented a wondrous assemblage of offal, each element prepared separately according to its needs. Paul Grimes was teaching at Peter Kump's cooking school and asked me to speak to his students; Nick Malgieri was teaching pastry there and joined us.

Fortunately, the American Institute of Wine and Food (AIWF) began to pick up the bills. They invited me to Dallas, early November, for a four-day Conference on Gastronomy in the newly opened, grandiose Hotel Crescent Court and, from there, flew me to southern California and to San Francisco for receptions and book signings.

I arrived at the Hotel Crescent Court late in the day. The lobby was aswarm with people checking in and another conference checking out. I saw no one I knew and went for a walk in the gardens. Three dejected-looking figures, slouching toward me from afar, were suddenly animated by yelps of delight at seeing a familiar face: Gérard Besson, Jacques Cagna and Jean-Pierre Billoux had been invited to present meals for the conference. They had been met, neither at the airport nor at the hotel. Jacques spoke a little English, Gérard and Jean-Pierre none at all. Gérard had arrived with a stock of little Puy lentils to garnish his turbot. Customs officials broke open and emptied all the packages, undressed him and poked around indiscreetly.... He was glum and angry about his reception in our wonderful democracy; all three were feeling very lost. We headed for a bar and they were soon laughing about their misadventures. Later that evening was a pre-conference mainfestation with hundreds of people milling around, a dozen stands, each manned by a chef from the Southwest serving out his specialties, thirteen wine stalls, and interminable queues everywhere. I knew some of the chefs by reputation—Dean Fearing, Stephan Pyles, Robert Del Grande.... The only one I knew personally was Mark Miller, at whose stand I took refuge behind the scenes. In the days to come, Gérard, Jacques and Jean-Pierre received ovations for their efforts and were once again stars instead of abandoned waifs.

In San Diego, I was passed around among members of the Institute. I remember a visit, with Anne Otterson, to the Chino family vegetable farm which, I learned, is one of Chez Panisse's principal suppliers. In Santa Monica, my host and another couple invited me to Chinois on Main. They had told Danny Kaye that I would be there. He arrived, emaciated and unsteady, fiddled with a cup of tea while we ate and asked me to visit him the following morning. He was very proud of his two kitchens, one Chinese, with an installation of giant woks, the other French, with a professional cookstove and a battery of copper. The walls were crowded with photos of famous chefs, Alexandre Dumaine, Paul Bocuse, the Troisgros brothers, Michel Guérard, Roger Vergé...posing with Danny, in a tailored chef's costume and tall toque, his face split with a deliriously happy grin. We separated after a long, sentimental hug which, I thought, had less to do with me than with the fact that he was preparing to take leave of the world. He died not long afterward.

Elizabeth David who, until a year or so earlier, had shown no interest in visiting America, was in San Francisco for the second time, staying with Gerald Asher, whom she had known during his wine merchant days in London. I had not visited the Bay Area since 1981. In 1983, Steve Sullivan had left the Chez Panisse kitchens to open The Acme Bread Co. on the premises of Kermit's wine emporium in Berkeley, while continuing to furnish Chez Panisse with beautiful sour dough bread, Alice had opened Café Fanny, fitted neatly between Kermit Lynch Wine Merchant and The Acme Bread Co., and, in San Francisco, 4 July 1984, Jeremiah had opened Stars, a glamourous brasserie reminiscent of a 1930s Paris which exists only in our imagination.

I stayed with Jeremiah and lunched often with Elizabeth, either at Stars or at Chez Panisse. Chuck Williams and the AIWF collaborated to organize a reception for me and *Yquem* at Williams-

Sonoma; I spoke about the history of the vineyard, noble rot and had begun to explain the vinification when a young man demanded to know the "brix readings." I knew nothing about brix. He launched into a brix lecture to an increasingly hostile audience and, with no preamble, shifted to the subject of cookbooks and his favorite cookery writer, Elliot Roosevelt. Hands were raised with questions, but the words would not be stopped. At evening's end, Greg Drescher, AIWF program director, Robert Clark, editor of the AIWF newsletter, and I went for a late supper to Stars, where the young man suddenly materialized, a tattered copy of Elliot Roosevelt's cookbook in hand, installed himself at our table and ploughed ahead with his exposition. Greg took him aside and returned alone to the table.

Alice wanted to organize a lunch in Elizabeth's honour. Elizabeth begged her not to, so she named Elizabeth guest of honour at a lunch given to celebrate the publication of *Yquem*. Paul Bertolli was chef. The menu opened with a salad of bulb fennel, firm raw cèpes, white Piedmont truffles and fresh Parmesan cheese, each shaved thinly, anointed with olive oil and a few drops of lemon juice, exquisitely simple and pure. In *Chez Panisse Cooking*, Paul wrote, "For Richard Olney, friend and mentor of the restaurant, I wanted to create a menu that would illustrate the idea that in the best of cooking, the cooking itself does not show...." We drank Yquem 1976 for dessert. Three days later at Joseph Phelps Winery, AIWF, with Jeremiah and his staff, organized "Jeremiah's Dinner for Richard Olney." This time the white truffles were scattered over pinkly roast mallard breasts and we finished with Yquem 1980.

November Lunch for Richard Olney

(The hand-painted menus, opposite page, were finished when the freshly fished, unshelled sea scallops arrived on the morning of the lunch to replace the black sea bass.)

Fennel, Mushroom, Parmesan Cheese, and White Truffle Salad
Vintage Tunina, Jermann
§
Sauteed Maine Sea Scallops
Raveneau Chablis (Blanchots), 1984
§
Saffron Risotto
Rubesco riserva in magnum, Lungarotti, 1975
§
Spit-Roasted Veal and Straw Potatoes with Chanterelles
Chateau Margaux in jeroboam, 1966
§
Garden Salad
§
Cheese
Nuits Meurgers, Henri Jayer, 1978
§
Yquem, 1976

Chez Panisse, 16 November 1986

I spent Christmas in Rochester with Byron and family and accompanied Mother to Washington to see in the New Year with Margaret, Elizabeth and James.

1987. During my absence from Solliès, Mary had settled into the house but, because she had never mastered the technique of filling the chickens' feeder and watering can, Henri came up to care for the chickens. One morning he reported to Mary that a fox had carried the chickens away. At 3 a.m. Washington time, she rang Margaret, who refused to awaken me. I returned to discover

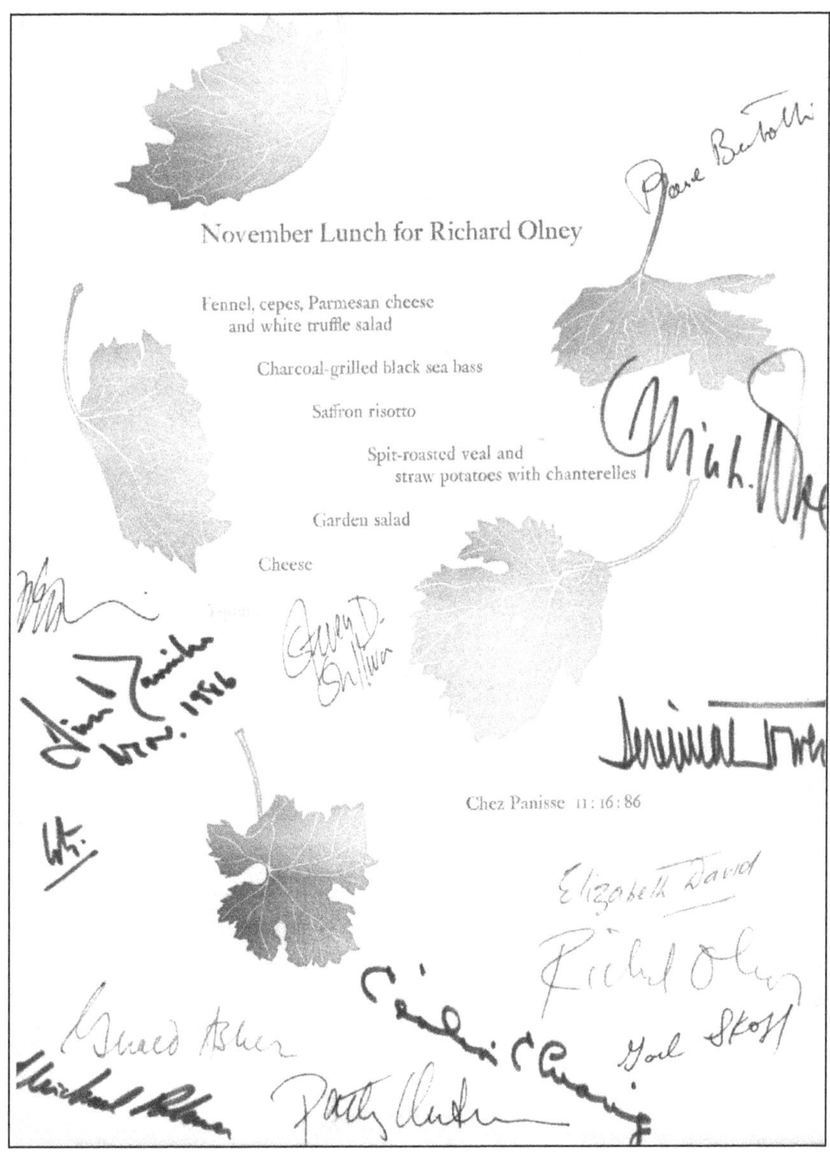

November Lunch for Richard Olney

Fennel, cepes, Parmesan cheese
and white truffle salad

Charcoal-grilled black sea bass

Saffron risotto

Spit-roasted veal and
straw potatoes with chanterelles

Garden salad

Cheese

Chez Panisse 11 : 16 : 86

that the electricity had been off for two months. Instead of pushing a button to put it back on, Mary had been content to drink away the evenings by candlelight. In the deep freeze, the young roosters and a kilo of truffles were in a state of semi-liquid putrescence. I

With Alice Waters and Elizabeth David, Chez Panisse, 16 November 1986.

threw out the deep freeze, repaired the chicken yard and bought new chickens.

Bipin Desai asked me to organize another dinner in collaboration with Jean-Claude Vrinat at Taillevent, this time to fête both Yquem and the wines of the Domaine de la Romanée-Conti:

Bienvenue au Château d'Yquem et au Domaine de la Romanée-Conti
Menu organisé par Bipin Desai et Richard Olney
18 Mars 1987, Le Taillevent, Paris

Foie Gras d'Oie et de Canard au Naturel
Château d'Yquem 1948
§
Rougets de Roche en Escabèche
Champagne Dom Ruinart 1979
§
Coquilles Saint-Jacques aux Moules
Montrachet 1967
§
Noix de Ris de Veau aux Primeurs
Côte de Boeuf à la Moelle
Romanée-Saint-Vivant 1971
Grands Echézeaux 1971
§
Pigeonneau de Bresse en Becasse
Richebourg 1966
§
Truffe du Quercy en Cocotte
Romanée-Conti 1959
§
Fromages de nos Provinces
La Tâche 1949
§
Glace au Lait d'Amandes et au Coulis de Groseille
Chateau d'Yquem 1959
§§§

AIWF

Jeremiah's Dinner for Richard Olney

Joseph Phelps Winery

November 19, 1986

1980 Schramsberg Reserve

Vegetable Salad

1982 Robert Mondavi Fumé Blanc Reserve

Black Bass with Lobster Sauce

1980 Trefethen Chardonnay

Roast Mallard Breast with Celery and White Truffle

1981 Jaeger Cellars Inglewood Vineyard Merlot

Grilled Mallard Leg with Curly Endive

1975 Joseph Phelps Vineyards Cabernet Sauvignon, in Magnum

1977 Joseph Phelps Vineyards Insignia

American Cheeses

1974 Chalone Vineyard Pinot Noir

Stewed Apples with Pistachio Cream

1980 Château d'Yquem

The American Institute of Wine & Food

12 April 1987. No bottles of Romanée-Conti 1927 remained in the Domaine's private cellar; instead, they offered me a bottle of Romanèe-Conti 1926 "for the anniversary of my conception."

Sheldrake Press, a small packaging publisher in London, asked me to write *Ten Vineyard Lunches*. I broke viticultural France into ten regions and presented a menu with recipes and wine suggestions for each region. The editor, Eleanor Lines, and the photographer, Bob Komar, both of whom had worked with me on *The Good Cook*, arrived in Solliès for the first of several cooking-photography sessions.

I had known Janet and Yannick Cam, proprietors of Le Pavillon restaurant in Washington, D.C., for several years. Janet and Dorothy Cann were traveling in Europe and suggested that we celebrate the Fourth of July in Solliès. They arrived with sparklers and reams of red, white and blue bunting to drape around the grapevine arbor, beneath which we passed a couple of days eating and drinking grand wines. The multicoloured lights which permanently surround the terrace lent festive support in the evening.

As therapy for the pain of Jean's death, Simca needed to keep busy under pressure. She thrust herself into work on a last book, *Food and Friends*, to which I donated a few pages, entitled *A Homage to Simca*. Michael James spent a couple of months at Bramafam. He was supposed to be co-author, taking notes and writing the English text. Simca complained that he borrowed her car every night to visit the bars in Cannes, returned late and slept all morning; no work was getting done. One night, returning from Cannes, Michael ran out of gas, abandoned the car on the roadside and took a taxi to Bramafam. That, she said, was the last straw. Michael returned to California and Suzy Patterson collaborated on the book.

My nephew, Johnny, arrived with an Italian girl, Anna Crosta, whom he had met at a German summer school for foreigners. Lulu asked us for bouillabaisse. We tasted in the cellars and spent the afternoon at table. Anna stayed for a week or so. I bought a car so that Johnny could move freely between Solliès and Aix, an hour's drive. He joined the Toulon ice hockey team and became an instant local star. Without quite realizing it, he was also enrolled in an intensive winetasting course, both from my cellar and during visits to vigneron friends.

Early October, at grape harvest time, I went to Burgundy to meet a prospective photographer for Romanée-Conti. Johnny joined me, we stayed with Aubert and Pamela, spent days at the Domaine, lunched with a hundred pickers, cellar staff and other personnel in a rambunctious ambience, visited the ancient ruins of the Saint-Vivant monastery and dined at Aubert's in Bouzeron with more pickers, mainly students. Neither Gisou nor I was happy with the photographer's work, but I came away with a clearer picture of the photos we needed and Johnny's fascination with the wine-maker's métier was deepened.

Gisou visited Harold Acton at La Pietra and left a copy of *Yquem*. I received a letter of praise for "the superbly produced and informative *Yquem*, which makes my mouth water and fills me with nostalgia (...) But I hope you are not too absorbed and can find time for other tastes." It might have been a letter from my father. Harold believed in the table and all the good things in life, but he was an aesthetic puritan, convinced that Art moved on a higher plane.

1 December. Jimmy Baldwin died of cancer. Peter Price died the day after Christmas; I had not seen him since winding up the Time-Life work in London, when he told me the doctors gave him five years to live.

I flew with Johnny to Saint Louis, Anna joined him there and I continued my holiday family rounds.

1988. 12 January. In Washington, Janet and Yannick Cam invited Margaret and me to Le Pavillon for a "Dégustation de Bourgogne 1985," ten grand Burgundies built around a menu of exquisite purity.

8 February. Gail Skoff gave birth to a girl, Marly.

The Toulon hockey team was playing Roanne on the latter's rink. I reserved a room for the night and a table for lunch the next day at Troisgros. At midnight, after the match, Johnny and I found Pierre Troisgros at the restaurant bar. "Still teaching in Avignon?" He had asked the same question a dozen times over the preceding fifteen years; the answer was always "no." "What are you doing?" "Working on *Romanée-Conti*." "Oh yes," he said, "Wasn't it (he mentioned the name of a French journalist)—or someone like that—who recently wrote a book on Yquem?" I exploded. Pierre had been present two years earlier at the Relais et Châteaux reception when Yquem received the annual prize, his son had been on the jury, the restaurant was a member of the Relais et Châteaux

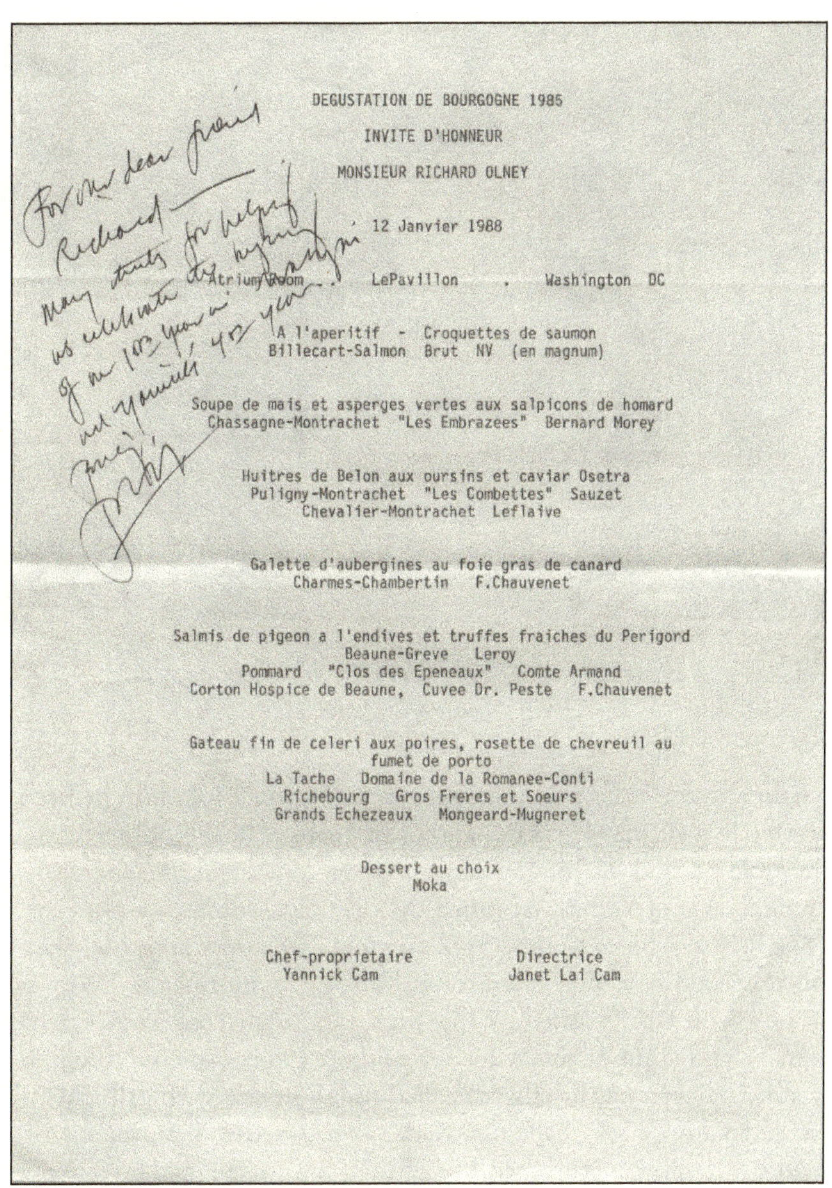

DEGUSTATION DE BOURGOGNE 1985

INVITE D'HONNEUR

MONSIEUR RICHARD OLNEY

12 Janvier 1988

Atrium Room . LePavillon . Washington DC

A l'aperitif - Croquettes de saumon
Billecart-Salmon Brut NV (en magnum)

Soupe de mais et asperges vertes aux salpicons de homard
Chassagne-Montrachet "Les Embrazees" Bernard Morey

Huitres de Belon aux oursins et caviar Osetra
Puligny-Montrachet "Les Combettes" Sauzet
Chevalier-Montrachet Leflaive

Galette d'aubergines au foie gras de canard
Charmes-Chambertin F.Chauvenet

Salmis de pigeon a l'endives et truffes fraiches du Perigord
Beaune-Greve Leroy
Pommard "Clos des Epeneaux" Comte Armand
Corton Hospice de Beaune, Cuvee Dr. Peste F.Chauvenet

Gateau fin de celeri aux poires, rosette de chevreuil au fumet de porto
La Tache Domaine de la Romanee-Conti
Richebourg Gros Freres et Soeurs
Grands Echezeaux Mongeard-Mugneret

Dessert au choix
Moka

Chef-proprietaire
Yannick Cam

Directrice
Janet Lai Cam

Dégustation de Bourgogne 1985
Invité d'Honneur
Monsieur Richard Olney, January 12, 1988.

With Ghislaine (Gisou) Bavoillot and Lulu Peyraud
AIWF, New York, April 1988.

chain and the book was on display at Troisgros. I told him he knew perfectly well that I was the author of *Yquem*. He affected to eat humble pie and sat Johnny and me down to a terrine of foie gras and a bottle of Volnay. At lunch the next day, I ordered a pig's ear. The maître d'hotel seemed to be in pain: "One does not order that kind of food in a three-star establishment," he murmered. "Why is it on the menu?" I asked, "I like pigs' ears." Any cook knows that ears should simmer gently for several hours to become succulently tender. My ear was briefly parboiled tough gristle with gribiche smeared atop. I asked the maître de'hôtel to return it to the kitchen and bring me something edible. "I told you so," he said triumphantly. The rest of the food was banal.

In early April, the AIWF held a colloquy in New York City, to which they flew Lulu, Laurence and Jean-Marie Peyraud, Gisou and me. Alice organized a grand reception on the theme of Provence for which, it seemed to me, she had solicited the help of every rising star in the American food world. On all sides, familiar

With Alice and Jill,
French Culinary Institute, April 1988.

figures were offering raw sardine fillets, tapénade or anchoïade on garlic crusts, opening sea urchins and dishing up octopus daube with aïoli. One wall was devoted to a blow-up photo of Lulu's kitchen fireplace. Kermit presented Domaine Tempier.

Margaret's show, "Solliès Landscapes," opened 10 April in Washington at the Susan Conway Carroll Gallery. Lulu and I went down from New York for the opening. There were garden, terrace and tablescapes, as well as landscapes, vivid memories of Solliès summers. Susan Conway gave a reception at her home that evening at which Lulu recounted a complicated tale to a group of guests who knew no French. I tried to translate, speaking slowly and enunciating carefully. Lulu was enchanted, she said, "I understood every word!" The others were puzzled: my "translation" had been delivered in French instead of English.

With Ghislaine (Gisou) Bauoillot and Nora Carey
AIWF Colloquy, April 1988, New York.

12 April. Dorothy Cann gave me a birthday dinner at the French Culinary Institute. There were balloons and streamers aplenty, Lulu, Laurence and Jean-Marie, Lydie and Wayne Marshall, Mary's niece, Carolyn, Gisou, Alice, Nora, Jill, Kermit.... We finished with Yquem.

Kit was leaving Time-Life. George Constable asked me to London to cook a farewell dinner in the Time-Life kitchen. He came over from Alexandria. Sybille joined us and Johnny worked with me in the kitchen. We were eighteen in the "executive" dining room for scrambled eggs with asparagus, roast leg of lamb, gratin Dauphinois, salad, cheeses and glazed apple and crêpe roulades, with the hallowed suite of Champagne, white Burgundy, clarets and Sauternes. The next evening, Kit, Tony, Johnny and I dined with Elizabeth David at Bibendum. A beautiful evening. Elizabeth was radiant, tasted her food and enjoined Johnny and me to finish her plates, lest they be returned full to the kitchen to trouble Simon. She was, then, nourishing herself more on conversation and wine and less on food.

Each year, during the Bordeaux May Music Festival, an evening chamber music concert was organized in the courtyard of Château d'Yquem, followed by a formal reception in the château. I profited from the invitation to plan a week's visit with Johnny to the Bordelais vineyards. In the Médoc, we stayed at Loudenne. Josette was in the kitchen, Sylvain was as attentive as ever but, without Martin, it couldn't be the same. We had lunch with Alexis Lichine and he joined us the next day for lunch at Ducru-Beaucaillou with Jean-Eugène and Monique Borie. We tasted in the cellars of Margaux, Latour, Mouton and Lafite. In Graves, at Malartic-Lagravières, Jacques Marly showered us with bottles, books and fossil seashells from the vineyard, we lunched at Domaine de Chevalier and tasted at Haut-Brion. In Saint-Emilion we dined with the Manoncourts at Figeac, tasted the next morning at Cheval Blanc and had lunch at the Hébrards' home. Everywhere, we drank 1961 with the cheese.

Alexandre asked us to spend the weekend with him and his sons, Bertrand and Philippe, then 14 and 11 years old, at Uza, an ancestral forest property in Les Landes, between Bordeaux and Biarritz. Bertrand was growing up and very self-possessed; Philippe was irrepressible and ecstatic to be in the presence of a hockey player. White asparagus from the property was wonderful.

Kermit and Gail were married in April. On May 30th, the day that Margaret, James and Byron arrived to spend the month of June with Johnny and me, the Peyrauds gave a Grand Aïoli marriage celebration at Domaine Tempier. Alice, Stephen, Fanny and a crowd of Côtes-du-Rhône and Burgundy vignerons were present—Aubert and Pamela, Gérard and Monique Chave, Jean-Marie Raveneau (Chablis), the Bruniers (Domaine du Vieux Télégraphe, Châteauneuf-du-Pape), and I forget.... Fanny painted the menu.

On the hillside, lunches were mostly melon and prosciutto, composed salads and cheeses, washed down with Corbières blanc and Tempier rosé. Johnny chose the dinner wines. On June 23rd, we drank the Romanée-Conti 1926. It was magical:

Richard Olney

Solliès-Toucas
23 June 1988

Apértif: Krug 1979
§
Filets de Sardines Crues en Marinade
Hermitage Blanc (Chave) 1981
§
Onglet Grillé
Gratin de Pommes de Terre aux Truffes
Echézeaux (DRC) 1978
§
Fromages
Romanée-Conti 1926
§
Château Ricaud (Loupiac) 1929
§

13 July 1988. (Me to Byron) "Johnny is taking a 6-week painting course in Aix, returns here Thursday evenings and goes back to Aix Sundays after dinner. I went to Aix last Thursday, spent the night and the next morning we tasted our way through the cellars at Château Simone, had lunch with the owners, René and Monique Rougier, and returned here Friday evening. Johnny's classes are over the 21st but he has rented the flat until the end of the month. The 22nd we are driving to Hermitage for a couple of days of winetasting, cooking and eating with Gérard and Monique Chave and he then plans to receive Anna in Aix before returning here…."

John arrived in August. Dîner 11 August 1988, with Kermit and Gail:

Apéritif: Krug 1973	
§	
Hermitage Blanc 1981	Soupe de Poisson à la Baudroie
§	
Latour, Magnum 1968	Gigot, Haricots Panachés
§	
Ducru-Beaucaillou '61	Fromages
§	
Yquem 1982	Crêpes aux Pommes
§	

Kermit asked Johnny to work in the Berkeley wine shop, beginning the first of September. Nora, who was working in London while preparing a book on preserves, arrived on vacation a few days before John returned to Saint Louis and Johnny headed for Berkeley. Autumn figs were ripe and grapes were ripening; she tested several versions of a fig and reduced grapejuice compote for the book. We exchanged meals with the Peyrauds. *Ten Vineyard Lunches* appeared simultaneously in England and the United States.

Alexandre and Bérengère asked me to lunch at Yquem with Bernard Pivot. Michel Guillard and the Lur-Saluces children, Isabeau, Bertrand and Philippe, were at table—the others were new to me. Two of the guests had a prolonged and heated argument about whether or not Louis XVI was responsible for the collapse of the Ancien Régime. The rest of the company seemed to have no opinion. Philippe was avid for news of my nephew. We finished with Yquem 1934, Alexandre's birthyear.

24 November. Anton Mosimann had left the Dorchester to create a "membership-by-subscription" restaurant. James wanted to gather British and American friends and colleagues around a dinner table. I met him, Margaret and Nathan in London, we discussed the menu with Anton over a bottle of Champagne and reserved a

With Anton Mosimann,
London 1986.

table for twelve in a private dining room. Elizabeth David and Valerie Eliot were amongst the guests. Nathan had a very good time, drank a bit too much wine and regretted it later.

In December, my round of family visits began in Berkeley. Johnny gave me a buffet dinner party at his newly rented basement flat in Bob Clark's house. John arrived and we made a number of trips to the Salvation Army store to furnish the flat. Jeremiah and Dick Graff joined forces to receive us at Stars, in the newly created

Margaret and Elizabeth David, Mosimann's, November 24, 1988.

private dining room and, at Chez Panisse, a perfect menu opened with Paul Bertolli'a intoxicating wild mushroom and truffle tart.

7 January 1989. In Washington, Janet and Yannick Cam again invited us to an evening of subtle food flavors and venerated vintages.

I don't know when I began to populate the aviary. One spring day, I stopped in a Toulon pet shop and bought three sprightly and inquisitive red-billed Leothrix, presumably a male and two females, though they have never reproduced. I installed giant bouquets of broom from the hillside, moulded a birdbath in concrete and built an electrically heated winter shelter, which most of the birds shun. Elizabeth offered me three-tiered feeders, designed to contain different grains at each level, and I fashioned dozens of nesting homes from the wooden cases of Yquem,

150 REDWOOD, SAN FRANCISCO, CALIFORNIA 94102, 415 · 861 · 7827

WELCOME BACK RICHARD OLNEY
FROM THE STAFF OF STARS & CHALONE VINEYARD
DECEMBER 20, 1988

***

Champagne, Veuve Clicquot, 1982
Pinot Blanc, Chalone Vineyard, Estate Bottled, 1983

***

DUCK PROSCUITTO WITH CONFIT OF GIZZARDS & CELERY SALAD

Pinot Blanc, Chalone Vineyard, Estate Bottled, 1981

***

GRILLED DUNGENESS CRAB WITH LOBSTER BUTTER

Chardonnay, Chalone Vineyard, Estate Bottled, 1981

***

SWEETBREAD TIMBALE WITH PIGEON SAUCE

Pinot Noir, Chalone Vineyard, Estate Bottled, 1981

***

STARS' PASSION FRUIT FANTASY CREAM WITH HOT GINGER COOKIES

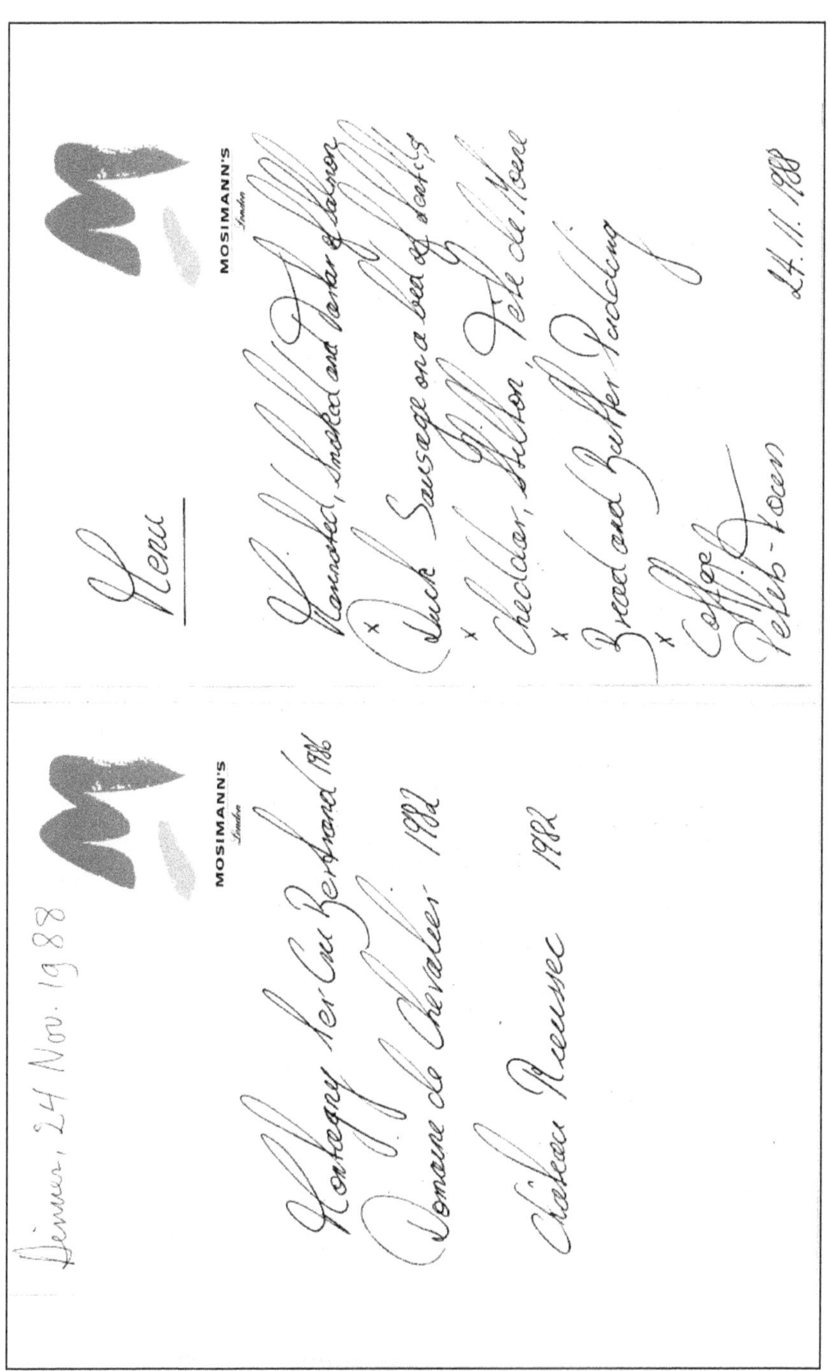

Dinner, 24 Nov. 1988

MOSIMANN'S
London

Montagny 1er Cru Bertrand 1986

Domaine de Chevalier 1982

Château Rieussec 1982

MOSIMANN'S
London

Menu

Marinated, Smoked and Tartar of Salmon

Duck Sausage on a bed of lentils

Cheddar, Stilton, Tête de Moine

Bread and Butter Pudding

Coffee

Petits-Fours

24. 11. 1988

Romanée-Conti and other growths unknown to most birds. In a few years time, a couple of paddas—Indonesian rice birds—increased fifty-fold, a pair of cockatiels swelled in number to forty-odd and several small finches crossbred to produce amusing hybrids. Unlike the other birds, whose young remain in the nests until they are ready to fly, the miniature Chinese quail are nidifugous. The moment they break out of their shells, they begin to lurch around like drunken bumblebees. The chickenwire mesh was not small enough to prevent their escape. From the first batch, two floundered into the chickenyard and were gobbled up by bloodthirsty hens; the others I gathered up outside and sequestered long enough to install a band of fine mesh around the borders of the aviary. A year later, they were twenty. Most enchanting are the little African parrots called lovebirds, brightly coloured and talented clowns.

Mary didn't care too much for my solitary habit of a light snack for lunch. On days that Henri worked, I prepared a serious meal and she joined us. Part of her established ritual was to drive first to a neighbouring village to "shop." The shopping was always the same—a bundle of radishes and some charcuterie, which she could have bought down the street from her house. Upon arriving, she would exclaim, "Whew! Shopping was so terrible! I've got to have a whisky!" Then we would "do the accounts"—a silly game, I thought, but, to Mary, it was of primordial importance that, for a bunch of radishes, she be reimbursed neither a centime too much nor a centime too little. It was her job to trim the radishes. By lunch's end she was drunk. When I cut off the whisky supply, she decided to hit the wine harder and was convinced I was cheating her. I poured to the same level in each glass but Mary would then snatch the bottle to fill her glass, pour wide of the mark and soak the tablecloth. One day, Mary arrived by foot, saying she could no longer shop, she had sold her car to a neighbour. That was wonderful news, although, henceforth, Henri had to drive her home after lunch. A few weeks later, she recounted a tale which seemed to puzzle her as much as it did us, though I think she believed it: she said she had sold her car and stopped driving many years earlier because she realized her eyesight was failing. Henri wasn't here

RICHARD OLNEY

le 7 Janvier 1989

Atrium Room . LePavillon . Washington . DC

Dom Perignon . 1973

A l'aperitif - Beignets d'huitres de Belon au vinaigre

Le Montrachet . Domaine Thenard . Remoissenet . 1982

Petit macaroni a la becasse et truffes fraiches du Perigord en salade

Quenelles de brochet gratinees a la creme d'asperges vertes

Chassagne Montrachet . Caillerets . B. Morey . 1983

Consomme aux ris de veau, raviolis aux lentilles

Homard du Maine roti a la ciboulette

Chateau Lynch Bages . 1949

Noisette d'agneau aux tetes de brocolis, fumet aux olives

Chateau L'Evangile . 1961 & Chateau Haut Brion . 1962

Fromage de chevre et sa salade de mache

Chateau Climens . 1983

Croquettes de fraises des bois et mangues aux pistaches, glace au caramel, jus de fruit de la passion

Moka

when she climbed the hillside with an awful woman whom she introduced as her neighbour, the wife of the man who had bought the car. She yapped like a lapdog, said she loved birds, her husband loved them even more and must come up; she pointed, screamed, waved her arms about, scared the birds to death and seemed convinced that I needed lots of company to fill in my solitary hours. I asked Mary never to bring the woman back and to make certain that her husband didn't call.

April 1989. I received from Jimmy Merrill a book called *A Catafalque for David Hill*, composed of reproductions of David's paintings and of short eulogies and expressions of affection for the artist's eccentricities by his friends. David died 31 August 1977. There were a couple of notes by B.V. (Bernie) Winebaum and at the end of the book is a two-page composition entitled "A Conversation with David Hill: 18.ix.1977," signed David Jackson and James Merrill, an unusual sort of interview across "The Great Divide" through the medium of an Ouija board. I sent Jimmy a copy of *Yquem*.

When the telephone rang at 4 a.m., I knew it was Bernie Winebaum: "Hello, pet. I'm just having a little cocktail before dinner." "For heaven's sake, Bernie, don't you know what time it is?" "Oh, pet, you know how I am, I get everything mixed up." He didn't get anything mixed up but every evening before a late dinner he was potted and began compulsively to ring up friends around the world. He was always on the line for an hour or more, babbling about the beautiful boys who worked in his garden, the landscape, his evening menu and so forth. No response was required. I could lay down the receiver, wander around the room, light a cigarette, pour a drink, return to the phone and the monologue continued.

9 June 1989. A note from Jimmy Merrill, mostly about *Yquem*, which finishes, "David saw Bernie last summer (first time in a decade—I was out of town) and got an impression of—well, call it pourriture noble. (He was wearing plus fours without stockings.)"

Bernie came to visit—first time in several years. He emerged from a rented car in an ankle-length, moth eaten bear coat (a junkshop *trouvaille*), leaning on a rustic cane, said he was crip-

Johnny picking grapes at Domaine Tempier, 1989.

pled—in an Athens hotel room, his legs had suddenly locked at the hip to punish his mother for making him homosexual. I thought if the punishment were intended for his mother, Freud should have locked her legs instead of his. I told him to stop being silly. The extent of his affliction was never clear to me—he seemed to walk more easily when not aware of being observed. In years past, Bernie had been a gentle, considerate companion, civilized and amusing. Now, he was a tyrant. He carried a portable radio whose wake-up station began blaring hideous music at 5 a.m.; at 10 or 15 minute intervals, he would then call, "C'mon pet, time to get up!" He was proud of his drawings, mainly of Greek men in various stages of undress, in which I could discern no trace of talent, and discovered that, by photocopying them and adding a couple of pen strokes, he could painlessly create new "originals," a pile of which he offered me. A couple of days into his stay, he informed me that his old and very dear friend, the painter, Sylvia Braverman, was expecting us for lunch in Vence. I had forgotten how terrifying his driving was. After lunch, Sylvia asked if we would like to visit her studio, a few stone steps distant from the house; Bernie thought he couldn't face the steps. When Sylvia and I returned from the studio, he figured it was the cocktail hour. Several hours and a dozen drinks later, he thought we should stay to dinner. Sylvia said there was nothing in the house to eat. "Oh, that's no problem," said he blithely, "Richard can always stir something up." Several drinks after dinner, in the early morning hours, he was struck by the urge to start ringing up friends in America. Sylvia was helpless. We stayed the night. The day of his departure, I learned that there was no question of his driving alone to the airport in his crippled condition. He would need my help to return the car, to find him a wheelchair and see to it that he was in good hands. I could take a taxi back home. We arranged with the rental car attendant to drive him to the airport entrance while I went ahead to find a hostess and prepare a wheelchair. The young lady was quite snotty. There were no wheelchairs, she said, except at the gates, for people who really needed them. When a crouching, bear-skinned specter suddenly materialized, teetering, lurching, swaying precariously, falling forward on a cane to retrieve its balance in extremis before thrusting ahead a stiff leg, she fled in horror and returned with a wheelchair. Bernie was very pleased with the effect he had produced. "Now," he said, "you can leave me, pet."

James first met Laura O'Connor in spring 1988 while in Ireland to deliver a Yeats lecture. They met again in London in Summer 1989, then in the south of France, and have been meeting and traveling together ever since.

Simon Hopkinson and a friend came to lunch. "One of my most memorable meals was enjoyed at the home of Richard Olney.... He lives at the end of an almost impossibly steep road.... I arrived for lunch after a death-defying drive on the back road from St. Tropez...in a nervous state and in need of a drink. Domaine Tempier rosé was very forthcoming while we watched Richard cook a fish soup made from very small Mediterranean fish." (*Roast Chicken and Other Stories*, Simon Hopkinson, 1994) I like to prepare fish soup from scratch after guests arrive to share with them my own awe at the beauty and the magical transformation from an array of brightly coloured, sparkling, freshly netted little rockfish—miniature versions of all the traditional bouillabaisse fish and many others, little slipper lobsters and live, scuttling crabs—into a limpid rose and amber, saffron-hued essence of the Mediterranean. It must never be the heavily cayenned and tomatoed fish purée commonly served in Mediterranean coast bistrots, but the Provençal dictum, forbidding the addition of wine to a fish soup, may be taken with a grain of salt—a half-bottle of white wine always improves it.

Apart from organizing regular wine tastings at the shop in Berkeley, Kermit encouraged the sales staff to keep working during the annual vacation period by paying travel expenses to Europe on condition that they visit and taste in vineyards. This permitted Johnny to divide his vacation between Solliès and vineyard visits, when I often joined him. In 1989, he chose the month of September, to coincide with the grape harvest at Domaine Tempier, where he picked and assisted at the vinification. Kermit, Gail and I joined the Peyraud family, Johnny, the other pickers and the cellar staff for the repas des vendanges, the annual meal celebrating the end of picking.

In Paris, I often stayed in a vast loft, which Pamela and Aubert had transformed into a comfortable apartment. At the kitchen end was a full-wall trompe l'oeil mural of Burgundian vineyards with, in the foreground, a marble tabletop on which were a dish of grapes, two volumes of Proust's *A la Recherche du Temps Perdu* and *Simple French Food.* 17 October, Aubert and I met there to assist later at Peter Thustrup's Romanée-Conti tasting at the Plaza-Athénée. He explained that the books in the mural had been chosen because Proust was his favorite author and *Simple French Food* was Pamela's favorite cookbook. He had naturally wanted the dish to contain typical small oval bunches of blue-black Pinot noir and golden Chardonnay, the noble grape varieties of the Cote d'Or. Instead, the artist had illustrated large, rambling loose clusters of gross ovoid pinkish table grapes. An eyesore.

Since building a road to the property, neighbouring landowners had profited to sell bordering pieces of land. It now fed four new houses and the mayor decided to twist the road sharply up to a higher half-hectare of hillside, where he built and sold four more houses. A strip of abandoned hillside bordering my terrace and wine cellar, which was not mine but which served to park Johnny's car and others, when family visited, was now inundated with neighbours' parked cars—one was a second-hand car dealer who parked, amongst others, a ghastly bus with cowboys and sunsets painted on each side—and children were invading the garden with pet rabbits, dogs and cats. I had tried years earlier to buy this land but, because it was worth nothing at the time and the owner had little to gain, he refused to sell. Now the old man (who was young when I first knew him) was willing to sell, but his son (whom I had known since he was a baby) was asking too much. ("Oh, Michel does exaggerate," exclaimed his mother.) I had no choice. If I didn't buy it immediately, someone else would and another new house would rise up in my face. There was another problem. The strip of land led down to the mouth of the ancient tunnel, down which a century earlier stones from the quarry were hurtled to be baked into quicklime far below. The tunnel was in bad shape and atop it, a cabin in ruin was perched on the edge of a cliff, which had already partially collapsed. I asked my friend, Frank Pittaluga, through whose services I had bought the property thirty years earlier, for advice. He assured me that, if I were to become proprietor of the tunnel, the community could either oblige me to render it safe (humanly impossible) or to sell my entire property to them at an imposed insignificant price. I told Vincent Canova (Michel's father) that I would accept his son's price but that I could not accept to buy the tunnel. He said, "But, Monsieur Richard, if you don't want the tunnel, we won't include it in the sale."

31 January 1990. (Me to Byron) "I signed a compromise last evening to buy the property.... Canova has to gather together a number of documents, including a recadastration of the parcel containing the tunnel to eliminate it from the sale. The contract will be signed whenever the surveyors get the work done.... Spent the day at a big bouillabaisse-Tempier tasting for a busload of Kermit's clients. Lucien was in a high state of euphory and kept me busy translating some extraordinary hands-across-the-ocean, wine-equals-peace-and-love philosophy."

9 April 1990. Alexandre, a dozen journalists and I assisted at a "One Hundred Years of Yquem" dinner at Gaston Lenôtre's restaurant, Elysée Lenôtre, preceded earlier in the day by an exposition, in a Place Vendôme jewelry store showroom, of the bottles of Yquem soon to be sold at auction in Monaco. Gaston confided to me that my recommendation, in *Yquem*, of the Sauternes-oyster marriage had prompted him at the last minute to add Marennes oysters to the menu. They were fresh and wriggly, the Yquem was vibrant; everyone was seduced by the alliance which, a century earlier, had been traditional before being mysteriously abandoned in favour of oysters and dry white wine. I have often served Sauternes with other bivalves, sea urchins and vioulets to my guests' ravishment. Its encounter with the delicate, lemony insides of vioulets is explosive.

Jane Grigson died.

Byron spent his vacation with his daughter, Elizabeth, in the wilds of Africa, amongst the elephants, lions and gorillas.

Two menus, with dates but no indication of guests, help me to reconstruct the summer of 1990. Margaret and James were here in June, John and Johnny in August:

2 June 1990

Apéritif: Krug Clos du Mesnil 1982
§
Vioulets, Olives noires, Amandes fraîches
Corbières blanc 1989
§
Soupe de Poissons; Baudroie
Corbières blanc 1989
§
Fromages
Echézeaux DRC 1978
§
Château d'Yquem 1985
§§§

9 August 1990

Apéritif: Krug, Grande Cuvée
§
Soupe de Poissons
Hermitage Blanc (Chave) 1982
§
Artichauts à la Barigoule
Hermitage Blanc 1982
§
Pintadeaux Grillés; Paillasson au Gratin
Griotte-Chambertin (Ponsot) 1983
§
Fromages
Romanée-Saint-Vivant DRC 1979
§
Château d'Yquem 1985
§§§

Kermit and Gail returned earlier than usual to Berkeley; Tonio was born 12 November.

23 November 1990. (Me to Byron) "The purchase of the Canova land has had miraculous results. I immediately put up a chain at the entrance and the public parking lot disappeared. Henri and I installed a fence all the way up the hillside and the neighbours' children stopped overrunning the property and tearing apart the ancient stone walls. I had the huge pine in the middle of the parking area cut down, we tore out the root, leveled the ground, built a garage and storage shed, cleaned up the Canova hillside, planted alleys of oleander, etc. Margaret suggested that she would like to spend more time here and that a studio would be a good thing for both of us—so plans are being made to build a studio beside the new garage.... The last couple of weeks have been dramatic. Mary finally had the fall which everyone has been expecting for years. She is in the hospital with a broken hip. The decline has been rapid in the last year or so—she is nearly always drunk or

unconscious, has no memory and, at least when drinking, no bowel or bladder control. A neighbour couple had more or less taken over her life—it was they who found her and took her to the hospital—somewhere between the fall and the hospital, her identity papers and jewelry disappeared. Suddenly, Bernard has begun to turn up at the hospital—I have, fortunately, missed him. The proprietor of Mary's house rang me to say that I should get rid of the neighbours (who found her) as they have a bad reputation and are known to make up to aging, lonely persons and take off with everything they own. With so many vultures circling around, I rang Mary's sister in Minneapolis and her nieces in New York and told them it was imperative that someone from the family be here as soon as possible. All three arrived here Monday morning—they leave Monday next and are trying to empty the house of valuables, arrange for Mary to move into a 'retirement home'—also trying to discover the state of Mary's finances, about which she is very secretive. Her sister and nieces understand, in any case, that there can be no question of her moving back into that house and that she must be put into a position where she is cared for, fed, and has no opportunity to get at any alcohol. Before she can go to a home, she must pass at least three months in a clinic learning to walk again.... Apart from working with Henri and visiting the hospital, I continue to spend all my time on *Romanée-Conti*. Still must get together the tasting-notes chapter called 'Vintages.' In the week to come, I should begin to receive sections of translation to edit—have been to Paris twice recently to work with editors and to choose photographs from the thousands that have been taken for the book. I will not come to the U.S. this year—the three-week break is not good for work."

Carolyn, Mary's niece, supervised the emptying of the house. She wanted the 27 volumes of *The Good Cook*, I bought a couple of pieces of furniture and recuperated four garden chairs that I had lent the Garins when they moved to Solliès; the awful neighbour woman took everything she could make off with—linen, towels, bedsheets and Mary's entire library. (She knew no English but must have imagined the books were valuable.) Nora was visiting me and wanted to buy a rocking chair (I am still holding it for her). The dreadful husband of the awful woman rang me: "Did you take those chairs?"; "Yes"; "They belong to me!"; "You are in error, I lent them to the Garins." "Oh," said he and hung up.

15 January 1991. (Me to Byron) "I profit from Henri's presence to be driven to the hospital weekly to visit Mary, whose leg came out of the sling, the skewer and the weights yesterday, after a month and a half—the mind is still in the mists and she is not likely ever to walk normally again.... Henri also keeps me up on world events, i.e. "Bush's war"—the French are hoarding in preparation for another World War; there is no more rice, pasta or sugar on the supermarket shelves (fortunately the whisky supply is not diminished) and gas stations are closed.... Flammarion has decided that *Romanée-Conti* must appear (in French) by October, so the months ahead promise to be packed."

For the "Vintages" chapter of *Romanée-Conti*, I had planned to assemble tasting notes culled from wine publications. Lalou and Aubert chose to organize a day-long tasting of every vintage of Romanée-Conti in the Domaine's vinothèque, several of which represented the last remaining bottle and many of which neither of them had tasted. I was horrified, but Aubert assured me that, if we didn't do it for the book, no future occasion could possibly justify a Romanée-Conti tasting of that amplitude and the precious old bottles might die in their dusty corners.

28 March 1991. Present, in addition to Lalou, Aubert and myself, were Serena Sutcliffe, director of the wine department at Sotheby's, Michel Bettane, "France's answer to Robert Parker," editorial adviser to *La Revue du Vin de France*, and Michel Dovaz, wine-book author, also associated with *RVF*. Forty-five vintages, from 1989 to 1918, were served in decade relays with a break for lunch. I don't enjoy marathon tastings, I am temperamentally incapable of taking notes and have never found other people's notes of any use to me, but the assembled notes of our three guests carried a fascinating message: winetasting notes define more clearly the personality of the taster than that of the wine.

Mary moved from the clinic to the home. It was as pleasant as a "retirement home" can be, a handsome old farmhouse set off from a country road by a courtyard, overlooking, from behind, pastures of grazing sheep, beyond which flowed the Gapeau river. She hated it. She was pampered by the owner and his young assistant. She refused to eat with the other pensionnaires; all her meals were served in her room. The doctors had forbidden all alcoholic beverages, but the owner discreetly included a small carafe of wine with each meal. Once a week, his assistant drove her to my place for lunch (with wine) and once a week Henri drove me to the home to visit. Margaret, James and Byron were with me in June, we visited the home and often drove Mary up the hillside for lunch.

Mother fell, broke her hipbone and was now in a nursing home in Iowa.

28 July 1991. (Me to Byron) "...have written several times to the nursing home but Mother has apparently abandoned her once conscientious habit of answering letters.... Mary makes no effort to improve her walking. She never leaves the chair in the corner of the room and, when she has to move, still hobbles in little inch-steps with a cane as when you were here. She is beginning to plot ways of getting out of the home.... A couple of weeks ago, American friends visited Mary and left a bottle of whisky—she was apparently out of control for three days.... Construction of the studio is under way.... The pressure has been intense to pull the book together—dramatic because August is a dead month with everyone on vacation so everything must be done within the next 2 or 3 days. I went to Paris for a day, returned and Gisou rang up at 11 p.m.—the entire staff was still at work and she wanted me to rewrite all the legends for the illustrations 'adding more honey'—spent two 15-hour days doing my best and several 2-3-hour-long phone calls dictating legends to an assistant. The miracle is beginning to happen.... John arrives 19 September, Johnny plans to pass the last week of September here and Nora (who is now in charge of creating menus and wine lists for the hotel-restaurants of the Euro-Disneyland project) rang up to say that she would like to spend the end of August here...."

Kit and Tony van Tulleken came by with Jonathon, age 10. They planned, the following day, to leave Jonathon with me while they went to pick up Alexander and Christopher, who were vacationing in the Alps, and return here for dinner. Jonathon entertained me for hours recounting the history of the Roman Empire and the reprehensible activities of its emperors, then suddenly lost interest in the Romans and said he thought maybe he needed a new toy. We walked to a neighbouring village on a back road, bought a couple of baubles and returned. ("We'd better walk more slowly, Mr. Olney, I think I have a stitch," said Jonathon.) That kept us busy for a couple of hours. At dinner time, Kit rang to say that they couldn't make it back before midnight—would I fix something for Jonathon's dinner and put him to bed? I prepared my solitary supper standby, picked a bay leaf and a branch of thyme in the garden, added them, with coarse grey sea salt and a smashed garlic clove to a pan of water over heat, added leek, onion, carrot and potato as they were sliced, boiled for 15 minutes, added broken-up spaghettini and sliced courgette and, 5 minutes later, a handful of little green beans cut into 1/4-inch lengths. When I dished up Jonathon's soup, I ground over pepper, grated over Parmesan and drizzled over olive oil. "Oh, Mr. Olney," he exclaimed, "this is the most wonderful soup I've ever eaten—I can taste every vegetable separately!" That was one of the nicest compliments I've ever received. Jonathon had no intention of being put to bed; several hours later, he joined us for a four-course dinner.

Bernard Pivot was the first person to receive an advance copy of *Romanée-Conti*, which would be officially published 14 October. I met Gisou in Dijon. We stayed at La Cloche, which housed Jean-Pierre Billoux's restaurant, where we were treated like stars—I hadn't seen Jean-Pierre since our Dallas encounter. The next day we met Pivot and his TV crew at the Domaine.

6 October 1991. (Me to Byron) "Returned day before yesterday from Burgundy where Bernard Pivot was filming the picking and vinification of Romanée-Conti—also some shots of tasting in the cellars—for his TV program to be shown the first days of November. I thought the Burgundy excursion would wrap the thing up but he told me I would have to come to Paris to appear 'on the plateau'...will have to go to Paris also the preceding week for radio and newspaper interviews; November 8 and 9, two long days of lunches, dinners, local television and round-table talks with journalists; booksignings, etc. are scheduled in Dijon and Beaune. Unnerving, but not nearly as bad as an American tour.... The car-

cass of the studio is built up to the roof level and the genoise—the protruding tiles above the façade—are in place."

Food and Friends, the book on which Simca had been working since Jean's death, was published, with illustrations by Paul Grimes. American friends asked me to join them to celebrate the event at a restaurant in Mougins. Simca rang. Her voice was terrifying—no longer a voice. She begged me not to come: she could see no one, she was too ill. She died a few weeks later.

Mary was hospitalized for internal bleeding. When I visited, her condition had improved and she expected to return to the home in a couple of days. The next day, Charlotte rang: Mary was dead; she had left instructions that her ashes be scattered in my garden; I promised to store them until family could visit the following year for a scattering ceremony. The owner of the home and his assistant drove me to the hospital to view the body, the coffin was then closed and we followed the hearse to Vidauban, where a slimy cremtory attendant addressed us in oily, whispered tones, intended to suggest respect for the dead, the coffin was hoisted onto rails and slid into the oven, where an explosion wrapped it in flames. Hideous.

Alice and Kermit were dreaming of a book about Domaine Tempier and Lulu's cuisine, to be written by Alice and illustrated by Gail. I agreed to write the wine chapter. They sent a proposal to Alice's agent, Susan Lescher, and were told that publishers found it too sketchy. Alice said, "You have to write the book, Richard." Susan asked me for a proposal. In my experience, publishers proposed to me, not I to them. I have no memory of what I wrote, but two months of silence followed, during which Lulu and I began to work in a pattern that was to last for two years: she drove to Solliès twice a week for three-hour sessions of culinary stream-of-consciousness conversation, punctuated by questions, while I took notes.

I received a telephone call from an editor in the San Francisco offices of Weldon Owen, an Australian publisher-packager, who was producing the large format, elaborately illustrated *Beautiful Cookbook* series. She asked if I would write *Provence the Beautiful*. I thought not. She said she would ring back. Susan

Lescher told me it was not an interesting proposition. (I didn't ask why, but I think packagers are not liked in the profession because they don't pay royalties.) I had more than once promised myself not to write another cookbook. Now, I was already working on another, with no contract in sight, and I figured that, as far as *Provence the Beautiful* was concerned, I knew all the material by heart, there was no reason that the text for a glossy coffee-table book should not be serious...and $40,000 might come in handy. I signed a contract, dated 26 November 1991, "To write the work consisting of: 1) 225 authentic recipes of Provence, each with an introductory paragraph of two or three sentences describing the history or origin of the recipe. 2) To write a 700 word introduction to each food category." The deadline for the finished manuscript was 30 April 1992.

Nine

1992-1999

Provence the Beautiful, Australia.

Lulu's Provençal Table.

Good Cook's Encyclopedia. French Wine and Food.

January 1992. As a result of unorthodox commercial activities, which resulted in a large proportion of the 1988 production of Romanée-Conti being siphoned onto the Japanese market while the American grey market was flooded with the Domaine's other growths of that vintage, Lalou was deposed as co-director of the Domaine de la Romanée-Conti and her family firm, the Maison Leroy, relinquished its rights to world distribution of the Domaine's wines outside of Great Britain and the United States, where other firms held exclusive contracts of distribution. The "scandal" broke in all the French newspapers and in specialized wine publications the world round; *The Wine Spectator*, devoted pages to it. Black clouds had been visible for some time on the horizon—I hoped they would dissipate. At dinner with Lalou, before the publication of *Romanée-Conti*, she had told me, "You cannot be my friend, Richard, if you are Aubert's friend." I answered, "That's ridiculous," but she was serious. Her absence at the promotional manifestations for the book's publication was conspicuous.

21 January 1992. (Me to Byron) "I am working hard on *Provence the Beautiful Cookbook*, with a 30 April deadline. Meanwhile, it seems that Alice's agent (who will also be mine) is getting together a contract with HarperCollins for the Domaine Tempier book...."

Saint-Vincent is the patron saint of vignerons. Each year, in a different village, the Confrérie des Chevaliers du Tastevin organizes, in collaboration with the community, a two-day celebration, the "Saint-Vincent Tournante." Thousands of people crowd into the streets of tiny villages, vignerons and négociants compete to produce spectacular displays, the Church and the Confrérie, all in grand robes, carrying dozens of statues of Saint-Vincent, form a cortège, a mass is held in the local church, the vignerons open their cellars to the public, banquets are held in the village and at the Château de Vougeot, wine flows free and freely everywhere, folkloric musical groups play and sing drinking songs in the cellars and rowdiness can become dangerous. It is a scene that I find sympathetic at a distance but of which I don't enjoy being an integral part. In 1992, 25 and 26 January, the Saint-Vincent Tournante was held in Vosne-Romanée. Aubert asked me to sit on a jury awarding prizes to young sommeliers. Portraits of the prince de Conti were everywhere, on giant posters, on the village banquet menu and on the wine labels; in the ancient courtyard, once the property of the Saint-Vivant monastery's prior, the Domaine had created a stage-set peopled with life-size figures of the prince de Conti, Madame de Pompadour, the monks of Saint-Vivant, and so forth.... Milling in the congested streets, we encountered Lalou and Marcel Bize. They failed to recognize the de Villaines. I automatically shook hands with Marcel and embraced Lalou. We moved on. I haven't seen them since.

I received the contract from HarperCollins, dated 27 January 1992, "with reference to a work tentatively titled 'Domaine Tempier, Food and Wine from a Provençal Vineyard'" (which became *Lulu's Provençal Table*). The manuscript was due 1 July 1993.

20 May 1992. In December, at the AIV assembly in Geneva, I had received whispered premonitions from Jacques Puisais and André Parcé that I was to be honoured by The Académie du Vin de France at their annual dinner the following spring. Official confirmation came from Christian de Billy (Pol-Roger Champagne), who was responsible for the organization of the dinner and the award ceremony at the Hôtel Meurice. I stayed with Nora, who came as my guest. Gisou, Lulu, Laurence and Michel Lemonnier were there. Amongst my friends in the Academy were Alexandre, Gérard Chave, Jacques d'Angerville, Michel Gouges, Jean-Pierre Perrin.... Speeches were made and I was asked to pose (awkwardly) for photographers, a glass of Champagne in one hand, the certificate in the other. It read: "Le Prix de l'Académie du Vin de France est décerné à M. Richard Olney pour l'ensemble de son oeuvre et pour son action internationale en faveur du vin." After dinner, Avis Bohlen, representing the U.S. Ambassador to France, spoke. I was dreaming when it became apparent that the entire dining room was waiting for me to rise and speak. Aubert, seated opposite me, was in torture, convinced that I would make a mess of it. As I began, he grimaced, gestured, shook his head in desperation.... Finally, all of the requisite clichés came pouring out: "...profoundly touched...greatly honoured to be recognized by such a distinguished body...eminent ambassadors of the world's greatest wine," etc. When I sat down, Aubert was beaming with pleasure. It had not been so difficult, for it was all true.

22 May 1992. Elizabeth David died. She was 78 years old.

Romanée-Conti, until the Revolution, was La Romanée; when the revolutionary government imprisoned the prince de Conti and confiscated his properties, they affixed the aristocratic name to La Romanée. Lying above Romanée-Conti today is a two-acre vineyard known as "La Romanée." Between 1815 and 1827, before vineyard appellations were protected by law, Lieutenant-Général Louis Liger-Belair, ancestor of the present owner, acquired, one by one, six adjoining fragments of vineyard, which he assembled into one and declared as "La Romanée." When I was working on

Romanée-Conti, bottles of "La Romanée" carried a blatantly false legend, which read: "Originally, there was only one Romanée.... La Romanée was broken up during the 15th century as a result of some sale or inheritance or other: the eastern section, bought in 1760 by the prince de Conti, still bears his name. The western section, or simply Romanée, as you see it today, has been since 1815 the monopoly of the Counts LIGER-BELAIR, Châtelains of Vosne-Romanée." La Romanée had never been broken up; its boundaries in 1512 were identical to those of Romanée-Conti today. I thought I should set the record straight. In the introduction to *Romanée-Conti*, I recounted the above history, in greater detail, and wound up with the observation, "In sum, Romanée-Conti is the only Romanée which possesses the historical right to the name La Romanée."

27 May 1992, 11:40 a.m. I was visited by an huissier (bailiff) from Toulon, come to serve a writ, which he had received from a lawyer in Strasbourg, representing the present Général Liger-Belair. He noted on the document the date and hour of his arrival and proceeded to read the text aloud. The gist of the writ was that I would be taken to court unless I immediately made amends by publishing retractions of my claims in *La Revue du Vin de France*, *Cuisine et Vins de France*, and *The Wine Spectator*. The huissier was supposed to record my response but, as he could make no sense of the text he had just read me, he first asked what it was about. I explained and showed him the passage in the book. He suggested that I refer the general to my publisher. He wrote: "TO WHICH the above-named responded that he was not in agreement with the demands and allegations contained in the body of the summons and that this demand should be addressed to the publishing firm, Flammarion...." In subsequent communications with Flammarion's lawyer, Maître Bourget, the general seemed to be especially incensed because I had included his name and that of his uncle, the Chanoine Just Liger-Belair, since deceased, in the list of acknowledgements, à propos of information received concerning La Tâche, a vineyard which had once belonged to the Liger-Belair family. This, he thought, was tantamount to suggesting that he and his uncle condoned my view of history. I asked M. Bourget to express

my willingness to remove his name and the chanoine's from the thank-you list in further editions of *Romanée-Conti*.

Mike Freeman was in Provence to photograph the scenic, cityscape and folkloric spreads for *Provence the Beautiful*. Most of the food, prepared and styled by Janice Baker, was shot by Peter Johnson in his Sydney studio, but they and the book's editor, Anne Dickerson, settled into the region for a couple of weeks to incorporate Provence into the photography.

Dick Graff and a friend came to lunch (fish soup); Mary's family arrived to scatter ashes—her nieces bore news by the grapevine of Bernard's death in a car accident; I joined my brothers and sisters in Iowa to visit Mother; Général Liger-Belair periodically renewed and compounded his demands....

17 September 1992. (Me to Byron) "The studio is beautiful, pristine white with an ancient hand-hewn stone sink. I have just finished installing the pine floorboards.... The tomato crop was huge.... Sent off several crates with Lulu, put up sauce, ratatouille, etc., still have some which go into daily sautés, soups and salads. Not very interesting for salads—low acid, not the taste I was looking for—will try something else next year."

Gérard Chave's son, Jean-Louis, had been studying in California. He and Johnny were friends, so Johnny arranged to take his vacation during the grape harvest and pick at Hermitage before spending a week with me. He wrote about the perilous adventure of picking on the sheer Hermitage hillside in Kermit's November brochure.

Johnny sent me the October issue of *Bay Food*. The cover was a photo of Paul Bertolli, inside was a long and touching interview: after ten years, he was leaving the Chez Panisse kitchens. A lump formed in my throat and I shed a tear.

6 November 1992. Jeremiah asked me to help celebrate his 50th birthday in Paris and Bordeaux. He arrived in Paris with Stars' pastry chef, Emily Luchetti, its chef, Mark Franz and other California friends. Clifford Harris came over from London. Gerald Asher, who moved back and forth between his Paris and San Francisco flats, was in Paris. The birthday dinner was at l'Ambroisie in the Place des Vosges, recently granted a Michelin

third star, whose owner had once worked in Claude Peyrot's kitchens. The food was disappointing. We wanted a drink after dinner. At our hotel, the Montalembert, the bar was closed; next door, at the Pont Royal, the bar was closed, the Flore was closed, les Deux Magots was closed.... We had an indifferent meal in a bistrot, Joséphine Chez Dumonet, known for its wine list. I chose a Charles Rousseau Clos de la Roche. The smart-ass English sommelier assured me it was bad and imposed another Burgundy that really was bad. I was disgusted with myself.... It was not the Paris I had once known. The Bordeaux tour was organized by Seagram. We were put up at Château de Pichon-Longueville Baron, of which Jean-Michel Cazes is director for the AXA insurance firm. He and Théréza received us there for dinner. I remember lunch at Beychevelle and, in Saint-Emilion, a wonderful, human family dinner and evening with Thierry and Marie-France Manoncourt at Figeac. At a bistro, known for its wine list, in the outskirts of Bordeaux, I discovered, framed behind the bar, the menu from the Rodenstock splurge at Yquem. The patron reminded me that he had been one of the sommeliers at that event. At another bistro, in the village of Sauternes, we recognized the patron's origin by his American accent. It dawned on me that I had met him many years earlier when he was married to Nicole Tari, proprietor in Barsac of Château Nairac.

11 December 1992. (Me to Byron) "The studio is finished, except for treating the floors with linseed oil. Electricity and heating installed. Now I have to finish the Tempier book. The largest part—the recipe section—I will finish in the week to come, then a couple of chapters about the wine, the appellation, the family, etc. I have to spend the first half of September next in Australia, on a promotion tour for *Provence the Beautiful* (James or Johnny—or both—will feed the birds in my absence)."

21 February 1993. André Guillot died.

22 February. (Me to Byron) "I have just finished the Domaine Tempier book.... The last month has been dramatic in the aviary. Birds disappeared mysteriously—one day, I found a half-devoured quail carcass, suddenly there were no more quails. Then the paddas began to disappear. I figured it must be rats. Henri and

I dug out the earthen floor, layered it with fine, strong wire mesh, cemented at the borders, and returned the earth. The birds continued to disappear. I removed all the nests to clean them. A weasel shot from one of the deep wine-case nests. Inside was a disgusting soup of half-devoured birds, blood and grass—the other nests contained freshly killed birds in waiting. I checked everywhere, could find no trace of the beast. The birds continued to disappear. Finally discovered that two holes at the bottom of the wall of the heated shed, cut there to permit quails to enter, led to hollow cement blocks above, from which protruded birds' toe-tips—filled the holes with rocks and stiff cement.... I hope the last remaining weasel has been cemented into its tomb. More than a hundred birds disappeared—and some of the prettiest."

17 March. (Me to Byron) "I think I've blocked out the weasels. The remaining birds are happier, spring is on the way, the nests have been cleaned and reinstalled, there is still a healthy padda population and none of the cockatiels were destroyed. They all want to start breeding and are constantly in and out of the nests."

Byron hoped that his youngest son, Christopher, who was about to graduate from college, would visit me during the summer, but thought that Christopher might be intimidated by the idea of traveling alone and thrust into a country where no one spoke his tongue.

24 April 1993. (Me to Byron) "I have written to Christopher suggesting that, except for a few hours' plane ride, he would not be traveling alone—unless he wants to be alone. That I would be happy to meet him in Paris, show him the town and that he could settle in here with the use of a car—we will see what effect the letter has.... The aviary has been extended to include a 5x2 metre section of the chickenyard and dozens of deep-box-nests are installed...."

May. *Provence the Beautiful* appeared early to coincide with a Williams-Sonoma "Provence Festival." I was impressed.... By the layout, the quality of the photos and the presentation of the food, which always looked exactly right. For the cover, a photo taken at the entrance to François Peyraud's house in Le Castellet was chosen.

Alice, Stephen, Fanny and their friend, Bob Carrau rented a cliff-top house in Bandol for the month of July; from a large terrace overlooking the sea, steep steps led to a private rock beach. They were a few minutes' drive from Domaine Tempier, from Kermit and Gail or Jean-Marie and Catherine in the hills above Le Beausset, from François and Paule in Le Castellet, and a half hour from Solliès. Susan Friedland, my editor at HarperCollins, and her cousins were vacationing in the region. Alice's friends, Eleanor Coppola and Tom Luddy, who were working on a documentary film about Alice and Chez Panisse, arrived with a crew of film technicians. And, of course, Lulu thought the circumstances were right and the time ripe for a great bouillabaisse lunch. I think we were twenty-eight at table. Bouillabaisse at Domaine Tempier is always good theatre: rosé flows, tapénade and anchoïade crusts circulate and François tends the outdoor fire, over which fish soup is heated in the old copper cauldron. This day was especially dramatic as cameras clicked and turned, while great cork platters of saffron-stained, oil-anointed rascasses and a dozen other varieties of striped, spotted and speckled fish emerged from the kitchen to be slipped into the caldron. The long table on the terrace was lined with freshly drawn bottles of cool red Tempier 1992. With cheese, Jean-Marie poured old vintages. I passed the night at Tempier. The next day, Alice, family and friends, Kermit and family and I, a good dozen, drove to Solliès for lunch. There was no time to cook, we emptied Lulu's refrigerator, picked up charcuterie and bread along the way—my larder may be empty, but the cellar is always well stocked. The lunch will not be recorded in gastronomic history, but we had a good time, tomatoes from the garden.

It may have been on this same occasion that Alice's friend and colleague, Anne Isaak, and her little boy, Elio, joined us. Elio was enraptured by the aviary. I let him in, he moved gently, silently, in awe—the birds thought he was one of them. He desperately wanted an aviary on the roof of their New York apartment building—his mother was not convinced that it was a practical idea. I mailed him a book, *You and Your Pet Bird*, but never learned if he got his aviary.

The following day, Susan and her friends came to lunch, bearing gifts. We ate my favorite summer lunch on the terrace: melon and prosciutto, composed salad, cheeses and fresh fruit. Before leaving, Alice wanted to invite all the Peyrauds, the Lynchs and me to dinner. She picked me up in the morning to help her shop in Bandol. We found freshly fished large shrimp, called gambas, and went by the butcher where she had ordered in advance a lot of quail to be split down the backs and flattened in preparation for grilling over wood embers. The butcher proudly presented his work. Alice gasped and burst into tears. He had split them along the breast-bone. I said, "Don't worry, sweetheart, everything will be all right," but I knew that, had our roles been reversed, I, too, might have been close to tears. For lunch, Fanny prepared a tomato salad, generously scattered with torn up basil. That evening, the ambience was joyous; Lucien, who suffered increasingly from rheumatoid arthritis, was nonetheless in high spirits. The shrimp were grilled dry in fiercely heated frying pans thickly layered with coarse sea salt, less than a minute on one side, then on the other, only until the translucent shells turned pink and opaque; I have never since prepared them any other way. The quail looked funny but they tasted good. Many vintages of Tempier were poured—the oldest was 1968.

Christopher spent three weeks with me. The day before leaving, he realized that he needed a cooking lesson. He loved the slices of rustic sour dough bread that I grilled, rubbed with garlic, dribbled with olive oil and cut into small squares to accompany pre-dinner drinks and he thought the flat zucchini omelette (shredded zucchini, salted in layers, squeezed, sautéed in hot olive oil, stirred into eggs, beaten with chopped butter and fresh marjoram, returned to the hot pan with more olive oil, Parmesan grated atop and finished beneath a grill) was very special. He returned to Rochester and proudly treated the family to olive oil-anointed garlic crusts and zucchini omelettes.

James and Laura settled in to care for the birds during my absence in Australia.

The Australian experience was brief but intense: a week in Sydney and a week, split between Melbourne and Brisbane, of organized lunches and dinners, based on *Provence the Beautiful*, with interviews and TV demonstrations tucked into the morning hours. Sundays and Mondays, when there were no organized meals, were booked with private lunch and dinner invitations. Pam Seaborne, whose agency organized the tour, and Anne Dickerson, who had come from San Francisco to assist, were my constant companions. I arrived on Monday, met everyone at Weldon Owen and was awaited for dinner by Guy Griffin, who had interviewed me by telephone a couple of weeks earlier.

Tony Bilson, who created the first week's menus in the Intercontinental's Treasury restaurant, treated me to a morning in Sydney's fish market, where I saw great banks of rascasse, the cornerstone of bouillabaisse, believed in Provence to exist only in the Mediterranean; they were labeled "rock cod." Slipper lobsters, called "bugs," and John Dory were abundant.... We swallowed a half-dozen varieties of wriggling oysters as they were shucked.

The only unpleasant experience was at one of the Sydney dinners. Bookselling and signing were dispensed with as guests milled around with drinks before going to table. I asked people to print their names on scraps of paper to avoid spelling mistakes in the dedications. The dinners were not formal, but one couple, perhaps American, arrived in evening dress. When we went to table, he removed his jacket, flung it over the back of the chair and undid the black tie. I was expected to speak about the food and the wine. He persistently interrupted me to ask imbecile, unanswerable questions which he thought were funny. I told him not to interrupt. He waited until the meal was half over to ask me to dedicate a book to his wife, Cheryl. I asked him to print the name on a piece of paper. "You know how to spell," he said. I didn't and spelled the name with an "S." His wife, who appeared to be constipated, wailed, "God, yewer Umurucun! Yeew know how ta spell ma name!" Had I acted correctly, I would have replaced the book, but I was irritated; I crossed out the misspelling and scribbled "Cheryl" in its place. The idiot continued to be loud and funny to the embarrassment of the other guests. The maître d'hôtel whispered to me that the chef would like to see me in kitchen. Tony, who had been following the nonsense from behind the scenes, poured me a tumbler of whisky, saying, "Here, you need this." I nursed my whisky in the kitchen until the pests left, then returned to the table to say goodnight to the other guests.

On the weekend, Anne, another editor and I drove to Hunter Valley to have lunch with Len Evans and his wife. He, extroverted, gregarious food and wine personality, chairman of Rothbury Vineyards and owner of the Evans Family Vineyards, immediately hustled us into a jeep to lurch around the vineyards sighting bounding families of kangaroos, an activity which he enjoyed immensely. All of his overflowing energy was devoted to entertaining; he was superbly indifferent to the fact that the leg of lamb had remained an hour too long in the oven. He had no idea who I was or why he had been asked to invite us. After lunch, he proudly showed me a copy of *Yquem*, "offered by the Count de Lur-Saluces," was nonplussed to discover that I was the author and hastened to dedicate a copy of *Len Evans' Cookbook*.

In Melbourne, the day before a banquet at the Grand Hyatt Hotel, at which Rita Erlich, food editor for *The Age*, was to be master of ceremonies, we had lunch at Stephanie Alexander, in suburban East Hawthorn. The restaurant is housed in a mansion of the last century; the ambience is civilized and the food was sublime. The sommelier, Craig, was determined that we should taste the best the cellar had to offer of Australian wines. Except for the oldest, a 1966 Tulloch "Pokolbin Dry Red, Private Bin," built to last, modern, synthetic glues refused to release the labels; Craig sketched those of a Sauvignon blanc '92, a Pinot noir '91 and an "Auslese Tokay" '92. That evening, Stephanie joined us at Rita Erlich's home for braised oxtail.

Stephanie reserved a table at the banquet for her business partner, Dure Dara, Craig and several other members of the staff, while she remained at the restaurant. At the far end of the dining room, on a raised platform, a lectern and a long table at which Rita, three or four dignitaries and I were seated, faced the audience. Rita was introducing me, while I pondered the means of disappearing without everyone thinking me crazy. I spoke into the microphone, "Excuse me, I have to pee," and fled through the wings. When I returned, Rita claimed that I had upstaged her. My speech

Byron.

was brief; for the most part, it was a question and answer session. The only question I remember—because it took me by surprise—was, "Have you eaten kangaroo?" The answer was no.

Back in Sydney on Sunday, the day before my departure, Peter Johnson and Janice Baker asked me to lunch with friends in Peter's vast, two-story loft-studio. We began with a platter piled high with "yabbies"—fresh water crayfish—hot from their court-bouillon, bigger, fatter, sweeter, more succulent than any of the American or European crayfish varieties.

2 October 1993. In 1593, Jacques de Sauvage acquired the right of tenure to Château d'Yquem, property of the king. In 1711, Yquem became a fiefdom of the Sauvage family. In 1785, Françoise-Joséphine de Sauvage, by her marriage to Louis-Amédée de Lur-Saluces, brought Yquem into the Lur-Saluces family. Alexandre wanted to celebrate the 400th anniversary of his family's presence

at Yquem by inviting a few passionate, commercially unbiased Yquem enthusiasts from around the world. There were no merchants, auctioneers, restaurateurs, sommeliers or journalists present. The guests numbered twenty-seven.

We were put up in a Bordeaux hotel. Alexandre had often spoken of his friend, "Tubby" (Robert) Bacon, from Chicago. Tubby Bacon ("skinny as a string bean") asked me to join him and a few other guests who were inviting Alexandre, the evening before the Yquem celebration, to Francis Garcia's Chapon Fin. It was a pleasant evening; Alexandre relaxed while his hosts searched out the greatest wines the restaurant had to offer in magnums. The next evening, I met Dr. Nils Stormby, who had translated and written the foreword to the Swedish edition of *Yquem*. After dinner, the cellarmaster, Guy Latrille, opened the only Yquem 1847 in the cellar, a bottle that had been offered years earlier to Alexandre by Nils Stormby.

James mailed me a copy of *A Different Person*, by James Merrill, a memoir of two and a half years spent in Europe in the early '50s, mostly in the company of Robert Isaacson. The language was intelligent and witty, the organization impressive and a number of the figurants were people I knew or had known....

25 December 1993. (Me to Jimmy) "My brother sent me *A Different Person*.... I adored it. I was wowed by the vision of conversational graffiti defacing noble ideas, 'so reasonable and intelligent,' and giggled at the jellyfish Madonna and Child. 'Who wanted a father, let alone a hamburger!' 'My dear—we must do this more often,' and 'Italicized' are vintage and delicious Robert. Hubbel (Pierce) and his long-ago songs thrust me into melancholy." In a Naples aquarium, "...a jellyfish of live, fringed crystal big as a skull, hovering over a much littler one. 'Madonna and Child,' Robert murmured." (*A Different Person*) The "father-hamburger" quote is a reference to a man of German origin, one of Robert's early admirers. "My dear—we must do this more often," was his observation at the culmination of what must have been an excruciatingly boring party where the guests played a parlour game called "Murder." "'What will it be like to meet in New York?' she wondered brightly. 'What will New York have to say to us or we to one

YQUEM LE

Samedi 2 octobre 1993

Dîner en l'honneur des Grands Amateurs d'Yquem

Réunis pour le 400ème anniversaire

Nage de Homard aux Mousserons

Consommé

Pigeonneau aux Pommes et Pointe de Cannelle

Fromages

Frangipane

Yquem 1988

Champagne Krug Grande Cuvée

Château d'Yquem 1982

Château Latour 1961

Château d'Yquem 1937

Yquem 1899

Yquem 1847

another? Now, I mean, that we've all become—' 'Italicized,' said Robert...."

Christopher moved to Berkeley. Johnny helped him get settled.

I spent a few days, between Christmas and the New Year, in Paris with Nora. Gregory Usher and his friend, Patrice Bachelard, came to dinner. Both were under the cloud of AIDS. Gregory was distressingly thin but in good spirits. Kit, Tony and the boys were in town and came to dinner. The twins were very grown-up. Jonathon recalled the "wonderful soup" he had eaten in Solliès.

3 January 1994. (Me to Byron) "Lulu's book is winding up...received this morning all the photos to be captioned.... Federal Express will come tomorrow to pick up corrected copy and photos with captions added...spoke with Margaret, who said that she and Elizabeth were working on a plan to come over this summer—and would work on other members of the family. I have to do a 'tour' when Lulu's book appears, theoretically in May, so family should be warned to visit later—"

8 January. A note from Jimmy Merrill, vaguely troubling: "Your letter gave me great, great pleasure. You are certainly one of the happy (I hope) few I was writing 'for'.... David is OK—emphysema and won't stop smoking; a junk TV addict. I'm not sure I can face it another year (but then I always do). A third address you might keep in mind is: 164 E 72 St....where I more and more hole up—as if there were any escape." (Two months later, a letter: "Forgive me if I've already answered your very welcome letter, but things are topsy turvy in whatever room I may find myself. I'm so pleased that you like the book. There is only a mere handful of ideal readers, and you are one. I seem to be gravitating more and more to life in New York. I came into an apartment that my grandmother bought in the early 40s...and I must say it's a godsend. The little Connecticut village that used to be a godsend is now stripped of pharmacy and tailor and green grocer; one has to virtually get into a car to buy a carton of milk. But younger or newer friends have begun moving in, ideal for those who enjoy an active social scene—as I do less and less....")

4 February. Gregory Usher died. He was 43 (a year later, Patrice died, same age).

10 February, a note from J.D. ("Sandy") McClatchy, editor of *The Yale Review*: "I happened to be sitting across the table from our dear mutual friend Jimmy Merrill in Key West recently when he opened your letter to him—a letter he was delighted to have. I asked him for your address, because I'm an admirer of your work and hope that someday you might have some of it to send us at *The Yale Review*...." (*La Romanée and the Prince de Conti* was published in the July 1995 issue.)

20 February 1994. (Me to Byron) "*Lulu's Provençal Table* is scheduled to appear May 2.... Kermit rang last night for news about the tour, I told him it would begin in New York and wind up in Berkeley-San Francisco the last half of May. 'Impossible,' he said, 'I must be here when you come and I have to be in France after May 15.' So I gave him the fax and the name of the HarperCollins promotion person and they will have to work it out.... I suppose that most of the month of May will be swallowed up by this business.... James plans to sit in for me during the tour—if he could stay on and the rest of the family arrive in June, it would be marvelous. Johnny plans to come this summer also."

27 February 1994. Harold Acton died at 89. He left La Pietra to New York University.

28 April. (Me to Byron) "...after much confusion, I think that Lulu and I will fly to San Francisco on May 11.... Lulu was torn between wanting to do everything and not daring to leave Lucien too long (daughters are replacing her). She is returning from New York May 20 and I return May 24."

4 May. Marion Cunningham and Abby Mandel came to lunch. I scoured the hillside to collect the last tender shoots of wild asparagus for an omelette—Daube en Gelée, Salad, Cheeses, Yquem for dessert.

11 May. Johnny and Christopher met us. We drove from the airport to the Alexander Book Company, San Francisco, for a book-signing, followed by a buffet-reception, where Bizou Restaurant presented preparations from the book, many to be accompanied by aïoli—the octopus stew was lovely and Tempier

flowed. Dinner at Alice's home in Berkeley. Lulu stayed with Alice, I stayed with Johnny. The next day, a press lunch at Reed Hearon's Lulu restaurant in the "bis" dining room, dominated by a fireplace before which suckling pig turned, was followed by the first of two Chez Panisse dinner-book-signings. Saturday was an all-day signing at Kermit's; clients brought in old vintages of Tempier to keep us going. Dinner with Jeremiah, lunch the next day, catered by Chez Panisse staff, at Kermit's and Gail's home in the Berkeley hills and, that afternoon, Johnny and Christopher put us on a plane for Los Angeles.

In Los Angeles, while signing books at Campanile, Janet Cam appeared bearing a pair of eyeglasses that I had lost or forgotten at Le Pavillon several years earlier. She and Yannick were separated; the Pavillon was closed. (Janet is now maître d'hôtel at the Lutèce, in New York.)

In New York, Dorothy Cann Hamilton organized a press party at the French Culinary Institute, lots of people milling around, in and out of the kitchens, finger-food, Tempier, friends and journalists.... Lulu and I chatted with Paul Grimes's students at Peter Kump's Cooking School; Lulu had to return before the Beard House dinner, conceived mainly in her honour. I met Lucia a couple of times for breakfast—she was being treated for cancer, but was in good spirits. Otherwise, my only free time was a Sunday evening: Lucia and I had dinner with Robert Isaacson and Jimmy Draper. Robert cooked. A beautiful evening—fifty years of memories and giggles. I learned from Robert that Bernie Winebaum had died a year earlier. One day, with Marion Cunningham, we shot five TV shows. In another TV studio, I ran into Paula Wolfert, brimming with spunk and enthusiasm, on the first leg of a several-month promotion tour—I wondered how she could do it.

I hadn't been in good form throughout the tour and was pretty much a basket case when James collected me on my return to France. The rest of the family arrived, I cooked, we ate and drank grandly and had a good time, but Byron was worried about my health and suggested that I come to Rochester for a check-up. I spent ten days mid-July there. Except for degenerative arthritis in the back, which was no news, the doctors found nothing amiss.

With Lulu Peyraud, Baywolf Restaurant, Oakland, California, May 1994.

On one of the first days of August, Lulu rang up. I had a high fever and was vomiting—I don't remember much else. She and Kermit arrived, packed an overnight bag, drove me to a Toulon hospital and Kermit telephoned Byron in Rochester.... I heard voices, opened my eyes and discovered John, James, Byron and Johnny at my bedside. The rest was recounted to me later: Before leaving, Byron had consulted a colleague at the Mayo Clinic—the symptoms suggested Rocky Mountain Spotted Fever. Toulon hadn't succeeded in diagnosing the illness. Byron confided his thoughts to the doctor in charge, who said she was leaving for the weekend and would worry about my problem when she returned. Byron said, "We have to get him out of here!" I was put into an ambulance and driven to Timone, the Marseille University hospital, where Professor Weiller, the doctor in whose ward I was established, met with the family's enthusiastic approval; the diagnosis concurred with Byron's suspicions. My brothers brought in a French edition of *Yquem* and suggested that I dedicate it to Professor Weiller.

John, James and Byron had to return to their professional duties. Byron would be in Europe with Marilynn in October and made an appointment to see Dr. Weiller at that time. Johnny, who, after six years in Berkeley, had enrolled for a year in a professional viticulture-oenology program in Beaune, stayed on until September, driving each morning from Solliès to Marseille with jars of freshly squeezed orange juice, decent bread and cheese and an occasional bottle of white wine. Lulu or another Peyraud furnished me daily with edible food, often from the sea, and red Tempier. The nurses told me if I didn't eat the hospital food, I would starve to death. I asked them if they ate it. Jean-Marie's daughter, Valérie, was studying medecine in Marseille and visited me daily. The spots didn't begin to appear until several days after I had entered Timone. My legs and feet were densely strewn with small black spots, a hideous sight. I left after two weeks—it could have been two days or two months.... Johnny drove me to Marseille for a check-up and an interview with Dr. Weiller before leaving for Beaune.

A month and a half later, when Byron and I visited Dr. Weiller, he congratulated me for the beauty of *Yquem*, the quality of the writing, etc., but, he said, if I was passionate about "les boissons," it might be a good idea to devote my time to a study of mineral waters. He recommended that I limit my wine consumption to a half-bottle per day and asked Byron if he did not agree. Byron mumbled (intending, perhaps, not to be understood) that maybe I should cut down a bit on the whisky but that he saw no problem with the wine. (I attributed Dr. Weiller's suggestions to dry humour and laughed politely but, a year or so later, François's son, Jérome, for whom Dr. Weiller is a hero, observed that, at gatherings of doctors and medical students, he has never been known to accept a drink.)

Sybille rang from London. "Dearest Richard," she said, "I hope you haven't given up wine. Doctors are frightful—the first thing they do is forbid you to drink wine.... It is very, very important that you continue to drink wine." I reassured her.

Bob Haas, American wine importer, long-time member of the Académie Internationale du Vin, and I co-sponsored three

California vintners, Dick Graff (Chalone), Paul Draper (Ridge Vineyards) and Josh Jensen (Calera) for membership in the *docte* society; they were to present their papers at the annual conference held at the Hôtel du Rhône in Geneva the first week of December. Dick had asked me to choose a restaurant where we could dine the evening preceding the opening of the conference. I have never had wonderful meals in Geneva, but those at the Rhône are respectable; I held a table in their "restaurant gastronomique," serviced by a different kitchen from that of the large dining room. Next to us was a table of academicians. Alexandre arrived alone, joined us for Champagne and insisted on offering the white wine (Yquem). We drank Chave's Hermitage with the cheese. Our neighbours were fascinated by the choice of wines—the next day, Léon Beyer assured me that he really could not condone drinking Yquem with turbot.... I was shattered. At the conference, plans were made to visit Champagne the following spring and California in the spring of 1996, this tour to be organized by Bob Haas and the three new academy members.

Except for Johnny and a young French-Canadian sommelier, Jean-Philippe Lefebure, the class in Beaune was composed of vignerons, mostly Burgundian, varying in age from 20 to 50. The studies were divided between classroom work and practical experience; Johnny assisted at the vendanges and several times spent periods working in the cellars with Aubert in Bouzeron, worked in Jacques Seysses's cellars at Domaine Dujac in Morey-Saint-Denis and at several vineyards whose proprietors I didn't know. At Christmas vacation, Johnny drove south with a fellow student, Virginie Taupenot-Merme, whose family owns vineyards in Gevrey-Chambertin, Morey-Saint-Denis and Chambolle-Musigny, and another young woman. They arrived for dinner at midnight—marinade of sardine fillets and a steaming daubière of tripe—Virginie produced a bottle of Chambolle-Musigny to accompany the cheeses and the girls left at 2 a.m. for Carqueiranne, a coastal village between Toulon and Hyères. A few days later, Jean-Philippe arrived with his friend, Danielle, restaurant proprietor in Montreal; then Anna arrived from Italy to help us see in the New Year.

6 February 1995. Jimmy Merrill died.

15 March. For Nora's fortieth birthday, her friends asked me to a surprise party in Paris; because I always stay with Nora when in Paris, the surprise element was dissipated by my arrival. I was unable to find a bottle from her birthyear in my cellar so chose the oldest bottle there as a birthday gift—an 1834 Port (and was relieved to learn a year later that it had been in perfect condition). Her friend, Erna Frachon, whose qualities had often been extolled also by Pamela and Aubert, prepared the dinner, crowned by legs of lamb, perfectly rose throughout, and an abundant ragoût of creamed baby fava beans and morels.

In late April, Johnny was in Solliès—it must have been Easter vacation. Guy Griffin was arriving from Australia to lay the groundwork for an article on Guy Julien's auberge, La Beaugravière in Mondragon near Orange. He asked us to accompany him there for dinner and lunch the next day. I had met Julien a year earlier at an AIV banquet in the cellars of Château de Beaucastel (Châteauneuf-du-Pape). In the region, he is celebrated for his truffle preparations and a spectacular wine list. Aubert had been there a couple of days earlier and offered him a copy of *Romanée-Conti*, which he produced for me to sign. A visit to the cellar revealed many treasures absent from the wine list.

I rang Lucia, who was in great pain and spoke with difficulty. "It's very, very bad...." She died in her studio.

The AIV Champagne tour, early June, coincided with the end of Johnny's studies. Jean-Marie drove, we stopped in Beaune to pick up Johnny and found a message from Aubert—we were expected for lunch at the Domaine de la Romanée-Conti. We ate simply, drank Montrachet, Romanée-Saint-Vivant and La Tâche. The Champagne visit was organized by Rémi Krug, Christian de Billy and Leclerc-Briant. Lunch at Gérard Boyer's was a symphony.

Margaret, Elizabeth, Byron, John, James and Laura arrived in Solliès. Every day was a celebration of fresh things and grand wines. Johnny, who was our sommelier, recorded the following menu:

With Lucien, Summer 1995.

James—Kitchen, Summer 1995.

Dinner at Richard's, June 17, 1995

Green Beans with lemon and olive oil
1991 Morey-Saint-Denis (blanc), Domaine Dujac
§
Grilled Sea Bass Pommes Vapeur
1982 Puligny-Combettes, E. Sauzet
1981 Chevalier-Montrachet, M. Niellon
§
Cheese Platter
1987 Clos des Lambrays, Taupenot-Merme
1987 Close de la Roche, Domaine Dujac
§
Strawberries
1989 Jurançon Vendanges Tardives, Domaine Cauhapé
§

Johnny stayed through the summer before returning to California for a temporary job at Firestone Vineyards, near Santa Barbara. Alice, Stephen, Fanny and Bob Carrau again rented a house in Bandol for the month of July. Paule and François organized a Grand Aïoli for twenty-some of Alice's friends, Peyrauds, Lynches and others. Lucien, who moved with difficulty, wanted to be there to embrace everyone—he and Lulu left before the aïoli, but not before an hour of drinking Tempier rosé and sucking at mussels, opened alive, peppered, drizzled with olive oil and grilled for less than a minute over the embers of vine prunings, a genial preparation of which François is past master.

27 July 1995. We invited (Fanny stayed with Marly and Tonio) Alice, Stephen, Bob, François, Paule, Kermit and Gail to dinner:

Reflexions

Aperitif: Krug

Sardines Crues à l'Hysope
Roque Sestière (Corbières) blanc 1994
§
Gambas Grillés sur Lit de Gros Sel,
Salade Composée
Domaine de Chevalier blanc 1983
§
Poulets de Bresse en Cocotte
Clos de la Roche (Ponsot) 1980
§
Fromages
Echézeaux (DRC) 1978
§
Pêches au Sauternes
Yquem 1985
§ § §

Jackie Morlon, who, twenty years earlier, as a sixteen-year-old mason's apprentice, had worked with me weekends pulling my house together, had moved to work with his wife's family in the southwest of France, the heart of foie gras country. He arrived with a gift—an enormous goose with a two-pound pale, blond liver. I was very touched, but I didn't know what to do with it. Johnny had left for California. I was alone. The carcass was no problem—I cut it up, salted it down with herbs overnight and transformed it into confit d'oie. I didn't want to sterilize the liver because I like my foie gras rose, but I couldn't see living off foie gras for the next ten days. I seasoned it, packed it whole into an earthenware terrine, tucked fragments of goose fat all around, splashed over ancient Cognac, covered the terrine tightly, poached it for twenty minutes in a bain-marie and left the terrine to cool in its water bath. When cold, it was firm, dense velvet and pink throughout. I rang up François and Paule. Paule answered. I explained that I had a serious problem and needed their help. She exclaimed, "Yes, anything!

What is it? Can we drive you somewhere?" "No," I said, "I have to get rid of a foie gras and you must come to lunch." They brought vioulets.

Déjeuner, 19 Août 1995, François et Paule

Apéritif: Krug 1976

Vioulets
Tempier rosé 1993
§
Eventails de Courgettes et Tomates
Tempier rosé 1993
§
Terrine de Foie Gras, Salade du Jardin
Lafite 1968
§
Fromages
Latour 1953
§
Suduiraut 1962
§ § §

Paule claimed that, whenever I called for help, it was always a question of helping me to eat and drink.

Labor Day, I flew to Rochester to join the rest of the family, arriving from Baton Rouge, Washington and Saint Louis and we drove to Iowa to visit Mother. She could no longer leave her wheelchair. It was not possible to take her out for a meal, but she kept busy reading and painting and was very happy to have her aging offspring around for a moment. She claimed to be 97 but was only 96. We finished the day at the Marathon Park, Father's creation from the early '30s. Byron had packed his bus full of firewood, flank steak, sweet corn and wine, John had brought other wines, Norris and Fran furnished garden tomatoes and other vegetables and we had a picnic.

After more than a decade's absence from Chez Panisse, Jean-Pierre Moullé was returning as chef of the downstairs restaurant.

Romanée-Conti finally appeared in English (Rizzoli), four years after the French publication.

Marion Cunningham asked if I would receive Edna Lewis and Scott Peacock for lunch. Of course, I was delighted. We had a composed salad, a pot of tripe and a platter of cheeses. Plenty of wine and lots of talk—I think they enjoyed themselves.

Simon Hopkinson had left Bibendum's kitchens (although he remained co-proprietor) to devote himself to writing. Jill had edited his first book, *Roast Chicken and Other Stories* (Ebury Press, 1994). They came bearing gifts, Jill a smoked eel and Simon a jar of rice in which were embedded three white truffles. Lulu asked us to lunch with Catherine and Jean-Marie. We drank a glass of rosé with Lucien, who had made an effort to come downstairs. Days often passed without his descending and he no longer joined others at the lunch table.

Aubert asked me to join him, late November, for a program of dinners and a vertical tasting at the Domaine of Romanée-Saint-

Margaret, James—Terrace, Summer 1995.

Vivant, to which wine authorities from around the globe had been invited. I begged off...and again, in December, when he was to meet Jacques Seysses in the south of France and suggested they pick me up to taste our way through the Loire Valley before returning to Burgundy. We made plans for me to visit in January when no special events were projected.

9 January 1996. Guy Griffin came to lunch, spent most of the day reading the first 500 pages of manuscript for this book. I worry lest it be boring and was pleased that he seemed fascinated.

Lulu was receiving about thirty of Kermit's American clients—restaurateurs, distributors and wine merchants—for bouillabaisse; many were the same that I had met six years earlier under similar circumstances. The dining room had been transformed into a mess hall and, because weather didn't permit preparing the bouillabaisse out of doors, François was occupied at the kitchen fireplace. Paule and Catherine were busy preparing rouille, tapénade and anchoïade and Jean-Marie was sommelier. Lucien was not visible—I went up to his bedroom to embrace him. The group was moving toward Burgundy. I followed them a couple of days later, arriving the day after their visit in Bouzeron.

Aubert had promised me a quiet, relaxed time with a few close friends. After returning, I tried to assemble my impressions, with pathetically inadequate results:

"Burgundy, 25-29 January 1996.

Jan. 26, Lunch:	Domaine de la Romanée-Conti (wines chosen by Bernard Noblet): Montrachet 1977, Richebourg 1952, Grands Echézeaux 1948.
Dinner:	Domaine Dujac with Jacques and Rosalind Seysses. Jacques d'Angerville and several other guests. St.-Jacques, ragoût de légumes, filet de boeuf truffé, paillasson—Morey blanc, Bonnes Mares, vieux Clos de la Roche....
Jan. 27, Tasting:	Jacques d'Angerville. Beautiful Volnays, Clos des Ducs, Champans.

Dinner: Pam and Aubert. Jacques d'Angerville, Hubert and Christiane de Montille. Aligoté 1994, Montrachet 1980, Echézeaux 1992, Romanée-Conti 1978.

Jan. 28, Lunch: Hubert, Christiane, Jacques d'Angerville, Pam, Aubert. Tasted in cellar '95s, '94s and '93s, Pommard and Volnay, Rugiens, Taillepieds, Champans and others, finished with '72 Champans, divine. At lunch, charcuterie, quiche, gigot, Meursault, Champans 1971, Rugiens 1969.

(DUMB-BELL—no memory two days later)"

14 February 1996. John wrote that he had a medical conference in Nice and planned to visit me afterward, 14-20 April.... "I was in Carmel, California, the first week of January, got together with Johnny for a tour of the Napa/Sonoma region and we got fairly seriously into some plans to start up a family winery.... He has been offered a good job at Ridge Winery which will begin March 1st...."

23 March. From Jack Fullilove: "Edna Lewis called and invited us to her 80th birthday party in Atlanta April 14. It sounds to be a big blow-out and we will go...a great many people have been asked. Scott, she tells me, will do a lot of cooking on the hearth...."

25 March. From Scott Peacock: "I am busily planning an 80th birthday celebration in honor of Miss Lewis...if you would care to express a thought or impression about this great lady, we would love to include anything you might say in a program that we are putting together for the event." I expressed my admiration for her beauty, her reserve and her gift of understatement.

The AIV California wine tour was scheduled for 16-21 May. Saturday evening in San Francisco and Sunday were free. Because he had so recently begun to work at Ridge, I didn't think it possible to invite Johnny to join the tour. I asked John and James; Byron was busy at a medical conference but free for the San Francisco weekend; Margaret and Elizabeth thought they might not have the stamina to support day after day of winetasting from 9 a.m. to midnight, but planned to meet us in San Francisco. Alice and

From left to right: Margaret, James, John, Elizabeth, me and Byron. Chez Panisse, 19 May 1996.

Kermit wanted to organize a lunch at Chez Panisse "For Richard Olney, Family & Friends" on Sunday, the restaurant's closing day. Upon receiving the final program, I discovered Johnny's name on the list of participants; he had been asked to share with Bob Haas's secretary, Jacqueline Léonard, the task of translator and problem-solver.

The vineyard meals were very good. At Au Bon Climat, Jim Clendenen treated us to a rustic meal of grilled things, wonderful sour dough bread and elegant wines, Pinot blanc and Pinot noir; at Chalone, Dick Graff had built an airy, spacious Provençal style villa since my last visit—we drank his Mourvèdre rosé at the swimming pool while eggplant slices and skewers of fresh sardines were grilling; in the rarified air on the ridge of the Santa Cruz Mountains at Ridge's Monte Bello Vineyard, the staff prepared old-

CHALONE VINEYARD

Académie Internationale du Vin

Déjeûner

du 17 mai 1996

Les Hors d'Oeuvre

1994 Mourvèdre Rosé, Richard Graff Vineyard

La Salade de Crevettes Rouges

1990 Pinot Blanc, Chalone Vineyard
1990 Chardonnay, Chalone Vineyard

Le Plateau de Fromages

1985 Pinot Noir, Chalone Vineyard

Les Tartes aux Fruits

1994 July Muscat, Richard Graff Vineyard

With Margaret and Elizabeth in Kitchen
Solliès, June 1996.

fashioned family food—cold poached salmons with sauce tartare, glazed pot-roasted legs of lamb, parsleyed potatoes.... Chardonnay 1994, Cabernet Sauvignon Monte Bello '92, '91, '90, '81 and, with the cheeses, magnums of 1971. Two days later, at Lytton Springs, Ridge's Sonoma Valley winery, where three neighbouring Zinfandel producers collaborated to present their wines, the lunch, built around an aîoli and grilled chickens, was catered by Kathleen Wheeler, proprietor of The Downtown Bakery in nearby Healdsburg. The breads were delicious—bread was good everywhere. Napa Valley was less interesting. At Silverado Vineyards, property of the Disney family, we tasted oenologically immaculate wines. Maybe, like people, if they are too perfect, they are boring—or maybe the lurking presence of Mickey Mouse distorted my judgment. At the Domaine Chandon banquet, the food was too complicated, the sauces too sweet and the red wines too warm.

The Chez Panisse lunch was magic. Among the guests were a dozen academicians and seven Olneys. Jeremiah was in Chicago. Alice had asked Marion Cunningham, Shirley Sarvis and Denise, Jean-Pierre Moullé's wife, whom I hadn't seen since Kermit and I had visited them many years earlier in the Bordelais (spitted game birds turned in the fireplace, Brane-Cantenac 1928). Kermit furnished the wines, four of which were academicians': Domaine Tempier rosé 1995, Hermitage blanc (Chave) 1993, Château Thivin, Côte de Brouilly (Geoffray) 1994, Domaine Tempier "La Migoua" magnums 1981, Côte-Rôtie (Gentaz-Dervieux) 1982, Clos Nicrosi Muscatelli 1994.

The printed menu was deceptively simple. Unmentioned were the local salmon, cold in a film of natural jelly, which accompanied the warm white asparagus, the platters of grilled lambs' kidneys and sweetbreads, the little new potatoes ("dug last night," Alice confided) and the cheeses. The guests were in awe at the purity of the food. Jean-Pierre and his staff received a long ovation. Late that night, we went to Zuni for dinner. Judy Rogers knew all about the Chez Panisse lunch; one of Jean-Pierre's assistants had come by and described it in detail.

26 June 1996. (Me to Byron) "A few days after returning from California, Lulu asked me to lunch with the owner (Reed Hearon), his chef and a couple of members of the staff from Lulu restaurant in San Francisco. I told them I had just been there (they knew from the grapevine) and that my nephew had tried unsuccessfully to hold a table at their restaurant for our Saturday evening meal. Impossible, they said, for you, there will always be a table…."

29 June. Nora and Dr. Gérard Chabal celebrated their marriage at a very grand château in the Loire Valley, near Blois. The religious ceremony was held in a private chapel on the grounds. Nora arrived in a horse-drawn barouche and a whirl of gossamer, just like the movies. Jean Bardet catered the dinner, after which an orchestra played waltzes for the old folks and was then replaced by a rock band. Nora and Gérard flew off to Capri.

Family planned to arrive mid-July. Johnny, who had been at Ridge for only a few months, had no vacation. 8 July. (Me to

Byron) "July in Provence has never been so crazy. Yesterday wild thunderstorms beat up the garden. This morning the mistral struck, laid the beans flat, tore up the tomatoes' stakes, etc. *Christian Science Monitor's* editor and wife for lunch, we huddled inside to eat as the garden was being destroyed. Weather has prevented me from preparing the swimming pool. The wind is still whipping what is left alive. It is cold."

13 July. The day of Byron's arrival, the weather turned human. Margaret, Elizabeth, James and Laura arrived the 14th, John the 15th; we celebrated James's birthday three days late and slipped into the annual pattern of light lunches and serious dinners on the terrace, punctuated by meals with Lulu and other Peyrauds. Lucien was bedridden and no longer came downstairs. Byron stayed ten days, promising to return briefly late September, the others stayed two weeks, except for Margaret, who remained with me until 20 August, working in the studio while I fiddled with my souvenirs.

3 August. A letter from James enclosing Sam Aaron's obituary from the *New York Times*.

3 August 1996. Pamela and Aubert were preparing to leave for Big Sur. He and Kermit had been plotting a meal in Solliès for weeks. Kermit announced that they would arrive for lunch. (Foolhardy, I thought, for Aubert, on the eve of his departure, to sacrifice ten hours on the road for the pleasure of sitting on my terrace—but it was good to see him.) We drank Aubert's young Rully with a salad of green shallots, little garden lettuces, rocket, purslane, basil, parsley and hyssop, green beans, garden tomatoes, boiled eggs and freshly salted anchovies:

Salade
Rully 1995
§
Gigot, Cocos (white shell beans)
Château Simone 1983
§
Fromages
Domaine Tempier magnum 1971
§
Château de Fargues 1984
§

7 August. (Me to James) "Lulu, Laurence and her new friend, Dominique, came for lunch with a loup, which I prepared in the oven—delicious with a Chave white, then a magnum of Latour '68." (Margaret's P.S.) "We have a surfeit of tomatoes—we're freezing them hand over fist. I've started quite a few ptgs—will take them with me half-baked & see what I can do in VA."

18 August. Paule, François and Jérome came to lunch. 20 August. Margaret left at the break of dawn with a huge carton of paintings. (I rang late that night—she and the paintings had safely arrived in Washington.)

Years earlier, before their children were born, Kermit and Gail had invited François, Paule and me to join them for two or three days on a sailboat, a pleasant experience that Kermit wanted to repeat on a grander scale, now that the children were old enough to enjoy it. François, Paule and I were again invited; the dates were set for 26 August - 2 September. Meanwhile, Chez Panisse was planning to celebrate its 25th anniversary with a week of "Provençal dinners accompanied by music and toasting," 22 to 28 August.

19 August. (Alice to me) "I wish I could join you on that 'Kermit cruise.' I'm afraid I will be trying to feed the 1800 people coming to dinner over the six day 25th birthday celebration.... We will be toasting to you. After all you inspired all this insanity, you know!"

Our cruise was a roundtrip to Corsica, anchoring overnight at small ports along the island's east coast. The boat, *Lelantina*, described in the brochure as a "gaff schooner," built in 1937-38, was beautiful. The crew was composed of the skipper, another young man and two young women, one of whom was cook, both of whom were kept busy serving us drinks, adjusting rigging and performing other mysterious chores associated with sailing. François brought along cases of Domaine Tempier, rosé and red, and a supply of Tempier olive oil, I brought cases of garden tomatoes and a litre of my herb vinegar. Kermit wanted me to take over the kitchen but I preferred not to offend the cook, who was proud of her talents. A week of far niente; I kept busy reading mindless books of the sort usually reserved for air travel. I learned from Kermit that Aubert, Pamela and Johnny had assisted at one of the Chez Panisse celebration dinners ("Wonderful!" Johnny told me later).

9 September. Hiroshi Yamamoto, Tokyo attorney and impassioned wine-lover, who, ten years earlier, had translated *Yquem* into Japanese, sent me his newly published translation of *Romanée-Conti*, elegantly boxed, the epitome of deluxe presentation.

21-24 September. Byron and family arrived from a week in Tuscany to pass three days in Solliès. We spoke with Johnny, who was busy with the vendanges in Lytton Springs, teaching ice hockey weekends and had bought grapes to crush and ferment in space adjacent to the ice rink.

5 October. Early morning, Lulu rang: "Lucien nous a quitté."

9 October. (Me to Byron) "Lucien's funeral was yesterday. Alice arrived from Berkeley the evening before. François picked me up at 9 a.m. When we arrived at the Domaine, there was already a crowd of family, vignerons from all over France, local dignitaries and friends. Lulu was upstairs with the coffin as people went up in turn to view the body. Finally, the coffin was closed and carried down the precarious, winding staircase, slipped into the hearse and the cortège began to inch its way toward the local church. Along the way, people left their gardens and doorsteps to follow.... The church ceremony was amateurish and interminable. I thought the priest must have taken acting lessons—not much left of the old Catholic ritual, but a lot of raising and swinging of arms, raising and lowering of voice. He noted that Lucien's friends counted many

believers and non-believers; when it came to passing around the bread wafers, he was very astute at distinguishing between them and us.... Lucien was buried, by special dispensation, at the Domaine, between the kitchen and the cellars, next to his beloved vines.... On the return journey, the cortège had multiplied several fold and we moved along by centimetres instead of inches. When we arrived, Lulu stumbled into the house instead of following the procession to the open grave. Someone had to go find her before the religious ceremony could continue. It was long. Then we cued up as one of the daughters held a vast bouquet of roses at the grave, each of us picking out a rose and tossing it over the coffin.... It rained all day. My umbrella and two or three others were black, all the others were multi-coloured memories of cubism and impressionism. Too bad they were not photographed for eternity—it was a fantastic umbrellascape. The house was packed, a buffet was set out, Tempier rosé and rouge were poured.... It was obvious that a couple of hundred people were going to be eating and drinking for several hours to come. Alice, friends of hers from Nice, Kermit, Gail and I fled to Kermit's to lunch on pasta and Tempier '87, returned several hours later to find the crowd still there. Lulu was grey and weak with pain and exhaustion. Finally returned, delivered by Alice's friends on their way to Nice, at 7 p.m.... Alice leaves Saturday. She, Lulu, Kermit and Gail will come to dinner Friday, I will bring up some grand wines, they will shop (Lulu said, 'I must bring the fish'), maybe I will prepare shellbeans with cuttlefish in their ink, I don't know—I only hope that it will be a gentle and relaxing moment."

11 October. When my guests arrived, red peppers had been grilled, peeled, seeded and torn to narrow strips, baby squid cleaned and shelled, fresh white beans put to cook. Kermit and Gail brought Safranés (wild milk-cap mushrooms), which I marinated with pounded garlic, sea salt, pepper, hillside herbs, lemon juice, olive oil and chopped parsley. Lulu brought Daurades Royales (Gilt-head Bream), gutted but unscaled. The mushrooms were grilled in the fireplace until crisp at the edges; the peppers and their juices were added to an olive oil vinaigrette with the drained beans, the squid were tossed over high heat with garlic persillade

for less than a minute and emptied over the beans; the fish were grilled, the charred sheath of skin and scales removed, the moist fillets lifted from the bone.

Alice, Lulu, Kermit, Gail, 11 October 1996

Apéritif: Krug
Safranés au Gril
Château Simone blanc 1986
§
Salade Tiède de Cocos aux Encornets
Château de Beaucastel blanc 1989
§
Daurades Royales au Gril
Château Cos d'Estournel 1988
§
Fromages
Château Lafite-Rothschild 1948
§
Château Voigny (Sauternes) 1945
§§§

Alice wrote, "...that perfectly lovely dinner with my dearest friends. I think you can understand why I thought everything was just right (those mushrooms massaged with garlic, the coco bean-squid ragout and that simply pure fish). But the 1948 Lafite—I can still taste it! I will always remember it and how I felt in your house that night!"

21 October. Johnny had spoken to me of Jim Harrison, the American novelist, who regularly visited Kermit's shop in Berkeley to order several cases of Tempier each time. Lulu had received him several months earlier. She said that he arrived in a chauffeured Rolls and wanted to drive to Solliès to collect me for lunch—she told him the Rolls would never make it up the hillside. He was expected again for lunch with his French translator. Kermit picked me up. Jim Harrison seems to have devoted his life to writing, hunting, eating and drinking; he has a healthy contempt for the modern world. We stood around the kitchen table drinking

Champagne and devouring vioulets while François basted a grape-leaf-wrapped 2-1/2 kg Daurade Royale in the fireplace.

7-12 November. James came for four days—to see Lulu, to visit Lucien's grave and to renew sentimental memories of talking and drinking all night long.

25 November. (Byron to me) "John is in the newspapers and on TV these days with his brain cancer-aspartame alarm. His publication has generated a lot of hostile response from a variety of sources, but I'm sure it's about what he expected. He's been through it before."

26 November. (Me to Byron) "Had a letter from Margaret who reports that John has just been in Washington and has been elected to the National Academy of Science. I'm sure his publication has generated hostile response. That's fine—John adores hostile response."

28 November 1996. A journalist telephoned from London, wanted the "inside story" on the sale of Château d'Yquem. I spluttered, "The What!?" She pronounced a jumble of letters. "What's that?" I asked. "Oh, you must know," she exclaimed, "It's the Louis-Vuitton-Moët-Hennessy group!" Vague misgivings congealed into a vision of disaster. I moaned, "Oh, no…how awful…." Yquem, which has been in the same family for four centuries, abandoned to the whoredom of a take-over conglomerate? One of the pillars of my fragile world was crumbling.

While Alexandre de Lur-Saluces was absent at a conference in the far east, Louis Hainguerlot, retired Commercial Director of the Champagne firm, Moët & Chandon, a major tentacle of LVMH, and his son, Bertrand, cousins of the Lur-Saluces family, issued the media release as if the sale were a fait accompli. They explained that they represent approximately fifty cousins, shareholders of 43% of the Yquem stock, and that Alexandre's older brother, Eugène de Lur-Saluces, had accepted to relinquish enough of his stock to give LVMH a majority of 55%. In their haste to get into the news, the father and son team didn't wait for LVMH to register a subsidiary company (2 December) designed to absorb Yquem. 13 December, fifteen days after the Hainguerlot press release, LVMH publicly announced its intention to acquire 50.66% of the capital.

Déjeuner - Lulu, Guil, Kermit
Tues. 29 oct. 1996

Pol Roger

Vioulets, radis,
olives noires
Ch. de Fargues 1983

Artichauts à la Barigoule
Dom. de Chevalier '78

Gigot rôti, cocos au beurre
Dom de Chevalier '78
Dom de Chevalier '70

Fromages
Dom de Chevalier '70

Fargues '83

(Six months later, an LVMH spokesman suggested that there had been "an unfortunate leak.")

23 December, an Yquem communiqué states, "The joint ownership, which exists since 1968 between Alexandre de Lur-Saluces and his brother, Eugène, effectively forbids any transfer of shares without the unanimous consent of the two brothers." Alexandre has taken the affair to court. The sale has been blocked until the court makes its decision, which could be in a year—or two, or more.

A Menu by Richard Olney for Charles Joguet

Truffled sausages with pistachios in court-bouillon
Small potatoes boiled in their skins
Chinon Rosé 1995

Squid and leeks in red wine
Chinon, Clos du Chêne Vert 1995
Chinon, Clos de la Dioterie, Vielles Vignes 1995
Chinon, Les Varennes du Grand Clos 1995

Stuffed braised lamb shoulder
White purée
Chinon, Clos du Chêne Vert 1990 (en magnum)
Chinon, Les Varennes du Grand Clos 1990 (en magnum)

Cheeses
Chinon, Clos de la Dioterie, Vielles Vignes 1986 (en magnum)

Pears in Chinon

Chez Panisse November 11, 1996 $90.

Thurs. 14 Nov. 1996
Kermit Lunch

Corbières blanc '95
Saucisson, olives noires
Salade Composée
Gambas grillés gros sel
Corbières

Poulet de Bresse grillé
girolles et Cèpes
Sautés, Persillade
Griotte-Chambertin
(Ponsot) 1983

Fromages
Griotte-Ch

At Gisou's suggestion, I wrote an "open letter" to the Premier Ministre, expressing my outrage and my belief that, if this sale were permitted to take place it would be a bitter blow to the prestige of the National Patrimony. A journalist, who had just interviewed Louis Hainguerlot, rang to ask if missing names in my Lur-Saluces genealogical tree (published eleven years earlier in *Yquem*) were due to malevolent intent. Someone is crazy, I thought, but I explained that my subject was Yquem, not peripheral personalities, and that the purpose of the tree was to clarify for the reader the line of Lur-Saluces descendents responsible for the direction of Yquem. He rang Gisou and received a similar answer. No mention of the tree occured in his article. (Six months later, an article in *La Revue du Vin de France* mentioned a "troubling lapse of memory" in the genealogy, proof to me that the Hainguerlots were still nit-picking. I wrote the author: "I would like your readers to know that there was neither memory lapse nor (as the Hainguerlot cousins pretend) malevolence in the conception of the genealogy, deliberately simplified, the purpose of which was to present to the reader, as clearly as possible, the direct lineage of Yquem directors. An updated edition of *Yquem* will be published in autumn 1997; the genealogy will remain unaltered.")

For Christmas, to increase their collection of antique kitchenware and table service, Byron and Marilynn received from friends, who had found it in Stillwater, Minnesota, a copper restaurant cloche to which was affixed a brass plaque bearing the legend, "La Mère Poulard, Depuis 1888." I was pleased to be able to place it in context:

"La Mère Poulard was a famous restaurant on the Mon-Saint-Michel, in Normandy. Mme Poulard was known for her omelettes. During the first thirty years of the century, much was written about the secret of her marvelous omelettes. I ate there once, over forty years ago. Mme Poulard was then long since dead. The omelettes were made in an iron omelette pan with a handle over a yard long, shaken over flames in the dining room fireplace. They had a pleasant, smoky taste. Elizabeth David recounts that, after decades of articles by different authors, claiming to be in sole possession of Mme Poulard's secret, a Monsieur Viel wrote to the old lady, then retired, asking for her secret. She answered: '6 June 1932. Monsieur Viel, Here is the recipe for the omelette: I break some good eggs in a bowl, I beat them well, I put a good piece of butter in the pan, I throw the eggs into it, and I shake it constantly. I am happy, monsieur, if this recipe pleases you. Annette Poulard.'"

22 January 1997. (Me to James) "François and Paule came to dinner Monday evening bearing truffles. I have never prepared such a radically simple meal for guests—scrambled eggs (half truffles, half eggs) and cheese platter (Pol Roger, Chevalier-Montrachet '94, Ducru '64).

14 February 1997. (Me to James) "Sheldrake, the packager for whom I wrote *Ten Vineyard Lunches*, writes that Interlink, the U.S. publisher, and they, under their own imprint, want to reissue the book as a paperback, with a new cover and a new title, *Richard Olney's French Wine and Food.* At my suggestion, they will get rid of the silly neo-cubist artwork; with a happier title and a cleaner look, maybe it will find a new life."

25 February 1997. Byron faxed that Mother was failing. I flew to Rochester but she died before we could reach her bedside. She was 98. Margaret, Elizabeth, John and James arrived. Because Marathon has no Catholic church, the service was held in the anonymous gloom of a funeral home. To Father Ziegmann, who came from the neighbouring town of Laurens to conduct the ceremony, Byron wrote a letter, which concludes, "You succeeded in lifting the spirits of a group of aging and sometimes skeptical offspring who did not come in expecting to have their spirits lifted. You must believe me when I say that this was a remarkable accomplishment and we are deeply grateful to you for it. It was a service entirely befitting the simple grace and dignity with which Mother lived her life. Thank you so much." The "skeptical offspring" is a reflexion of one of Mother's frequent observations: "I don't know how I ever managed to raise such a pack of heathens!"

13 March 1997. Johnny faxed that James Robertson, at The Yolla Bolly Press in Covelo, California, planned to publish a limited edition of *Babette's Feast* and to ask me for an "afterword." The next day, Kermit, Gail, a couple of other Americans and I were lunching at Domaine Tempier. I asked who knew anything about *Babette's Feast*. "Oh," they chorused, "it's a famous movie." But no one knew the author.

James Robertson faxed. The author was Isak Dinesen (fifty years earlier, I had read and forgotten *Seven Gothic Tales* and *Out of Africa*). *Babette's Feast* was one of a collection of short stories,

Anecdotes of Destiny. Thanks to James, faxes and FedEx, I rapidly received two biographies, a volume of letters and *Anecdotes of Destiny*.

Babette's Feast is a tale of high fantasy. Briefly, it concerns a woman, once worshiped by international aristocratic society as the supreme culinary genius of the period, chef de cuisine at the Café Anglais, Paris's most fashionable restaurant (1802-1913), and creator of the most sublime dishes known to the fastidious world of gastronomy, who, having joined her husband and son during the Parisian Communards' uprising, crushed in May 1871, escaped to Norway with a letter of introduction to a couple of puritan spinster sisters, while her husband and son were sent before the firing squad by General Galliffet, exquisite gastronome and her greatest admirer. She remained a silent and humble servant to the pious sisters until, twelve years later, to commemorate the 100th anniversary of the birth of the sisters' dear, departed father, saintly founder of an unusually abstemious puritan cult, Babette begs to be permitted to prepare a meal for the dissipating members of the cult, who hold food in horror. The menu is exposed by the exclamations of a worldly guest, formerly a client of the Café Anglais: "Amontillado! And the finest Amontillado I have ever tasted; ...Surely I am eating turtle soup—and what turtle soup!; ...Incredible! It is Blinis Demidoff!; ...But surely this is Veuve-Clicquot 1860!? ...But this is Cailles en Sarcophage!; ...Beautiful grapes!" And they drank Clos de Vougeot 1846.

My task, relaxing and amusing, was to fill in a few gaps about 19th century gastronomy, the history of the Café Anglais (which could fill a fascinating book) and to define the dishes in *Babette's Feast*. There are plenty of 19th century books describing the slaughter of 250 kg sea tortoises and their transformation into soup with the addition of chickens, meats and "turtle herbs"; Blinis Demidoff sounds like old Russian aristocracy but, in culinary parlance, "Demidoff" means truffles—pancakes and truffles are silly; Ali Bab's Ortolans en Sarcophages was the inspiration for Cailles en Sarcophage. The birds are boned, stuffed with foie gras, briefly sweated in a braise of mirepoix, the juices of roast and pounded thrush, demi-glace and Madeira, before being fitted into hollowed-out truffles, closed with truffle lids, wrapped in bards, enclosed in papillottes, buried in hot wood ashes until done, unbarded and served with the braising juices.

3 April 1997. Hubert and Christiane de Montille and their daughter, Isabelle (whom I had last seen twenty-one years earlier, a shy child) came to lunch. I was pleased with my salad of parboiled broccoli florets, rapidly sautéed baby squid persillade, green shallots and black olives. It was followed by a pot of tripe and a cheese platter. We drank Krug 1973, Domaine de Chevalier Blanc 1983, Domaine Tempier La Tourtine 1993, Domaine Tempier 1967 and Taylor Port 1924. Hubert wrote, "We will not soon forget that one must, alas, wait for more than 70 years to drink a great Port like the Taylor 1927."

Kermit wants to buy a vineyard; he sent Johnny over in late April to check out possibilities in the Languedoc and the Roussillon. Kit wanted me to visit London to discuss video-cassettes. 4 May, I flew with Johnny to London, where he was changing planes, and spent a few days with Kit and Tony. The twins are both at Oxford, studying medicine. Jonathon is over six feet tall, still growing and hasn't forgotten "the wonderful soup." I saw Sybille for dinners at Jill's, at Kit's and Tony's and at Bibendum. She is frail, moving carefully with the help of a cane, but in good spirits and working on a new book; delicate health has not cooled her passion for wine and conversation.

A British firm, Quadrille, published *The Good Cook's Encyclopedia*, a single volume condensation of the 27-volume Time-Life series. They asked me to write a foreword and to promote the book during the last week of May. Sybille again joined us for dinners prepared by Jill and Kit. The tour embraced London, Birmingham, Manchester and Edinburgh. In Edinburgh, at Rafaeli's, I ate the best restaurant food of my visit. That evening, a reception organized by Clarissa Dickson-Wright at The Cook's Bookshop overflowed into the streets.

I returned to Solliès late Sunday, 1 June. Elizabeth's daughter, Sarah, and her companion, Michael, were due Monday evening for a two-day visit. Henri, who had cared for the birds during my absence, came Monday morning to collect his pay. I said, "Shall we do some shopping?" He answered, "Your niece can drive you. The doctors found a spot on my lung." He died six weeks later.

Family arrived, Byron with a container of freshly dried blond Minnesota morels. We were eight. The garden disgorged tomatoes. Lists of everyone's favorite dishes were compiled. For James's birthday we ate: Marinade of Raw Anchovy Fillets, Sautéed Cuttlefish, Poulets de Bresse with Morels, Cheeses; Johnny brought up Montrachet '85, La Tâche '85, Romanée-Conti '89 and Yquem '83.

Lulu came to lunch. I prepared a thick, flat omelette with shredded, salted, squeezed and sautéed zucchini, a bowl of shelled mussels and a crumbling of freshly dried oregano flowers—it tasted of the garrigue and of the sea. Stuffed chapons de mer were laid on a bed of wild fennel branches, crowned with lemon slices, moistened with the mussels' marinière liquid, anointed with olive oil and baked. Lulu likes red Domaine Tempier with her fish: we drank Pol Roger, Domaine de Chevalier blanc '83 with the omelette, Tempier '92 with the fish and Tempier '82 with the cheese.

I received a carton bursting with documents—photos, articles, speeches, menus, recipes—from Monique (Allégrier) Becquaert, who hoped that I could write a book in homage to her grandfather, Francis Carton, creator of the restaurant Lucas-Carton and one of the great figures on the Parisian culinary scene during the first half of the 20th century. In 1905, he was 26, when he lost a leg from a disastrous accident with a tray of pastry hot from the oven. The Société des Cuisiniers de Paris (renamed La Mutuelle des Cuisiniers de France), a benevolent mutual aid society, furnished him with a wooden leg. He became director of La Mutuelle in 1912 and president in 1923. In 1920, he created *La Revue Culinaire*, the society's official journal, with his friend, Prosper Montagné, as editor; in 1925, he bought La Taverne Lucas and baptized it Lucas-Carton. In 1926, his daughter, Andrée, married Alex Allégrier, who shared the direction of Lucas-Carton until Francis Carton's death in 1945. Alex was patron until his death in 1977; Andrée and Monique directed the restaurant until Andrée's death in 1983. In 1984, Lucas-Carton was sold to a conglomerate; Alain

Senderens is in the kitchen; Roland, who was maître d'hôtel Chez Garin until it closed, is maître d'hôtel.

Forty years ago, in a weekly Parisian journal, Simon Arbellot wrote an article entitled "Monique a Vingt Ans...," evoking the vast cellars of Lucas-Carton, whose farthest reaches, concealing their greatest treasures, lay beneath the nave of the Madeleine church and were walled up during the war to deceive the German occupants. Lucas-Carton's chef and the sommelier officiated at Monique's twentieth birthday dinner at the Allégrier's country home. The menu was: "Marennes Extra, Saumonneau au Clos Vougeot, Timbale de Ris de Veau Financière, Noisettes d'Agneau 'Madeleine,' Pâté de Bécasses 'Brillat Savarin,' Gerbe de Lauris (asparagus), Fromages, Glace Monique, Gâteau Anniversaire, Corbeille de Fruits." The wines: "Porto et Xérès Mackensie Réserve Francis Carton, Chevalier-Montrachet 1945, Magnum Château Ausone 1914, Magnum Château Latour 1904, Romanée-Conti 1937, Impériale de Krug 1928, Armagnac 1884, Grande Champagne 'Les Joussons' 1777, Vieilles Chartreuses Jaune, Verte et Blanche 1875."

I couldn't write the book. Francis Carton's life-long passion for La Mutuelle and its philanthropic projects might, I thought, be meaningless to readers outside the profession and I had no faith in the success of a "Lucas-Carton Cookbook"—the cuisine was extraordinarily rich, unadaptable to a home kitchen and intimidating to a calorie-conscious public. Moreover, the present Lucas-Carton could only confuse the picture; only the art nouveau woodwork and the bronze maidens emerging from tulips have not changed.

1 December 1997, from Byron: "...good news on the medical front...not really new news but further confirmation that oleomargarine is poisonous and does exactly the opposite of what it was supposed to be doing. It's very painful for all the nutrition experts of the world to come to terms with this revelation. They can't give up altogether so they suggest that maybe 'tub margarine,' whatever that is, is a reasonable substitute.... They have the same kind of problem dealing with the issue of wine and the health.... They will all go to their graves with butter and alcohol free bodies."

27 December. Lulu fetched me to join Alice and Fanny at Tempier—truffles under ashes and loup fresh from the sea, unscaled and grilled high over wood embers, moist and sweet. Fanny is a lovely girl, very grown-up and gourmande. Lunch the next day with Jean-Marie and Catherine, wriggly Breton oysters and soupe de poisson with poached monkfish. Jean-Marie drove me home, while Lulu accompanied Alice and Fanny to Le Castellet for dinner with François and Paule. They flew from Marseille at dawn the next day.

1 January 1998. Andre Parcé died.

8 January. François picked me up to join the annual pilgrimage of Kermit's American clients, organized and led by Bruce Nyers. After tasting five cuvées from each of several vintages in the cellar, the group filed through the kitchen to admire legs of lamb à la ficelle twisting in the fireplace with potatoes baking in the ashes. The table was set on the terrace, soupe de poisson, croûtons and rouille mounted with monkfish livers to start.

12 January, from Johnny: "Dick Graff died last Friday—flew his plane into a power line and crashed on the way to his hillside retreat." I don't know when Dick first visited me in Solliès—twenty years ago, maybe more—but I remember checking the year of his birth and opening a Château Latour Blanche 1937.

3 February 1998. (Me to James) "John and Johnny should by now have signed purchase papers for the Sonoma Valley property—it will soon be time to plant vines. Received faxes yesterday from Gisou (giving me the go-ahead for an update of *Romanée-Conti*—Flammarion wants it in the bookshops by May) and from John Colby (Brick Tower Press) who would like to publish *Reflexions*.

22 February 1998. (Fax from Marilynn) "Do you know of a restaurant in Paris called Lasserre? Yesterday at an antique shop I found a little copper sauté pan (3-inch diameter) with the name Lasserre on the handle and a crest with the name on the pan itself. The address, 17 Avenue Franklin Roosevelt, is also on the handle. Quite heavy and quite sweet." A summer evening in the mid-sixties, long since forgotten, began to etch itself in my memory: Garin, Mary, James, Judy and I had held a table for dinner chez

Lasserre. I remember that I was irritated by the grinding roof-ceiling which slid open to expose a star-lit sky. The food was not memorable and the wines I've forgotten, except for the Mouton-Rothschild 1953, which I'd asked to be served at cellar temperature. (Garin was always pleased to let me order the wines, probably because he enjoyed the ensuing scandal concerning the temperature.) It was decanted and poured at 80°F.; I had the usual battle with the obstinate sommelier until the decanter was finally, but resentfully, put into an ice-bucket. Judy thought it would be cute to lift one of the miniature copper saucepan ashtrays; with all the subtlety of a silent screen star, she glanced furtively to all sides before slipping the coveted object into her bag. Nothing was said, but the little copper pan was added to our bill at an astronomic price. (Over the years, Lasserre must have made a fortune from light-fingered souvenir-seekers.)

I opened *Truman Capote*, George Plimpton's chronologically ordered book of quotes, to a photo of a lugubrious Victorian mansion, spooky and eerily familiar. I had forgotten how ugly it was, the mansion at Yaddo, an artists' colony in upstate New York, where Margaret and I were guests during the summer of 1951, a few months before I sailed. Most of the guests were writers. There were two or three painters' studios and two studios for composers. The head mistress, director of Yaddo, was Mrs (Elizabeth) Ames. I thought she was 80 (but, at 24, everyone between 60 and 90 is the same age). She stood rigidly upright; her conversation, punctuated by electrical storms in a hearing aid, was polite and impersonal, untainted by critical observation. But, each morning, certain guests were delivered succinct little notes concerning their reprehensible behavior. The rules at Yaddo were draconian but, in practice, rarely respected. Lunch boxes were labeled and laid out to be picked up and carried to studios or workrooms at 8 a.m. Socializing was forbidden until after 4 p.m., dinner was at 8 and all lights were supposed to be out by 10. The guests formed cliques, each organizing cocktail parties before dinner and, often, after hours drinking sessions. Margaret and I lived in the West House annex, its lights unfortunately visible from Mrs Ames's house, and regularly received notes forbidding us to stay up late. Polly Hanson (poet) and Clifford Wright (painter) were year-round guests and assistants to Mrs Ames. They, and other guests who had visited before, provided us with anecdotes about preceding years, many from the 1946 spring session, when Carson McCullers, Katherine Anne Porter, Marguerite Young, Truman Capote, John Malcolm Brinnin and Leo Lerman were amongst the residents. Mrs Ames's note, delivered one morning to Truman Capote and Leo Lerman, "Would Mr. Capote and Mr. Lerman stop committing nuisances on the bathroom floor?" became famous.

I moved into Clifford Wright's flat in New York. The FBI thought Yaddo was a "nest of commies." Two G-man clones with slouch hats, trench coats and mean, slit eyes pounded on the door one morning, burst in, pushing FBI badges in my face and said, "You are Clifford Wright!" I said, "No." They were checking on someone who had been at Yaddo, suspected of being communist. I had never met him but knew his wife, editor on a fashion magazine, and rang her. "Oh yes," she said, "we know, they've been all over the place." Clifford surprised his friends by marrying a Danish writer in residence at Yaddo, Elsa Gress, and moving to Denmark. He visited several times, in Paris, Clamart and Solliès, dreamt of creating another Yaddo in Denmark, but I could never bring myself to travel that far north.

15 April 1998. (Me to Byron) "I received the biography of Beauford (*Amazing Grace*, David Leeming) in today's mail. Also, from James, an article from the *Tampa Tribune*, "Florida Family Finds Long-Lost Dancer Brother," all about Arthur Bell, age 71, out of touch with his family far nearly fifty years, found half frozen in the streets of Brooklyn, "homeless and disoriented," now recuperating and learning to walk again in a New York City nursing home, about to be reunited with his younger brothers and sisters. It would be nice if Arthur found a few years of serenity with an adoring family.

"François rang last week to ask if Lulu, Paule and he could bring some food and help me celebrate my birthday. They brought vioulets, gambas and a loup. Grilled the prawns on a bed of coarse sea salt and grilled the unscaled bass 10 inches above the bed of coals—all very clean and pure. Drank Pol Roger 1989, Château de

Fargues '83 with the vioulets, Muscadet sur lie '96 with the prawns, Chevalier-Montrachet '91 with the loup, Bourgueil '89 with cheese and finished with the remainder of the Fargues."

Byron: "When you grill a large fish 10 inches from the coals do you follow the same general rule of cooking it for about 8 to 10 minutes per inch of thickness or does it take longer? I assume cooking further from the coals is a good idea for larger fish. When I have grilled fish it has always been 4 or 5 inches from the coals. For large fish, this means they end up quite black on the outside."

Me to Byron: "I was very pleased with my fish grilled high over the coals—it takes a bit longer, at a guess 40 minutes for a bass 3 1/2 inches thick behind the gills. I shoved a bouquet of wild fennel into the gut cavity and smeared a bit of oil on the scales to make sure they wouldn't stick, turned the fish 2 or 3 times on the grill, the scales and skin formed a firm, brittle, lightly browned sheath, which lifted like a lid to reveal glistening white fillets. When the scale-skin sheath appears, suddenly less rigid and a viscous essence begins to form a teardrop beneath the body of the fish, it is done."

19 May 1998. A letter, signed by the director of the prime minister's Information Bureau, soliciting cooperation with a government press service for foreign journalists assisting at the 1998 World Cup, was addressed to:

Monsieur Jacques de Sauvage
Château d'Yquem
4. château Yquem
33210 Sauternes

Alexandre de Lur-Saluce's ancestor, Jacques Sauvage, lived four centuries ago. Alexandre's proposed answer: "Returned to the Eternal Father in 1609; see book by Richard Olney...."

7 June. (Me to James) "Gisou (carrying copies of the updated *Romanée-Conti*) and Joe Fitchitt came to dinner and spent the night. She was on a diet, so we sat down to jambon de Parme, hot green bean salad, unscaled, ungutted rougets wrapped in grape

leaves and grilled, a cheese platter, and drank Aubert's Rully les Saint-Jacques '96, La Tâche '91 and Yquem '82...."

8 July. A letter from Denis Mollat, publisher of *Pour Yquem* (testimonies of loyalty to Alexandre de Lur-Saluces and Yquem), enclosing a newspaper clipping: Bernard Arnault, LVMH director, had lodged an "abuse and slander" complaint in court against Monsieur Mollat and two of the letter writers. Air France bumped Arnault's lawyer from his Paris-Bordeaux flight because the plane was overbooked—the next flight was retarded by two hours; case deferred until autumn.

Because interminable rains in California had prevented planting vine rootstock at the Sonoma property until mid-summer, Johnny postponed his visit to Solliès until late autumn, after the grape harvest at Ridge.

10 July. Byron flew into Hyères, arrived for lunch. Nathan's friend, Bennet, was expected to meet James and Nathan at 10 a.m. in the Nice airport. James rang at noon—no Bennet. Bennet faxed Solliès—he had missed a train in Marseille...more uncoordinated faxes and phone calls. James and Nathan spent the day at the airport, drove into Nice to meet another train that Bennet had missed and arrived at dusk without Bennet. A lady, who sounded cross, rang from the information counter at the Nice airport, asked if I knew someone named Bennet. She put him on the line, I told him to take a train to Toulon and a taxi to Solliès. We sat down to dinner at midnight. Christopher arrived a couple of days later, in time to share James's birthday dinner (sautéed squid, grilled guinea fowl, potato paillasson, cheeses; Krug NV, Bouzeron Aligoté '97, Tempier La Tourtine '87, Latricières-Chambertin '83, Yquem '80). Nathan, Christopher and Bennet discovered a common passion for an animated cartoon TV show with a character named Homer. All three had memorized precious lines of dialogue, which they recited in turn. Bennet wanted to discuss Freud; "fraud" misspelled, I suggested. When he left, he tried to express his pleasure at having been exposed to uncommon ideas.

Margaret and Elizabeth arrived 15 July. Laura rang from California to say she would like to be married on the terrace the following Saturday, 25 July: James didn't seem surprised. Byron and Christopher had to return before the marriage.

31 July. (Me to Byron) "Ten days ago Laura arrived from Ireland with her mother. Her sister and a child flew from Australia, a friend came from Germany, then two brothers from Ireland. Lulu produced a priest, who performed admirably. The O'Connors read passages from the Scriptures. Lots of Pol Roger (white and pink); smoked salmon, roast leg of lamb, potato-sorrel gratin, cheeses, wedding cake de rigueur; Rully '96, Romanée-Conti '90, Yquem '83. Margaret and Elizabeth left the 28th, James and Laura left this morning, Nathan stays until 10 August."

18 August (Fax from Johnny). "Aubert called last week from Big Sur to ask if he could come by Ridge to taste on his way to San Francisco. Paul and I were expecting him today, however he had to return abruptly to France. His father had a bad fall, may have broken some vertebrae."

29 August. (Me to Johnny) "Aubert's father died a week ago. 89 years old, a kind and gentle person."

8 October 1998. (Me to Byron) "A year or two ago, Nora arranged for Marion Cunningham to teach a week of baking classes at the Ritz Hotel cooking school. Marion asked me to speak to the students. Because I didn't know what to say, my speech became a question and answer session. Marion claims that, in answer to a question concerning the importance of authenticity in the kitchen, I said, "I don't know anything about authenticity—the important thing is that the food taste good." I have no idea what other nuggets of wisdon I let drop, but Marion was impressed. She exclaimed, "Your voice must be heard, Richard!" "But Marion," I said, "My voice has been heard repeatedly and, anyway, I'm so dumb, I say the same things over and over again," to which she answered, "Some things can't be repeated too often!" Since then, she and her friend, Peggy Knickerbocker, food journalist and cookbook author, have been plotting with *Gourmet* magazine to "get my voice heard." They, Reed Hearon and his friend, Nina Ebert, arrived Tuesday for lunch. (Peggy reminded me that we had met in 1975 when I demonstrated at Williams-Sonoma, San Francisco, and again in 1994, when Reed organized a suckling pig reception for

Lulu Peyraud and me.) *Gourmet* had faxed me that the photographer, Jean Cazals, would be with us Thursday and Friday. He rang Wednesday evening—he and his assistant had just arrived at the Nice airport, had to fly out again late Thursday. I asked them to drive straight from the airport for a drink and some soup. I think Jean fell in love with the place the moment he set foot in the kitchen. He remembered me from the loony Rodenstock extravaganza at Château d'Yquem in September 1986, described the nervous tension as he photographed the sommelier's trembling hands easing the cork from the 1750 bottle of Yquem.

"Today we shot composed salad, leg of lamb hung from a cord before the fireplace, potato and sorrel gratin, a cheese platter and Marion's bread pudding, sat down to eat at 2 and, since the shoot was finished, the others decided they wanted to visit St. Tropez. Everyone left at 4."

25 October 1998. (Me to Byron) "Aubert rang. He and Pamela would be in the midi 18 October. Could they take me to lunch? Before leaving for the Lingousto, I opened a half bottle of Trockenbeerenauslese 1990, a gift from a German friend, grower unknown to me. Pink-grey-purple squared tablecloth, surmounted by a splashy, spreading bouquet of cosmos in the same colours, more vivid. The wine was deep gold, the nose explosive. "A very great moment," said Aubert. At the restaurant, we ate sautéed wild mushrooms (cèpes, girolles, trompettes de la mort, lactaires délicieuses) and rare roast wild mallard. With the duck, said Aubert, we should drink a Bandol. He mumbled inaudibly to the sommelier, who returned with a DRC Grands-Echézeaux 1988. It was lovely.

"Reed and Nina, on a continuing gastronomic tour, came by next day with chefs from two of Reed's San Francisco restaurants: Cèpes en persillade, Smoked salmon, Garden salad (Aubert's Aligoté); Tripes au vin blanc, Rattes (Hermitage, Chave '90), Cheeses (Clos de la Roche, Ponsot '83); Yquem '90 for dessert....

"James's book, *Memory and Narrative*, official publication January '99, will be in print next month. An excerpt from *Reflexions* will appear in the January issue of *The Yale Review*. No more visits in sight until Johnny arrives sometime in November."

6 November 1998. (Me to James) "Jean-Eugène Borie died. Drank a bottle of Ducru 1961 in his memory.

"In desperation, prowling for something to read, I dragged out Yeats;

'Whence did all that fury come?
From empty tomb or Virgin womb?
Saint Joseph thought the world would melt
But liked the way his finger smelt.'

A lovely epitaph to the Second Millennium."

12 November 1998. (Letter from Jimmy Draper) "I have the infinitely sad job of telling you that we lost our beautiful Robert a week ago today...."

17 November. (Me to Byron) "Robert Isaacson's death has depressed me.... Lulu and Kermit to lunch today, simple perfection—Kermit brought cheeses and a bottle of Chablis (Ravenneau, Montée de Tonnerre 1978), Lulu brought vioulets, salad ingredients and a daurade royale (gilt-head bream). Sent Kermit to the cellar to choose a red wine, he returned with a Domaine de Chevalier 1981 (said to be a small vintage—both the Chablis and the Domaine de Chevalier were monuments of balance and complexity)."

5 December 1998. (Me to Byron) "Jeremiah telephoned—he has sold Stars and is preparing a trip around the world to wind up other affairs, will come by Solliès in January. Just returned from the AIV conference in Geneva, had dinner with Michel Lemonnier (retired), Hubert (retired) and Christiane de Montille, Pierre (who has sold Château Giscours and retired) and Mme Tari, Bruno (who has sold Château Cos d'Estournel) and Mme Prats...and Michel Bettane, France's answer to Robert Parker. Shared a table the next day with Paul Draper (Ridge), who waxed eloquent about Johnny's talents.

"Received from Gisou an article, first page, date, name of publication and author's name missing, the latter obviously Jancis Robinson, à propos of an event in Germany: Rodenstock out-Rodenstocking Rodenstock with a week-long tasting, including amongst other wines, 125 vintages of Yquem; Alexandre was not invited."

22 December 1998. (Me to James) "Johnny left this morning after five days spent mostly at table, primitive food (salads, squid this way and that, duck gizzards, chanterelles, freshly dug rattes...) and what he happened to find in the cellar—'53 Latour, '47 Cheval Blanc, '71 Forts de Latour, '74 Tempier, '83 Montluisants (Ponsot), '86 Simone blanc, '89 Richebourg (DRC), '93 Pommard Rugiens (de Montille), '96 Rully (Aubert) and, of course, plenty of Bouzeron Aligoté to splice it all together.

"At Tempier, Lulu served bourride and Jean-Marie poured rosé '98, Cabassaou (the lower slope of La Tourtine, planted to 50 year old Mourvèdre) '97, Cabassaou '88 and Tourtine '82. Two days later, with François, Paule and family, we drank still prickly Cabassaou '98 with braised squid and aïoli, Cabassaou '89 with leg of lamb roasted pinkly before the fireplace, Tempier '72 with cheeses and finished with a bottle of Yquem '82."

A man telephoned late one afternoon, said it was urgent, could he make an appointment to see me the next day. "A propos of what?" I asked. He said. he represented one of the most distinguished wine firms of Bordeaux. I told him it would be a waste of his time and of mine—I was not a potential client. He insisted it was not in the interest of selling wine that he so longed to meet me, he would love to simply discuss wine with me...could he come by the next day at 4 p.m.? I met him as he drove up the hillside. He radiated grey respectability and was accompanied by his teenage son, dressed for the occasion with a tie and jacket in which he was visibly uncomfortable. As we entered the kitchen, the largest and only comfortable room in the house, a thread snapped, not only the thread of self-control, but something more scary. He claimed, "You told me you lived in a house (une maison)–this is not a house, it's nothing but a shack (une cabane)!" I had told him nothing at all. I reminded him that he had invited himself with no encouragement from me. The boy was flushed with embarrassment and dared look neither at me nor at his father. He was frightened. I pulled out copies of *Yquem* and *Romanée-Conti* for my unruly guest's inspection. This did not sooth him; on the contrary, he was outraged that an American should be permitted to publish books about France's greatest wines. I asked if he would like to visit the wine cellar. "Non!" he snapped and led the trembling boy away. I tried to figure out what had happened. The firm, whose wines he represented, must have informed him that a wine writer lived in his region. Perhaps he had a vision of a grand seigneur in a fine château, surrounded by devoted servants. I imagined that the discovery of an unkempt hermit in a hillside "shack" was the last straw after years of frustration in the life of a traveling salesman.

Reactions vary. Recently, a young man, who had delivered a truckload of logs for the fireplace, came into the kitchen to settle the note. His eyes opened wide and his face stretched to a huge smile as he caressed the ancient marble sink and the tiled work surface, gazed in rapture at the fireplace, the rows of copper, piles of earthenware and the cookstove. His voice was reverent: "This is the most beautiful kitchen I've ever seen...."

19 April 1999. A communiqué from Château d'Yquem indicates that LVMH has won the battle and now owns 64% of Château d'Yquem. In hollow phrases, the take-over artist, Bernard Arnault, expresses his admiration for Alexandre de Lur-Saluces and his satisfaction that Alexandre will remain at Yquem "to ensure the durability of this prestigious growth." Ugh.

20 April 1999. (Me to Byron) "Just read an unauthorized biography of Elizabeth David by Lisa Chaney, who didn't know E.D. It is not a nice book. Duplicitous. The author is appropriately enamoured of the food writing but doesn't like the person she has invented. The delivery through pursed lips is that of the complacent puritan: the sniff of disapproval is audible. The language is mealymouthed and pompous, the psycho-jargon depressing.

"Innuendos and gratuitous remarks are scattered arbitrarily throughout the text: 'It was hard, for women particularly, to like her....'; she was 'not inclined toward self-reflection'; 'not able to sustain a relationship'; she had 'an unerring ability to associate herself with men who could be relied upon for unreliability'; 'her forte lay more in the area of courtesanship than in the sometimes duller but more enduring one of conjugality.' She is said to have 'a drive to control and manipulate, a disciplined schizoid behaviour,' to be 'feline' and 'predatory.'

"The author hammers away relentlessly at her subject's 'heavy drinking' ('lived the life of a femme fatale, drinking to excess...abused her body with too much alcohol,' etc.) and her 'capacity for insensitivity' ('repeated lapses of sensitivity...breathtaking disregard for others' sensitivities'; abrasive to the point of rudeness....')

"The reader is told that E.D. preferred the company of homosexuals. Elsewhere, one reads, 'In common with any number of other women, Elizabeth appears to have believed that they were ultimately more respect-worthy than men. She may also at some point have had a romantic liaison with another woman.' Wishful thinking.

"The Elizabeth I knew preferred the company of intelligent people. She loved conversation and she loved to laugh. Her wit was pointed but never cruel. She loved five-hour-long lunches with several wines. Naturally. The best conversation is always at table."

Afterword

Summer 1999. Solliès-Toucas.
by James Olney

April 20. (Richard to James) "I am looking forward to our summer. As you know, it is always the most precious moment of my year. Perhaps I am just feeling gloomy, but I wonder if it will be our last summer together on the hillside. I have never considered leaving it, but my legs, my back and my excessive tiredness are not improving—and, of course, they won't."

30 April. (Richard to Byron) "Very confusing, family's projects for visiting—it is wonderful when everyone is together, but if it stretches out that's all right with me. The most beautiful time of the year is when I am with family."

3 May. (Richard to Jill Norman) "The family has done a bad job of coordination this year. Byron arrives 3 July, Margaret

and Elizabeth arrive (I think) 8 July, James, Laura, Nathan and the new baby girl, Gobnait, arrive 15 July in time for dinner; Byron leaves the next morning, Margaret, Elizabeth, and Nathan leave 21 July, James, Laura, and Gobnait leave the 28th (they hope to sail to Corsica and back 22-25 July). So, the place will be packed from 15 to 21 July, but I could put you up before or after."

17 May. (Richard to Elizabeth) "I guess that you have been in touch with other members of the family. You are all apparently stretching yourselves out through the month of July. Only yesterday received approximate schedules from Byron and James. Byron arrives 3 or 4 July, leaves 16 July. James, Laura, Gobby, and Nathan arrive the 15th, in time to have dinner with Byron before his departure the next morning. You and Margaret, I understand, plan to arrive the 8th and leave 21 July at the same time as Nathan. James, Laura, Gobby leave the 28th. Of course, you and Margaret could stay on a week and still have a ride to the aerport with James. I cannot have enough of family."

24 May. (Richard to James) "I think that, finally, everything is (almost) together. Your hotel room in Corsica is confirmed, I have your boat tickets in hand. Adjoined a fax from Jill. I have told her that I will have space when she and Paul are here. Will have to think about the lunch she wants to organize, it may be more practical and easier on Lulu to do it here, which would mean the 26th, after your return from Corsica and before your departure.... I think that I can promise fresh tomatoes from the garden; as for the rest, I trust we will have a good time and drink some super wines."

24 May. (James to Richard) "Received the fax with Jill's adjoining.... We're contemplating a small, decidedly secular ceremony in Solliès to give Marina Gobnait her name formally and to have it include the French portion of her identity—i.e., Lucie. I've asked Nathan to stand not as godfather but as a sort of protector in big-brother form and wonder if Lulu would consent to be something of the same on the motherly side. The idea is a very brief ceremony around the fish basin, a few drops of water sprinkled, the names pronounced, and then a glass of wine. I think the only thing it would mean would be assuring that Lulu could come over one

Gobnait and R.O., July 1999.

day during the week that Nathan, Elizabeth, and Margaret are there. I *wish* Byron and John could be there, but that's obviously not possible.... We're greatly looking forward to the time in Solliès. I'm sure that, as you say, we'll have a good time and drink some super wines—and shouldn't be surprised if we talk some nonsense as well."

26 May. (Richard to Lulu) "Quant au baptême 'laïque' de Marina Gobnait Lucie O'Connor Olney le 18 (il y aura un autre baptême très Catholique en Irelande), dont tu sera désigné comme Marraine et Nathan comme le Grand Frère Protecteur (j'ignore si je serai prêtre), cela se passera à côté du bassin aux poissons. James indique que la cérémonie sera simple, quelques gouttes d'eau aspergées sur l'enfant, les noms prononcés, suivi d'un verre de vin. On pourrai, sans doute, se mettre à table ensuite."

27 June. (Letter, Aubert de Villaine to Richard) "Je te vois très peu, mais cela ne m'empêche pas de penser souvent à toi. N'ayant malheureusement pas de possibilité immédiate d'aller jusqu'à Solliès, je me permet de t'envoyer un 'signe de vie' sous la forme de quelques bouteilles qui, j'espère, te feront plaisir."

Invoice (marked "Cadeau Domaine") from the Domaine de la Romanée-Conti, dated 2 July 1999:

1 Bouteille de MONTRACHET 1969
1 Bouteille de LA TACHE 1979
1 Bouteille de ROMANEE SAINT VIVANT 1991
1 Bouteille de GRANDS ECHEZEAUX 1993
1 Bouteille de GRANDS ECHEZEAUX 1989
1 Bouteille d'ECHEZEAUX 1990

Byron arrives 4 July, John (plans uncertain until the last moment), Margaret and Elizabeth on the 8th, James, Laura, Nathan and Marina Gobnait the 15th.

6 July. (Richard to Byron, late night on the terrace) "I don't know, but I feel this may be the last summer on the hillside." Byron: "I don't know why you say that. Given the family medical history, you should live and thrive here for another twenty years." Richard: "We'll see."

10 July. (Letter from Joan Aiken to Richard) "Good about all those family visits. I read some piece of research that said people who live in the south & have strong bonds with family live to over 100."

15 July 1999. Dinner on the terrace, Solliès-Toucas. At table, Richard, Margaret, John, Elizabeth, Byron, James, Laura, Nathan—and Gobnait alongside.

Marinade d'anchois à l'hysope
Rully les Saint-Jacques d'Aubert de Villaine, 1997
§
Moules à la marinière
Montrachet 1969
§
Gigot à la ficelle
Pommes de terre aux truffes
Romanée-Saint-Vivant 1991
§
Fromages
La Tâche 1979
Château d'Yquem 1992
§§§

The atmosphere one of euphoria, of well-being and joy at being all together at last; the menu a kind of distillation of Richard's feelings and beliefs about food and wine: the friendly Rully an ideal partner to the delicacy of the raw anchovy fillets, sprinkled with purple hyssop flowers; the deep, golden Montrachet playing off against the tiny mussels and their taste direct from the sea; the vibrant Romanée-Saint-Vivant fully capable of supporting the robust flavors of the gigot and the heavily truffled potatoes; the complex La Tâche splendid with an array of cheeses—Comté, Reblochon, Roquefort, Saint-Nectaire, Tomme de Savoie, two or three fresh goat cheeses; the Yquem unique and standing alone, gathering into its incredibly rich depths the experience of the entire evening—the full glory of the meal lying, however, not in single dishes or wines but in the symphonic harmony of the whole progression of dishes and the suite of wines. A magic moment enshrined now in individual memories and in a single, integral family memory.

16 July. Byron and John depart.

18 July. Around the fish basin, with Nathan as Big-Brother Protector and Lulu as Godmother, Richard pronounces these words: "Nous, amis et famille de cet enfant, nous sommes réunis aujourd'hui pour lui conférer des noms qui signifient son héritage et sa nature. Elle s'appelle Marina parce que son signe du zodiaque est Le Poisson, son élément spirituel est l'eau. Elle appartient à la mer. Elle s'appelle Gobnait parce qu'elle est d'Irelande et elle partage avec la Sainte Gobnait de Kerry un rapport avec les abeilles. Elle s'appelle Lucie par sa liaison intime avec la France en la personne de sa marraine, Lucie Tempier Peyraud. Elle s'appelle O'Connor car elle est le corps et l'âme de sa mère. Elle s'appelle Olney car, comme la Marina du *Périclès* de Shakespeare, elle est la rédemption de son père et l'objet de l'affection de son grand frère et protecteur, Nathan. Ainsi, avec ces gouttes d'eau, nous te baptisons *Marina Gobnait Lucie O'Connor Olney*. Pour couronner cet événement, un verre de rosé du Domaine Tempier est indiqué."

21 July. Margaret, Elizabeth and Nathan depart.

Scribbled notation in R.O.'s hand of the menu prepared by himself and Jill Norman at Domaine Tempier 26 July: "vioulets, octopus daube, gigot à la ficelle, green beans, salad, cheeses, fruits—Jean-Marie furnished the wines, spread over two decades."

28 July. James, Laura and Marina Gobnait depart.

29 July. (Richard to Byron) "Jill and Paul arrived during James's and family's absence in Corsica (with which they were very pleased), they returned Sunday evening for a guinea fowl dinner. Jill and I had spent the day preparing for her bash at Tempier (we were 12), cooking ahead of time an octopus daube (I had splashed in some marc, then added bottle ends of Châteauneuf, Tempier, etc., thought it was not enough, snatched another Tempier bottle and poured in half before realizing it was the marc bottle—after 3 hours' gentle simmering and being reheated the next day, everyone thought it was spectacular and, from now on, will add more marc to their daubes), preparing the gigot to be roasted à la ficelle, there was little to do at Tempier except to taste for two hours in the cellar. Lulu had bought vioulets to start with. A great success and I was done in by the end of the day. We ate left-over octopus with shell beans for supper, Jill and Paul left the next day after a big salad, James and family left yesterday and I collapsed, short of breath with chest pains, no doubt a nervous reaction to pressures...now, things seem to be looking up."

28 July. (Fax from Jill to Richard) "I hope you had a good day with James, Laura & Marina—I imagine they are on their way to Ireland by now. It was lovely to see you & to be on your peaceful hillside again—it is one of the best places in the world. Thank you so much for wonderful meals & wines & talk; the memories will last a long time."

31 July. (Fax from Byron to Richard) "Do you often have chest pains? It always makes a cardiologist nervous to hear about chest pains. The more I think about your legs and the problem you have with walking any distance, the more it seems to me that an impaired circulation may be at least part of the problem—not the balance part but the discomfort that comes with walking. It should be looked into."

29 July. (Richard to John Colby) "My summer is over. Family and friends have left...."

Two final pictures of Richard, burned into memory: of him holding Marina Gobnait in a rocking chair and comforting her as her parents finish packing—a good and loving uncle to the end; and of him, seen in a rearview mirror, disconsolately waving them down the hillside.

* * * *

3 August 1999. (Byron, in Rochester, by telephone to James in Dublin) "Richard was found dead in his bed this morning."

4 August. Byron arrives in Hyères and James in Nice, they proceed together to Solliès and find gendarmes from Solliès-Pont at the gate to the property, identify themselves, receive the keys to the house and enter to find a picture of perfect order: a dish with traces of a tomatoed pilaf on it, the pan in which the pilaf was warmed, and a wine glass, all placed next to the sink for washing (the remains of the pilaf neatly stored in the refrigerator); on the table an open book with Richard's glasses alongside, the fax from Byron of 31 July, received at 2:54 p.m., still in the machine.

Conversations with a man who did some gardening unfold this narrative: after talking briefly with the gardener at noon on Saturday (July 31), Richard ate a light lunch, read a bit, went to take a nap, suffered a heart attack in his sleep and never awoke. The gardener discovered the body on Tuesday (August 3). Byron and James, with Lulu and Kermit, to the morgue in Cuers 4 August; they arrange for cremation without ceremony the next day, return the ashes to the house, and plan a ceremony celebrating Richard's life for next summer when family and friends from France, America and England can gather in his memory on the hillside he loved so much.

5 August. (Jill to James and Byron) "I hardly know what to write to you; I have barely grasped that Richard is no longer there on the hillside. Sorrow, grief, frustration, anger are all mixed up. I cannot imagine what a loss it must be for you and the rest of the family. I loved Richard, and admired and respected him greatly.

Those words of Norman Douglas to Elizabeth come to mind: 'Whoever helps us to a greater understanding deserves our eternal gratitude.' Richard certainly did that for me, and for many people."

Byron to James at table on the terrace in Solliès 9 August (Menu: brochettes of lamb's hearts and kidneys, the remains of the pilaf found in the refrigerator, a bottle of Château de Beaucastel 1986 from the cellar): "Do you realize what we're doing?—eating the last meal Richard will ever cook for us."

Silence.

§ § §

—Kitchen. Silent, August 1999.

Reflexions

Biography

Aalto (Bill). Poet, friend of poets.
Aaron (Sam). Wine merchant. President of Sherry-Lehmann, Inc. (679 Madison Avenue, New York, NY) He is succeeded by his nephew, Michael Aaron.
Acton (Sir Harold). British novelist, historian, memoirist. Precocious poet and aesthete at Oxford. Born, grew up and died at Villa La Pietra, near Florence.
Alexander (Stephanie). Restaurant proprietor (Stephanie's, Melbourne, Australia), cook and writer. Author of *Stephanie's Menus for Food Lovers*, *Stephanie's Feasts and Stories*, *Stephanie's Australia*, *Stephanie's Seasons....*
Allégrier (Alex). Proprietor and director, with his wife, Andrée (née Carton), of the restaurant, Lucas-Carton, Place de la Madeleine, Paris. Lucas-Carton was sold in 1984.
Anger (Kenneth). Independent, underground film-maker–Fireworks, Scorpio Rising.... Author of *Hollywood Babylon*.
Angerville (Jacques, marquis d'). Vineyard proprietor in Volney (Côte de Beaune, Burgundy), sole owner of the clos des Ducs. Owns parts of Champans, Taille Pieds, Les Caillerets, Les Frémiets, Les Angles, Meursault Santenots, Les Combes (Pammard)....
Arbellot (Simon). Journalist (*Figaro*, *Le Temps*, *Paris-Midi*, *Aux Ecoutes*, *Cuisine et Vins de France*, etc.), director of the Guide Kléber Colombes da Touristes Gastronomes.
Ashbery (John). American poet.
Asher (Gerald). Wine merchant, London, New York, San Frencisco. Wine columnist for *Gourmet*. Author of *On Wine*.
Auden (Wystan Hugh). British poet, naturalized American. His poems, published in collections include "The Dance of Death" (1933) and "The Double Man" (1941).
Baldwin (James). Black American novelist and essayist. Fled to France in 1948, age 24. Author of *Go Tell It on the Mountain* (1953), *Giovanni's Room*, *Another Country*, *Notes of a Native Son* (1955), *The Fire Next Time* and many other books and essays.
Bamford (Martin). Director of IDVF (International Distillers and Vintners, France), who lived and received at Château Loudenne. His table was famous in the Médoc and the international wine world.
Barnagaud (Jean). Proprietor, director of the restaurant Prunier, rue Duphot, in Paris. His wife, née Prunier, managed the restaurant of the same name in London; their son still manages Prunier-Traktir, rue Victor-Hugo, in Paris.
Barry (Naomi). American, food and travel writer, established in Paris.
Bavoillot (Ghislaine). "Directrice du Département Art de Vivre," with the publisher, Flammarion, responsible for all books which reflect the pleasure of living.
Beard (James). American, author of many cookbooks.
Beck (Simone). Kown to everyone as "Simca." Co-author, with Louisette Bertholle and Julia Child, of *Mastering the Art of French Cooking*. Held regular cooking classes for Americans at her home in Plascassier near Cannes.
Bedford (Sybille). English novelist (*A Legacy*, *A Compass Error*, *A favorite of the Gods*, *Jigsaw*), travel writer (*The Sudden View*), essayist ("The faces of Justice," "As It Was"), biographer (Aldous Huxley).
Benny (Norma). Registrar for Lubéron College, Avignon cooking classes.
Bernachon (Maurice). Celebrated chocolatier, Lyon.
Bérot (Charles). Proprietor-chef of l'Escale, in Carry-le-Rouet, near Marseille. Today Mme Bérot's nephew is in the kitchen.
Bertolli (Paul). Chef, Chez Panisse, Berkeley, California. Co-author, with Alice Waters, of *Chez Panisse Cooking*.
Besson (Gérard). Chef de cuisine Chez Garin until the restaurant was closed in 1973. Now proprietor-chef of Gérard Besson, Paris.
Bettane (Michel). Wine writer. Editorial consultant to *La Revue du Vin de France*.
Beyer (Léon). Alsatian vineyard proprietor.
Billoux (Jean-Pierre). Restaurateur in Dijon, formed by Alexandre Dumaine.
Billy (Christian de). Director of the Champagne firm, Pol-Roger. Retired.
Bize (Lalou Leroy). Co-proprietor of Domaine de la Romanée-Conti, former co-director.
Blanc (Georges). Proprietor-chef of the restaurant in Vonnas that bears his name. It was created by his grandmother and once known as Chez la Mère Blanc.
Bocuse (Paul). Proprietor of the restaurant that bears his name in Collonges-au-Mont-d'Or, near Lyon.

Borie (Jean-Eugène). Proprietor in Médoc of Château Ducru-Beaucaillou (St.-Julien), Château Haut-Batailley (Pauillac) and Château Grand-Puy-Lacoste (Pauillac).
Boyer (Gérard). Proprietor-chef of Les Crayères, in Reims (Champagne).
Braverman (Sylvia). American painter.
Brée (Germaine). French literature scholar, teacher, author. Born in France, moved to U.S. 1926. Served with French army during World War II.
Broadbent (Michael). Director of wine department, Christies, London. Author of books on wine.
Brown (Dale). European editor Time-Life Books, London. Later transferred to Alexandria, Virginia. Retired.
Brownstone (Cecily) Associated Press food editor. Retired.
Cagna (Jacques). Restaurateur, Jacque Cagna, Paris.
Cam (Yannick, Janet). Proprietors of Le Pavillon, Washington, D.C. Le Pavillon closed, they separated, Yannick has formed other projects in Washington, Janet is maître d'hôtel at Lutèce in New York.
Cann (Dorothy–later Hamilton). Effervescent proprietor-director of The French Culinary Institute in New York City.
Carey (Nora). Researcher, *The Good Cook*, author of *Perfect Preserves* (1990), public relations director, Hôtel Ritz and Ritz-Escoffier Cooking School, Paris.
Cavanaugh (Inez). Night club entertainer
Cazes (Jean Michel). Vineyard proprietor: Château Lynch-Bages (Pauillac), Ch. Les Ormes de Pez (St.-Estèphe). Managing director of AXA-Millésimes: Château Pichon-Longueville Baron (Pauillac), Ch. Suduiraut (Sauternes), Ch. Cantenac-Brown (Margaux), Ch. Petit-Village (Pomerol), etc.
Chalmers (Irene). Publisher-author, food subjects.
Chave (Gérard). Vineyard proprietor in Hermitage and Saint-Joseph (both central Côtes-du-Rhône). The labels bear the name of his father (and son), Jean-Louis Chave.
Child (Julia). Cookbook author, television personality.
Claiborne (Craig), Cookbook author. Former restaurant reviewer for the *New York Times*.
Clark (Robert). Socio-historical food and wine chronicler. Former editor of the Journal of Gastronomy, author of *James Beard, a Biography* (1993).
Clos-Jouve (Henri), Gastronomic journalist.
Cofacci (Gino). Longtime companion and calvary of James Beard.
Colby (John). American. Publisher, Brick Tower Press.
Colquhoun (Joan). Passionate admirer of Bill Aalto.
Constable (George). European editor, Time-Life Books, subsequently chief U.S. (Alexandria) editor.
Cottin (Philippe). President of the board of directors of the Baron Philippe de Rothschild Company: Châteaux Mouton-Rothschild, d'Armailhac, Clerc-Milon (all Pauillac), the brand-name, Mouton-Cadet, etc.
Courtine (Robert). French gastronomic journalist.
Craxton (John). British painter.
Cunningham (Marion). James Beard protégée, author of the revised *Fanny Farmer Cookbook*, *Cooking with Children*.
Curnonsky (pre-name of Maurice Sailland). Journalist, native of Anjou, born 1873. 1927: in France, the poets had elected a "prince de poètes," the singers a "prince de la chanson," and so forth. The gastronomic journalists decided to elect a "prince de la gastronomie." From 3388 voters, Curnonsky received 1823 voices (Simon Arbellot). He was the prince until his death in 1956; the journalistic brotherhood swore there would never be another prince, although some hankered after the title.
Dannenbaum (Julie). Cooking school, Philadelphia. Author of cookbooks: *Julie Dannenbaum's Creative Cooking School*, *Menus for All Occasions*.
David (Elizabeth). British cookbook author, food and travel writer. Her style enchants those who love the table and frustrates the adherents of mechanical recipe presentations. In England, hers is a name apart, admired above all others.
Davis (Douglas). Expatriate American painter, lover of Edith Piaf.
Decure (Madeleine). Founder, editor of *Cuisine et vins de France*, 1947, in collaboration with Curnonsky.
Delaney (Beauford). Black American painter, arrived in Paris in 1953.
Delmas (Jean). Director of Château Haut-Brion (Passac, Graves). Retired.
Desai (Bipin). Nuclear physicist, ardent wine collector.

Didier (Jean). "Secrétaire général" of the Guide Kléber Colombes des Touristes Gastronomes; he became director at Simon Arbellot's death in 1966.
Dovaz (Michel). Wine writer. Regular contributor to *La Revue du Vin de France*.
Draper (James). Curator, The Metropolitan Museum of Art, New York City.
Draper (Paul). Director of Ridge Vineyards, California.
Drouhin (Robert). Director of the Burgundian wine firm, Joseph Drouhin, in Beaune.
Dumaine (Alexandre). Proprietor-chef of l'Hôtel de la Côte d'Or, in Saulieu (Burgundy), from 1931 until his retirement in 1964.
Escoffier (Pierre). Grandson of the famous chef.
Eliot (Valerie). Widow of the poet, T.S. Eliot.
Fisher [M(ary) F(rances) K(ennedy)]. 1908-92. Writer, essayist, whose. subject was often food including *Serve It Forth* (1937) and *With Bold Knife and Fork* (1979).
Fitchett (Joel) . Journalist. the *International Herald Tribune*.
Flammarion (Charles-Henri). President-director of the French publishing firm, Flammarion.
Florsheim (Sue). Her husband, Harald, inherited Florsheim Shoes.
Ford (Charles Henri). American poet, long-time companion of the Russian painter, Pavel Tchelitchew. Publisher-editor, during the 1940s (in collabaration with co-editor, Parker Tyler, and managing editor, John Myers) of the avant-garde art and literary revue, *View*.
Frechtmam (Bernard). American. Scolarly translator of Jean Genet's books into English.
Garcia (Francis). Proprietor-chef of Le Chapon Fin, Bordeaux.
Garin (Georges). Celebrated restaurateur, Nuits-Saint-Georges, Paris, Solliès-Toucas.
Geoffray (Yvonne). Proprietor of Beaujolais vineyard, Château Thivin (Côte de Brouilly). Succeeded by her nephew, Vincent Geoffray.
Gerfroit (Rose). Proprietor of olive oil mill, Solliès-Pont.
Giacometti (Alberto). Swiss sculptor and painter, lived and worked in Paris. Died 1966.
Gingold (Hermione). English comedienne.
Goldstein (Julius). American painter. Married to Joan Aiken, author of children's books and thrillers.
Gouges (Michel). Burgundy. Vineyard co-proprietor with his brother, Marcel, of Domaine Henri Gouges, Nuits-Saint-Georges (Côte de Nuits). Includes Clos des Porrets and parts of les Saint-Georges, les Vaucrains, les Pruliers, les Chaignots, Les Perrières (Pinot blanc)....
Graff (Richard). Califonia vineyard owner.
Greenberg (Noah). American conductor. Creator of Pro Musica Antiqua.
Greene (Gael). Food journalist, restaurant critic, *New York Magazine*.
Grigson (Jane). English cookbook author. Her husband, Geoffrey, was a well-known literary critic.
Griffin (Guy). Australian food and wine writer, resturant critic, based in Sydney.
Grimes (Paul). Artist, cooking teacher.
Gruber (Lester and Cleo). Proprietors of The London Chop House, Detroit.
Grunewald (Henry). Editor-in-Chief, Time Inc. (retired).
Guillard (Michel). Photographer for *Yquem*. Editor of the periodical, *l'Amateur de Bordeaux*.
Guillot (André). French chef. Teacher of chefs. In 1972, because of delicate health, he closed his restaurant, l'Auberge du Vieux Marly, but continued to conduct annual cooking classes in the south of France. He was unconditionally worshipped by all of his students.
Hacker (Ernst). Viennese, naturalized U.S. citizen, married to Lucia Vernarelli. They divorced but never really separated. Ernst moved to Florence and Lucia divided her time between New York and Florence, where she lived with Ernst.
Haeberlin (Jean-Pierre). L'Auberge de l'Ill, Illhaeusern, Alsace. Jean-Pierre is in charge of the dining room and of public relations. His brother, Paul, who was for many years in the kitchen, has ceded that responsibility to his son.
Harper (Allanah). British writer, who settled in the south of France (La Roquette-sur Siagne, near Grasse). Sybille Bedford and Eda Lord rented the ground floor of her villa for many years.
Harrison (Jim). American novelist, adventure with a surrealist edge. Hunter, fisher, gastronome and impassioned lover of the wines of Domaine Tempier.
Hessell (Bernard). American. Black dancer, Folies-Bergère
Hazelton (Nika). Cookbook author, cookbook reviewer.

Hébrard (Jacques). Co-proprietor former director of Château Cheval Blanc (Saint-Emilion).
Hiély (Pierre). Chef-proprietor of Chez-Hiély, Avignon. Today, he is in semi-retirement and shares the proprietorship with his chef and his maître d'hôtel.
Hill (David). American painter, made his home in Paris.
Hahnsbeen (John). Witty, urbaine friend of artists. Curator of Peggy Guggenheim's collection in Venice.
Holmes (Mary). Art history lecturer at the University of Iowa, Iowa City, during the 1940s; later moved to California.
Hone (Russell). British consultant far the *Wine* volume in *The Good Cook* series. Married to Becky Wasserman, lives in Burgundy.
Honoré (Marcel). Backer and silent partner of *Cuisine et Vins de France* and *La Revue du Vin de France* until the death of Madeleine Decure (1968), when both revues were sold to Odette Kahn, Madeleine's assistant editor.
Hopkinson (Simon). 1983, chef at Hilaire, Old Brompton Road, London; 1987, co-proprietor-chef at Bibendum; remains co-proprietor but has since retired from the kitchen to write. Author of *Roast Chicken and Other Stories*.
Howard (Brian). American parents. Precocious, brilliant, beautiful, outrageous young poet at Eton and Oxford, close friend of Harold Acton (from whom Harold later attempted to distance himself).
Isaacson (Robert). Former art dealer (Robert Isaacson Gallery), Collector, art historian, harpsichordist, wine connoisseur, accomplished cook....
James (Michael). Food entrepreneur, one-time assistant for Simone Beck, organized cooking classes at Robert Mondavi Vineyards, Napa Valley, etc.
Jerome (Carl). Assistant in James Beard.
Jones (Judith). Cookbook editor, Alfred A. Knopf.
Kahn (Odette). Proprietor-editor of *Cuisine et Vin de France* and *La Revue du Vin de France* from 1968 to 1979 when, under pressure to make ends meet, she injudiciously sold 51% of the shares in both revues, with the verbal agreement that she remain editor-in-chief. The buyer put her out and resold the reviews.
Kallman (Chester). Friend and colleague of W.H. Auden.
Kaye (Danny). Comedian. Impassioned amateur cook.
Korn (Jerry). Former editor-in-chief of Time-Life Books, Alexandria, Virginia.
Krug (Rémi). Co-director, with his brother, Henri, of the Champagne firm, Krug.
Ladenis (Nico). Proprietor-chef, Chez Nico at Ninety, Park Lane, London.
Lemonnier (Michel). Journalist. Collaborator, with Madeleine Decure and Odette Khan, on *Cuisine et Vins de France* and *La Revue du Vin de France*.
Lenôtre (Gaston). Pastry chef, caterer, founder of l'Ecole Lenôtre, Paris restaurateur (Le Pré catalan, Pavillon Elysée), author of cookbooks on pastry, ices and confectionery, desserts, etc.
Levy (Paul). American journalist, food writer, based in London.
Lewis (Edna). American cookbook author.
Lichine (Alexis). 1913-1989. Born in Moscow. Moved with his family to France after the Russian Revolution and to the United States in 1934. Wine grower, wine merchant, author of *Alexis Lichine's Guide to the Wines and Vineyards of France* and of *Alexis Lichine's New Encyclopedia of Wines and Spirits*. Proprietor of Château Prieuré-Lichine (Margaux). Succeeded by his son, Sacha.
Lord (Eda). American-born writer. Lived mostly in France and England. Author of *Childsplay*, *A Matter of Choosing* and *Extenuating Circumstances*.
Lougee (Jane). American. Publisher, in Paris, of the English language, underground literary magazine, *Merlin*, launched in 1952.
Lur-Salucas (comte Alexandre de). Vineyard director, co-proprietor of Château d'Yquem (Sauternes) and Château de Fargues (Sauternes).
Lynch (Kermit). Wine merchant, importer and distributor, Berkeley, California. Divides his time equally between California and France. Author of *Adventures on the Wine Route*.
Malgieri (Nick). Pastry cook, teacher, author of *Nick Malgieri's Perfect Pastry*, *Great Italian desserts* and *How to Bake*.
Manoncourt (Thierry). Proprietor, Château Figeac (St.-Emilion).
Marly (Jacques). Former owner of Château Malartic-Lagravière (Léognan, Graves).
Maroc (Daniel). French underground poet.

Marple (Leslie). Friend of Sybille Bedford. Once married to film-maker John Huston. Sister of Joan Black (later married to Peter Churchill), friend of Eda Lord.
Marsauche (Didier). Apprentice-cook with Garin at Le Lingousto, Solliès-Toucas; later, chef de cuisine at the country auberge, l'Aiguebrun, near Bonnieux, in the Lubéron.
Marshall (Lydie). French, married to American, Wayne Marshall. Her cooking school, La Bonne Cocotte, in Greenwich Village, is famous. Author of *Cooking with Lydie Marshall* and *A Passion for Potatoes*.
Martin (Ailene). Alumnus of the Avignon cooking classes. Since married to French chef, Jean Berrard.
Marty (Suzanne). My landady in Clamart, 1953-1966.
Maza (Herbert). President of American University, Aix-en-Provence, and of Lubéron College.
McCully (Helen). Food editor for *McCalls* magazine and, later for *House Beautiful*. Died 1977.
Merrill (James). "A great American poet–winner of every major prize America can offer its poets, from the Pulitzer to the Bollingen." (from the book jacket of *A Different Person*).
Michaelis (Tommy). International lawyer, established in Paris during the early 1950s.
Michelson (Annette). American. Lived in Paris during the early 1950s. Teaches film at New York University.
Miller (Henry). American writer (1891-1980), lived in Paris during the 1930s. Author of *The Air-conditioned Nightmare*, *Tropic of Cancer*, *Tropic of Capricorn*, *Sexus*, *Plexus*, *Nexus*, etc. Greatly admired in France, his books were banned in the United States until 1960.
Montille (Hubart de). Lawyer, vinyard proprietor and wine-maker. Vines in the neighboring Burgundian (Côte de Beaune) villages of Volnay (Champans, Taillepieds, Mitans) and Pommard (Rugiens, Pézerolles).
Mosimann (Anton). Formerly chef de cuisine, Hotel Dorchester, London. Proprietor-chef at a private club (by subscription), Anton Mosimann, at 11B Halkin Street, Belgrave Square, London.
Maullé (Jean-Pierre). Chef at Chez Panisse, Berkeley, California. Married to Denise Lurton, daughter of André Lurton, Bordelais vineyard proprietor in Graves, Entre-deux-Mers and Saint-Emilion.
Mouquet (Monsieur) Former president of Le Club de Cent.
Neuville (Sacha). Born Albrecht Niederstein in Germany. Lived in the south of France during World War II with papers in the name of Sacha Neuville.
Noblet (André). Cellar master, Domaine de la Romanée-Conti (Vosne-Romanée, Côte de Nuits). Succeeded by his son, Bernard.
Norman (Jill). British editor and publisher. Close friend and editor of Elizabeth David's books.
Oberlin (Russell). Counter-tenor with Noah Greenberg's Pro Musica Antiqua, music professor.
Ollard (Richard). British historian. Editor at Collins Publisher, London.
Painter (Mary). American economist, employed by the U.S. government (Marshall Plan) in Paris, 1947-1956, later for the OECD (Organization for Economic Cooperation and Development), Paris. Married Georges Garin, 1969.
Peacock (Scott). Cook, partner of Edna Lewis.
Perrin (Jean-Pierre). Co-proprietor, with his brother, François, of Château de Beaucastel (Châteauneuf-du-Pape), proprietor of La Vielle Ferme near Orange. Chancellier of the Académie Internationale de Vin.
Peyraud (family). Vineyard proprietors, Domaine Tempier (Bandol), near the Mediterranean coast. The domaine was inherited by Lulu (née Tempier), developed by her husband, Lucien (died 1996) and is now operated by their two sons, Jean-Marie, who is in charge of the cellars and the vinification, and François, who cares for the vines. Approximately a third of their entire production it exported to Kermit Lynch in Berkeley, California.
Peyrot (Claude). Proprietor-chef of Le Vivarois, Paris.

Pivot (Bernard). One of the most famous figures in France. Essayist, novelist, literary editor for several publications, publisher, television personality and producer, purveyor of culture to the masses. For fifteen years his hour-long, weekly literary television round table, l'Apostrophe, was immensely popular, until he abandonned it for another television formula.

Place (Robert, Ninette). Former proprietors of Château Bouscaut (Cadaujac, Graves).

Ponsot (Jean-Marie). Burgundy vineyard proprietor in Morey-Saint-Denis (Côte de Nuits). Vines in clos de la Roche, Clos Saint-Denis, Latricières-Chambertin, Griotte-Chambertin, Chapelle-Chambertin, etc.

Price (Peter). English film-maker. Lived in Paris during the early 1950s. Retired to his father's dairy farm, in Tibberton, near Gloucester, to lead the life of a "gentleman-farmer."

Puisais (Jacques). Oenologist. Director of the Laboratoire Départemental et Régional d'Analyses et de Recherches in Tours. President of the Union Nationale des Oenologues, president of the Institute Français du Goût, honorary president of the Union Internationale des Oenologues, honorary president of the Académie Internationale du Vin, etc. Author of books on wine and gastronomy.

Raine (Kathleen). British Poet.

Read (Pat). Cookbook editor, Simon & Schuster.

Ricard (Claude). Former proprietor, wine-maker, Domaine de Chevalier (Léognan, Graves).

Ricard (Marie, née Fournier). Born in Salon-de-Provence, daughter of an olive-oil merchant. She shared a house on a vast, wooded property, Les Plaines, in the Salon countryside, with her son, Jacques, and his companion, Rosette.

Rice (William). American food journalist, now with the *Chicago Tribune.*

Robinson (Jancis). British. Wine corresponent for several newspapers, columnist for *The Wine Spectator*, author of books on wine, editor of *The Oxford Companion to Wine*, created a popular series of television programs on wine.

Rodenstock (Hardy). Wealthy German wine collector, famous for his annual, organized winetasting events.

Rogers (Judy). Co-proprietor of Zuni Café, San Francisco.

Rolfson (John). ABC Television European Bureau Chief.

Ronsheim (John). Composer, music professor, Antioch college. Wine collector, lover of the table. Dreamt of moving gastronomy into the arena of higher education, a dream that failed.

Rorem (Ned). American composer.

Rothstein (Serena). American painter.

Rougier (René). Vineyard proprietor, Château Simone (Palette), near Aix-en-Provence.

Rousseau (Charles). Burgundy vineyard proprietor (labels bear his father's name, Armand Rousseau) in Gevrey-Chambertin (Côte de Nuits). Vines in Chambertin-Clos de Bèze, Chambertin, Mazy-Chambertin, Charmes-Chambertin, Mazoyères-Chambertin, Ruchottes-Chambertin (Clos des Ruchottes), Clos Saint-Jacques, Clos de la Roche....

Rusconi (Natale). Former manager of the Gritti Palace, Hotel, Venice.

Salzfass (Jane–later Freiman). Member of the Avignon cooking class, 1972. Assistant in my classes at James Beard's, 1974. Journalist, cookbook author.

Sax (Richard). Studio assistant, *The Good Cook.*

Seysses (Jacques). Burgundy vineyard proprietor, Morey-Saint-Denis (Côte de Nuits). Vines in Chambolle-Musigny. Charmes-Chambertin, Clos St.-Denis, Clos de la Roche, Echézeaux, Bonnes-Mares....

Shoffner (Robert). Food editor, restaurant critic for the *Washingtonian*, Washington, D.C.

Sohmers (Harriet). American writer.

Sontheimer (Carl). Creator of the trademark, "CuisineArts."

Stein (Elliott). Arrived in France in 1947, age 19. Launched a literary magazine, *Janus* (short-lived for lack of funds). Returned to New York in the late 1950s. Film critic for *The Village Voice*, New York. Contributor to *Sight and Sound.*

Stern (James). Short story writer. Born in Ireland, educated at Eton. Lived in Rhodesia, Berlin, Hawaii, London, Paris, New York and, finally, in Wiltshire. With his wife, Tania, translated books by Brecht, Freud, Kafka, Mann, Zweig, etc.

Sullivan (Steve). Apprenticed in the kitchens of Chez Panisse, became the Panisse baker, then established the Acme Bakery next to Kermit Lynch Wine Merchant, in Berkeley.

Sutcliffe (Serena). British, married to David Peppercorn, wine authority. Director of the wine department, Sotheby's, London. Editor of *Wines of the World*, author of books on Burgundy, Champagne, etc.

Taittinger (Claude). President, managing director of Champagne Taittinger, Reims.

Tchelitchew (Pavel). Russian. Painter, ballet set designer.

Tobias (Doris). Food editor, *Woman's Wear Daily* (*WWD*).

Tower (Jeremiah). Chef, Chez Panisse; worked on the early volumes of *The Good Cook*; proprietor of Stars, the San Francisco brasserie.

Triplette (Clay). Housekeeper, kitchen assistant, shopper and cook for James Beard.

Troisgros (Jean, Pierre). Brothers, co-proprietors of the restaurant, Troisgros, Roanne. Jean is dead, Pierre's son is in the kitchen.

Tulleken (Kit van). European editor of Time-Life Books during The Good Cook years.

Turel (Lili). Swiss. Met Sacha (Albrecht Niederstein) and Eda Lord in Berlin; they all moved to France in 1933. After the war, Lili shared a house with Philippe Wehrlé in Magagnosc, near Grasse.

Usher (Gregory), Director, under Anne Willan, of the La Varenne cooking school, Paris. Later, director of the Ritz-Escoffier cooking school, Paris.

Vernarelli (Lucia). Painter whom I met, at the same time as Julius Goldstein, in Rufino Tamayo's painting class at The Brooklyn Museum Art School, 1945.

Viliaine (Aubert de). Co-proprietor and co-director of the Domaine de la Romanée-Conti, Vosne-Romanée (Côte de Nuits). The Domaine is sole proprietor of the vineyards, Romanée-Conti and La Tâche and owns parts of Echézeaux, Grand-Echézeaux, Richebourg, Romanée-Saint-Vivant and Montrachet. Aubert de Villaine also owns vineyards with his wife, Pamela, near their home in Bouzeron (Côte Chalonnaise) and in Rully (Côte Chalonnaise).

Vimont (Pierre, Pierrette). Proprietors of la Guinguette, in Clamart during the 1950s and 1960s.

Vrinat (Jean-Claude). Proprietor and brilliant director of the restaurant, Le Taillevent, created by his father, André Vrinat, immediately after the war.

Walter (Eugene). American writer.

Wasserman (Becky). American wine broker, based in Burgundy. Married to Russell Hone.

Waters (Alice). Creator and proprietor, once chef, now director, of the restaurant, Chez Panisse, in Berkeley, California, dedicated to fresh, biologically uncontaminated produce and simple cooking procedures. Author or co-author of *The Chez Panisse Menu Cookbook*, *Chez Panisse Pasta*, *Pizza and Calzone*, *Chez Panisse Desserts*, *Chez Panisse Cooking*, and *Fanny at Chez Panisse*.

Watson (Peter). British. Art collector. Friend of artists, commissioned portraits from Tchelitchew and Giacometti, funded *Horizon*, the literay magazine edited by Cyril Connally, and the ICA (Institute of Contemporary Art). Intelligent, gentle, witty, relaxing companion.

Waxman (Nahum). Proprietor of Kitchen Arts & Letters, New York City ("A Bookstore and Gallery Devoted Exclusively to Food and Wine.")

Wehrlé (Philippe). French Intellectual, his passions were divided amongst physics, opium, the table and the court of Louis XIV. Shared a house in Magagnosc with Lili Turel.

Williams (Chuck). Devotee of the table, creator of Williams-Sonoma.

Wilson (Garland). Pianist, night-club entertainer.

Wilson (José), British journalist, moved to the U.S., food editor, *House and Garden* 1963 to 1965, began to collaborate with James Beard and rapidly became his ghost writer; wrote his sindicated columns, based on taped chats and polished his books with Judith Jones until her death by suicide in 1980.

Winebaum (Bernard). Poet, friend of poets, world traveler.

Winebaum (Sumner, Helen). Brother and sister-in-law of Bernie.

Wolfe (Suzanne). American. International lawyer, Geneva.

Wolfert (Paula). Serious cookbook author: *Couscous and Other Good Foods from Morocco*, *Mediterranean Cooking*, *The Cooking of Southwest France*, *Paula Wolfert's World of Food*, etc.

In the United States:
Brick Tower Press
1230 Park Avenue
New York, New York 10128
Tel: 212-427-7139

bricktower@aol.com

For sales, subrights information,
and international distribution,
please call 1-800-68-BRICK

or visit our website
www.BrickTowerPress.com
www.bookmanuscript.com
www.Ingram.com

"Mr. Olney's influence in the culinary profession was profound...."
-*New York Times*

"...an unparalleled view of French food and wine."
-*Chicago Tribune*

"Olney was well ahead of his time. He was without doubt, one of the most influential of modern writers about food. He has a very strong claim to be considered the best."
-*Times*, London

Richard Olney, one of the first food writers to introduce the simple joys of French cooking to American readers was an American who lived in Europe for almost 50 years. He died unexpectedly July 31, 1999. Author of more than 35 titles and inspiration to hundreds more his works include *French Menu Cookbook, Simple French Food, The Good Cook, Yquem, Ten Vineyard Lunches, Romanée-Conti, Provence the Beautiful, Lulu's Provençal Table, Good Cook's Encyclopedia*, and *French Wine and Food.* A resident of Solliès-Toucas, France, Olney was close to his art and family and friends.